T0305605

FARMING FUTURES

This book studies the management challenges and possibilities in sustaining farmer producer organisations (FPOs). It goes beyond the conventional metrics of cost-benefit analysis by drawing on 15 case studies of diverse FPOs spread across India to fill a significant knowledge-practice gap in the domain of producer collectives. The book explores issues of ownership and governance, studies the empirical basis for policy decisions on FPOs, and provides actionable insights and knowledge, keeping in mind the complexity of the institutional design of an FPO. It also discusses the envisioned role of civil society organisations in supporting FPOs and looks at the kind of institutional innovations that are needed to create a cohesive ecosystem for FPOs.

A unique collaborative project jointly authored by academics and development practitioners, the book will be of use to students and researchers of agricultural economics, environment and business, agricultural development, environmental economics, rural studies, entrepreneurship, and South Asian studies. It will also be of interest to development professionals, civil society organisations, and policymakers.

C. Shambu Prasad is Professor, Strategic Management and Social Sciences, the Institute of Rural Management Anand (IRMA), India. His expertise and research include several interdisciplinary fields such as social entrepreneurship, science and technology studies, rural livelihoods, innovation management, managing producer collectives, and sustainable agriculture. He has been a Fulbright senior research fellow at Cornell University. He founded IRMA's incubator in 2016 and mentors and advises several social enterprises, producer organisations, and start-ups. He is a co-editor of *Farming Futures: Emerging Social Enterprises in India* (2019). He is a member of expert committees of the Government of India on science and technology and agriculture. He currently coordinates a project on "Small Farm Incomes" that explores co-creation of knowledge in agriculture by academicians and development practitioners.

Ajit Kanitkar is a visiting faculty at Indian Institute of Management (IIM) at Udaipur, India. With a career spanning decades of work in the development sector, he was a senior advisor and researcher at VikasAnvesh Foundation, Pune. He has also served as the programme officer at Ford Foundation and Swiss Agency for Development and Cooperation, both in New Delhi, and a faculty member at IRMA. He is associated with many civil society organisations across the country. His co-edited book in 2019, *Farming Futures: Emerging Social Enterprises in India* (2019), is a unique collection of 15 contemporary case studies documenting in detail social enterprises in agriculture. In 2021, he co-edited *Sowing Impact: Agri Entrepreneurs in India Stories of Innovation, Hope & Resilience.*

Deborah Dutta was a Senior Research Fellow at the IRMA, India, following her PhD from the Homi Bhabha Centre for Science Education, Mumbai. Her research areas span the field of environmental education and sustainable transitions with a focus on community-practice-based approaches such as urban farming. Her work explores community engagement, socio-technical systems, and sustainable food systems. She is a member of the South Asian Learning Sciences Collective and a 2021–22 fellow of the Education for Sustainable Development (ESD) Leadership programme hosted by Engagement Global, Germany. She is also the recipient of a grant under "Transforming Education for Sustainable Futures" (TESF), a research network supported by the UK Global Challenges Research Fund (GCRF).

FARMING FUTURES

Reimagining Producer Organisations in India

Edited by C. Shambu Prasad,
Ajit Kanitkar and Deborah Dutta

Routledge
Taylor & Francis Group
LONDON AND NEW YORK

First published 2023
by Routledge
4 Park Square, Milton Park, Abingdon, Oxon OX14 4RN

and by Routledge
605 Third Avenue, New York, NY 10158

Routledge is an imprint of the Taylor & Francis Group, an informa business

British Library Cataloguing-in-Publication Data
A catalogue record for this book is available from the British Library

ISBN: 978-1-032-31098-5 (hbk)
ISBN: 978-1-032-31101-2 (pbk)
ISBN: 978-1-003-30803-4 (ebk)

DOI: 10.4324/9781003308034

CONTENTS

v

CONTENTS

CONTENTS

FIGURES

TABLES

CONTRIBUTORS

Abhishek Saxena is a doctoral (fellow programme) scholar at the Institute of Rural Management Anand (IRMA). His work involves looking at governance and management of producer organisations through the lens of stakeholder theory. He has disseminated his research regularly at several conferences and through popular media such as blogs. His wider interest lies in social entrepreneurship; grassroots innovations in agriculture; health and education domains; collective action; governance of people's institutions; diversity in research communication; and anthropological and participatory action research in health, food, and education.

Animesh Mondal is a post-graduate in social work from the Delhi School of Social Work. He leads the Sustainable Agriculture and Livelihoods Programme at Samaj Pragati Sahayog (SPS), an organisation that works with women on interventions related to sustainable farming and other areas. In his association with SPS, for over 20 years, he played a vital role in developing the SHG model promoted by SPS. He was the programme coordinator of SHG-led livelihood intervention from 2010 to 2014 at SPS. He served as the CEO of Ram Rahim Pragati Producer Company Limited from 2012 to 2015 and again from April 2022 to present.

Anita Paul has a master's degree in social work from Delhi University and has been involved directly with community development programmes. In 1992, she co-founded Pan Himalayan Grassroots Development Foundation, a voluntary organisation which spearheads sustainable mountain development initiatives in the Indian Himalayan Region. She holds the portfolio of Director (Community Initiatives) in Grassroots and has promoted Mahila Umang Producers Company with marginalised women farmers as shareholders engaged in sustainable livelihoods improvement efforts. She is actively engaged in championing for mountains as an important ecosystem that matters for all with focus on gender-inclusive policies for sustainable development in various forums nationally, regionally, and internationally.

Astad Pastakia works as a freelance consultant in the area of rural livelihoods, innovations, and collective enterprise. With a basic degree in agricultural sciences, he completed post-graduation and fellowship in management both from the Indian Institute of Management, Ahmedabad. His doctoral research was focused on grassroots innovations for sustainable agriculture. His paper "Grassroots ecopreneurs: change agents for a sustainable society" in the *Journal of Organisational Change Management* (1989) was judged Outstanding Paper of the Year by MCB University Press, London. He has published three books, including a four-volume open-access handbook on livelihood strategies for rain-fed areas.

Balakrishnan S. is CEO of Vrutti, having more than 22 years of experience in creating wealth and building resilience for marginalised and vulnerable communities such as farmers, women, fisher folks, and micro and nano entrepreneurs through livelihood transformation models. He has experiences in building models for scale, developing various financial products and services, building and nurturing community organisations, producer collectives, value-chain establishment, and enterprise development. He did his graduation in science and completed post-graduate diploma in business management (PGDBM) from Indira Gandhi National Open University (IGNOU).

Debanjan Ghatak is working with PRADAN and primarily looks after the Farmer Producer Organisation Resource Center hosted under PRADAN. He has 14 years of experience in social mobilisation, livelihood, renewable energy, and other rural development activities. He was a Research Advisory Committee Member in Ambedkar University Delhi (Development Studies). He completed his BTech in electrical engineering from West Bengal University of Technology and MA in rural development from IGNOU.

Gautam Prateek is an assistant professor at the School of Rural Management, XIM University, Odisha. Gautam holds a PhD in community resources and development from Arizona State University.

Gouri Krishna is a development professional and has worked as the CEO and managing director of BASIX Consulting and Technology Services Ltd. (BCTS). She holds a post-graduate diploma in rural management from the IRMA. She has over three decades of experience working with grassroots-level community-based organisations such as cooperatives, self-help groups, and farmer producer organisations (FPOs). She was associated with promoting and nurturing over 200 farmer producer companies in Uttar Pradesh, Maharashtra, and Chhattisgarh. She co-authored *Different Models of Financing Small Farmers' Agricultural Value Chains*. She has anchored the state of sector report on FPOs for NAFPO in 2022.

Hareesh Belawadi is a business consultant to commercial and social enterprises, serving diverse clients, ventures, and projects across sectors, industries, and domains in urban, rural, and tribal India since 2008. He works closely with client teams to co-develop and implement strategies and tactics in their pursuit of customer-centric solutions, marketing, growth, profit, and impact. He has 12 years of prior work experience as engineer, manager, leader, facilitator, and partner in a variety of entities across sectors – corporate companies, development catalysts, producers' collective, consulting firm, and family farm. He has a bachelor's degree in mechanical engineering in 1995 from MIT Manipal. He also has a postgraduate diploma in management in 2002 from EDI Ahmedabad.

Milee Parmar, a graduate from IRMA, is a development practitioner. She's currently associated with Looms of Ladakh – a cooperative of women herders and artisans. She has worked on women's socio-economic empowerment initiatives and strengthening of farmers' collectives with organisations like Rajasthan SRLM, EY, and FWWB. Her passion lies in the areas of producer collectives, social entrepreneurship, environmental sustainability, and improving livelihoods of the artisans.

Naveen Patidar is Chief Executive Officer of the Aga Khan Rural Support Programme (India), a pioneer development agency working on rural livelihoods. He has more than 15 years of experience in designing and managing large development projects in the areas of water, sustainable agriculture, rural livelihoods, energy, and women empowerment. He has expertise and experience of working with communities living in extreme poverty. Climate change mitigation and adaptation, and farmers collectives are his areas of current interests. He is leading the transformation of programmes through promoting innovations, better designing of programmes, and use of digital technologies. He is a computer engineering graduate followed by post-graduation from the IRMA.

Nikhila Shastry currently works as a team lead in Livelihood Practice at Catalyst Management Services (CMS) in Bangalore. She has a unique blend of six years of experience in the livelihoods domain area, across the functions of grassroots implementation, consulting, research, and technology. She holds a master's degree in livelihoods and social entrepreneurship from the Tata Institute of Social Sciences, Mumbai. She is passionate about developing and implementing inclusive and sustainable solutions for the community and creating significant positive impact.

Niraj U. Joshi is Senior Research Associate with the Global Economic Development and the Biosphere programme at the Royal Swedish Academy of Sciences in Stockholm, Sweden. He has earlier led the research and education programmes at two flagship organisations of the Aga Khan Development Network in India and Mozambique. He has more than two decades of experience in management of environmental and rural development programmes as well as monitoring and evaluation of these programmes. Over the past decade he has also led research projects on managing common pool resources, climate change adaptation in agriculture, and ecological entrepreneurship and has also written and presented several peer-reviewed papers on these themes.

Pallavi G. L. is a doctoral (fellow programme) scholar at the IRMA. Her research interests include sustainability of collective enterprises and issues of credit access and market access for small farmers.

Parthasarathy T. is a rural management professional, is alumnus of the IRMA, and is currently the CEO of Skillgreen Global Private Limited. He was previously coordinator of the Green College initiative of Welthungerhilfe and was heading the Livelihoods vertical at the Maharashtra State Rural Livelihoods Mission. He works on skill building of FPOs and rural entrepreneurs and has contributed to open source facilitation manuals for capacity building of FPOs.

Pranamesh Kar is a development sector professional who holds a master's degree in rural management from XIM University, Odisha. He has experience in strengthening community collectives (SHGs, FPOs, FPCs, and so on), livelihoods promotion, improved agriculture, and government-NGO collaboration. He has co-authored research papers focusing on the third sector's contribution to public policy, and displacement and rehabilitation of slum dwellers of Odisha. Currently his association with Professional Assistance for Development Action (PRADAN) contributes to the vision of doubling small farmer's income in Odisha.

Rajat Tomar is a rural management professional currently working with eKosh Financial Services Pvt Ltd. Prior to joining eKosh, he was the CEO at Ram Rahim Pragati Producer Company Ltd. (RRPPCL). At RRPPCL, he worked with Samaj Pragati Sahyog and the farmer members to ensure that the company's revenue grew by three times and enabled it to become self-sustainable in many ways. He is a trained mechanical engineer and worked at United Breweries Limited before taking up rural management as a career after his post-graduate education from IRMA.

Rajesh Verma is a development professional working as the CEO of UPPRO (state-level federation of FPOs of Uttar Pradesh promoted by Small Farmers Agribusiness Consortium (SFAC) Delhi). He holds a PG in business administration with a specialisation in agribusiness. He has more than 15 years of experience in the development sector including 11 years in inclusive finance and community institutions building (FPOs). He has worked at Taylor Nelson Sofres MODE, Religare Securities Ltd., and BASIX Consulting. His expertise includes agri-produce market linkages; FPO development; and management, HR, and finance management.

Ritesh Pandey is a practitioner, currently leading strategic partnerships in a social business centred around potato value chain named Siddhi Vinayak Agri Processing Pvt Ltd. He has graduated from BIT Mesra in computer applications and further from IRMA in rural management. He has worked with Mother Dairy, PwC, Microsave, and so on, wherein he has gained experience in marketing agri- and allied produce as well as promotion and strengthening of FPOs, especially in Bihar. He has led multi-stakeholder-oriented projects and activities. His goal is to conceptualize and execute ideas wherein wealth could be locally generated and captured in the rural economy.

Sachin Oza is Executive Director of DSC Foundation, an organisation involved in capacity building, research, documentation, and policy advocacy. Oza has done his master's in social work from the M.S. University, Baroda, and is associated with the natural resource management sector since 1990. He is a practitioner, trainer, and researcher. He has conducted several studies and presented papers on community involvement in water management, sustainable agriculture, and participatory groundwater management. He is a member of several state- and national-level forums related to policy influencing in Participatory Natural Resources Management (PNRM) in India.

Shilpa Vasavada is a gender and livelihood professional with experience in gender mainstreaming in livelihoods, largely with the non-profit sector in India. She is a graduate from Tata Institute of Social Sciences, Mumbai, India. Her specific areas of interest include gender and climate resilient agriculture, gender mainstreaming in FPOs, gender, and Women's Land Rights. She is the founder Convener of a state-level network of Civil Society Organisations (CSOs) on women's land rights where she led the network for about 15 years. Ms Shilpa is a certified master trainer of IFC-Learning Performance Institute, UK.

Sudha Narayanan is Research Fellow, International Food Policy Research Institute (IFPRI), New Delhi. Narayanan's research interests straddle agriculture, food, and nutrition policy; and human development in India. She is particularly interested in survey-based research using microeconometric approaches to understand broader questions of agrarian change and state delivery systems for nutrition security. Narayanan holds a PhD in agricultural economics from Cornell University and MPhil and MA degrees in economics from the Delhi School of Economics, India.

Sudipto Saha is a financial inclusion and livelihood professional having varied experiences including agribusiness support, promotion of farmers producers companies (FPCs), and building their systems and processes. He has also reviewed and assessed more than 150 institutions working in financial inclusion for facilitating financial linkages and capacity building support. He has promoted more than 30 FPCs in the states of West Bengal and Assam and facilitated convergences with several government schemes and marketing companies. He is a post-graduate diploma holder from the IRMA, post completion of bachelor in engineering (BE) from Malviya National Institute of Technology (MNIT), Jaipur.

Tara Nair is the director of research at the Work Fair and Free Foundation headquartered at Bangalore. She completed her MPhil (Applied Economics) and PhD (Economics) from the Centre for Development Studies, Thiruvananthapuram, affiliated to the Jawaharlal Nehru University, New Delhi, India. She was previously part of the faculty at the Entrepreneurship Development Institute of India, MICA (formerly Mudra Institute of Communications, Ahmedabad), and IRMA and has also headed research at Friends of Women's World Banking, India. Her current research mainly concerns policy and institutional aspects of micro and inclusive finance, social economy of small-scale fisheries, and feminist approaches to development.

Vaibhav Bhamoriya is Faculty and Assistant Dean (Development) at IIM Kashipur. He has earlier served as faculty at IIM Ahmedabad and IIM Indore. He graduated from IIT (ISM) Dhanbad and did his master's from IRMA. He has worked closely with community-based organisations (CBOs) and FPOs as a researcher and consultant over the past two decades. His research and consultancy interests are agri-entrepreneurship, sustainability, and producers organisations. He is the first recipient of Page prize (global mention) for sustainability curricula from India and has won the IIT-IIM professor of the year in 2020.

FOREWORD

This volume is an important compilation of cases of upcoming farmer producer organisations (FPOs) in various geographies of India. Its timing is apposite too since the Government of India has put much store in promoting FPOs of all hues to serve as a vehicle for rural development. In her 2018 Union Budget, the finance minister set the country a target of incubating 10,000 producer organisations. This is ambitious, especially so because even after a century's experience in promoting farmer cooperatives of various types, the alchemy of catalysing energetic, self-sustaining producer organisations remains a source of endless charm and frustration for researchers and practitioners alike. Producer cooperatives we celebrate today in dairying, sugar, and a few other sectors were all created more than 50 years ago by some political entrepreneurs as well as a motley band of self-less Gandhians dedicated to constructive nation building work. That tribe has vanished, but their work has been taken over by a new generation of development professionals and NGOs, most of whom view cooperatives as instruments not only of development but also of inclusion of the marginalised – women, adivasis, and landless and marginal farmers. These often have little to sell other than their unskilled labour; as a result, organising these into viable producer organisations of scale and significance is a challenge, but it is also an opportunity for discovery in curating an incubation protocol, as this book suggests.

Ever since its formative years in the 1980s, energetic farmer organisations have been an enduring interest for IRMA faculty and students. What passed off then as mainstream farmer cooperative system in India – mostly PACS – was little more than an appendage of the state and offered little role to farmer members in its governance or management. For IRMA – under the spell of early dairy, sugar, and cotton cooperatives of western India – a true cooperative is governed by members through its elected leaders and managed by professionals accountable to them. A messy political process of articulating and synergising conflicting interests of varied member groups is the quintessence of a true cooperative. As protagonists of this cooperative ideal, IRMA's founders argued that a rural economy teeming with such

cooperatives in various fields would not only lay the foundation for wholesome socio-economic development but also underpin our political democracy with a groundswell of village-level democratic institutions. No wonder,
the idea of self-governing farmer cooperatives was a foundational element
of IRMA's genesis which, in following years, gave birth to a tradition of
research that IRMA can claim to be uniquely her own.

The received theory until then was that strong cooperatives are built by
charismatic and sagacious leaders. But during the 1960s and 1970s, many
dairy, sugar, and cotton cooperatives were founded and made successful
by founders known for neither charisma nor sagacity. A competing theory
offered by leading sociologists B. S. Baviskar and D. W. Attwood argued that
dairy and sugar cooperatives in western India, mainly Gujarat and western
Maharashtra, succeeded in large numbers because *Patidars* in Gujarat and
Marathas in Maharashtra – who spearheaded and led these to success –
were close-knit farming communities with sharp economic instinct, high
entrepreneurial quotient, and social capital. The theory seemed compelling
since one found then (and finds even now) hardly any example of a large,
successful cooperative enterprise of adivasis or fisher folk or any of the marginalised communities. For those – such as the authors of the case studies in
this volume – seeking guidance on how to organise producers among adivasis, women, or marginal communities into robust, self-sustaining FPOs, the
Baviskar-Attwood theses presented a blind alley.

IRMA studies of the 1980s and the 1990s accepted that social contexts –
social capital, entrepreneurship, cohesiveness, leadership – do indeed matter
as enablers of success in cooperative entrepreneurship; but what matters
even more is the *design* of a cooperative enterprise as a member-controlled
economic organisation. It argued that *Patidar* leadership in early years did
doubtless play a key role in the success of Amul and other dairy unions in
Gujarat; however, these would have hardly succeeded as Uttar Pradesh's
milk supply unions of the 1940s in which the cooperative merely collected
farmers' milk while a private businessman undertook its processing and
marketing. Likewise, with *Marathas* or without, sugar cooperatives in
Maharashtra would have amounted to little as cane supply unions of Bihar
where the cooperative merely coordinated cane harvesting and transport
while all processing was controlled by a third party with no accountability
to farmers. No wonder Dr Kurien insisted that a farmer cooperative can
succeed only if the entire value chain – procurement, processing, and marketing – were unified under cooperative governance.

IRMA research also hinted, though not explicitly, that leadership role
in successful cooperatives may well be overrated since within a sector, successful cooperatives are remarkably alike to the original model. This is how
Amul developed into Amul pattern. Sugar cooperatives as a class are different from dairy cooperatives; but within sugar or dairy sector, the likeness
among cooperatives in their design is exceptional. This suggests that the real

hard and costly work of innovation, experimentation, trial and error on what works and what does not was done mostly by early pioneers. Founders of dairy unions in Mehsana, Banaskantha, Vadodara, Surat, and other districts merely copied what Amul did in all things that mattered to their success as farmer-owned businesses. Under Operation Flood, state governments tried but failed to recreate Amul pattern in other states because the core of the design was emasculated. Had some social entrepreneur, backed by a patient funding partner but untrammelled by bureaucratic procedures, made a sincere attempt to recreate Amul design in Uttar Pradesh, chances are that she would have built a successful dairy farmer organisation without *Patidars* or *Marathas* as members and leaders. Forty years ago, when IRMA advanced this hypothesis, there was no counterfactual to test it. But the success of new-generation cooperatives (NGCs) with a modified Amul design that the National Dairy Development Board (NDDB) has promoted in Saurashtra, Rajasthan, Vidarbha, Uttar Pradesh, and Punjab attests to the IRMA hypothesis. It signifies that getting the *design* right is central to building robust producer organisations.

This rather long introduction to the IRMA tradition of cooperative research is apposite because it hints that, if designed right, a producer organisation can succeed even in harsh social conditions in its domain. If FPOs can succeed only if their members and leaders belong to an enterprising farming community with high social capital, as the Baviskar-Attwood thesis implied, FPOs studied here would have no hope whatever to build economic muscle and achieve techno-economic success. All FPOs studied here prioritised women, adivasis, and small and marginal farmers, that too, in harsh, rain-fed tracts. Of the 12 individual FPOs studied, six are completely women owned, and three are led by woman chief executive officers (CEOs). They purposely chose difficult settings with many challenges but few business opportunities. To top it all, many FPOs covered also pursued larger social goals which might not be necessarily consistent with their members' immediate priorities. Thus, Samaj Pragati Sahayog (SPS) wanted its FPO to promote pesticide-free farming by poor adivasi farmers in poorest parts of tribal Madhya Pradesh. Krishidhan advocated environmentally sustainable farming in arid north Gujarat. Sahaja Samrudhdha wanted Desi Seeds to support only desi seed savers. Some FPOs had the benefit of pre-existing social capital through long collaboration with promotional NGO. Many others, however, were created overnight without any prior work on mobilisation and social capital creation. Can these become economically strong member-controlled producer organisations? IRMA research would suggest they can if they were *designed* right.

So what indeed has IRMA research meant by *design* in this particular context? Is it a magic bullet that guarantees success? Certainly not, but good design does guarantee collective will among members to succeed. The first test of a good design of an FPO is that its members develop a 'skin in the game', as it were. Design for a self-governing FPO is best understood as a member-centred process of problem solving that strengthens the collective agency of its membership. Such a design infuses in it a will to survive and grow and to seek internal locus of control. It enjoins the FPO to find ways to harmonise priorities of intense minority and apathetic majority in its membership and strive to accumulate member allegiance by constantly innovating to further their shared priorities. FPOs designed thus manifest behavioural patterns distinct from investor-owned firms (IoFs) which maximise Return on Equity (RoE). Quintessentially, successful FPOs seek three kinds of centrality: in their members' livelihood systems, in their chosen line of business, and in the economy of their domain. Not all FPOs succeed equally in this endeavour; nature of business and its social context determine inter alia how central they become.

IRMA's deployment during the 1980s of the term *design* for cooperatives in some ways presaged the vast and exciting field of 'design thinking' that has opened up since around then (see Liedtka, 2018). However, innovation, experimentation, trial and error in 'design thinking processes' are costly and time-consuming. As a result, as alluded earlier, new cooperatives tend to emulate the design evolved by a successful pioneer rather than rediscovering the wheel all over again. This does not by any means imply that there is a unique design to build a successful FPO in a sector. New-generation dairy cooperatives have undertaken a new round of design thinking process and evolved a somewhat different design for organising dairy farmers. They have done away with village societies, modified electoral rules, and adopted an asset-light capital structure. For now, the new design seems to be working as well as the Amul pattern. Another good example of robust design is the women's self-help group (SHG) movement that has taken rural India by storm.

In sum, then, designing a high-performing FPO involves creative engagement in five spheres: (a) constantly improving the value creation model including the technology of transformation as well as transaction; (b) enhancing member-centredness of the operating system; (c) ensuring patronage-cohesive governance system; (d) creating and sustaining favourable external task environment; and (e) nurturing member allegiance. In all FPOs, design is always work in progress. A fledgling FPO struggling to survive, as well as an established one seeking centrality, will gain by directing its thinking and energies on these five spheres. Researchers and field professionals in promotional and funding agencies too can help FPOs better by focusing their inputs on these five spheres.

Regretfully, in the past 50 years, the field of research on cooperatives in India has been as barren as that of cooperative entrepreneurship, governance, and management. With little Indian material of significance, the recent wave of research on FPOs therefore draws heavily on European and North American literature on cooperatives where the focus is primarily on business performance. The irony is that farmer cooperatives in industrialised countries are so fundamentally different from FPOs of the kind we study in this book – in the relevance of inclusivity, in their business goals and objectives, in average size of their member's business, in their dependence on government and NGOs, and so on – that Western literature can be of little value in understanding challenges facing FPOs. Therefore, this volume of FPO case studies is well suited to build upon and extend the IRMA tradition of research on cooperatives in today's context.

The methodology of this study – emphasising co-creation approach to knowledge building – is uniquely suited for this purpose. Academics were paired with development practitioners as well as consultants to initiate a process of joint inquiry, and the abstracts were peer-reviewed and discussed in a subsequent workshop that included the case protocol. Throughout, the study stressed iterative and reflective process, collective enquiry, and democratic forms of participation.

Producer organisations covered in this volume represent great variety in size, membership, scale of business, locale, and especially their normative underpinnings. Membership varies from 500 to over 5,000; age varies from six to 15 years; business turnover ranges from a few lakhs per year to some crores. There are village-scale, single-tier collectives, but the volume also includes Maha FPC that federates over 600 primary collectives. Krushidhan in North Gujarat has a three-tier structure with SHGs and farmer clubs at hamlet level, cluster committees at sub-regional level, and the FPC board at regional level.

Inclusion of the marginalised sections is the defining aspect of the FPOs covered. Little surprise then is that economic success has not been their hallmark, and many of the FPOs studied have much ground to cover as robust, self-sustaining producer-owned business enterprises. A few have crossed the financial viability threshold, but many are struggling to get there. All suffer capital and capability constraints. Developing a stable anchor activity to pay for fixed costs is a key concern, and many keep shifting businesses in an opportunistic manner. In some sense, these infirmities represent the price paid for high level of social, especially gender inclusion, rather than chasing socio-economic performance and vitality as FPOs. The case study authors are sensitive and empathetic to this predicament. The key takeaway for the FPOs is that, in many ways, their journey itself is their destination so far. But in the times to come, a valid question these will all have to contend with is: can inclusive FPOs of the marginalised transform themselves into successful enterprises with economic muscle? If IRMA research is any guide, these sure can by proactively adopting design features that help grow economic muscle.

Significantly, much design thinking about the shape FPOs would take occurs not in its membership but among promoters and other stakeholders. In early cooperatives in western India, this was done by Gandhian workers like Tribhuvandas Patel. Today, their role is taken up by promotional agencies – NGOs, governments, donors who found FPOs to achieve development outcomes. What kind of member-organisation does an FPO grow into a few years after its establishment is profoundly affected inter alia by the foresight and sagacity that promoters and other stakeholders bring to their incubation. This volume will hopefully set into motion a debate on how these and other FPOs can use design thinking to become successful enterprises without sacrificing their inclusivity.

Tushaar Shah

Reference

Liedtka, J (2018). Why design thinking works. *Harvard Business Review*, September-October. Retrieved from https://hbr.org/2018/09/why-design-thinking-works

ACKNOWLEDGEMENTS

This book is a culmination of in-depth and long-term collaborative associations between academics, development practitioners, professionals working in FPOs, and farmers who form the literal backbone of the country. We would like to thank the case authors for their patience, generosity, critical inputs, insightful data based on ground experience, and their whole-hearted support in making the work on collective enterprises a truly collective effort over the last two years.

The authors are especially grateful for the time and patient engagement provided by the board members, CEOs, and other stakeholders of the FPOs covered in the volume. A special mention of the contributors includes Mohan Sharma, Executive Director, Development Support Centre (DSC), Jaswant Chauhan (Chief Executive Officer (CEO)), and Vasant and Nitin Patel from Krushidhan; Shivendra Kumar, Ram Krishna Satyam of Jeevika; Vijay-shankar P S, Animesh Mondal, Rajat Tomar (CEO), support staff at Ram Rahim FPC and Samaj Pragati Sahyog; Indranil Mazumder, Md Jabbar Khan, Sahid Ali, and Ismail of the Bhangar FPC, as well as the Director, Department of Agriculture-Marketing, Government of West Bengal; Balakrishnan, Pramel Gupta, Satish Chandra Mishra from Vrutti, as well as agriculture and horti-culture departments of the state government of Chhattisgarh for the Maha-nadi case; all team members and office bearers of Umang Mahila and Krishi Bagwani cooperative; Krishnagopal, Sarat Kumar, and Waseem from Access Livelihood Consulting who were involved in incubation and management of Hasnabad FPC; Bharat Mogre and Vivek from AKRSP(I) for the Pandhana FPO case; Alagesan P (Dr), Senior Scientist & Head, ICAR – Krishi Vigyan Kendra, MYRADA, Arvind Risbud, Executive Director, and Gayatri Lal, Pro-gramme Officer, MYRADA, Gokulnathan – Director, Kazhani, Kavitha, K P, CEO, Kazhani FPC; D. Sattaiah, CEO BASIX and Rajnikant Prasad, for the Navyug FPO case in Uttar Pradesh; Krishnaprasad, the founder, and other staff and board members of Desi Seeds; Kuldeep Solanki, board members of Gujpro including Kavita Mehta, Kirit Jasani, Dalsukhbhai, and other staff of Ambuja Cement Foundation, board members, CEO and farmer members of Somnath FPC, Kodinar for the Gujpro case; Mr Yogesh Dwivedi, CEO

Madhya Bharat, Board of Directors of MBCFPCL, and Sanjay Pandya, production manager for the Madhya Bharat case; Yogesh Thorat, CEO, Prasant Pawar, Hanumant Wadekar and Medha Adhikari in MAHAFPC.

Critical and constructive feedback provided by Dinesh Awasthi, Sankar Datta, C. S. Reddy, Shirish Joshi, Emmanuel Murray, and others helped in sharpening the arguments presented in the volume through their continuous engagement with the project during the workshop during the Kurien Centenary celebrations on 25 November 2022. The last mile work in the book, involving proofreading, updating citations, and language editing, was made easier thanks to abiding support of Arnab Chakraborty and Aneesh Mohan. The administrative backend of formalising the collaborative process was admirably handled by Chintan Patel. Astad Pastakia, K. V. Gouri, Dr Tara Nair, and Abhishek Saxena went well beyond their role as chapter authors to provide critical inputs for the introduction and synthesis chapter. Their meticulous engagement with the book is much appreciated.

Dr Tushaar Shah has been a constant source of inspiration and support during the workshop, and we are immensely grateful to him for agreeing to go through the manuscript and present his insightful foreword brining continuity with the IRMA research on collective enterprises in the 1990s and re-interpreting these for today's times. We thank IRMA's Director, Prof. Umakant Dash, and the academic community of IRMA for their constant support and encouragement throughout the project. Profs. Preeti Priya, Hippu Nathan, and Aashish Argade contributed through reviews of cases and by also taking up cases that unfortunately could not fructify due to the pandemic. Srinivasan Iyer, programme officer, of Ford Foundation has been a silent but significant source of support for backing the idea and investing in the process of co-creating new knowledge through the Living Farm Incomes project. His empathetic involvement, despite the pandemic, and the emphasis he placed on the ground-level understanding of ideas through collaborations were critical for the project.

We sincerely hope the book inspires constructive discussions and generative policy directions, building on the collaborative spirit that gave birth to this volume. We dedicate this volume to Dr Verghese Kurien, whose pioneering work on producer collectives has been an inspiration for us as editors and all those listed earlier.

ABBREVIATIONS

Abbreviation	Full forms
AAPCL	Aranyak Agri Producer Company Ltd.
ACCESS	Access Development Services
AEs	Agri-Entrepreneurs
AGM	Annual General Meeting
AIC	Agriculture Insurance Company of India Ltd
AKRSP (I)	Aga Khan Rural Support Programme (India)
ALC	Access Livelihoods Consulting
ALDF	Access Livelihoods Development Finance
APEDA	Agricultural and Processed Food Products Export Development Authority
APL	Above Poverty Line
APMC	Agricultural Produce Marketing Committee
APPI	Azim Premji Philanthropic Initiatives
ASA	Action of Social Advancement
ATMA	Agricultural Technology Management Agency
B2B	Business to Business
B2C	Business to Customer
B2G	Business to Government
BAIF	Bharatiya Agro Industries Foundation
BAIPP	Bihar Agriculture Investment Promotion Policy
BASIX	Bhartiya Samruddhi Investments and Consulting Ltd
BAU	Business Acceleration Unit
BISCOMAUN	Bihar State Co-operative Marketing Union Ltd
BMGF	Bill & Melinda Gates Foundation
BoD	Board of Directors
BoI	Bank of India
BPL	Below Poverty Line
BRGF	Backward Regions Grant Funds Programme
BRLPS	Bihar Rural Livelihoods Promotion Society
BSFL	Bhartiya Samruddhi Finance Limited
BVPCL	Bhangar Vegetable Producer Company Limited
CAR	Capital Adequacy Ratio
CAs	Chartered Accountants
CBBO	Cluster-Based Business Organisation

ABBREVIATIONS

Abbreviation	Full forms
CDF	Cooperative Development Foundation
CDFI	Centre for Digitization of Financial Inclusion
CEO	Chief Executive Officer
CHCs	Custom Hiring Centres
CIF	Community Investment Fund
CIP	Cooperative Initiative Panel
CLF	Cluster-Level Federation
CMRC	Community Managed Resource Centre
CMS	Catalyst Management Services
COFCO	China Oil and Foodstuffs Corporation, and formerly COFCO International Limited
CRPs	Community Resource Persons
CSO	Civil Society Organisations
CSR	Corporate Social Responsibility
DAP	Di-Ammonium Phosphate
DBT	Direct Benefit Transfer
DCMS	District Cooperative Marketing Society
DHO	District Horticulture Officer
DIN	Digital Identity Number
DKVPCL	Dhari Krishak Vikas Producer Company Ltd
DMF	District Mineral Foundation
DoA	Department of Agriculture
DOPRD	Department of Panchayat & Rural Development
DPIP	District Poverty Initiative Program
DSC	Development Support Centre
F&V	Fruits and Vegetables
FAGs	Farmer Affinity Groups
FAO	Food and Agricultural Organisation
FCI	Food Corporation of India
FGD	Focused Group Discussions
FIGs	Farmers Interest Groups
FPCs	Farmer Producer Companies
FPOs	Farmer Producer Organisations
FSF	Food Security Fund
FSSAI	Food Safety and Standards Authority of India
FWWB	Friends of the Women's World Bank
FYM	Farmyard Manure
GBMs	General Body Meetings
GCMMF	Gujarat Cooperative Milk Marketing Federation
GDP	Gross Domestic Product
GGPCS	Gumla Gramin Poultry Co-operative Society Ltd.
GoI	Government of India
GPA	General Power of Attorney
GREEN	Genetic Resource, Ecology, Energy and Nutrition
GRGs	Goat-Rearing Groups
GRKM	Gujarat Rajya Krushak Manch
Gujpro	Gujpro Agribusiness Consortium Producer Company Ltd.
HDI	Human Development Index
HFSPC	Hasnabad Farmers Services Producer Company Limited
ICAR	Indian Council of Agriculture Research

Abbreviation	Full forms
ICRIER	International Centre for Research on International Economic Research
ICRISAT	International Crop Research Institute for the Semi-Arid Tropics
ICTs	Information And Communication Technologies
IDWG/OA	Inter-Departmental Working Group on Organic Agriculture
IFFCO	Indian Farmers Fertiliser Cooperative
IIRR	Indian Institute of Rice Research
INM	Integrated Nutrient Management
IPM	Integrated Pest Management
IRMA	Institute of Rural Management Anand
JLG	Joint Liability Groups
JOHAR	Jharkhand Opportunities for Harnessing Rural Growth Project
JVs	Joint Venture
JWAPCL	Jeevika Women Agri Producer Company Limited
KBSSSL	Krishi Bagwani Swawlambi Sahakari Samiti Limited
KCs	Kisan Clubs
KFPCL	Kazhani Farmer Producer Company Limited
KPCL	Krushidhan Producer Company Ltd.
KVKs	Krishi Vikas Kendra
LDM	Lead District Manager
LEPNRM	Livelihood Enhancement through Participatory Natural Resource Management
LRPs	Local Resource Persons
MABIF	Madurai Agri-business Incubation Forum
MACP	Maharashtra Agriculture Competitive Project
MAHAFPC	MAHA Farmers Producer Company Ltd.
MANAGE	National Institute of Agricultural Extension Management
MATCS	Mutually Aided Thrift Cooperative Societies
MBCFPCL	Madhya Bharat Consortium of Farmer Producers Company Limited
MCA	Ministry of Corporate Affairs
MFP	Mega Food Park
MFPCL	Mahanadi Farmer Producer Company Limited
MINI	Millet Network of India
MPDPIP	MP District Poverty Initiative Project
MSP	Minimum Support Price
MT	Metric Tonne
MVMs	Mahila Vikas Mandals
MYRADA	Mysore Resettlement and Development Agency
NABARD	National Bank for Agriculture and Rural Development
NAFED	National Agricultural Cooperative Marketing Federation of India Ltd
NAFPO	National Association of Farmer Producer Organisations
NBFC	Non-Bank Finance Company
NCDC	National Cooperative Development Corporation
NCDEX	National Commodities and Derivatives Exchange
NCML	National Commodities Management Services Limited
NDDB	National Dairy Development Board
NeML	Network Element Management Layer
NFSM-A3P	National Food Security Mission-Accelerated Pulses Production Programme

Abbreviation	Full forms
NGC	New-Generation Cooperative
NGO	Non-Governmental Organisation
NIC	National Informatics Centre
NKFL	Nab Kisan Finance Limited
NPK	Nitrogen-Phosphorus-Potash
NPM	Non-Pesticide Management
NPOP	National Programme for Organic Production
NRLM	National Rural Livelihoods Mission
NRM	Natural Resource Management
NSC	National Seed Corporation
NTFP	Non-Timber Forest Produce
NVIUC	National Vegetable Initiative for Urban Clusters
NYPCL	Navyug Kisan Producer Company Ltd.
ODOP	One District One Crop
P2C	Producer to Consumer
PACS	Primary Agricultural Credit Societies
PAT	Profit After Tax
PBT	Profit Before Tax
PCA	Primary Census Abstract
PCMC	Producer Company Management Committee
PCS	Produce in the State
PDS	Public Distribution Scheme
PGs	Producer Groups
PGS	Participatory Guarantee System
PI	Promoting Institution
PIM	Participatory Irrigation Management
PKVY	Paramparagat Krishi Vikas Yojana
PMFBY	Pradhan Mantri Fasal Bima Yojana
PNRM	Participatory Natural Resources Management
PODF	Producer Organization Development Fund
PoP	Package of Practice
POs	Producer Organisations
PPP	Public-Private Partnership
PPPAID	Public Private Partnership-Integrated Agriculture Development
PPPCL	Pandhana Pashupalak Producer Company Limited
PPS	Pashu-Palak Samuhs
PRADAN	Professional Assistance for Development Action
PRODUCE	Producers' Organization Development and Upliftment Corpus
PSF	Price Stabilisation Fund
PSS	Price Support Scheme
RAF	Rajya Ajeevika Forum
RF	Revolving Fund
RGB	Representative General Body
RIs	Resource Institutions
RKVY	Rashtriya Krishi Vikash Yojana
RKVY-RAFTAAR	Rashtriya Krishi Vikas Yojana – Remunerative Approaches for Agriculture and Allied Sectors Rejuvenation
RML	Reuters Market Light
RoC	Registrar of Cooperative
RoCs	Registrar of Companies

Abbreviation	Full forms
ROCE	Return on Capital Employed
RRPPCL	Ram Rahim Pragati Producer Company Limited
RTI	Right to Information Act
RTRS	Round Table on Responsible Soya
SAUs	State Agriculture Universities
SB	Sufal Bangla
SBY	Savayava Bhagya Yojane
SEBI	Securities and Exchange Board of India
SEWs	Skilled Extension Workers
SFAC	Small Farmers Agribusiness Consortium
SGSY	Swarnjayanti Gram Swarozgar Yojana
SHG	Self-Help Group
SHPL	Safe Harvest Private Limited
SLPC	State-Level Producer Company
SOPs	Standard Operating Procedures
SPS	Samaj Pragati Sahyog
SPVs	Special-Purpose Vehicles
SRI	System of Root Intensification
SRLM	State Rural Livelihood Mission
SROI	Social Returns on Investment
SS	Sajjata Sangh
SSE	Social and Solidarity Economy
TL	Truthfully Labelled
TNAU	Tamil Nadu Agriculture University
TNIAMP	Tamil Nadu Irrigated Agriculture Modernization Program
TNOCD	Tamil Nadu Organic Certification Department
UPBSN	Uttar Pradesh Bhumi Sudhar Nigam
UPPRO	Uttar Pradesh Producer Company Ltd
VAMNICOM	Vaikunth Mehta National Institute for Cooperative Management
VAPCOL	Vasundhara Agri-Horti Producer Co. Ltd
VO	Village Organisation
VLOs	Village-Level Organisations
VPFPC	Vaishanavdham Parunde Farmers Producers Company
VRPs	Village Resource Persons
WARDA	Women's Advancement in Rural Development and Agriculture
WHR	Warehouse Receipt
WSHGs	Women Self-Help Groups

1

PRODUCER ORGANISATIONS AS 21ST-CENTURY FARMER INSTITUTIONS

*C. Shambu Prasad, Ajit Kanitkar,
and Deborah Dutta*

The Covid-19 pandemic has laid bare the existing fault lines of our inequitable economic systems. Eighty-four per cent of Indian households suffered a decline in their income even as the number of billionaires and their wealth increased leading to calls for introducing global wealth taxes to address this crisis (Chancel et al., 2021; Oxfam, 2022). Could alternative economic systems that embed the distribution aspects of wealth creation during production mitigate this problem? As member-owned, people-centred, and value-based enterprises, cooperatives are potentially better vehicles for promoting equality and inclusive economic development (Iyer, 2020). Members of cooperatives have shown greater resilience during crises like the pandemic and have withstood shocks and carried on their businesses despite widespread disruption (Hiriyur and Chhetri, 2021; Billiet et al., 2021). Despite an overwhelming focus on investor-owned firms as *the* economic organisations in management research, cooperatives have begun to feature in recent discussions on management paradigms beyond profit maximisation (Adler, 2016). Cooperatives are part of community wealth-building strategies that could broadly include consumer cooperatives, worker cooperatives, or producer cooperatives (Dubb, 2016). Cooperative enterprises, according to Verghese Kurien, the founder of the dairy cooperative movement in India, "constitute a model for a people-centred and sustainable form of societal organization based on equity, justice, and solidarity" (p. 103, Chakraborty et al., 2004).

1. Smallholder agriculture and producer organisations

Cooperatives that were an integral part of rural development policy witnessed a decline in the 1980s. Producer organisations (PO) are replacing the older category of farmer organisation and cooperatives with a greater emphasis and policy orientation on market orientation, the enterprise nature, and as rural businesses (Bijman, 2016). POs, in rural areas, have been seen to play an important role in alleviating poverty and supporting development that led to organisations like the World Bank increasing their capacity development support for agricultural POs. POs are seen as key actors for integrating small farmers into economic production chains, important for democracy and human development, as essential actors in bringing about innovation and as vehicles to overcome social dilemmas (Gouët et al., 2009).

Smallholder farmers account for between 30 and 70% of global food production. Small farms in India are defined as holdings with size less than 2 hectares, while operational holdings greater than 10 hectares are classified as 'large'. However, 70% of farms in India are 'ultra-small' – less than 0.05 ha. Further, between 1990–1991 and 2015–16, the share of small and marginal farmers rose from 78 to 86% (Giller et al., 2021; Kumar et al., 2020).

Activities that were traditionally farm-centric like production of seeds, animals, feed, and fertiliser are all increasingly being integrated within consolidated agribusiness value chains. For instance, three global market leaders in seeds that control over 50% market share are also major pesticide producers. These agribusiness conglomerates can dictate prices, conditions of production and exchange, and the direction of government policies (Econexus, 2013). Individual peasants or subsistence farmers are connected in complex ways with global agribusinesses through local retail markets (Aga, 2018). Food sovereignty movements seeking greater autonomy of peasant agriculture have emerged across the globe since the 1990s, often using the lens of 'food regime' to better understand the complex intersections at play in the food and agriculture system (McMichael, 2021).

Small producers suffer from high production and market risks emerging from lack of capital and capacities; high operational costs; poor or costly access to services like technology, training, and credit; and weak bargaining power. Also, they largely remain invisible in the policy prescriptions. Right from the mid-19th century, cooperatives have played a vital role in helping small producers overcome these challenges, and collective action has been seen to flourish while providing a social, economic, and political alternative to profit-maximising capitalism (Ratner, 2009). Different forms of formal and informal collectives under the broad canvas of social and solidarity economy (SSE) have emerged that seek to reassert social control or 'social power' over the economy by giving primacy to social and environmental objectives above profits. They rethink economic practice in terms of democratic self-management and active citizenship with the potential to provide decent work (Utting, 2016).

POs are seen as the only institutions which can protect small farmers from the ill effects of globalisation or make them participate successfully in modern competitive markets by provisioning various services, which enhance member engagement and lead to producer agency and empowerment (Penrose-Buckley, 2007; Trebbin and Hassler, 2012). Unlike private agribusiness(es) that create value only for investors, POs are needed to capture value for farmer members (Gersch, 2018). POs are seen as institutional innovations that can reduce transaction costs, provide technical help in production and creating social capital, offset scale disadvantages faced by small farms in supplying to the modern value chains, help in farm diversification and better price realisations in output markets, strengthen bargaining power, and raise the voice of smallholders in the policy process (Ton et al., 2007; Kanitkar, 2016; Singh, 2021a, Pingali et al., 2019).

The 2008 World Development Report, the World Bank's first report on agriculture after 1982, emphasised the need to improve the competitiveness of smallholder agriculture and popularised the narrative of "making markets work for poor people" (World Bank, 2007; Cooney and Shanks, 2010). POs were seen as the favoured vehicles for improving farm income ever since. However, the policy prescriptions for POs in developing countries sit uncomfortably with the literature on agricultural cooperatives predominantly from the North American and European contexts where new-generation cooperatives (NGCs) have been explored for greater engagement with markets and value chains through mechanisms like joint ventures and alliances (Cook and Iliopoulos, 1999). Smallholder farm sizes in the developing world though are vastly different from the hundreds to thousands of hectares in the Western world to fractional or less than few hectares in the developing world. Member equity is substantially lower, and thereby their access to and control of value chains too is limited.[1] Understanding contextual differences is critical for effective design of POs.

1.1 Agrarian distress and POs in India

No national occupational group in the world contains more people, or more poor people, than India's agricultural sector. Moving beyond the post-independence pangs of production deficit, India today is a leader in agricultural commodities in the world in vegetables, buffalo meat, rice, wheat, and sugarcane.[2] While crop yields have increased over time, farm incomes have stagnated or declined. Agriculture's contribution to GDP in India has fallen to around 14%, yet 50% of the workforce continues to partially rely on agriculture for their livelihoods. Rising input costs and stagnating output prices coupled with low yields make for low returns. Rural households in several Indian states experience negative growth in real net incomes. Productivity growth in field crops appears to have stagnated owing to a combination of poor soils, water constraints, and unbalanced fertiliser use. The current crisis in Indian agriculture is often attributed to a historical policy that privileged self-sufficiency over sustainability (Kumar et al., 2020).

Any discussion on farming and agriculture in India is incomplete without reference to the long-standing agricultural crisis and distress of farmers. The number of farmer suicides in India during 1995–2012 was more than 300,000 (Nagaraj et al., 2014).[3] In recent years this distress has manifested in terms of farmer protests forcing state and central governments to reconsider their policies, most significantly the contentious farm bills of the Government of India (GoI) in 2020 that led to the largest and longest sustained non-violent movement in Indian history (Singh, 2021; Narayanan, 2021; Nandakumar, 2022).

Farming is a high-risk business, and financial returns fluctuate wildly between years. An average Indian farmer is estimated to be earning Rs. 3,140 per month in 2016–17 from cultivation activities that constitute only 36% of the total monthly household income of about Rs. 8,931 (including income from non-farm sources, salaries, wages, and the like). Estimates suggest that a rain-fed farmer taking a crop loan of Rs. 300,000 in a year could easily become a defaulter with a crop loss in two seasons and would need Rs. 31,500 to restart his/her account (Saini et al., 2021). Despite highly subsidised rates at which loans can be availed, a significant number of small and marginal farmers depend on non-institutional sources of credit at higher interest rates.

The Indian government renamed the department of agriculture to include farmer welfare and constituted a committee to double farm incomes. Farmer producer organisations (FPOs) were seen as a critical instrument that would transform agriculture from subsistence to an enterprise. There are over 280 references to FPOs in its 14-volume report, and FPOs are seen as one of the more effective institutions to reach out to small and marginal farmers and build their capacities to collectively leverage their production and marketing strength for enhancing farmer income. FPOs in India thus face multiple expectations from stakeholders to provide solutions to smallholder agriculture. These include being a 'voice' for farmers against corporate interests and takeover, enabling markets to work for the poor, and a vehicle to increase farm income. They are expected to be institutions that could present a middle path between otherwise polarising narratives that tend to see this as a corporate takeover by the opponents of the farm bill or 'the 1991 reform movement' by proponents of the farm laws (Prasad, 2021). In the next section we trace the evolution of FPOs in India to help situate the set of cases in the book from rain-fed regions of India.

2. POs in India: from cooperatives to producer companies

In the decades following India's independence, there were several farmer leaders who spearheaded POs registered as cooperatives. Stalwarts such as Tribhuvandas Patel in Gujarat (for dairy farmers), Vitthalrao Vikhe Patil in Maharashtra (sugarcane farmers), and Viswanath Reddy in Mulkanoor in Telangana/Andhra Pradesh (paddy farmers) seeded cooperatives, nurtured them in initial years, and ensured that the emerging cooperative grew in both business and membership. Cooperatives also had significant support from the academia with the setting up of many cooperative management training centres and specialised institutions such as the Vaikunth Mehta National Institute for Cooperative Management (VAMNICOM) in 1967 and the Institute of Rural Management Anand (IRMA) in 1979 to create professional manpower for the growing dairy sector following the Anand pattern of cooperatives through Operation Flood. New knowledge combining practice and theory followed with scholars like Baviskar and Attwood (1995) positing that fertile grounds for cooperatives emerged in places where the regional political economy was considered favourable.

Researchers at IRMA led a series of workshops and books on rediscovering cooperation, and alternative explanations were sought to explain the performance of cooperatives. The seminal work by Tushaar Shah (1995a, 1996) presented an alternate explanation for driving cooperative performance with an aim to seek a minimal blueprint that brought greater attention to the design, governance, and management of cooperatives as self-governing organisations. Shah's six principles of the Anand pattern have been invoked to drive better cooperative performance going beyond dairy into other sectors. There was however a significant change in the external environment since the 1990s with the liberalisation of the Indian economy and the opening up of commodity markets to global players. Unlike the dairy and sugar industries, that had built significant capacity and competence to cope with these changes, cooperatives in other agricultural commodities had significantly lower market shares and were insufficiently organised to expand or respond effectively to the sweeping changes of the agricultural sector.

While state support for cooperatives was high in post-independence India, it declined over the years with few new cooperatives being established since 1980s. High dependence and excessive interference by the state produced "a vast but spineless cooperative movement" (Shah, 1995b) that was central to government policy on rural credit but becoming entrenched power centres for doling out patronage, financial help, and political support (Vaidyanathan, 2013). Leading thinkers of the cooperative movement such as Mohan Dharia, L. C. Jain, Verghese Kurien, and the Cooperative Development Foundation (CDF) as part of the Cooperative Initiative Panel (CIP) pushed for a liberal law that would enable greater member control and autonomy of cooperatives and a reduced role of the registrar of cooperatives in cooperative functioning in the 1990s. This led to the formation of the Mutually Aided Thrift Cooperative Societies (MATCS) and self-reliant cooperatives in a few states, especially in Andhra Pradesh, where this change in the law also coincided with the growth of the self-help group (SHG) movement. While the larger thrust of these new cooperatives was in the microfinance sector (Nair and Gandhe, 2011), there were also some in later years that became strong agricultural cooperatives, such as the Dharani Mutually Aided Cooperative Society (Sathish Kumar and Prasad, 2020).

2.1 Producer companies as NGCs in India

Traditional cooperatives were increasingly seen as unsuccessful in linking small farmers to the global market. The ground for a new set of cooperatives with greater autonomy and democratic control by members continued through the concerted efforts of the CIP. A need was felt for a central enabling legislation that would respond to new challenges posed by the liberalisation of the Indian economy. A committee for the formation and conversion of cooperative business into companies under the chairmanship of Dr Y K Alagh was constituted by the GoI in 2000. The committee highlighted the need for new institutions that would enable rural producers as equal partners in the new economy, who could market their produce in a modern and professional manner. The committee reviewed cooperatives and companies with the cooperative ideal from Denmark, Switzerland, Zimbabwe, and the United States and recommended that the government enact a legislation to enable registration and operation of producer companies in India. An amendment of the Companies Act, 1956, provided for registration of 'Producer Companies' by primary producers. This has been hailed as an Indian version of a NGC (Singh, 2008), a new form of collective action (Trebbin and Hassler, 2012) and an institutional innovation (Singh, 2021a) while also criticised for being 'old wine in a new bottle' (Shah, 2016).

Table 1.1 highlights the key differences between a producer company, a cooperative, and a private company. As is evident, the producer company format enables greater 'ease of doing' business for POs but can also come with

Table 1.1 Comparison of Indian cooperatives, producer, and other companies

Feature	Cooperative	Producer Company	Other Companies
Registration	Co-op Societies Act	Companies Act	Companies Act
Membership	Open to any individual or cooperative	Only to producer members and their agencies	Any person who wishes to invest
Area of Operation	Restricted	Throughout India	Throughout India
Professionals on Board	Invitees only	Can co-opt experts as directors	Provision for independent directors
Shares	Not tradable	Tradable within membership	Freely tradable
Voting Rights	One member one vote; registrar (govt. rep) has veto powers	One member one vote; non-producer cannot vote	Proportional to shareholding
Government Role	Significant, excessive	Minimal	Minimal

Feature	Cooperative	Producer Company	Other Companies
Compliance	Annual reports to regulator	As per Companies Act (2013), high and challenging	As per the Companies Act
External Equity and Other Entity Relations	No provision; transaction/ contract based	No provision; can form JVs and alliances	Allowed JVs and alliances
Profit Sharing	Limited dividend on capital	Based on patronage and with priority on building reserves	As decided by board with no restrictions
Income Tax	Trading surplus exempt under Section 80P	Section 80P(A) exempts income from eligible businesses up to Rs. 100 crores till 2024–25	25% corporate tax rate

Source: Compiled by authors from Singh and Singh (2014) and Phansalkar and Paranjape (2021)

greater compliance requirements – a challenge for an ostensibly first-generation, and even illiterate, farmer board of directors (BoD) in remote corners of India.

While the phrase 'producer organisation' is common internationally, in the Indian context the more common phrase is 'farmer producer organisa-tion' (FPO). This is a much broader category that includes several legal forms of collectives of farmers that could be formally registered as a traditional cooperative society under various state governments, the new-generation self-reliant cooperatives operational in a few states, a section 8 company, a public trust, or a society. However, the most preferred organisational form has been the producer company under 2003 Act that was later modified in 2013, following opposition from an industrial chamber and counterargu-ments by proponents of company legislative reform in favour of farmers.[4] Figure 1.1 shows the registration of FPCs since inception. Technically, the number of FPOs is larger than this. However, there are challenges with put-ting together data across multiple implementing agencies and formats that need to be collated at each state level for cooperatives.

The evolution of Farmer Producer Companies (FPCs), which began with a trickle with fewer than 50 FPCs registered per year until 2010, has now become the most favoured form of PO in India. It is estimated that there are 22,388 FPCs registered until March 2022.[7] One can broadly discern four phases of FPO evolution in India. The first phase, roughly from 2003 to 2010, was the gradual acceptance of this new form with the biggest thrust coming from Madhya Pradesh that pioneered the registration of 18 FPCs through the World Bank–funded District Poverty Initiative Program (DPIP) with a generous support of Rs. 2.5 million each for working capital and administrative costs over five years. Further, Civil Society Organisations

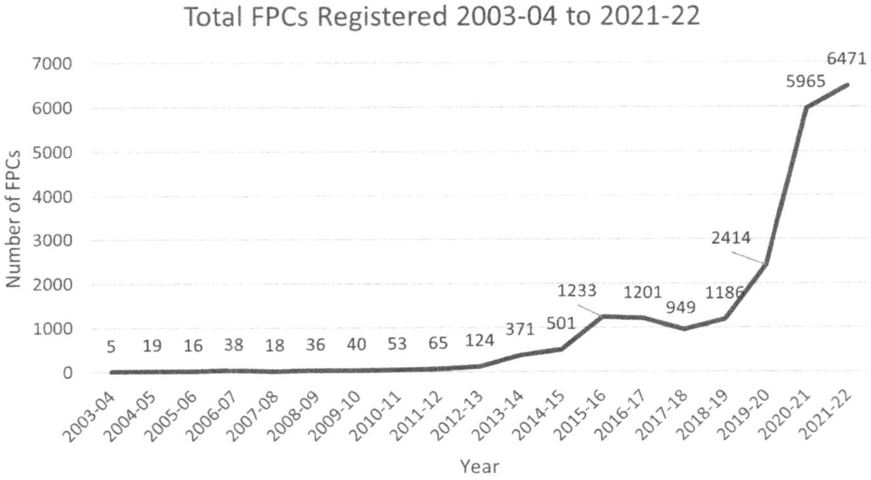

Total FPCs Registered 2003-04 to 2021-22

Figure 1.1 Trajectory of FPC registration
Source: Collated from Ministry of Corporate Affairs database[5,6]

(CSO) were actively involved in the mobilisation of farmers and executing the programme (Chauhan, 2016). Many leading CSOs such as Professional Assistance for Development Action (PRADAN), Bharatiya Agro Industries Foundation (BAIF), and Rangsutra began experimenting with this new form in *tassar* (Masuta), agriculture (Vasundhara Agri-Horti Producer Co. Ltd (VAPCOL)), and handicrafts, respectively.

The second phase governing the trajectory and growth of FPOs has been largely due to the policy thrust at the national level, first from the Small Farmers Agribusiness Consortium (SFAC), an entity under the Ministry of Agriculture, through a pilot programme from 2011 to 2013. This led to mobilisation of 0.25 million farmers into 250 FPOs (about 1,000 members) drawing from the MP DPIP model. Resource Institutions (RIs), largely CSOs, were empanelled with a two-year period to invest in capacity building and handholding of FPOs.

Policy guidelines for the spread of FPOs were formulated in 2013[8] that enabled a larger spread in the third phase (2014–17) through the active engagement of the National Bank for Agriculture and Rural Development (NABARD) through its Producers' Organization Development and Upliftment Corpus (PRODUCE) Fund of Rs. 20 million for the creation of 2,000 FPOs (both cooperatives and companies). NABARD is currently the biggest player in the FPO ecosystem with an estimated 55% of all FPOs registered in the country (Suryakumar, 2022).

The fourth phase (2017–20) witnessed a greater uptake of this model by many state governments through World Bank and other support that led to an acceleration of FPC formation in states like Maharashtra, which today constitutes over 30% of the FPOs in the country. During this period there has also been a concerted policy thrust reflective of the shift in understanding of farming or agriculture as a 'value-led enterprise' as articulated in the Doubling Farmers' Income (DFI) report. The last and ongoing phase can be seen from 2020 with the central government's thrust for creation of 10,000 FPOs by 2024–25 (Prasad, 2019; NAFPO, 2022). The massive expansion of FPOs across India has also revealed structural shifts in the FPO movement with little investment in state capacity, a greater role of consultants and a diminishing role of CSOs, especially at the grassroots, that were at the forefront in embedding the FPO movement in India (Prasad, 2021; Singh, 2022). This phenomenal growth of FPOs in India has not been matched with sufficient academic engagement, and we explore what this means for new knowledge on POs.

3.   Co-creating new knowledge on POs in India

Mainstream academia has been slow to respond to the rapid spread of FPOs and explicating what it means for Indian agriculture. Studies, as is increasingly common in academia, depend solely on online database searches and tend to ignore significant insights from critical reflections and knowledge grounded in practice or practitioner experiences and run the danger of ignoring the significant contextual differences between POs in India and the rest of the world. Significant knowledge continues to emerge from chapters in annual livelihood reports[9] and the more recent state of sector reports by the National Association of Farmer Producer Organisations (NAFPO) (Phansalkar and Paranjape, 2021; NAFPO, 2022). Critical challenges highlighted in these reports include the perpetual capital and capability constraints faced by FPOs (Mahajan, 2015), the need to recognise diversity and complexity and build ecosystems that could enable the 'ease of doing' business for FPOs (Prasad, 2019). The reports also describe the undercapitalisation, lack of business acumen, and unsuitable operating models (Govil and Neti, 2021) widespread among FPOs. An annotated bibliography covering the period between 2003 and 2019 looking at the literature on FPOs in India found a preponderance of cases on Western India and limited work on the inclusive participation of marginalised sections and women in POs (Prasad, 2019). We suggest that a co-creation approach to knowledge, which seeks to create spaces for dialogue between academics interested in PO research and development practitioners, is more likely to produce newer insights, and this volume attempts to address this research gap.

It is pertinent here to briefly review the relevant literature that provided us with critical insights while embarking on our journey towards discovering collaboratively newer and contemporary frames to understand the dynamics of FPOs in India and elsewhere. Tushaar Shah's framework (1995a, 1996, 2016) highlighted the importance of designing member-owned institutions as interacting sub-systems of members, their governance, and operating systems. As POs seek domain centrality and if good POs are member-central, they would be empowered to both guide and assess performance of the professionals involved in day-to-day operations. This opportunity for dairy cooperatives' business to be significant in the economic domain has been possible for historic reasons but has rightly been questioned for its applicability in non-dairy agricultural POs in contemporary times, where the market already has significant established players that the FPO must compete with (Ganesh, 2017). Importantly though, Shah's work anticipated more recent shifts in the theory of cooperatives that go beyond the rigid conceptualisation of cooperatives as an independent firm to the complex and multi-dimensional nature of agricultural cooperatives, or in short from 'economic analysis' to 'economic design' (Cook and Grashuis, 2018).

Cooperatives' performance has largely been assessed based on neo-classical theories that essentialise the aim of the cooperative to maximise member return (and patronage refund) while minimising costs of production. Cooperatives, however, optimise among multiple goals rather than only maximising profits. They also face constraints beyond production, related to institutional structures, property rights and the need to consider transaction and adjustment costs (Royer, 1999, 2014). While the New Institutional Economics literature incorporates some of these failings and has been used to better understand the governance challenges of cooperatives (Cook and Iliopoulos, 1999; Chaddad and Cook, 2004) their extension to Indian contexts of agricultural cooperatives owned by a large number of smallholder farmers necessitates a rethink beyond the cooperative, and a closer look at the ecosystem and the promoting or incubating institution in particular. Recent work looking at the governance-strategy link in organisational management (Busco et al., 2007) suggests a greater focus on diffusion of governance principles throughout the organisation with the BoD needing to be more involved in strategic planning and monitoring implementation in day-to-day operations.

Newer understandings of cooperatives need to look beyond agricultural economics' literature and point to the need to accommodate the 'world of farmers' and the 'world of managers' as the prime task of the BoD and management (Bijman et al., 2013). Cornforth (2004), in his review of various theories of governance, argues for a multi-paradigm paradoxical view of cooperative governance. Furusten and Alexius (2019) suggest that achieving multi-vocality can be regarded as a strategic goal of the board members and the management of cooperatives. A framework that may help in looking at multiple processes at the same time, increasingly popular in understanding the firm, but less applied to POs, is the stakeholder theory (Freeman, 1984). Freeman showed that the firm was operating in an environment where there were more entities that were interested (or had stake) in the business. This idea of the 'firm' embedded in a system of actors/stakeholders' view has been pursued by some scholars in strategic management (Ghosh, 2010). The conception is however not entirely new within cooperative literature. Mary Follett (see Fox, 1968) has articulated this quite early, but it has not been pursued by cooperative scholars proactively since. Mapping and understanding the cooperative or a PO as part of a multi-stakeholder ecosystem has, we suggest, greater explanatory power.

Within the Indian context there have been a few landscape studies from the Azim Premji University that have sought to characterise the fast-evolving FPO ecosystem by demystifying the numbers and exploring the capital structure and levels of inclusion of these new institutions (Govil et al., 2020; Neti and Govil, 2022). Nayak (2016) points to organisation design issues behind the below-par performance of FPOs in terms of financial returns to individual producers and argues for an 'optimal' design as a single-window service at the level of Gram Panchayat or a group of villages. There is however little empirical evidence for such an ideal architecture of sustainable FPOs.

Singh and Singh (2014) offered the first detailed business performance of FPCs across four states and highlighted growth challenges due to their weak financial performance and poor ecosystem support. A larger and more recent study by Singh (2021b) extends this discussion on performance by exploring the impact of producer companies in five states, with Madhya Pradesh and Rajasthan common across the two studies. The study found performance linked to location (ecosystem and policy support varied widely across states) as well as the quality and capability of the promoting agencies in linking farmers to modern markets. An action research study on market linkages in 49 clusters in 52 districts was done by Arya Collateral for the Tata Trusts (2020). Only 40% of the 1,833 FPOs surveyed were active, an indication of the challenges in selection of FPOs for long-term studies.

A tested way for smallholder cooperatives to ensure greater presence in domains like milk and fertilisers has been to have a market-facing federated cooperative as Gujarat Cooperative Milk Marketing Federation (GCMMF) and Indian Farmer Fertiliser Cooperative (IFFCO). Federating collectives, it is argued, can solve the problems of economies of scale, fair-priced market access, integration and upward mobility of the producer in the value chain, and reduction of the production and market uncertainty/risk faced by farmers. Pooling resources, defining property rights, creating and nurturing ownership among primary producers are often achieved by POs. However, the goals of tackling risk, moving up the value chain, and gaining market through diversified product portfolio and advocacy at higher levels are often beyond the scope of individual POs and better achieved by second-order collectivisation to create apex cooperatives or federations of cooperatives.

A rather neglected area of research on PO in India has been the potential and examination of functioning of FPO federations. Between 2014 and 2020, 20 such federations were registered. These organisations are still evolving and only eight of them are active (Singh, 2021). Three of the cases in this volume explore the functioning of the three most active FPO/FPC federations in India fulfilling the need for grounded insights on market linkages for FPOs coupled with issues relating to the ecosystem and the 'ease of doing' business for FPOs.

The overview of literature above presents a case for a new inclusive frame to understand and make sense of the diversity and complexity of FPOs in India. These could help explore and, if possible, answer questions on appropriate frameworks, design, incubation, growth and management challenges, performance assessment and policies. The broad question driving the study is, are FPOs the organisations of the future that offer a potential strong vibrant alternative to the challenges faced by smallholder farmers in the market-based solutions? Specific dimensions of this question can be articulated as follows:

- Would newer perspectives drawing from stakeholder theory, social enterprise, responsible and inclusive businesses offer better explanatory power than the conventional typical transaction cost economics and agency theories?
- Would the frameworks developed based on the study of dairy cooperatives and the Anand pattern developed in the 1990s in pre-liberalised India still hold for non-dairy FPOs?
- What would be the new insights from fresh entrepreneurship literature that prioritises experimentation, failing forward and lean start-up ideas, and how could they be applied to the incubation of FPOs?
- How is the governance of these New Age social start-ups different from established organisations? Would the famed circle of responsibilities for Cooperative Boards (Baarda, 2003) and the arm's-length separation of governance from operations work well for FPO BoD, who are often first-generation entrepreneurs with limited business exposure and skills?
- How effective have the market linkages of FPOs been with growing interests of commodity exchanges and corporates showing interest to tie up with FPOs? What has been the experience of FPO federations in enabling market linkages and providing a voice for FPOs, and small farmers, in an ecosystem that is dominated by big players?
- Is there an empirical basis for many of the policy prescriptions on the optimal size of an FPO (1,000 members in the 2013 policy guidelines and 300 in the 10,000 FPO policy) and how are they linked to profitability? Given the multiplicity of objectives of FPOs that often have features of social enterprises with dual purposes (Kaushik, 2022), how effective are existing frameworks of assessing their performance?
- How realistic is the time frame of three years' project support for FPOs that has driven the massive growth of registrations in the last few years in India? Can FPOs provide a middle ground for an alternate route to agricultural reform in light of the contentious farm bills?

Through detailed studies of 15 FPO cases, this volume seeks to go beyond existing landscape studies and explores the multiple dimensions of FPO growth, management, and performance in diverse settings. Many questions, ideas, and concerns from several field-level interactions and workshops and national conferences (held at IRMA and other parts of India since 2015) provided the motivation for the study and helped shape the research questions.

4. FPOs as inclusive institutions of farmers

Greater market integration has implications for the inclusive nature of POs (Bijman and Wijers, 2019). In the Indian context, FPOs have been seen as inclusive institutions that exist primarily to strengthen the bargaining power of smallholder farmers through collective action, and these farm aggregation models can help smallholders by improving their access to credit, technology, and extension services (Sharma, 2013; Abraham et al., 2022). An estimate from the online database of Tata Cornell Initiative on FPOs of 13 states reveals that smallholders have been part of nearly 50% of all FPOs. This number, while not representative of the larger percentage of small farmers in India, is significantly higher than their representation in other institutions like the traditional cooperatives or their institutions for credit access – the Primary Agricultural Credit Societies (PACS).[10]

In the volume and the cases chosen for detailed analysis, inclusion has been an important criterion both as a framework and for selection of cases. By inclusion we explore the following dimensions. First, recognising the role of CSOs as important for inclusive institutions and creating the base for greater ownership of these first-generation entrepreneurs. Current policies tend to overplay the business acumen of external consultants over building capacities of CSOs to lead the FPO revolution (Prasad, 2021; Singh, 2022). Second, to ensure that not only is smallholder focus maintained in the choice of FPOs to study, but there is also an attempt to proactively explore the potential of FPOs both to go beyond becoming mere last-mile suppliers of agrochemical inputs and as institutions that would promote the greater use and adoption of sustainable farming. Finally, we explicitly attempt to explore gender roles in the running of these institutions.

4.1 Engendering FPOs

Women contribute an important but often unrecognised role in agriculture and allied activities. The lack of visibility is reflected in the fact that despite forming 55% of the agricultural workforce,[11] the percentage of female operational holdings in the country is only 14% as per the 10th agricultural census (2015–16). The urgent need for a gender-sensitive focus also stems from the increased trend in distress-induced urban migration, primarily by men, in search of employment. This has led to what is known as 'feminisation' of agriculture due to increased participation of women in several activities in the agricultural value chain (Vepa, 2005). The increased labour is rarely accompanied by equivalent remuneration. Instead, even as their role in agricultural activities increases, they have a limited role in agricultural decision-making, low representation in market-facing roles, and little control over price realisation of farm commodities (Agarwal, 2014).

FPOs have the potential to build on the framework and mobilisation offered by existing SHG networks to empower women from an entrepreneurial standpoint. Newer market opportunities and autonomy offered by FPOs can help transcend the sociocultural factors preventing women from actively participating in the agri-value chain. Since most schemes and benefits available to farmers are directly tied to landholdings, policies end up having a blind spot for gender-specific reforms. As a result, discriminatory social structures get reinforced due to lack of opportunities for women to access information, resources, extension services, credit, technology, land, and local institutions. Alluding to the male dominance seen in the cooperative movement, the NAFPO study (2022) suggests that the same pattern may continue into the FPO movement unless inclusive measures are implemented to ensure equitable participation and access.

The recent push by the GoI, to form farmer collectives and enable them to leverage economies of scale, needs to take cognisance of the gender constraints and opportunities to effect any sustainable change in farmer incomes (Bathla and Hussain, 2022). Pointing out the lack of representation in the FPO policy guidelines, Vasavada (2021) argues that there is no mention of the minimum number of women FPOs to be formed, nor any criteria for the minimum number of women shareholders in a mixed FPO. Without adequate capacity building and ecosystem support, the requirement of an FPO's BoD having at least one female number becomes a tokenistic gesture rather than bringing any ground-level transformations. Without empowering women to play a crucial role in managing FPOs, gender disparity is bound to widen as they would lose access to entrepreneurial levels of market engagement and remain restricted to field labour. As caretakers and people most closely related to the land, active participation of women can also help steer sustainable production practices, as they witness the ill-effects of chemical-laden practices first-hand. It is thus not a coincidence that many initiatives connecting social equity and environmental issues often have women at the forefront (Shiva, 2018). Envisioning FPOs as inclusive and sustainable initiatives thus needs active engagement and a supportive ecosystem to enable participation of women. We also suggest that there is a case for exploring, in the Indian context, the scope of FPOs as sustainable transition intermediaries (Groot-Kormelinck et al., 2022).

The availability of an opportunity through a new institution (such as forming an FPO) does not guarantee equitable participation because women face additional constraints and patriarchal norms, preventing them from exercising agency or control in the organisation. Understanding ground-level initiatives focused on supporting and enabling women-led FPOs can offer insights for designing policy recommendations and acknowledging the added dimensions of socio-economic complexities governing women's participation in male-dominated markets. In this book, seven chapters focus on various aspects of women FPOs, across different geographies, commodities, and promoting institutions. In many of these cases, the significance of pre-existing networks of women SHGs in mobilising the community is evident. In our concluding part of this introductory chapter, we describe the research process followed in light of the above concerns and frameworks highlighted.

5. Research approach and the process of co-creating knowledge

The cases featured in this collection are an outcome of extended and sustained forms of participative inquiry between academics, practitioners, and grassroots promoters of FPOs to collectively make sense of the dynamic and ever-changing socio-political and economic landscape. Characterisation of the management challenges in FPOs has a lot to gain from understanding the evolving processes and practices in these organisations. Given the complexity of the ecosystem governing these organisations, we chose approaches that allow for collaborations, methodological pluralism, adaptive iteration, and critical reflexivity (Chambers, 2015). The collaborative initiatives can be traced back to several stakeholder dialogues in the form of national workshops hosted by the IRMA since 2015 to co-create knowledge on these complex organisations.[12] These dialogues underlined the need for greater cross-learning between field and academia to foster 'nuance and interrogation' around the policy discourse emphasising collaborative research between development professionals, policymakers, and research organisations to jointly strengthen capacities, generate development outcomes, and identify future areas of research (Lomas, 2000; Lundy et al., 2005). This explicit partnership allows for contextual embedding of research problems (as opposed to abstract, theoretical questions) while providing the opportunity to learn across geographical and institutional boundaries. Characterising and understanding ground-level issues encountered by FPOs required an acknowledgement of the sheer diversity and contexts governing individual organisations. With inclusion being an important theme, scoping of cases was predominantly focused on rain-fed areas, and those with significant woman or tribal leadership, given their conventional invisibility in policy dialogues.

Prior networks built over workshops were tapped to seek collaborators who would be interested in conducting an in-depth study of selected FPOs. Nurturing a democratic space for collective inquiry translated into a slower process of relationship development and consultation. Some of the contributors were part of *Farming Futures*, a similar collaborative volume of 15 cases on agri-based social enterprises (Kanitkar and Prasad, 2019). At a workshop in March 2020, potential authors explored ways to improve on the first volume of *Farming Futures* and to work along a common case protocol to ensure greater alignment among individual cases. Three cases, with joint authors, were first developed as both a pilot and template for developing a case study protocol. Potential authors were then invited for online orientation workshops and brainstorming sessions to discuss the goals, values, priorities, and perspectives of each contributor in October 2020. The selection criteria of the cases included the need to have the FPOs in operation for at least three years and the aim was to cover as many regions as possible (with no more than one case per promoting institution) while reflecting a diversity of FPOs and their federations. Table 1.2 presents an overview of the cases chosen including their year of registration, promoting organisation and commodities that the FPO deals with.

Based on the initial consultation process, broad focal themes to study respective FPOs were decided.[13] Academics were paired with development practitioners and consultants to initiate a process of joint inquiry, and the abstracts were peer-reviewed and discussed in a subsequent workshop that included the case protocol. The iterative and reflective process aimed at bringing alignment and analytical consistency across the cases. The process was appreciated by the authors, as it offered them a safe reflective space. Excerpts of some feedback illustrate the point:

> In all the field interactions, the practitioners had the details, what they needed was a dialogue partner, someone who will sit with them, listen to their stories, get feedback and often respond to questions they were struggling with. . . . We went NOT to extract data from them but in return also offered our reflection.
>
> Teaming up with a development practitioner was very productive as it helped to get the internal processes followed and rationale-meaning logic of certain interventions – why SHGs in lieu of farmer interest groups . . . it also helped understand the ecosystem better . . . institutional knowledge and grassroots rapport building are challenges faced by outside researchers and having a practitioner as a co-author smoothened the journey.

Three cases that could not meet the criteria developed as part of the framework were dropped. Two of the FPOs were less than three years old, and the promoting institution of the third was reluctant to share data or be named. Field visits were a key part of the writing process as they allowed the authors a sense of FPO operations that usually remain unarticulated. Three promising FPO cases could not be pursued due to the difficulty faced in undertaking field visits by case authors. The idea that better theories can be put forward by academics and managers who are pragmatic and aware of the context being theorised (Wicks and Freeman, 1998; Freeman and McVea, 2005; Ghoshal, 2005) was pursued. Interim reflections by authors were encouraged to

Table 1.2 Snapshot of the 15 FPOs as on 28 April 2021

FPO Name	Chap No	Promoting Institution	State	Date of Registration	No. of Shareholders	Commodities (in order of importance)
Krushidhan	2	Development Support Centre	Gujarat	2013	4409	Potato, groundnut, wheat, paddy, maize, spices, cotton
Jeevika	3	Jeevika	Bihar	2009	1206	Maize, mango, wheat and mentha oil
Bhangar	4	Access Development Services	West Bengal	2012	1751	Fruits and vegetables
Ram Rahim	5	Samaj Pragati Sahyog	Madhya Pradesh	2012	5062*	Red gram, Bengal gram, wheat, maize, *jowar*, soybean
Mahanadi	6	Vrutti	Chhattisgarh	2014	613	Custard apple, non-timber forest produce
Umang Mahila	7	Grassroots	Uttarakhand	2009	1142	Spices, walnuts, pickles, preserves and hand-knits
KBS Coop	8	PRADAN	Jharkhand	2003	2680	Horticultural commodities
Hasnabad	9	ALC India	Telangana	2012	1004	Red gram, groundnut
Pandhana Pashu Palak	10	AKRSP	Madhya Pradesh	2016	552	Goats, back-yard poultry chicken
Kazhani	11	MYRADA	Karnataka	2016	1000	Banana, paddy, millets
Navyug	12	BASIX	Uttar Pradesh	2014	1005	Mangoes, wheat, paddy
Desi Seeds	13	Sahaja Samrudha	Karnataka	2013	500	Organic seeds – (paddy, horticultural crops, millets)
Maha FPC#	14	42 FPCs meet	Maharashtra	2014	600+ FPCs	Pulses, soybean, onions
Madhya Bharat#	15	Rajya Aajeevika Forum	Madhya Pradesh/ Chhattisgarh	2014	134 FPCs (11 Coops)	Certified seeds, soybean, wheat, pulses, paddy,
Gujpro consortium#	16	Sajjata Sangh	Gujarat	2014	30 FPCs	Groundnut, wheat, mango, cumin, coconut

* comprising 364 SHGs shareholders

FPO federations

capture everyday transactions, the local socio-political climate, market proximity, BoD dynamics, state of available infrastructure, and so on, and authors were encouraged to present their initial field impressions in the form of blogs. A compendium of blogs that included many of the ideas from the cases was released as part of the Kurien Centenary celebrations at IRMA (Prasad and Dutta, 2022). Some guiding questions that emerged over time through the iterative process of writing, field visits, and interviews were as follows:

- Incubation – How long should the incubation period of an FPO be? Who bears its costs? When is the right time to withdraw? How have promoting institutions handled post-project closures?
- Entrepreneurial quality – What are the makings of a vibrant FPC? Are FPOs today closer to social enterprises or start-ups than traditional cooperatives? How have the FPOs been balancing their financial and social objectives? Has the FPO movement led to a rise in rural entrepreneurship and enterprise?
- Capacity building and ecosystem support – How strong is the ownership by members of the enterprise? Are FPOs better led by professional well-paid staff, or should there be a thrust to develop business capacities of farmer members? Is an *atmanirbhar* (self-reliant) FPO a myth, and how can their governance be strengthened to reach this goal?
- Business model – How do FPOs evolve their business models given their capital and capability constraints?
- Performance assessment – What are the metrics that would help understand the impacts – economic, social, and environmental, and how are they viewed at the farmer and FPO levels?
- How do FPOs make decisions, and are the governance and management or operating systems able to undertake decisions with lesser involvement of the promoting institutions in the long run?

The 'Farming Futures' project attempted to leverage the different knowledge, skills, and values of the contributors through multiple rounds of peer review such that specific aspects of gender inclusivity, sustainability, and organisational dynamics within an FPO could be explicitly discussed. The exercise was perceived as being helpful towards opening newer vistas for looking at their own cases and being part of a collective inquiry.

The themes discussed in the synthesis chapter of this volume were derived based on a combination of inductive and deductive analysis of the individual chapters. A rigorous analysis of the business performance of the FPOs and emerging trends was done via the collection of balance sheets for all the FPOs until the year 2020–21. Categories were developed and discussed to articulate connections between aspects such as gender and sustainability, or FPO infrastructure and overall profitability. The overall timeline of critical events in the research process is outlined in Figure 1.2.

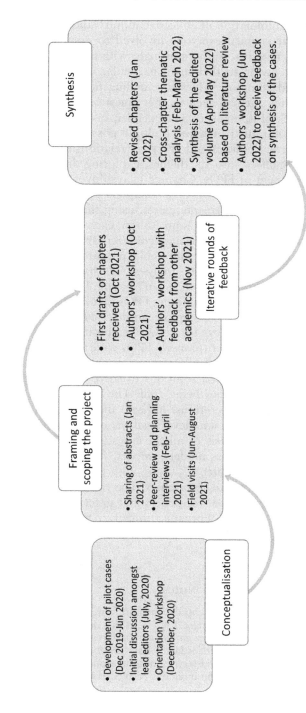

Figure 1.2 Illustrating the collaborative research and writing process

This volume is a culmination of collective inquiry and democratic forms of participation that enabled everyone involved to assume ownership of the project in different ways. Authors brought with them a flavour of epistemic heterogeneity owing to their own particular experiences and interests. Authors shared common values of enabling farmers to have decent livelihoods and better agency, even as they questioned each other about the emphasis, or lack of it, on aspects like gender, sustainability, and so on. The book is an invitation to imagine multiple possibilities that continue to exist between formal policies and everyday relationships that FPOs are a part of and is organised into six themes, exploring different areas concerning the management of FPOs. Chapter 1 lays down the context of the extant literature and research in the area. Chapters 2–5 explore the issue of market access through collective enterprises, using the illustrative cases of Krushidhan, Jeevika, Bhangar, and Ram Rahim, each having established a unique process for market access through contract farming, specific tie-ups with government or private bodies, and public procurement. The processes of building inclusive institutions are analysed in Chapters 6–9. We posit that prioritising participation of women can't be simply seen as an 'add-on' to other tasks of an FPO, and engendering FPOs involves designing institutions differently. Chapters 10–13 explore younger FPOs to explore their innovative practices and journeys for collective autonomy with a changed ecosystem that some of the older (pioneer) FPOs were unable to access. The cases demonstrate ways in which FPOs engaged with the wider ecosystem to develop unique, context-based solutions to solve specific issues within the organisation or commodities being sold. The management challenges and opportunities of FPO federations, hitherto unexplored, are taken up in Chapters 14–16 through a state-level analysis of MAHAFPC, Madhya Bharat, and Gujpro. A synthesis of all the cases along the parameters of incubation, inclusivity, business models, impact, financial and social performance is presented in Chapter 17, along with concluding thoughts for policymakers, practitioners, and researchers. The volume ultimately aspires to enthuse a new generation of researchers and practitioners to study the emergence of such novel forms of organisation, given their potential to offer a strong alternative towards farmers' prosperity and equitable, sustainable food systems as a whole.

Notes

1 Further, the share of population who depends on farming as primary livelihood option is significantly lower – a mere 1.4% – in the United States as compared to over 50% in India. The agrarian employment figures from United States have been referred from https://www.ers.usda.gov/data-products/ag-and-food-statistics-charting-the-essentials/ag-and-food-sectors-and-the-economy/. The estimate of population employed in farming in India has been cited from Kumar et al. 2020.

2 See https://www.rbi.org.in/Scripts/BS_ViewBulletin.aspx?Id=20750 as accessed on 12 August 2022.
3 Official data indicates a decline in farm suicides since 2016, but some suggest this has more to do with changed methodology than any ground-level changes. https://psainath.org/the-slaughter-of-suicide-data/
4 See Alagh's 'In the Right Company' (22 December 2015) for more details https://indianexpress.com/article/opinion/columns/in-the-right-company/
5 The data is dynamic, as a result of which the specific web links change with time. The main site accessed was https://www.mca.gov.in/MinistryV2/aboutmasterdata.html
6 All figures in the book have been created by the authors of the corresponding chapters.
7 The MCA database for year 2021–22 has figures missing for the months of November 2021 and January and March 2022. https://www.mca.gov.in/content/mca/global/en/data-and-reports/company-llp-info/incorporated-closed-month.html accessed on 13 July 2022.
8 See https://www.mofpi.gov.in/sites/default/files/fpo_policy_process_guidelines_1_april_2013.pdf
9 The annual State of India's Livelihoods (SOIL) report brought out by Access Development Services has had chapters on FPOs in 2015, 2017, 2019, and 2021. https://livelihoods-india.org/publications/all-page-soil-report.html
10 Collated by authors from https://tci.cornell.edu/?blog=assessing-indias-fpo-ecosystem#tables. There is variation across states with West Bengal, Tamil Nadu, Karnataka, Uttar Pradesh, and Telangana having less than 40% small farmers (accessed on 12 August 2022). The newly formed Ministry of Cooperatives has pegged its reforms on digitization of PACS that have known to be unrepresentative of small and marginal farmers.
11 According to World Bank data, retrieved from the International Labour Organisation (ILO) database. https://data.worldbank.org/indicator/SL.AGR.EMPL.FE.ZS?locations=IN
12 For more details, see https://www.smallfarmincomes.in/fpojourney as well as the deliberations of the various national FPO conferences in the website.
13 Facilitating open-ended discussions during the Covid-19 pandemic was a challenge, and innovative ways to seek responses were sought through Google forms, breakout sessions, and WhatsApp® groups.

References

Abraham, M, Verteramo, CL, Joshi, E, Ali Ilahi, M & Pingali, P (2022). Aggregation models and small farm commercialization – A scoping review of the global literature. *Food Policy, 110,* 102299. https://doi.org/10.1016/j.foodpol.2022.102299

Adler, PS (2016). Alternative economic futures: A research agenda for progressive management scholarship. *Academy of Management Perspectives, 30*(2), 123–128. Retrieved from https://www.jstor.org/stable/44645029

Aga, A (2018). Merchants of knowledge: Petty retail and differentiation without consolidation among farmers in Maharashtra, India. *Journal of Agrarian Change.* https://doi.org/10.1111/joac.12249

Agarwal, B (2014). Food sovereignty, food security and democratic choice: Critical contradictions, difficult conciliations. *Journal of Peasant Studies, 41*(6), 1247–1268.

Baarda, J (2003). *The circle of responsibilities for co-op boards* (USDA, Rural Business and Cooperative Services, Cooperative Information Report 61).

Bathla, S & Hussain, S (2022). Structural reforms and governance issues in Indian agriculture. In R Chand, P Joshi & S Khadka (Eds.), *Indian agriculture towards 2030: Pathways for enhancing farmers' income, nutritional security and sustainable food and farm systems* (pp. 251–296). Singapore: Springer.

Baviskar, BS & Attwood, DW (Eds.) (1995). *Finding the middle path: The political economy of cooperation in rural India*. New Delhi: Vistaar Publications.

Bijman, J (2016). The changing nature of farmer collective action: Introduction to the book. In J Bijman, R Muradian & J Schuurman (Eds.), *Cooperatives, economic democratization and rural development* (pp. 1–22). Cambridge, MA: Edward Elgar Publishing.

Bijman, J, Hendrikse, G & van Oijen, A (2013). Accommodating two worlds in one organisation: Changing board models in agricultural cooperatives: Changing board models in agricultural cooperatives. *Managerial and Decision Economics, 34*(3–5), 204–217. https://doi.org/10.1002/mde.2584

Bijman, J & Wijers, G (2019). Exploring the inclusiveness of producer cooperatives. *Current Opinion in Environmental Sustainability, 41*, 74–79.

Billiet, A, Dufays, F, Friedel, S & Staessens, M (2021). The resilience of the cooperative model: How do cooperatives deal with the COVID-19 crisis? *Strategic Change, 30*(2), 99–108. https://doi.org/10.1002/jsc.2393

Busco, C, Giovannoni, E, Riccaboni, A, Franceschi, D & Frigo, ML (2007). Linking governance to strategy: The role of the finance organization. *Strategic Finance, 89*(3), 23–28.

Chaddad, FR & Cook, ML (2004). Understanding new cooperative models: An ownership-control rights typology. *Review of Agricultural Economics, 26*(3), 348–360. https://doi.org/10.1111/j.1467-9353.2004.00184.x

Chakraborty, SK, Kurien, V, Singh, J, Athreya, M, Maira, A, Aga, A, Gupta, AK & Khandwalla, PN (2004). Management paradigms beyond profit maximization. *Vikalpa: The Journal for Decision Makers, 29*(3), 97–118. https://doi.org/10.1177/0256090920040308

Chambers, R (2015). Inclusive rigour for complexity. *Journal of Development Effectiveness, 7*(3), 327–335.

Chancel, L, Piketty, T, Saez, E & Zucman, G (2021). *World inequality report 2022*. World Inequality Lab. Retrieved from https://wir2022.wid.world

Chauhan, S (2016). Luvkush crop producer company: A farmer's organization. *Decision, 43*(1), 93–103. https://doi.org/10.1007/s40622-015-0121-1.

Cook, ML & Grashuis, J (2018). Theory of cooperatives: Recent developments. In *Routledge handbook of agricultural economics* (pp. 748–759). London: Routledge.

Cook, ML & Iliopoulos, C (1999). Beginning to inform the theory of the cooperative firm: Emergence of the new generation cooperative. *The Finnish Journal of Business Economics, 4*, 525–535.

Cooney, K & Williams Shanks, TR (2010). New approaches to old problems: Market-based strategies for poverty alleviation. *Social Service Review, 84*(1), 29–55. https://doi.org/10.1086/652680

Cornforth, C (2004). The governance of cooperatives and mutual associations: A paradox perspective. *Annals of Public and Cooperative Economics, 75*(1), 11–32.

Dubb, S (2016). Community wealth building forms: What they are and how to use them at the local level. *Academy of Management Perspectives*, 30(2), 141–152. Retrieved from https://www.jstor.org/stable/44645031

EcoNexus (2013). *Agropoly-A handful of corporations control world food production*. Zurich and Oxford: Berne Declaration and EcoNexus.

Fox, EM (1968). Mary Parker Follett: The enduring contribution. *Public Administration Review*, 28(6), 520–529.

Freeman, RE (1984). *Strategic management: A stakeholder approach*. London: Pitman Publishing.

Freeman, RE & McVea, J (2005). A stakeholder approach to strategic management. In M Hitt, E Freeman & J Harrison (Eds.), *Handbook of strategic management* (pp. 183–201). Blackwell Publishing: Oxford.

Furusten, S & Alexius, S (2019). Managing hybrid organizations. In S Alexius & S Furusten S (Eds.), *Managing hybrid organizations: Governance, professionalism and regulation* (pp. 333–360). Singapore: Springer International Publishing. https://doi.org/10.1007/978-3-319-95486-8_17

Ganesh, V (2017). Farmer Producer Companies: A response. *Economic and Political Weekly*, 52(40), 73–74.

Gersch, I (2018). Producer organizations and contract farming: A comparative study of smallholders' market strategies in South India. *Zeitschrift Für Wirtschaftsgeographie*, 62(1), 14–29. https://doi.org/10.1515/zfw-2017-0026

Ghosh, A (2010). *Embeddedness and the dynamics of strategy processes: The case of AMUL cooperative, India* [Doctoral, Montreal, McGill University].

Ghoshal, S (2005). Bad management theories are destroying good management practices. *Academy of Management Learning & Education*, 4(1), 75–91.

Giller, KE, Delaune, T, Silva, JV, Descheemaeker, K, van de Ven, G, Schut, AGT, van Wijk, M, Hammond, J, Hochman, Z, Taulya, G, Chikowo, R, Narayanan, S, Kishore, A, Bresciani, F, Teixeira, HM, Andersson, JA & van Ittersum, MK (2021). The future of farming: Who will produce our food? *Food Security*, 13(5), 1073–1099. https://doi.org/10.1007/s12571-021-01184-6

Gouët, C, Leeuwis, C & van Paassen, A (2009). Theoretical perspectives on the role and significance of rural producer organisations in development: Implications for capacity development. *Social and Economic Studies*, 75–109.

Govil, R & Neti, A (2021). Farmer producer companies: From quantity to quality. In B Sen (Ed.), *State of India's livelihoods report 2021* (p. 172). New Delhi: Access Development Services.

Govil, R, Neti, A & Rao, RM (2020). *Farmer producer companies: Past, present and future*. Bangalore: Azim Premji University.

Groot-Kormelinck, A, Bijman, J, Trienekens, J & Klerkx, L (2022). Producer organizations as transition intermediaries? Insights from organic and conventional vegetable systems in Uruguay. *Agriculture and Human Values*, 39(4), 1277–1300.

Hiriyur, SM & Chhetri, N (2021). *Women's cooperatives & COVID-19: Learnings and the way forward*. Ahmedabad: SEWA Federation.

Iyer, B (2020). Cooperatives and the sustainable development goals. In M Altman, A Jensen, A Kurimoto, R Tulus, Y Dongre & S Jang (Eds.), *Waking the Asian Pacific co-operative potential* (pp. 59–70). Cambridge: Academic Press.

Kanitkar, A (2016). *The logic of farmer enterprises (Occasional Publication 17)*. Anand: Institute of Rural Management Anand (IRMA).

Kanitkar, A & Prasad, CS (Eds.) (2019). *Farming futures: Emerging social enterprises in India*. New Delhi: Authors Upfront.

Kaushik, R (2022). Understanding cooperatives as social enterprises. *Economic and Political Weekly*, *57*(5), 24–30.

Kumar, R, Agrawal, NK, Vijayshankar, PS & Vasavi, AR (2020). *State of rural and agrarian India: Report 2020, rethinking productivity and populism through alternative approaches*. London: Network of Rural and Agrarian Studies (NRAS).

Lomas, J (2000). Essay: Using 'linkage and exchange' to move research into policy at a Canadian foundation: Encouraging partnerships between researchers and policymakers is the goal of a promising new Canadian initiative. *Health Affairs*, *19*(3), 236–240.

Lundy, M, Gottret, MV & Ashby, JA (2005). *Learning alliances: An approach for building multistakeholder innovation systems*. ILAC brief no. 8. Washington, DC: World Bank Group. Retrieved from http://documents.worldbank.org/curated/en/564521467995077219/Learning-alliances-an-approach-for-building-multi-stakeholder-innovation-systems

Mahajan, V (2015). Farmers' producer companies: Need for capital and capability to capture the value added. In S Datta, V Mahajan, S Ratha, et al. (Eds.), *State of India's livelihoods report 2014* (pp. 87–108). New Delhi: Oxford University Press.

McMichael, P (2021). Food regimes. In AH Akram-Lodhi, K Dietz, B Engels & BM McKay (Eds.), *Handbook of critical agrarian studies* (pp. 218–231). Cheltenham: Edward Elgar Publishing.

NAFPO (2022). *State of sector report: Farmer producer organisations in India*. New Delhi: Authors UpFront.

Nagaraj, K, Sainath, P, Rukmani, R & Gopinath, R (2014). Farmers' suicides in India: Magnitudes, trends, and spatial patterns, 1997–2012. *Review of Agrarian Studies*, *4*.

Nair, TS & Gandhe, R (2011). Liberal cooperatives and microfinance in India: Diagnostic study of a cooperative federation. *Journal of Rural Cooperation*, *39*, 19–34.

Nandakumar, T (2022). *Farmers, fam laws and ways forward: A report for The Food and Land Use Coalition India*. New Delhi: The Food and Land Use Coalition India.

Narayanan, S (2021). Understanding farmer protests in India. *Academics Stand against Poverty*, *1*(1), 133–140.

Nayak, AK (2016). Farmer producer organizations in India: Policy, performance, and design issues. In NC Rao, R Radhakrishna, RK Mishra & VR Kata (Eds.), *Organised retailing and agri-business* (pp. 289–303). New Delhi: Springer.

Neti, A & Govil, R (2022). *Farmer producer companies. Report on inclusion, capitalisation and incubation* (No. 2; p. 48). Bangalore, Karnataka: Azim Premji University.

Oxfam International (2022). *Inequality kills: The unparalleled action needed to combat unprecedented inequality in the wake of COVID-19*. Oxford: Oxfam International.

Penrose-Buckley, C (2007). *Producer organisations: A guide to developing collective rural enterprises*. Oxford: Oxfam.

Phansalkar, S & Paranjape, A (2021). *Making farmer producer organizations achieve viability: A practical guide*. New Delhi: Authors UpFront.

Pingali, P, Aiyar, A, Abraham, M & Rahman, A (2019). Linking farms to markets: Reducing transaction costs and enhancing bargaining power. In *Transforming food systems for a rising India* (pp. 193–214). Cham: Palgrave Macmillan.

Prasad, CS (2019). *Farming as an enterprise: Ten years of FPO movement in India. State of livelihoods report* (pp. 37–48). New Delhi: Access Development Services.

Prasad, CS (2021). Consultation or consultants? *Seminar, 748,* 46–50.

Prasad, CS & Dutta, D (2022). *Fields of change: Managerial insights on FPOs in India.* Anand: Institute of Rural Management Anand.

Prasad, SC & Prateek, G (2019). *Farming futures: An annotated bibliography on farmer producer organisations in India* (Working Paper 290). Anand: Institute of Rural Management Anand.

Ratner, C (2009). Cooperativism: A social, economic, and political alternative to capitalism. *Capitalism Nature Socialism, 20*(2), 44–73.

Royer, JS (1999). Cooperative organizational strategies: A neo-institutional digest. *Journal of Agricultural Cooperation,* 44–67.

Royer, JS (2014). The neoclassical theory of cooperatives: Part I. *Journal of Cooperatives, 28,* 1–19.

Saini, S, Hussain, S & Khatri, P (2021). *Farm loan waivers in India, assessing impact and looking ahead. NABARD research study 22.* Mumbai: NABARD and Bharatiya Kisan Sangh.

Sathish Kumar, CAV & Shambu Prasad, C (2020). Social innovations in organic foods in rainfed India: The case of Dharani FaM Coop Ltd. In *Cooperatives and social innovation* (pp. 165–182). Singapore: Springer.

Shah, T (1995a). *Making farmers cooperatives work: Design, governance and management.* New Delhi: Sage.

Shah, T (1995b). Liberalisation and Indian agriculture: New relevance of farmer cooperatives. Indian. *Journal of Agricultural Economics, 50*(3), 488–509.

Shah, T (1996). *Catalysing co-operation: Design of self-governing organisations.* New Delhi: Sage Publications.

Shah, T (2016). Farmer producer companies: Fermenting new wine in new bottle. *Economic & Political Weekly, 51*(8), 15–20.

Sharma, P (2013). Leveraging farmer producer organizations to boost production, mitigate risk and strengthen food security: Lessons and challenges. *Journal of Land and Rural Studies, 1*(1), 41–48.

Shiva, V (2018). *Development, ecology, and women. Living with contradictions* (pp. 658–666). New York: Routledge.

Singh, N (2021). Agrarian crisis and the longest farmers. Protest in Indian history. *New Labor Forum, 30*(3), 66–75. https://doi.org/10.1177/10957960211036016

Singh, S (2008). Producer companies as new generation cooperatives. *Economic and Political Weekly, 43*(20), 22–24.

Singh, S (2021a). Institutional innovations in India: An assessment of producer companies as new-generation co-operative companies. *Journal of Asian Development Research,* 1–18. https://doi.org/10.1177/2633190X211033510

Singh, S (2021b). *Understanding performance and impact of producer companies: Cases studies across States and promoters in India. Final Report.* Ahmedabad: Centre for Management in Agriculture.

Singh, S (2022). *How can India's farmer producer companies better serve small-scale farmers?* London: International Institute of Environment and Development.

Singh, S & Singh, T (2014). *Producer companies in India: Organization and performance*. New Delhi: Allied Publishers.

Singh, V (2021). *Understanding of Farmer Producer Company (FPC) Consortiums in the Indian context: Exploratory study on second level institutions in the FPC ecosystem*. New Delhi: Rajiv Gandhi Institute of Contemporary Studies.

Suryakumar, PVS (2022). The power of organisation through farmer producer organisations: NABARD's experiences. In *Aggregation model of sustainable farming for smallholder farmers in the Asia Pacific region* (pp. 1–6). Lucknow: Bankers Institute of Rural Development. Retrieved from https://birdlucknow.nabard.org/wp-content/uploads/2022/03/Aggregation-model-of-sustainable-farming-for-smallholder-farmers-for-the-Asia-Specific-Region.pdf

Tata Trusts (2020). *A comprehensive study for identification of vibrant FPO clusters for effective market integration*. Mumbai: Tata Trusts.

Ton, G, Bijman, J & Oorthuizen, J (Eds.) (2007). *Producer organisations and market chains: Facilitating trajectories of change in developing countries*. Wageningen: Wageningen Academic Publishers.

Trebbin, A & Hassler, M (2012). Farmers' producer companies in India: A new concept for collective action? *Environment and Planning A, 44*(2), 411–427. https://doi.org/10.1068/a44143

Utting, P (2016). *Mainstreaming social and solidarity economy: Opportunities and risks for policy change*. Retrieved from https://base.socioeco.org/docs/paper-mainstreaming-sse-12-november-2016-edit-untfsse.pdf

Vaidyanathan, A (2013). Future of cooperatives in India. *Economic and Political Weekly, 48*(18): 30–34.

Vasavada, S (2021, February 25). The 10,000 FPOs scheme ignores women farmers. *IDR*. Retrieved from https://idronline.org/the-10000-farmer-producer-organisations-scheme-ignores-women-farmers/

Vepa, SS (2005). Feminisation of agriculture and marginalisation of their economic stake. *Economic and Political Weekly*, 2563–2568.

Wicks, AC & Freeman, RE (1998). Organization studies and the new pragmatism: Positivism, anti-positivism, and the search for ethics. *Organization Science, 9*(2), 123–140.

World Bank (2007). *World development report 2008: Agriculture for development*. Washington, DC: The World Bank.

2

DYNAMICS OF INCUBATING A MULTI-COMMUNITY, MULTI-COMMODITY, MULTI-LOCATION FPO

The case of Krushidhan Producer Company in Gujarat

Astad Pastakia and Sachin Oza

1. Introduction

1.1 Context

Managing scarce water resources for farm productivity is critical for Gujarat's 60% population dependent on farm-based livelihood. Ahmedabad-based Development Support Centre (DSC) addressed this issue by supporting farming communities to implement participatory irrigation management (PIM) in irrigated areas and watershed management in dryland areas. It soon became a national resource agency for water management in agriculture, having extended its work to Madhya Pradesh, Maharashtra, and Rajasthan.

DSC realised that enhancing water management alone was not enough, as agriculture was plagued by several problems. Indiscriminate use of chemical fertilisers and pesticides affected soil health, micro-climates, and farmers' health. Uncertain weather conditions exacerbated by climate change had made it more risky. Lack of market information left marginal farmers at the mercy of traders. These issues were compounded by the near absence of an agri-extension system that could guide marginal farmers constituting 70% of farmers.

It is in this context that Krushidhan Producer Company Ltd. (KPCL), registered in December 2013, was visualised as the central part of a strategy that would transform agriculture. The slogan *"takau kheti – kamau kheti"* (sustainable farming – profitable farming) was adopted even before the company was born. Although KPCL had restricted the number of shareholders, its services were available to all farmers within the target area of 190 villages

DOI: 10.4324/9781003308034-2

in northern and central Gujarat. Given its unique mission KPCL became a multi-location, multi-commodity, multi-community farmer producer company (FPC) by choice. This case explores the challenges of incubating such an institution over a period of six years and making it financially independent. It also shows how the incubator and incubated organisations can support each other to achieve their common mission.

KPCL received early recognition at the state and national levels for its impact on marginal farmers of the region. It was conferred the Best Agripreneur Award at the 7th National Conference, Game Changer Awards (2017), and FPO Impact Award from Access Livelihood Services (2019).

1.2 DSC's theory of change

In 2008, DSC developed a systematic plan for promoting sustainable and profitable agriculture with the following key objectives: *productivity enhancement, cost reduction, risk mitigation, and increased price realisation through value addition and market linkages.* Collective action and enterprise was necessary to make its initiatives sustainable. It therefore visualised a three-tier organisation comprising farmer's clubs and SHGs at the hamlet level, organising committees at the cluster level and a FPC at the regional level (Figure 2.1).

The implementation of such a plan became possible with financial support from RBS Foundation through a ten-year programme called LEPNRM (Livelihood Enhancement through Participatory Natural Resource Management).

2. Incubation of the producer company

2.1 Overview

The first phase of four years (2008–11) represents the pre-KPCL phase, during which much of the spadework was done. In phase 2 (2012–16) the company was launched on 2 December 2013. During phase 3 financial and other supports to the company were continued while it explored various options for revenue generation. The company became financially independent from 1 October 2019. Figure 2.2 shows the overlap of the LEPNRM support during the incubation stages of the company.

The coverage of farmer participants and their institutions as of 2019:

- Farmers in targeted area   45,000
- Farmland covered (ha)   52,650
- Villages   190
- Kisan Clubs   338
- Woman SHGs   185 (78 engaged in productive activities)

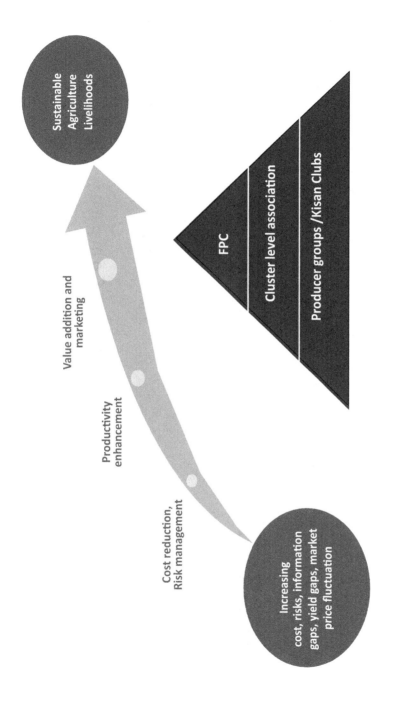

Figure 2.1 DSC's theory of change
(*Source:* Development Support Centre)

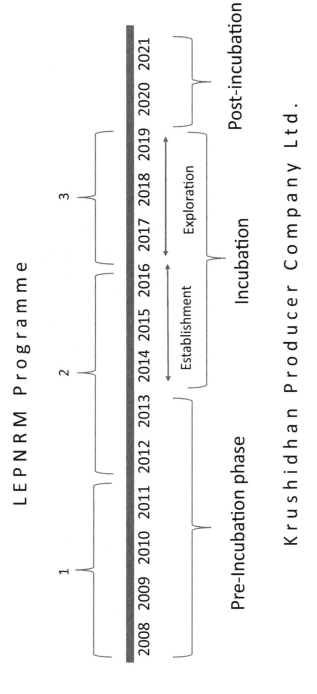

Figure 2.2 Timeline of LEPNRM including incubation of KPCL

- Farmers patronising KPCL   14,000
- KPCL shareholders   4,409

The total amount spent under LEPNRM was Rs. 27.8 million of which Rs. 21.4 million was towards extension work and Rs. 6.4 million towards incubating KPCL.

3. Phases of development

The story of KPCL's seeding and incubation is told in three phases, as described next:

1 Pre-incubation – Building the base
2 Incubation

    a) Establishment
    b) Exploration

3 Post-incubation – Financial independence

3.1 Pre-incubation (2008–11)

This was largely devoted to laying the ground for the farmer producer organisation (FPO) and rebuilding the agricultural system to make it viable and sustainable. It was used to build an agri-extension system consisting of a team of para-workers providing the latest information about non-chemical and organic methods of farming, to Kisan Clubs (KCs) and women's SHGs at the village level. This was achieved through demonstrations/trials in farmers' fields, exposure visits, farmer meetings/workshops, training, night video shows, awareness campaigns, among other methods of extension.

Package of practices (PoPs) and new technologies were demonstrated in more than 5,000 farmer's fields and adopted by 15,000 farmers, indicating a multiplier effect of three. Crop productivity increased from 20 to 70% generating increased interest and ownership among farmers.

3.2 Incubation (2013–19)

3.2.1 Establishment (2013–15)

This phase saw the strengthening and expansion of the agri-extension system. It also saw the formal *launch of KPCL in December 2013*. The Board of Directors (BoD) were provided suitable training, covering financial and legal literacy, collective decision-making, market exposure, and good governance. Backward linkages were established to deal with aggregated demand for agri-inputs.

The company promoted production of certified and foundation seed for wheat crop by its own farmers in 2015, thereby benefiting both farmer producers and farmer consumers. In the same year KPCL got into Minimum Support Price (MSP) scheme on behalf of groundnut producers on a pilot scale, aggregating 380 MT from 15 villages, valued at Rs. 15 million. The positive impacts through better price realisation prompted more farmers to become shareholders.

3.2.2 Exploration (2016–19)

This phase of incubation was focused on building strong networks with Krishi Vikas Kendras (KVKs) and agri-universities, so that para-workers and KCs could directly approach them for help and guidance in the coming years. Demonstrations and other extension activities were implemented through *convergence* with government agencies like KVKs and Agricultural Technology Management Agencies (ATMAs). A number of KPCL farmers were recognised and awarded by KVKs at the district level for their contribution to agriculture extension.

Special efforts were made to address the issue of climate change. Among these, short duration varieties of wheat and castor found ready acceptance. Solar-powered group fencing proved effective for protecting cash crops from wild boar and other ungulates. Innovative organic farmers were supported for both production and marketing. However, adoption of organic farming by 2019 was still partial and mainly for home consumption. Multiple reasons were identified and are being addressed to hasten adoption.

KPCL began aggregating produce for better price realisation. Having had a positive experience with MSP in the previous phase, it took this up on a larger scale. By 2017–18, the company's sales turnover reached Rs. 161.9 million. However, this time the company had negative experiences during implementation, including non-reimbursement of transport expenses, which affected its profitability. As a result, gross revenue fell to Rs. 19.45 million in 2018–19 due to non-participation in MSP procurement.

Two other initiatives taken during 2017 were significant. (a) Maize procured from Meghraj farmers by KPCL was used to produce cattle feed and supplied to Himmatnagar and Modasa farmers. Maize farmers got better prices while the others got cattle feed at cheaper rates. (b) There were production and sale of groundnut seed (without certification) to farmers in the same region. By 2018, the professional team of KPCL and the BoD were seriously looking for an *anchor activity* that would generate enough income for the company to cover its salary expenditure and overheads which were estimated at Rs. 0.25 million. In the rabi season of 2019, KPCL took up contract farming with Iscon-Balaji Pvt. Ltd. for potato crop, on a pilot scale, which turned out to be a success. The following year, this was scaled up four times, resulting in income that covered more than 50% of the salary and overhead expenses. At the time of writing, this activity was poised to replace MSP as an anchor activity that would keep the company financially viable. But Jasvant Chauhan, the CEO, was on the look out to develop more activities that had the potential. For instance, production of certified wheat seed by farmers had great potential to be scaled up. It would benefit both farmers and the company financially.

3.3 Post-incubation (October 2019 onwards)

As mentioned above, potato contract was scaled up to cover half the fixed expenses from its revenue. The rest was covered by the agri-input and seed business. With the onslaught of Corona pandemic, KPCL's activities were somewhat affected due to higher operating costs. Gross revenue decreased from Rs. 85 million to Rs. 63 million, that is, by 25%. However, from 2022 to 2023, it is expected to reach more than Rs. 70 million.

4. Functioning of agri-extension system

During the entire incubation period of six years, the agri-extension system worked as a partnership between the incubator and incubated institutions. DSC created the demand for new technology and associated agri-inputs while KPCL met this demand by establishing backward linkages and supplying quality inputs at the doorstep of the farmer. This process is captured in the diagram in Figure 2.3.

As shown in the figure, a team of para-workers link DSC to the farmers through KCs and women's producer groups, providing them information about the latest practices, technologies, and agri-inputs for sustainable agriculture. The technology is discussed within the group, and farmers draw support from each other, leading to higher adoption.

Farmers also go through stages of adoption. First-time adoption usually implies a trial. If the farmer does not get the desired results, he/she may discontinue. Here the role of the local resource person becomes critical in following through until the farmer takes more trial(s) and gets the desired results. After sustained adoption, the farmer is likely to encourage others to adopt as well. By September 2019, 45,000 farmers had been exposed to new technology and KPCL was actively serving 18,400 of them.

5. Evolution of marketing strategies

During the exploration phase, cluster committees were formed as a platform for KCs to express their needs and suggest ideas that would benefit their clusters. Company directors representing each cluster facilitated these

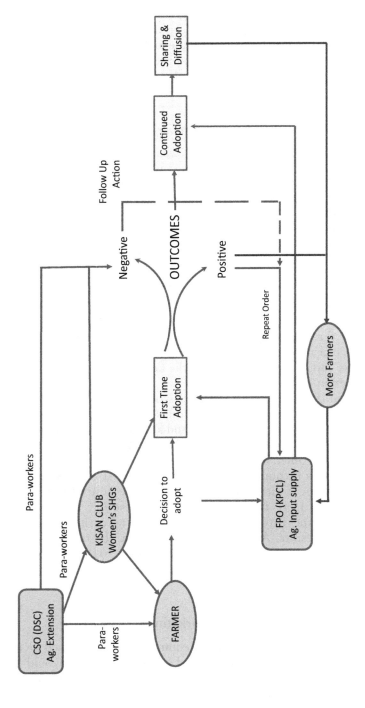

Figure 2.3 Agri-extension system – complementary action of civil society organisation and FPO

meetings and were given a free hand to test different ideas with a fund of Rs. 1,00,000. Several ideas were suggested by the expert director and DSC staff to see if these would appeal to the BoD.

Two brainstorming workshops, one in 2016 and another in 2020, were facilitated by external consultants. The criteria used for selecting promising ideas were (a) scalability, (b) profitability, (c) entry barriers, (d) growth potential, (e) strategic potential, and last but not the least (f) social benefits. Promising ideas were pilot-tested and later scaled up if successful.

Figure 2.4 summarises the mix of market initiatives on both backward and forward sides that have enabled growth of the company. Significantly, the backward side is well covered with three instances of backward integration. On the forward side, a few linkages have been made of which the MSP scheme in groundnut was the most beneficial. Currently the state government has banned FPOs from participating in it on account of a few instances of violation of norms. The spices processing initiative could never progress beyond local markets.

The potato initiative promises to replace MSP scheme as an anchor activity to increase profitability of the company (see Box 2.1).

5.1 Search for a suitable revenue model

Most of the activities undertaken so far were primarily aimed at meeting the felt needs of the marginal farmers. These also happened to provide low to moderate margins to the company (Table 2.1). However, an appropriate revenue model involves having at least one or two product lines that can contribute enough income to the company to cover its fixed costs. Selecting such an anchor activity has two main considerations: (a) what is the margin and (b) what is the existing or potential volume that can be achieved over a reasonable time frame.

Seeds coming through distributers (the regular supply channel) provide very low margins at around 3% as they have to accommodate many middlemen. Chemical pesticides provide better margins, but these are promoted as a measure of the last resort under responsible farming. Bio-products from distributors provide high margins but are not proven and therefore still under observation. Farm equipment provide moderate margins, but these are not very fast-moving items and require space and capital for storage. Bio-pesticides and bio-fertilisers produced by own farmers are mostly sold to other farmers at the village itself. Hence although margins are good, the volumes are limited and unlikely to grow in future. Margins on sale of cattle feed produced by KPCL itself are moderately good at about 15%, but at present volumes are not high and production is not even. On account of low entry barriers, 'me-too players' can provide stiff competition, making it unattractive in the long run.

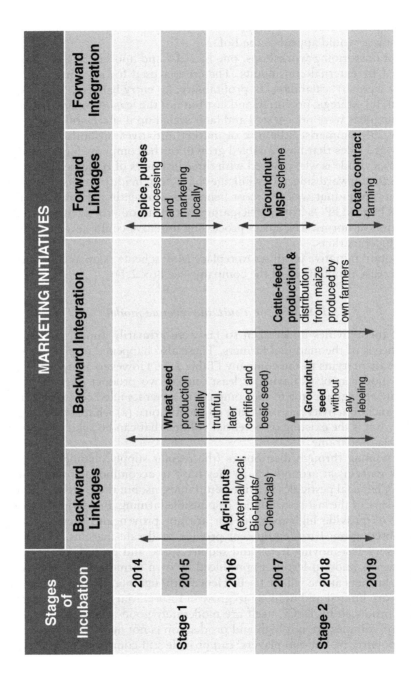

Figure 2.4 KPCL's market initiatives

Table 2.1 Margin analysis of products/product categories (%)

Details	2016–17	2017–18	2018–19
1 *Agri-inputs from distributors* (average margin)			
1.01 Seeds	3.25	3.50	2.89
1.02 Pesticides	12.50	12.35	12.93
1.03 Bio-products	27.30	23.54	22.56
1.04 Farm equipment	12.08	9.64	7.58
2 *Agri-inputs produced by own farmers or KPCL* (average margin)			
2.01 Wheat seeds	7.48	8.50	10.16
2.02 Groundnut seeds	5.20	6.00	7.56
2.03 Fodder seeds	15.00	15.00	16.36
2.04 Bio-fertiliser	12.00	12.00	11.78
2.05 Bio-pesticide	8.05	8.75	9.09
2.06 Cattle feed	15.22	12.67	16.67
3 *Aggregation and marketing of agricultural produce*	7.00	7.25	7.46
4 *MSP with government (groundnut)*	1.00	1.00	1.00
5 *Retail outlet – Ahmedabad/Himmatnagar (KPCL/Gujpro)*	0.50	0.50	0.72
6 *Potato – contract farming* (2019–20)	2.75		

Box 2.1 Potato contract farming: Emerging anchor activity

In 2018 –19, KPCL became a vendor for farmers of Himmatnagar on a pilot scale, with Iscon-Balaji as the partner company. The biggest advantage with Balaji was that it could procure under-sized potatoes as well as those affected by blight because it owned a manufacturing plant producing powder for industrial uses. Farmers were expected to respect the intellectual property rights of Iscon-Balaji and not sell their produce to other competitors. A contract was signed on 30 August 2019. The company provided 100 MTs of potato seeds of its patented variety *Santana* to 30 selected farmers, and the purchase price for the output was fixed in advance. Fifty percent of the seed material was provided on credit, and farmers had the option to have it deducted at the time of harvest. Farmers were provided technical support on site as well as through telephone during the farming period (November to March).

As per the PoP recommended by the company, the farmer was expected to put 20–25 MTs (about ten trolley loads) of compost/organic fertiliser in one acre of land. The returns would depend on his/

---

her ability to apply fertiliser. According to Dr Namita Oza of Iscon-Balaji, technically, *Santana* had the potential to produce potatoes of as much as 1 kg per piece!

KPCL supported the farmers with technical guidance, procurement, and transportation of potatoes after harvest and supervision of potato grading as per specified standards. By the end of March 2020, the harvesting was completed although marred somewhat by the Covid-19 pandemic.

Encouraged by the success of the pilot, the following year, operations were scaled up by four times (Table 2.2). KPCL came up with a service (optional) to supply agri-inputs as per the PoP specified by the company, for a small fee, resulting in an income of Rs. 0.25 million. KPCL also gave credit to the farmers for 3–4 months, which was recovered at the time of harvest.

Table 2.2 Results of contract farming with Iscon-Balaji

Particulars	2019–20	2020–21
Production (MT)	1090	4800
Average price realized (Rs)	9046	10,000
Gross value (Rs. Million)	9.86	48.00

The farmers were happy with the production, price, and timely technical support received. Farmers experienced, on an average, net profit of about Rs. 0.1125 m/acre. The profit/sales ratio was 52.9%, which was much higher than that of wheat, their main crop.

About 50–60% of the farmers involved are marginal, while the rest are relatively larger. This may appear to be a compromise with the original goal of working largely for marginal farmers. But in the absence of any other anchor activity that would ensure the economic viability of the company, a conscious choice was made. As it turned out, it led to a larger acceptance of the company within the farming community, even though 75% of its members were marginal (ownership of land < 2 ha).

Retailing of commodities, especially pesticide-free and organic produce in cities like Ahmedabad and Himmatnagar, has been initiated through Gujpro (the state-level FPO federation in Gujarat). As of now this option is not very attractive because of very low margins (<1%) and low volumes. In the distant future when consumers become more health conscious and are willing to pay a premium for certified produce this would become a viable option for the company.

5.2 *Promising product lines*

1   Certified and truthful labelled seeds produced by farmers themselves are promising as the margins are moderate and potential for volumes is high. As of now achieving higher volumes is constrained by lack of sales personnel. Jaswant Bhai, the CEO, is contemplating signing a B2B contract with Ankur seeds in the near future, in order to achieve higher volumes. If this works, it could become one of the future anchor activities which also benefit the farmers a great deal.

2   Aggregation and collective marketing of commodities provide low margins at around 7% and are a risky business. However, volumes can be high and social benefits are also high. The company has recently taken up a registered shop at the Himmatnagar *mandi*. KPCL farmers would have the option to sell their produce through this shop.

3   Selling commodities to government under MSP scheme has proved beneficial in the past. Even with a margin as low as 1% it works out well because of very high volumes. Farmers also gain substantially through assured and better price realisation. Whenever the state government reopens this option for FPOs it will be worth taking up.

4   The opportunity of potato contract farming has taken care of the present worry of covering salaries and overheads. It is promising because although it provides low margins (2.75%) volumes can be high with greater prospects for steady growth. Among the current players in the market, Balaji-Iscon is one of the few which understands the FPO and works with them as per their terms and conditions.

6. Financial performance

Table 2.3 provides a summary of financial performance of the company on key parameters. While sales revenue and profit after tax have fluctuated, it is worth noting that the losses of Rs. 0.734 million carried over from its previous form, the Dhari Krishak Vikas Producer Company Ltd (DKVPCL),[1] have finally been wiped out in 2017–18. By September 2019 the company had reserves and surplus of about Rs. 0.39 million. Its fixed assets had gone up from Rs. 0.075 million at the end of stage 1 to Rs. 1.224 million at the end of stage 2. These assets include a plot of land and a godown of 35 sq. ft. for storage of agricultural produce. A significant development during stage 2 is the accessing of long-term debt to the extent of about Rs. 1.83 million of which about Rs. 0.80 million has been contributed by large farmers and the remaining from KCs/SHG. The revolving fund of Rs. 1.0 million refers to the amount provided by SFAC as a matching grant for purchase of equity by marginal farmers. During 2020–21 the company was able to access another long-term loan from NABKISAN of Rs. 2 million at a reasonable interest rate of 8.5%.

Table 2.3 Summary of financial performance (Rs. in million)

Particulars	Incubation Stage 1			Incubation Stage 2			Post Incubation	
	2013–14	2014–15	2015–16	2016–17	2017–18	2018–19	2019–20	2020–21
Gross Revenue	2.91	4.63	10.63	56.58	161.94	19.45	32.75	85.05
Profit Before Tax	0.38	0.17	0.84	0.22	0.24	0.08	0.01	0.02
Profit After Tax	0.38	0.17	0.84	0.04	0.16	0.07	0.01	0.02
Share Capital	0.54	0.78	1.02	2.56	3.77	4.41	4.41	4.41
Reserves and Surplus	-0.35	-0.19	-0.14	-0.01	0.32	0.39	0.40	0.43
Long-Term Liabilities	–	–	0.30	–	1.51	1.83	1.14	2.53
Revolving Fund	1.00	1.00	1.00	1.00	1.00	1.00	1.42	1.42
Fixed Assets and Investments	0.03	0.03	0.07	0.15	0.20	1.22	1.25	1.58
Current Liabilities	0.97	1.26	2.10	1.29	12.97	1.76	6.94	15.71
Current Assets	1.96	2.64	3.77	6.38	19.03	8.17	14.56	21.90
Ratio Analysis								
Gross Profit/Revenue	0.1310	0.0360	0.0790	0.0040	0.0010	0.0040	0.0003	0.0002
Debt-Equity Ratio (Total Liabilities/Equity)	1.8110	1.6120	2.3620	0.5030	3.8450	0.8150	1.8320	4.1370
Debt to Asset Ratio (Total Debt/Total Assets)	0.4890	0.4720	0.6250	0.1970	0.7530	0.3830	0.5110	0.7770
Current Ratio (Current Assets/Current Liabilities)	2.0110	2.0980	1.7970	4.9520	1.4670	4.6350	2.0980	1.3940

The table also shows the trend of four key financial ratios over time. The profitability ratio has been consistently low with the second stage doing even worse than the first stage. Although the reserves and surplus now stand at Rs. 0.398 million for a company that is seven years old, this balance needs to be substantially increased. For the same reason the company has not been able to declare any dividends so far. After changes in the rules, during 2020–21 no tax has been deducted from profits as companies with turnover lower than Rs. 1,000 million are exempted. The remaining three ratios are well under control, thanks to the strategy of being asset light and raising funds from internal sources – such as savings of its network of SHGs and KCs. Current ratio has been consistently low, indicating use of internal resources as well as good working capital management. The debt/equity ratio in 2020–21 has shot up to more than 4.0; however, this is still well covered by total assets.

Mohan Sharma, Executive Director of DSC, who has served KPCL as an 'expert director' for three years, makes a significant observation regarding financial performance of the company:

> The present system of accounting tends to grossly underestimate the financial situation of the company, as there is no provision to show the economic benefits generated by the company for farmers (both members and non-members). Until such time that a new system of reporting is designed exclusively for social business enterprises such as FPOs, perhaps it will be best to carry out independent impact studies at regular intervals.
>
> (per.com)

Benefits to the farmers are both tangible and intangible. The tangible benefits can be traced and quantified under the four objectives of *cost reduction, risk reduction, productivity improvement* and *better price realisation through market linkages and/or value addition.*

6.1 Tangible benefits

To get a flavour of the benefits generated for the marginal farmer, rough estimates were made for the case of groundnut sold through MSP scheme.

In 2018–19, farmers benefitted to the tune of Rs. 31.8 million simply from better price realisation. The difference between MSP and prevailing market price ranged from Rs. 175 to 250 per 20 kg. For its services in organising supervision of quality standards and logistics, the company earned Rs. 1.413 million by way of commission. Hence for every one rupee earned by the company, it generated a benefit of Rs. 22.5 for the farmers! (Table 2.4).

Table 2.4 Estimate of benefits passed over to farmers through MSP

Ground Nut (MSP scheme)	2017–18	2018–19
Procurement (MT)	1021.70	3174.60
Value (million)	43.40	141.30
KPCL revenue (million)	0.43	1.41
Benefit to farmers (million)	10.20	31.80
KPCL returns as % of sales value	1.00	1.00
Farmers' benefit as % of sales value – higher price realisation	23.50	22.50
Ratio of Benefits to farmer/profits to KPCL	23.50	22.50

6.2 Intangible benefits

Considerable impact has also been made through intangible benefits such as *risk mitigation* in agriculture (dealing with climate change, improving soil health and sustainability, reducing negative impacts of chemicals on local micro climate) and health of farming communities (reduction in problems related to cancer induced by chemical pesticides). Most of these are difficult to measure as they may occur over a long time-frame.

7. Governance and its challenges

7.1 Decision-making at KPCL

KPCL found itself doing the balancing act on a number of fronts, as described next:

• Balancing social and commercial goals:

Choosing the right portfolio of activities that ensure commercial viability while meeting social objectives is a major preoccupation of the BoD and professional staff.

Another issue is to ensure that small and marginal farmers are the main beneficiaries and owners of the company. An analysis of member farmers based on size of their land-holding (2015–16) confirmed that more than 72% of the members were small and marginal. Only ten farmers representing 0.5% were large farmers. According to Mr Mohan Sharma, since there was an organic growth of the company, inclusion of certain farmers who fell in medium or big category was unavoidable. According to Sharma, "large farmers had not proved to be a problem – rather they were often helpful in their own ways. A few large farmers had even provided loans to the company in their individual capacity" (per. com.).

- Participation of members versus non-members

During the initial stages farmers were eager to get the services of the company but not so eager to put their money on it. Many of them adopted the 'wait and watch' policy even when DSC and KPCL had carried out drives to increase the shareholding. A stage has now come where farmers are eager to join, but there is cap on the extent of shareholding that KPCL can accept. This is because a share capital beyond Rs. 5 million would reclassify KPCL as medium scaled. This would have implications for compliances and taxes, which, for the time being, KPCL would like to avoid. In 2018 the company stopped taking new members. The peak participation of non-member farmers was in 2018 on account of the MSP scheme, when they were three times the number of shareholders (Figure 2.5).

- Balancing needs of geographical regions/clusters

The communities residing in different areas are different and so are the cropping patterns. Meghraj has tribal and OBC communities engaged in rain-fed farming. Dhari also has OBC communities and is rain-fed. In contrast, the others (Visnagar, Himmatnagar, and Modasa) have irrigated land and belong to upper- or middle-caste Hindu families. Their contribution is significantly higher as reflected in shareholding pattern and sales, because of which they have larger representation in the governing board. Out of a total

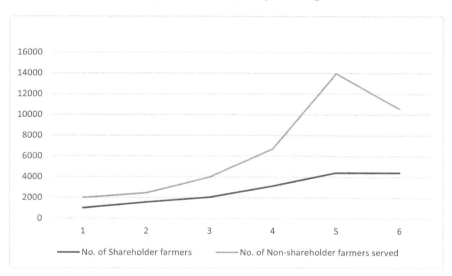

Figure 2.5 Shareholder versus non-shareholder beneficiaries

of ten directors in the BoD, Visnagar has three, Himmatnagar and Meghraj have two each, while the rest including Modasa, Vehlal, and Dhari have one each. One seat is reserved for the expert director. This gives Visnagar, Himmatnagar, and Modasa greater say in decision-making.

The ability of the representatives from larger and more successful clusters such as Visnagar and Himmatnagar to understand and accept the needs of relatively backward/smaller clusters like Meghraj would ensure future collaborations between clusters.

- Balancing participation of men and women

In 2015–16, only 19% of the members were women. By 2019 it had gone up to 27%. These women are mainly from SHGs that have taken up productive activities. The participation of women is much higher in tribal areas (60%) than non-tribal areas (all < 35%) as shown in Table 2.5. Upper-caste families feel that women have "no time for such activities" because they are engaged mainly in household work and animal husbandry.

As of 2019 there were two women representatives on the BoD. An initiative proposed by women representatives, aimed at making available grocery provisions in bulk for social occasions, was taken up at Himmatnagar in 2018. However, it was wound up within six months presumably because the assumptions made in the project did not hold. A special report from a gender specialist in the evaluation of LEPNRM 3 has come up with a number of measures to improve the gender balance.

The relationships between various participants in the FPC are depicted diagrammatically in Figure 2.6.

The diagram helps to bring out the complexity of the institution. It also shows why FPOs are so fragile and take so much time to incubate. Building from below is the key to stability, but this inevitably calls for investment in time, and capacity building of various constituents and power centres. KPCL is a product of such an investment. It has now reached a crucial stage where its leadership will be put to test as DSC's role is reduced to that of friend, philosopher, and guide.

Table 2.5 Women shareholders in different clusters

Unit	Female Shareholders	Total Shareholders	Percentage of Female Shareholders
Visnagar	358	1729	31.11
Himmatnagar	200	868	23.04
Modasa	290	855	33.91
Meghraj	330	545	60.55
Dhari	5	412	1.21
Total	1183	4409	26.83

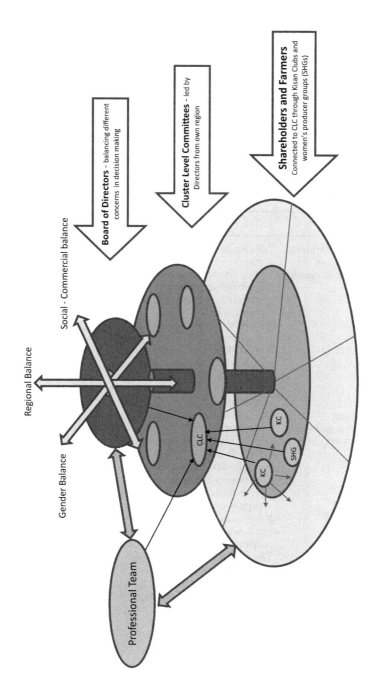

Board of Directors - balancing different concerns in decision making

Cluster Level Committees - led by Directors from own region

Shareholders and Farmers Connected to CLC through Kisan Clubs and women's producer groups (SHGs)

Social - Commercial balance

Regional Balance

Gender Balance

Professional Team

CLC

KC

SHG

KC

Figure 2.6 Relationships between participants in KPCL

7.2 Quality of leadership

Leadership has to come from the BoD, which is expected to volunteer considerable amount of its time to a multitude of tasks.

Two main criteria used for selecting board members were (a) membership with a KC and (b) active participation in the work of the company and KC. How has the leadership at KPCL performed so far? A preliminary assessment indicates that the BoD has been as active as the professional staff of KPCL and DSC staff during the years of incubation, although the areas in which they have been active are different. There were local issues that they could handle comfortably, but for some issues they needed DSC's support (Table 2.6).

Table 2.6 Leadership at KPCL during incubation period

No.	Function	BoD's Contribution	DSC's Contribution
1	Mobilising farmers and creating member allegiance	BoD leaders took responsibility for their own clusters and used their influence to improve shareholding as well as participation of both members and non-members. It has taken up the idea of decentralised governance by taking the lead in functioning of cluster-level committees.	DSC used its influence with SHGs and KCs to improve shareholding through specific drives; it used farmer meetings to raise awareness and create member allegiance.
2	Supporting professionals and implementation team	During the first stage of incubation BoD played a valuable role by identifying the felt needs of the farmers on the one hand and smoothening supply issues with farmers at the point of supply on the other. It has maintained customer relations and put in place a grievance-redressal system.	Implementation team, particularly the manager deputed by DSC, played a critical role in making the BoD understand its role. He provided market information and facilitated decision-making.
3	Mobilising resources	The board understood how difficult it was to access formal credit. It chose to rely on internal funding and mobilised funds from SHGs, KCs, and even individual farmers who were aligned with the company's goals and mission.	DSC was only partly successful in mobilising funds from external sources – for instance the equity grant provided by SFAC.

No.	Function	BoD's Contribution	DSC's Contribution
4	Dealing with external and internal threats	During the second stage of incubation, local vested interests, which felt threatened by the rising economic power of the company, threw a spanner in the works by using false accusations with National Agricultural Cooperative Marketing Federation of India Ltd (NAFED) to get KPCL blacklisted from becoming a vendor. It was the patient lobbying by Vasantbhai, the chairperson, that got the company out of this situation.	Since Vasantbhai was handling the situation in a mature manner, DSC only needed to support him in this case.
5	Identifying new market opportunities	Two ideas suggested by BoD were tested and selected for implementation. These included seed production (wheat, groundnut, and fodder) and contract farming of potato. Both these have promise for becoming anchor activities.	To improve their entrepreneurial orientation, DSC took several initiatives such as brainstorming sessions, feeding of ideas from time to time, and so on, which were evaluated by BoD and ultimately owned and implemented by it.
6	Financial and legal literacy for better compliance and administration	Since company laws are in English and rather complicated, this was an area where they needed help. Later couple of directors were made familiar with the rules and their implications.	This was a new area even for DSC staff, who had to rely on their auditor to learn the ropes before they could build the capacity of the BoD.

The issue of financial and legal literacy of the BoD is a major challenge. This is an area of capacity building, which should continue beyond incubation as the rules keep changing from time to time and need to be understood for specific situations before proper decisions can be taken.

The leadership demonstrated by Vasantbhai the chairman in the face of external threats was exemplary. These external forces cannot be underestimated, and a system of 'eternal vigilance' needs to be brought in place to safeguard the interests of the company. This is a leadership skill that is not very common and needs to be valued. It also needs to be built into the capacity-building agenda of the BoD. Dealing with internal threats is equally important. Maintaining transparency, ensuring democratic decision-making, and aligning members with the common goals, as done by KPCL, are among the measures to avoid internal threats.

A recent move has been to create cluster committees as a form of *decentralised management* where directors representing various clusters would take leadership for their respective areas. To this end, each director has been given a free hand to spend up to Rs. 1,00,000 on local initiatives which could drive change.

As of March 2021, KPCL had 11 employees apart from the CEO, who are organised in three categories: (a) finance and administrative, (b) supervisory staff, and (c) field staff (Figure 2.7). Jaswant Chauhan, who was deputed from DSC as the manager in 2013, continues as the CEO in 2021. The staff

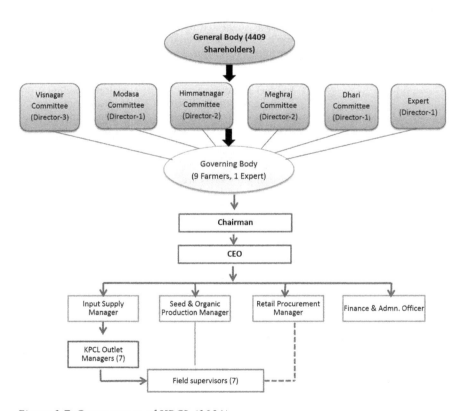

Figure 2.7 Organogram of KPCL (2021)

members at cluster level are accountable to the cluster committee. But they are also accountable to their executive managers and ultimately to CEO.

The present staff has demonstrated its commitment to the FPO over the past 7–8 years. During the Corona pandemic, it voluntarily deferred 20% of its salary until such time that company's financial condition improved. It received the pending amount only eight months later after the potato harvest.

8. Conclusion

KPCL has become financially independent since October 2019. After two years, it has demonstrated that it can keep its head above the water by covering all its fixed expenditure. Potato contract-farming has emerged as the current anchor activity. Scaling up of certified seed production by the farmers could become the second. The search for such activities by Jaswant Bhai, the CEO, will continue in order to meet the expectations of financial sustainability.

KPCL is making a huge social contribution towards farming communities in target areas, particularly marginal farmers – which is not reflected in its balance sheet. In the absence of suitable norms for reflecting these benefits in their annual reports, FPOs may find it practical to use two kinds of ratios to assess the depth and spread of social benefits realised by the farming community:

1   For every rupee of gross profit to the company, what is the average increase in gross profit to the farmer taking advantage of its services (through cost reduction, increase in productivity, better price realisation, reduced risk, and so on)?
2   What is the proportion of benefits passed on to non-members (other farmers accessing services of the company) as compared to members (shareholders)?

These ratios can be calculated for specific activities as well as for the services provided by the company as a whole. For better analysis the proportion of benefits passed on to farmers through backward versus forward linkages and through backward versus forward integration can be worked out. Non-tangible benefits that accrue over long term if any, such as improved soil health and better health of farming communities on account of shift to organic farming, could be taken note of with some quantification where possible. Periodic impact studies would serve the purpose and could be read along with the annual financial reports.

The lessons provided by this case study can prove invaluable to FPCs catering to the needs of entire farming communities, rather than a few hundred farmers cultivating a single crop. The latter can be taken up only by farmers with high-risk-taking ability or by FPCs that have access to support from government and other organisations. The KPCL model shows that multi-commodity, multi-community, multi-location companies can deal more effectively with risk on their own, while creating greater social benefits. However, this can only become possible when the support institution has made considerable investments prior to the launching of the company. More specifically these investments may include (a) creating an agri-extension system with the active participation of farmers and extension agencies, (b) promoting SHGs and KCs that become the building blocks for the future FPC, and (c) building the capacity of local youth who work as local resource persons, to build the extension system and who would join the professional management team when the company is launched.

Note

1 It may be noted that KPCL is a new form of Dhari Krishak Vikas Producer Company Ltd (DKVPCL), initiated by DSC in Amreli district of Gujarat in 2005. It was found more expeditious to transform DKVPCL into KPCL rather than to create a new FPC. As a result of this decision, KPCL inherited losses worth Rs. 0.73 million. On the other hand, DSC had gained practical experience which proved invaluable for incubating KPCL.

3

JEEVIKA WOMEN AGRI PRODUCER COMPANY LIMITED

The timid rise of an all-women state-promoted FPC in an "aspirational" district of Bihar

Sudha Narayanan, Milee Parmar, and Ritesh Pandey

1. Background

Khagaria district is located in the Indo-Gangetic plains of the Indian state of Bihar. It is overwhelmingly rural, with 94.7% of its population living in rural areas, according to Census 2011. Surrounded by seven rivers, the plentiful water resources and rich alluvial soil support high yields in agriculture. Parts of the district however also experience floods routinely when swathes of agricultural land remain submerged, restricting the cropping season to just one in the lowlands. Wheat and maize dominate the cropping pattern, along with some paddy and more recently soybean. Banana cultivation has expanded in three out of the seven blocks that make up the district, while mango and litchi orchards have for long been the preferred crops in certain clusters.

Despite its rich natural resources that can support a vibrant agriculture, Khagaria's social indicators put it among the worst performing districts in India. For example, the sex ratio of 886 women per 1,000 men is among the lowest in the country. At the turn of the millennium, in 2001, female literacy rate was a mere 29%, rising to only 49.56% in 2011. Despite improvements, the district still lags others in the country in terms of socio-economic development. Since 2015, Khagaria is one of 36 districts in Bihar receiving funds via the Backward Regions Grant Funds Programme (BRGF). In January 2018, Khagaria was designated an "aspirational district" under the Transformation of Aspirational Districts[1] intended to achieve rapid socio-economic progress.

1.1 Promoting rural livelihoods via farmer producer companies in Bihar

Long before these recent initiatives, in 2007, the Bihar Rural Livelihoods Project (BRLP) launched an ambitious state-wide initiative, aided financially by the World Bank to form self-help groups (SHGs) among women aiming

DOI: 10.4324/9781003308034-3

to alleviate poverty.[2] As in other districts, Khagaria too saw the formation of SHGs of 10–20 women members each in a village, together represented in a village organisation (VO) at the village level and several VOs further aggregating into a cluster-level federation (CLF) at the block level. The BRLP aimed to achieve financial inclusion for women and enable access to formal credit to support livelihood activities that would alleviate poverty via linkages with banks and training in livelihood activities. In Bihar, JEEViKA or the Bihar Rural Livelihoods Promotion Society (BRLPS) was formed as an autonomous institution of the state government to manage the BRLP and has emerged as a particularly effective steward of the programme.

As JEEViKA turned its focus to facilitating livelihood activities, in the field of agriculture, the formation of farmer producer companies (FPC) became a key strategy across the state with a dedicated vertical for farming-focused livelihoods within the organisation. JEEViKA has promoted ten FPCs so far. In Khagaria, the eponymous Jeevika Women Agri Produce Company Limited (JWAPCL), the focus of this case study, is one of them.

The strategy employed by JEEViKA for FPC formation was to leverage its frontline workers, including village resource persons (VRPs) and skilled extension workers (SEWs) to motivate SHG members to become members of producer groups (PGs). PG members are urged to become shareholders in the FPCs. In essence, this involved building a federated structure that mimicked and paralleled the SHG federation, building the FPC bottom-up. In form and purpose, the SHG-VO-CLF remained distinct from the PG-FPC system. It was believed that building sustainable and profitable women-owned FPCs would empower women by ensuring that they take advantage of economic opportunities for marketable work and gain control and say over household income (Tripathi et al., 2020).

Although the effort to form FPCs began in 2009, most FPCs were largely inert in the initial years. It was soon recognised that establishing sustainable agro-based livelihoods would be no easy task, especially in a context where women are mostly unlettered with little experience in active engagement in formal business. A technical assistance initiative called Women's Advancement in Rural Development and Agriculture (WARDA) was established in 2016 to facilitate the revival of FPCs (Tripathi et al., 2020). WARDA was supported financially by the Bill & Melinda Gates Foundation (BMGF). TechnoServe, a private consultancy firm, was roped in to help JEEViKA establish these FPCs and provide the necessary training in business capacity, production, and post-harvest management. In Khagaria as elsewhere, the focus was to establish market linkages for farmer members, bypassing middlemen, and securing better prices for the farmers' produce. Under the WARDA programme, TechnoServe worked with JEEViKA and the PG-FPC system to pilot approaches to develop value chains for identified crops. Its role soon became indispensable with TechnoServe's involvement extending well beyond training and capacity building to the execution of business plans and on occasion managing operations on the ground. TechnoServe's functions devolved on MicroSave Consulting in 2020, a decision taken by JEEViKA, but the essential design of the programme and role of the private technical consultant remain unchanged as of 2021.

The JWAPCL has 1,206 shareholder members with a share capital of Rs. 0.30 million as of 2021. Since 2009, more than 1,500 women farmers are collectivised as 52 PGs spanning all seven blocks in Khagaria district and one block (Pirpaiti) of Bhagalpur district of Bihar. In its lifetime, it has achieved a peak revenue and profit of Rs. 47.89 million and Rs. 1.69 million, respectively, in 2018–19, mostly derived from maize trading in both spot and futures markets. JWAPCL's experience holds the potential for many valuable lessons. We focus on four of them: How has an FPC in a resource-constrained context with unlettered members who have limited entrepreneurial skills managed to sustain themselves? In what ways do the FPC's SHG pedigree and JEEViKA's patronage influence the functioning and performance of the FPC? How far has the management of complex tasks of the FPC devolved or not devolved on the JWAPCL? What role does the recently installed professional management team play in ensuring active participation of FPC members?

2. The JWAPCL story

2.1 *The beginnings*

The Jeevika Women Agri Producer Company Limited (JWAPCL) was incorporated on 25 November 2009 under Part IXA of the Companies Act, 1956. It is one of the first women-only FPCs to be registered in Bihar, along with Aranyak Agri Producer Company Ltd. (AAPCL), and is the third oldest FPC in the state. Most of the 500 shareholders at that time subscribed to 50 shares of Rs. 10 each.

Most FPCs fostered by JEEViKA had the SHG-VO-CLF federations in place before venturing to form PGs. Interestingly, JWAPCL was formed even before the CLFs, a crucial component of the SHG-VO-CLF system, were formed. In this, the JWAPCL stands out as an anomaly, indicating early member interest in conducting business. As with most JEEViKA-promoted FPCs, there is a large overlap between SHG and PGs. For example, many PG members used the same name for both the SHGs that were formed first and the PGs that followed later. The PGs were conceived of as informal entities, whereas the FPCs they federate into constitute a formal entity. One member of the Board of Directors (BoD) of JWAPCL recalled the initial days and how they persuaded potential shareholders to join the FPC pointing out to them that their contribution was just like 'school fees for admission'. To get benefits from the operation of the company they would need to get 'admitted'. JWAPCL had modest beginnings, but its first members had clear goals and well-defined aspirations.

2.2 Quiet early days (2009–15)

"When we formed our company, our assessment was that considerable impact can be created in lives of our members through reducing cost of seeds and ensuring its timely availability," said Amrita Devi, a current BoD member of JWAPCL. The FPC responded to this need and undertook seed production activity of wheat and paddy during initial years of their existence. The activity was implemented on a very small-scale pilot level with about 10–12 member farmers with business less than Rs. 100,000 annually. Despite early success, however modest, they soon realised that systemic constraints, such as the absence of warehousing capability to store and maintain the quality of seed, prevented scaling up of seed production. The years between 2009 and 2015 were not particularly eventful with the FPC focusing on its original and core business of seed production on a limited scale (Figure 3.1). Indeed, there is little systematic information on the FPC for this period. During this time, the FPC was also engaged in facilitating access to agri-inputs for its members. In 2014, a mentha oil marketing pilot allowed members to go beyond their limited set of activities.

2.3 Pivoting to maize (2016–19)

A key turning point for JWAPCL came in 2016. TechnoServe came on board to assist JEEViKA-promoted FPCs with training and enterprise development under WARDA. Around this time, JWAPCL made a foray into maize marketing. It is useful to foreground this decision of maize as focal crop against the larger maize economy in the region. The area around Khagaria and neighbouring Purnia has been home to an 'unlikely' revolution in maize in the two decades since the 2000s. This was largely due to the introduction of high-yielding hybrid maize seeds, the region's proximity to rakes and arterial roadways, the rapid co-emergence of warehouses that collectively complemented the region's natural fertility (Singh and Damodaran, 2015). The growing importance of maize in the region prompted the National Commodities and Derivatives Exchange (NCDEX) to declare Gulabbagh in Purnia as a delivery centre in 2013. For farmers, although maize was potentially a lucrative crop, non-transparent trading practices including improper weighing and arbitrary grading for quality put farmers at a disadvantage. It seemed natural for JWAPCL to look to maize as a business proposition.

Another JEEViKA-promoted FPC, Aranyak, in neighbouring Purnia, had just tasted considerable success trading in maize, including hedging in the futures market with NCDEX, enabled by extensive support from TechnoServe. Inspired by this, JWAPCL decided to adopt this strategy but with an important difference – they had only limited support from TechnoServe (Figure 3.2). The JWAPCL CEO Shivendra states, "Drawing on learnings from Aranyak's experience, JWAPCL started maize marketing in 2016–17

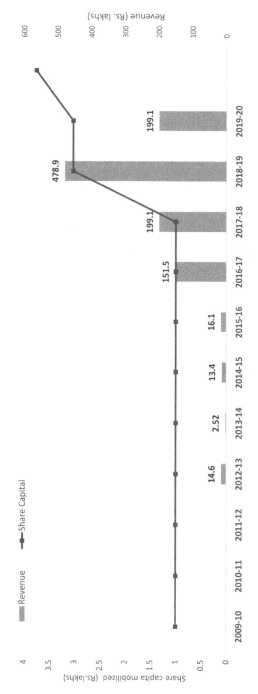

Figure 3.1 A timeline of JWAPCL's activities and membership

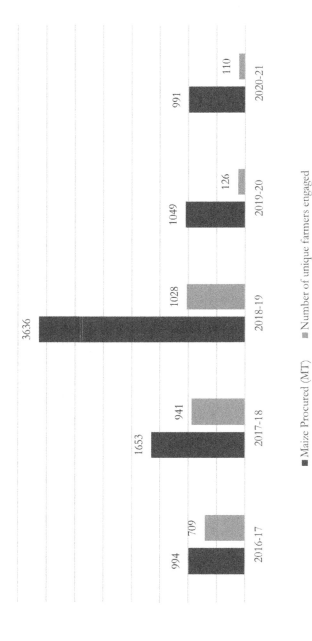

Figure 3.2 JWAPCI's maize business: warehousing and trading

without much of technical support from the TechnoServe. We were able to supply 1,000 tonnes of maize through suitable market linkages like NeML, NCDEX as well as Arya Collateral, etc." (interview). The company also distributed patronage bonus in 2016–17 among members as the company made profits during the year.

Aware that poor maize quality might be their undoing, JWAPCL had procured a maize dryer that year to ensure that members are able to get a premium for better-quality maize. There were not many takers, however. By most accounts, it appears that quality issues, for example, maintaining low moisture levels, continue to be a challenge even today, as it was then.

In 2017–18, the FPC scaled up its maize trading volume from about 1,000 tonnes to 1,650 tonnes (Figure 3.2). A short-term loan of Rs. 3.95 million and a long-term loan of Rs. 11 million in 2016–17 and 2017–18, respectively, enabled this. In 2018, a member of the BoD met Mr V K Sinha, the then president of Securities and Exchange Board of India (SEBI), in an event and requested him to facilitate opening of NCDEX-accredited warehouse in the district. On the suggestion of Mr Sinha, NCDEX opened one in Khagaria which led to substantial increase in business volume from about 1,650 MT in 2017–18 to about 3,600 MT in 2018–19. That year, however, JWAPCL made losses in maize trading due to a market-wide downturn in maize prices.

The NCDEX experience of JWAPCL and Aranyak has been highlighted often as glorious examples of FPCs leveraging the futures platform (Chatterjee et al., 2019). JWAPCL's success had several ingredients: technical inputs, even if limited, from TechnoServe and the NCDEX, timely availability of working capital, and the fortuitous access to the NCDEX leadership that enabled access to warehouses. The cautious approach adopted by JWAPCL ensured that their exposure to the risks of the maize futures platform through 2018–19 was limited; JWAPCL was selling maize to several other buyers as well at that time – including traders at the *mandi* prices.

The early enthusiasm for maize trading waned after the downturn in maize prices in 2018–19. There were other reasons as well. The first was the discontinuation of the NCDEX-accredited warehouse. Second, 2020 saw a transition in the technical assistance provider from TechnoServe to MicroSave. Third, Covid-19-induced lockdowns hampered operations of the FPC. Maize continues to be central to JWAPCL's activities, but their operational challenges have led them to consider new strategies that reveal maturity in negotiating the risks in value-chain participation. These include plans to secure warehouse space and the use of agri-entrepreneurs (AEs) to scale up procurement.

2.4 New directions: diversification and experimentation

Even in 2018, JWAPCL had systematically initiated other business activities in a bid to both reduce dependence on a single commodity and ensure a continuous year-round stream of income. This trend has intensified.

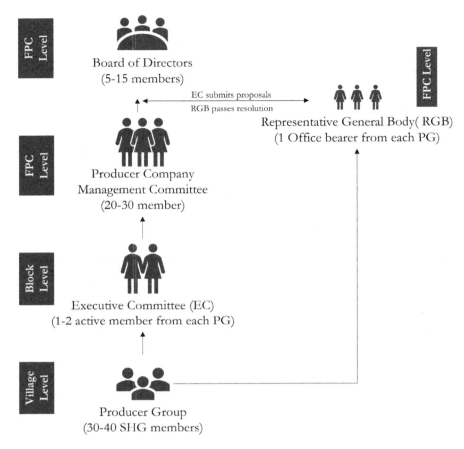

FPC Level — Board of Directors (5-15 members)

EC submits proposals
RGB passes resolution

Representative General Body(RGB)
(1 Office bearer from each PG)

FPC Level — Producer Company Management Committee (20-30 member)

Block Level — Executive Committee (EC)
(1-2 active member from each PG)

Village Level — Producer Group
(30-40 SHG members)

Figure 3.3 Governance structure of JWAPCL

The years since have been marked by diversification and experimentation (Figure 3.3).

For example, JWAPCL leased mango orchards in the pre-harvest period and undertook harvesting and marketing operations, linking up with online and brick and mortar retailers, such as Big Basket, Reliance Fresh, e-locals, and 99 grocers, for sale of the output. Banana has been identified as a focus crop for the district under One District One Crop (ODOP) initiative by Directorate of Horticulture, Government of Bihar. Subsequently, JWAPCL has recently ventured into banana value chain as well and has supplied around 34,000 banana saplings among its member farmers at subsidised cost. It has also piloted banana marketing with Patna-based firm Jitban. JWAPCL has recently started supplying food grains to JEEViKA's SHG

Table 3.1 Annual Action Plan of JWAPCL, 2021–22

Area of Business	Details	Target Volume (tonnes)	Total Revenue (INR million)	No. of Target Farmers
Agri-input business	Seed, fertiliser, pesticides, organic fertiliser	54.09	3.898	2,900
Agri-output business	Maize, mentha, mango, wheat	5,111.50	66.80	1,350
Value addition business	Katarni rice and *chura*	2.00	0.14	100
FSF/rural retail business	Rice, pulses, mustard oil, sugar, and so on.	60.00	2.540	300
KG Kit (No.)	Kitchen garden kit	15,000.00	1.05	5,000
Total business		**5,227.59**	**74.42**	**9,650**

beneficiary members under its Food Security Fund (FSF) programme. It has supplied 6 tonnes of food grains worth INR 0.25 million in two village organisations of JEEViKA in Khagaria districts under FSF programme of JEEViKA. The FPC has procured and marketed about 500 kg of mentha oil with revenue of INR 0.5 million in 2020–21.

The intent to continue diversifying business activities is reflected quite clearly in JWAPCL's Annual Action Plan for 2021–22 (Table 3.1).

3. A review of performance

Two key components are critical for the success and sustainability of any farmers' collective governance and management. Every other component of the business should ideally be designed such that both management and governance converge to enable the FPC to embody the true spirit of a farmers' collective. In this context, we explore five dimensions of performance of JWAPCL – governance, management, business capabilities, financial capabilities, and ecosystem support.

3.1 Governance

Under the guidance of JEEViKA, JWAPCL has adopted a comprehensive and a very representative governance structure described later (Figure 3.3).

- **Representative general body (RGB):** One office bearer from each PG is drawn to form FPC-level RGB. It convenes quarterly wherein JEEViKA's district project manager, livelihood manager, and other concerned staff from JEEViKA also join the meeting. The management team of JWAPCL presents progress in various business activities of the FPC as well as their next quarterly plan.

- **Executive committee:** Apart from the RGB, block-wise executive committees have been formed with 1–2 active members from each PG in a block. It meets every month to undertake reviews of production and business planning of PGs and plan future activities. PG representatives then carry out decisions taken in the EC meeting in their respective PGs.
- **Producer Company Management Committee (PCMC):** A PCMC at the FPC level comprises members from block level. The management team of the FPC, specifically CEO, as well as livelihood manager of farm theme of JEEViKA are also members of the committee. The PCMC meets monthly to discuss progress of existing business activities of the FPC and plans for future business initiatives as well. It provides the platform for aligning the business plans of the PGs with that of FPC and helps FPC streamline the flow of inputs and resources based on the requirements of the PG members.
- **BoD:** BoDs are elected from among PCMC members. BoD meetings convene quarterly wherein BoD reviews business progress against the formulated plan and takes necessary action on any resolution passed by RGB. Plans for the following month are also discussed in the meeting.

JWAPCL has in place each of these elements of the governance structure. JEEViKA continues to actively train and build capacity of various stakeholders to strengthen the governance structure. TechnoServe earlier, and now MicroSave, are similarly heavily involved in the business plans and operations. In the past year, Covid-19-related restrictions have limited the activities of the committees. Connectivity and limited use of communication technologies continue to limit the transition to virtual meetings, but the FPC has been far from dormant even in the face of such challenges.

The BoD of JWAPCL participates quite actively in the company's business operations, specifically in agri-produce marketing activities. Our interviews with BoD members revealed that they were up to date on the JWAPCL's activities and plans and engaged with the management in substantive ways. The BoD members also play a critical role in encouraging farmers to participate in the Company's procurement operations. In this too the current and past BoD members seemed to be quite active.

Amrita Devi, Shobha Devi, and Meera Devi are authorised signatories of the JWAPCL for any banking transaction along with the CEO of the FPC. The former two have served as directors since JWAPCL's incorporation. The FPC's emphasis on cashless transactions also ensures that authorised BoDs are engaged throughout the year to carry out various transactions.

Although BoD meetings are mandated each quarter, the board of JWAPCL meets more frequently to decide on business-related activities, especially as JWAPCL diversifies into new activities. An annual general meeting is conducted every year when shareholders elect or re-elect BoDs. In 2019, the general body has replaced three BoD members. Occasionally, the FPC conducts emergency general meeting to cater to more pressing needs.

In the case of JWAPCL, though BoD members are active, there is still a long way to go for them to act independently without JEEViKA's continuous engagement in training and capacity building and MicroSave's technical assistance and handholding. JEEViKA continues to support JWAPCL in the preparation of annual business plans, ensuring that it undertakes these as planned. The BoD and the management team are encouraged to take ownership of these activities.

From 2016 onwards when JWAPCL started maize trading, it has been able to increase the member participation in its business activities from 700+ unique farmers in 2016–17 to 1000+ farmers in 2018–19. Despite setbacks due to a rollback in maize business and later due to Covid-19, recent addition to business activities and renewed community mobilisation has led to member participation picking up.

3.2 Management

The structure of management and the team has evolved over the years in JWAPCL. The FPC started with a very basic management team structure wherein JEEViKA deputed its staff to perform various roles and undertake business activities. As the FPC started scaling up and diversifying their business activities, there was a need for a separate and more evolved management team. In 2019–20, JEEViKA decided to recruit highly qualified professionals in the JEEViKA-nurtured FPCs. As part of the initiative, JEEViKA appointed a marketing and procurement manager, governance and community capacity building officer, MIS executive, accountant, and an office assistant in the FPCs. Shivendra, the current CEO, has been in his position for eight years. The salaries and other reimbursable expenses of these professionals continue to be reimbursed by JWAPCL by JEEViKA.

Apart from the core management team, JWAPCL relies on a network of AEs or individuals who are trained in business operations to take the company's services to the farmers. They work on a commission basis wherein they procure agri-input from the FPC and provide to member farmers on prices as fixed by the FPC. They also procure agri-input from member farmers on behalf of JWAPCL. The cost of such resources is usually borne by JWAPCL.

JWAPCL has adopted the prescribed standard operating procedures (SOPs) developed by JEEViKA to standardise its management- and governance-related activities. These are common to all FPCs promoted by JEEViKA. Similar SOPs exist for financial activities as well including a clearly defined financial delegation matrix. For procurement of any assets, there is a procurement sub-committee whose members include two BoDs, CEO, district project manager, and livelihood manager. The committee convenes monthly to discuss any asset procurement. For instance, based on at least three quotations, the committee takes decisions related to vendor, rate, and quantity.

3.3 Ecosystem support

A chief source of strength for JWAPCL is the support from an ecosystem that JEEViKA enables. First, MicroSave supports JEEViKA's State Project Management Team and the FPCs in various business incubation processes as well as in scouting for market linkage actors. MicroSave has one district co-ordinator in Khagaria to provide technical assistance to the FPC and is supported by a cluster co-ordinator and state team of MicroSave. JWAPCL receives comprehensive support from JEEViKA's Farm Livelihood state and district team as well as its District Project Team of Khagaria for both community mobilisation and its operations. JEEViKA ropes in JWAPCL for several other initiatives it implements including, for example, supplying to its FSF programme. JEEViKA enables JWAPCL to leverage necessary funds in terms of short-term loans or revolving funds from CLF as well as PGs. Other JEEViKA-led activities in which JWAPCL is involved include extending inputs such as seeds and saplings to farmers. These provide a steady and captive business for JWAPCL. JWAPCL also secures informal support from local government institutions including agriculture colleges, Krishi Vigyan Kendras (KVKs), relevant district-level line departments, and so on. More recently, JEEViKA has partnered with Syngenta Foundation to train AEs that mentors and handholds these AEs.

3.4 Financial capabilities

The financial capabilities of the FPCs are a cumulative reflection of the three capabilities we have discussed thus far, that is, the FPC's governance, management, and the business initiatives. In this section, we present key financial indicators (see Table 3.2).

3.4.1 Share capital mobilisation

While most of the shareholders have subscribed 50 shares with of Rs. 10 each, ten of the board members who initially formed the BoD have subscribed 1,000 shares of Rs. 10 each. Currently share capital of JWAPCL stands at Rs. 0.3756 million with authorised share capital of Rs. 0.5 million. The number of equity subscribers was stagnant at 500 till 2017–18 but has been on the rise 2018–19 onwards. The increase in the number of subscribers likely indicates increased confidence in JWAPCL and effective mobilisation.

3.4.2 Books of accounts maintenance

The FPC uses the software Tally to maintain its accounts, backed by physical records. Since JEEViKA has facilitated appointment of full-time accountant, JWAPCL is able to maintain its books of records in a professional manner. Additionally, JEEViKA uses its own portal named "Supply Chain Management System" to record any transaction with PGs and beneficiary farmers. As of now, transactions at the last mile are not digitised, even though JWAPCL reports details of its activities in the MIS.

3.4.3 Accounting and auditing compliances

JWAPCL, being a JEEViKA-supported FPC, have been complying with accounting and auditing compliances without delays. Additionally, internal audits are conducted by district project management team as per set processes. Similarly various statutory and legal compliances have been systematically fulfilled with the help of qualified professionals as per the SOPs.

3.4.4 Financial linkages

Most of the short- and long-term credit requirements of JWAPCL are addressed by BRLPS or its promoted institutions like cluster-level federations, advance from PGs, and so on. These come at lower than the market cost. So far, BRLPS has provided Rs. 12.5 million as grant or revolving fund support to the FPC. While it has linkages with SBI and Bihar Gramin Bank to meet its banking needs, JWAPCL has thus far not leveraged the Matching Equity Grant Support provided by Small Farmers Agribusiness Consortium (SFAC) that offers financial support to FPCs. However, it has applied under Bihar Agriculture Investment Promotion Policy (BAIPP) 2020 for a 25% capital subsidy on a proposed 5,000-tonne warehouse with equipment for post-harvest processes to support its output marketing. It has already cleared the first stage of the application process of State Investment Promotion Board.

3.4.5 Financial performance

For the initial 6–7 years, the business turnover of the FPC remained in the range from Rs. 0.3–1.6 million per year. After infusion of funds (grant and debt) in the year 2016 and 2017, the FPC has shown improvement in terms of revenue and profits. As compared to the 2015–16, revenue grew by 844% in the financial year 2016–17. The impact of losses incurred on maize trading activity can be seen from Table 3.2; the reserve funds were wiped out after the loss in the year 2017–18, which was refuelled with some more funding in the year 2018–19.

Table 3.2 Financial performance of JWAPCL over the years (Rs. in million)

Years	2009–10	2010–11	2011–12	2012–13	2013–14	2014–15	2015–16	2016–17	2017–18	2018–19	2019–20
Revenue	–	–	–	1.46	0.25	1.34	1.61	15.15	19.91	47.89	19.91
Profit/Loss	–	–	–	-0.02	-0.14	-0.13	0.01	0.01	-3.37	1.66	0.002
Share Capital	0.1	0.1	0.1	0.1	0.1	0.1	0.1	0.1	0.1	0.30	0.30
Reserves and Surplus	1.0	1.04	1.03	1.01	0.87	0.74	2.25	2.26	-1.11	10.87	10.80
Long-Term Borrowings	–	–	–	–	–	–	–	3.95	–	–	–
Current Liabilities	0.01	0.22	0.04	0.44	0.22	0.22	0.27	0.45	11.22	0.82	0.29
Fixed Assets	–	0.01	0.02	0.01	0.01	0.01	0.01	0.01	0.03	0.03	0.08
Current Assets	1.11	1.37	1.17	1.59	1.23	1.11	2.67	6.78	10.27	11.97	11.38
Number of Members								500	500	952	1,064

Our analysis of key indicators of financial well-being of JWAPCL suggests modest performance with considerable scope for improvement.

- The current ratio remains reasonable due to relatively low borrowings. Profit margins have remained consistently low with significant decline in the last couple of years.
- The Return on Capital Employed (ROCE) was poor for the first seven years with some improvements after. In general, this suggests the inability of the FPC to increase profits relative to the amount of capital available with it.
- Capital Adequacy Ratio (CAR) remained high due to the revolving fund/grant support received from BRLPS. Without this support, raising debt fund for the FPC would be extremely difficult.
- Total assets and working capital turnover ratios are low while the fixed assets turnover ratio remains high because of the low fixed assets maintained by the FPC. Current assets are poorly managed from a revenue-generation perspective.

3.4.6 Tangible and intangible assets

The FPC has few tangible assets other than office equipment, weighing machines, moisture metres, and so on. On the other hand, the company has what are deemed intangible assets. A large network of PGs and the social capital derived from its links with JEEViKA. In addition, JWAPCL's vendor code due to forward linkages with major players like NCDEX, NeML, Roquette, and so on, and its licenses for retailing of fertiliser and seeds are among the other intangible assets.

4. Impacts of JWAPCL

JWAPCL has generated wide-ranging positive impacts for participating farmers.

JWAPCL adopted transparent and fair practices in procurement of agri-produce from beneficiary farmers. It trained its procurement mobiliser to assess quality using moisture metre and uses fair weighing scales while removing 'additional pouring' of the commodity per quintal (1–2 kg per bag on grains) that village-level aggregators typically charge from farmers. By virtue of bypassing multiple value-chain intermediaries and directly transacting through institutional buyers or big district-level trader, the FPC is able to capture additional value and offer better rates to beneficiary farmers. JWAPCL claims to increase price realisation by 10% due to effective dis-intermediation and fair practices. JWAPCL has institutional linkages with agri-input companies and district-level distributors of agri-inputs. As a result, the FPC is able to provide quality seeds and inputs that farmers trust. JWAPCL is able to disintermediate multiple layers of intermediaries to directly procure agri-input from district-level distributors or agri-input companies at reduced rates and pass these benefits on to farmers who purchase inputs.

Fair practices adopted by JWAPCL prompt other value-chain actors like input dealers or village traders to amend their business practices thereby benefiting other farmers in the operational area of the FPC as well. Further, with the recent strategy to create a cadre of AEs, the JWAPCL is likely not just to generate employment via its activities but has broader impacts locally on business practices.

4.1 Social impacts

JWAPCL has played critical role in empowerment of women farmers associated with FPC. Beyond membership, opportunities exist for women to become AE or VRPs. "No one used to know us and now JEEViKA has empowered us . . . we are able to converse with the Prime Minister of India," (interview) said Shobha Devi who is a BoD as well as an AE associated with JWAPCL. Another shareholder member named Amrica Devi said, "Now, we are so empowered that whatever the task, at the district or state level, we know that a couple of us would be able to complete it, be it obtaining any document from line departments or availing any financial services from banks" (interview).

In recognition of these many impacts, awards and recognitions have come its way. These play a critical role in motivating JWAPCL's BoD creating a greater sense of ownership of and enthusiasm for the FPC's activities, despite a heavy reliance on JEEViKA and MicroSave.

4.2 Current status and the road ahead

Although maize trading continues to dominate JWAPCL's activities, accounting for about 80% of its revenue in 2020–21, JWAPCL's diversified business activities have opened multiple interaction points with beneficiary farmers, while catering to diverse needs of members and across geographies. As on August 2021, there are about 1,206 women members from these PGs who have subscribed shares of the FPC. At the time of writing, efforts were being made to update the lists of shareholder members and mobilise more women to become shareholding farmers.

JWAPCL's business activities have evolved since inception; from a narrow focus on seed production to a diversified business portfolio including agri-input marketing as well as produce marketing activity of wheat, maize, mentha oil, mangoes, and so on, the challenge is to ensure that FPCs have some activity and cash flow throughout the year. JWAPCL has managed to forge effective forward and backward linkages, some nascent, others mature.

Forward linkages with a diverse array of buyers such as NCDEX, NCML, NeML, Arya Collateral, COFCO International, Roquette, Jitban as well as local traders provide reliable marketing channels. Noteworthy is that in terms of its market linkage partners, JWAPCL has transitioned successfully away from an overwhelming reliance on NeML and NCDEX. Backward linkages with IFFCO, BISCOUMAUN, and Unnati as well as district-level agri-input distributors support the FPCs input retail activity. JWAPCL procured a retail license for fertiliser as well as seed sales early on and has weight and measurement license required to operate agri-input shop or collection centres. As mentioned, a recent innovation in JWAPCL's operations is the use of a network of AEs. Going forward, this would enable JWAPCL to scale up and ensure that the last mile delivery of its services is effective.

The CEO Shivendra is optimistic about a continued focus on trading, noting that there is substantial scope in trading especially if JWAPCL can secure warehouse space. Expected margins range from 2 to 3% for inputs, 20% for vegetable seed kits, 3 and 5% for wheat/mentha and maize, respectively, to 10% for mango, Katarni rice, and *chura*, as also pulse supplies to FSF. Indeed, shareholders aspire to go beyond in the context of output marketing. "We want to have our own warehouse and our own transport vehicles," noted one BoD member. They believed this would be a game changer for their business. At the time of writing JWAPCL had cleared the first stage of securing a grant under the BAIPP for warehouse and had just opened its first agri-input store and was awaiting a licence for the sale of pesticides. Input trade would continue to form a modest, albeit key part of the operations, according to the CEO.

JWAPCL has not registered a spectacular growth like many successful FPCs; nor have they adopted an aggressive growth strategy. At the same time, there is a clear roadmap for steady, stable growth with diversification. A professional management team and strong financial, managerial, and technical support enabled by JEEViKA and MicroSave have been crucial to JWAPCL. At the same time, this has not crowded out the enthusiastic participation and ownership of its members. JWAPCL's ambitions are tempered by a cautious approach. Their strategy appears to rest on small pilots to test out feasibility and constraints as well as opportunities in various value chains. The FPC is well poised to continue and scale up activities that have yielded positive results into the future.

Notes

1 https://www.niti.gov.in/about-aspirational-districts-programme. Accessed 14 August 2021.
2 The BRLP is the designated institution to implement National Rural Livelihoods Mission (NRLM) of the Government of India – the NRLM, launched in 2011, restructured and replaced the Swarnajayanti Gram Swarozgar Yojana (SGSY) implemented since 1999 to focus strongly on capacity building, mobilization, and

skill development with a broader livelihoods approach than SGSY. The philosophy underpinning SGSY was that the poor need to be organised and their capacities built up so that they can access self-employment opportunities.

References

Chatterjee, T, Raghunathan, R & Gulati, A (2019). *Linking farmers to futures market in India* (Working Paper 383). International Centre for Research on International Economic Research (ICRIER). Retrieved from https://icrier.org/pdf/Working_Paper_383.pdf

Singh, S & Damodaran, H (2015). *Bihar: An unlikely corn revolution.* Retrieved from https://indianexpress.com/article/india/india-others/bihar-an-unlikely-corn-revolution/

Tripathi, S, Sengupta, P, Dubey, P, Rathinam, F & Gaarder, M (2020). *Evaluating the women's advancement in rural development and agriculture programme, 3ie process evaluation report.* New Delhi: International Initiative for Impact Evaluation (3ie). Retrieved from https://doi.org/10.23846/NRLMPE01; https://wdra.gov.in/web/wdra/maize

4

LEVERAGING INSTITUTIONAL ARRANGEMENTS IN ACCESSING MARKETS

The case of Bhangar Vegetable Producer
Company Ltd

Deborah Dutta and Sudipto Saha

1. Introduction – how can small farmers manage the risk of selling perishable produce?

The pandemic and increased awareness regarding the role of a healthy diet in improving immunity have led to increased demand for fresh fruits and vegetables (F&V). Recognising its importance, the United Nations declared 2021 as the international year of F&V to raise awareness of their nutritional and health benefits, as well as to draw attention to the need for sustainable and inclusive value chains to generate better livelihood and increase agro-biodiversity. India has diverse agro-climatic zones allowing it to produce almost all varieties of F&V. It is second only to China in F&V production, having nearly 6.66 million hectares under cultivation of fruits and 10.35 million hectares under cultivation of vegetables. Within the country, West Bengal is the largest producer of horticultural crops accounting for 9.6% of total production in the country. Vegetables comprise nearly 86.4% of the horticulture produce in the state (PCS, 2017). Estimates suggest that West Bengal produced about 33.24 million metric F&V over 1.76 million hectares (National Horticulture Board, GoI).

However, how much of this agricultural output translates into better incomes for the farmers? Studies indicate that due to the perishable nature of the produce, as much as 30–35% of F&V is wasted during harvest, storage, grading, transport, packaging, and distribution. Only 2% of these crops are processed into value-added products (Balaji and Arshinder, 2016). In West Bengal, where 90% of the cultivators are small and marginal, an increase in the price of agricultural inputs, uncertain price of perishable produce, lack of access to credit, and inadequate market infrastructure pose serious challenges to the sustainability of the farm sector in the state. Despite high productivity, farmers in the state have one lowest agricultural household

DOI: 10.4324/9781003308034-4

income in the country (Rs. 3,980) compared to the national average (Rs. 6,426) (Das and Mandal, 2021).

In an attempt to overcome these issues, a pilot project to create FPOs was initiated in 2011–12 under a programme called the National Vegetable Initiative for Urban Clusters (NVIUC) under the Rashtriya Krishi Vikash Yojana (RKVY). This was an initiative undertaken by the Department of Food Processing Industries and Horticulture, Government of West Bengal, in collaboration with the Small Farmers Agri-business Consortium (SFAC), New Delhi. Farmers based in Bhangar II Block of the district of South 24 Parganas were selected due to the area's proximity to Kolkata (about 40 km from the city).[1] As one of the resource institutions (RIs) for the SFAC programme, ACCESS Development Services (ACCESS) was tasked with mobilising farmers and incubating the collective enterprise.

2. Establishing a network of trust – the role of ACCESS as a promoting institution

2.1 "Not another chit fund scam"

When ACCESS began the task of mobilising farmers by holding village-level meetings, the farmers were very sceptical about the idea of an FPO. They thought ACCESS to be like other chit fund companies that had cheated many farmers of their savings in the past. They were also unsure of the benefits they would get by forming the collective. The mention of getting quality farm inputs, including seeds, pesticides, and fertilisers, through the intervention caught a few farmers' interests, but they were largely doubtful of assured quality. This was because of their earlier experiences of getting poor-quality subsidised farm inputs. So, the ACCESS team decided to build its credibility by asking the District Horticulture Officer (DHO) to chair a meeting at the block level where all Panchayat Pradhans were invited. The project activities and objectives were discussed at this meeting, chaired by the DHO. This helped in gaining some trust among the panchayat leaders, who were then more willing to participate in the activities of the project. Next, ACCESS identified some, who were essentially respected farmers from within the community to help them in convincing others. The demography of the villages being predominantly inhabited by people of Islamic faith lent to a homogeneity that was easier to leverage as people tended to conform to group-level decisions. To build rapport with them and connect better with the community, the project team screened movies about farmers' organisations elsewhere that had successfully marketed local produce.

Jabbar Khan, the then local resource person (LRP) of ACCESS, was also a farmer and acutely aware of the prevalent issues. He had completed graduation but took up farming along with his father due to lack of jobs. He, along with a few other LRPs, played a crucial role in mobilising farmers to form a company. Finally, after many rounds of discussions, the Bhangar Vegetable

Producer Company Limited (BVPCL) was registered in September 2012 and currently spans 23 villages with 1,751 farmers across 117 farmers interest groups (FIGs). The share capital per member is (average) Rs. 425. Farmers' trust in the idea of an FPO grew when ACCESS helped them participate in training programmes and buy farming infrastructure through government schemes and welfare support systems.

2.2 Creating a financial base

The next big challenge for ACCESS was to convince banks to open accounts for the FIGs, who mostly constitute farmers interested in establishing an FPC. This was difficult in the absence of banking guidelines for such groups. The team sought help from the lead district manager (LDM) and senior bank officials and conducted an orientation meeting for different banks. Most of the banks who participated in the meeting agreed to open accounts for the 15 FIGs initially formed by the project team. Today, each of the 117 FIGs under BVPCL has its own bank account where Rs. 100 collected from each member is deposited monthly as individual savings. Members commonly engage in inter-loaning and take loans from the common pool to purchase agriculture inputs such as fertilisers, pesticides, and seeds. The funds received are used by FPO representatives in the form of working capital. Even funds received in the form of subsidies are retained and used as a revolving fund to provide services to farmers. Once existing groups started benefiting, other farmers started taking interest and became members of existing FIGs or formed new FIGs.

2.3 Support beyond technical requirements – helping members find their way

ACCESS representatives worked with the farmers to iron out issues that typically don't form a part of training programmes but are of immense practical significance. For instance, while Bhangar FPC had been given permission to sell their produce in the city through a facilitated tie-up with Mother Dairy booths, most farmers did not know what such deliveries entailed. Indranil Mazumder, one of the key representatives involved in incubating Bhangar, spent long periods of time in the villages to understand the issues faced by the farmers. The following instance narrated by him is a telling example of things that might go unnoticed in broad arrangements of incubating FPOs unless attention is paid to smaller obstacles,

> Drivers, who are mainly farmers themselves, didn't know the city roads properly. Many times they would return with the entire truck still unloaded, and the vegetables would have to be sold at half the price in nearby markets. What we did was that we took out pictures of locations, and roads from Google map naming each location

with lanes by lanes; we taught them every detail. We trained the drivers. I got involved in all these things. This has no connection with the production, but this was important.

(Indranil Mazumder, ACCESS representative, interview)

Members were also explained how to sort and grade the produce, as well as pay attention to peak business timings in the city to sell their produce with the least possible wastage. In the early days, members would also be harassed by the police when the transport trucks moved into the city. This led to getting them signboards issued from the state that allowed them unrestricted entry.

2.4 Enabling access to subsidies and schemes to build assets

ACCESS enabled Bhangar to get timely subsidies and loans to buy assets such as motorised vending carts, power tillers, shade nets, poly-tunnels, and poly-houses. They have an impressive fleet of over 25 Tata Ace vehicles and over 125 power tillers at their disposal. To date, BVPCL has received a total investment of Rs. 60.32 million from the Government of West Bengal (details in Table 4.1), and the balance amount has been mobilised as loans from the banks as most of these schemes availed from the state government are credit-linked. As a result, farmers have been growing crops multiple times and even in off-seasons to avail better market prices. As Shahid, the CEO of BVPCL, explained,

Spinach is sold normally in 5 to 10 rupees per kg, but during the rainy season, it is grown in poly-house or poly-tunnel, and then it is sold for 40 to 50 rupees per kg.

(Shahid, CEO, BVPCL, interview)

Adoption of these techniques did not happen overnight, though. Farmers initially protested the building of poly-houses thinking they were just fancy

Table 4.1 Overview of financial support provided by the State Agriculture and Horticulture department

	Department	Total Amount (INR)	Support Provided (INR)
Financial Support Provided for Assets	Agriculture (Power Tiller, Power Weeder, Power Sprayer Set, Knapsack Sprayer)	1,000,000	400,000
	Horticulture (Tata Ace, Shade nets, Power Tiller Polyhouse)	120,039,112	59,919,556
	Total amount	121,039,112	60,319,556

tents. ACCESS then took seven lead farmers for an exposure visit to see a banana tissue culture poly-house to show them how poly-houses could be used to increase productivity. The farmers were eventually convinced and agreed to allow the construction of five common poly-houses on land jointly owned by farmer members. Eventually, 102 poly-houses were constructed. Unfortunately, the Amphan cyclone in 2020 destroyed all their poly-houses, thus making off-season cultivation difficult.

2.5 Enhancing productivity through access to premium inputs

ACCESS connected Bhangar with seed companies like Bayer and Syngenta to get quality inputs with nearly 20% discount to boost their productivity and grow niche, exotic vegetables like coloured capsicum, bok choy, celery, lettuce, and broccoli. They get a premium price for such products in urban markets. It also facilitated a link with Indofil Chemicals Company for procuring fertilisers and pesticides. Recently, in an effort to move towards sustainable cultivation, ACCESS also facilitated the installation of 12 vermicompost units and encouraged BVPCL to get the soil regularly tested by nearby Krishi Vigyan Kendras (KVKs) to add nutrients only as per requirements. Farmers have also been shown multi-cropping techniques to avoid the risk of monocrop failures, while supporting agrobiodiversity.

3. Timeline of BVPCL

Since its inception in 2012, Bhangar has managed a steady growth as a result of significant schemes and collaborations for quality inputs and access to markets. Its growth has been consistent since the tie-up with Sufal Bangla (SB), the sales assurance of which also allowed them to reach out to high-end hotels, government canteens, office cafeterias, and so on, to sell premium produce. Bhangar received the best FPO leader award in the East region by Samunnati in 2019 in addition to the Best FPO award conferred by Government of West Bengal. It has also garnered several recognitions for participating in local food festivals by the state government. Jabbar Khan and other BoDs are often invited to speak at other FPO meetings or other FPOs visit BVPCL. So eventually Jabbar decided to ask for an honorarium for the time devoted to such exposure visits and talks. Apart from gaining some revenue, the gesture also helped lend an ambience of professionalism to such activities. A timeline of the FPC indicating major milestones is shown in Figure 4.1.

4. Governance and leadership of BVPCL

BVPCL today comprises 1,751 farmers in 117 FIGs across six selected gram panchayats covering 48 villages. It has eight board members, including one woman though her presence is just meant to fulfil the board membership

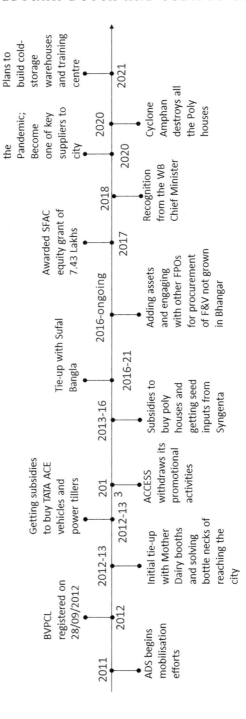

Figure 4.1 A timeline of Bhangar FPC

74

criteria laid out by SFAC. Given a traditionally conservative society, and the requirement of board members to interface with many private and public representatives, all interactions are done by male members. All farmer members are also mostly male because women rarely have landholdings in their name in that area. The average age of the board members is 38.

Abdul Jabbar Khan, the chairperson of BVPCL, has been associated with the organisation since the formation of FIGs and registration of the company. He, along with a few more people, has been a part of the board on a rotational basis, playing a key role in ensuring communication and unity among the members. According to Indranil, the real benefit of forming BVPCL has been the confidence instilled in the farmer members to actively seek opportunities and form a collective voice. The following incident narrated by him illustrates this point:

> During the season, capsicum is cultivated by many farmers and sold in huge quantities. But local traders were not ready to pay the right price for that. They were paying 5 to 7 rupees per kilo. This means farmers had to sell at a loss because capsicum seeds cost around 40 to 50 thousand rupees for a kg. . . . Then Jabbar told all the member farmers of BVPCL to stop selling the capsicum at the local market. He was even supported by non-members on this front. You know, when I first met Jabbar in 2011, he didn't say a word during the entire meeting. By 2019, when this incident happened, he had the confidence to call up the Horticulture department, asking them to allow BVPCL to sell their produce at the wholesale market in Kole and Howrah. . . . At these markets they were able to sell at 15 rupees per kilo. The next day, the local traders had to pay them the same amount because they realised that their business was being sabotaged if farmers started selling at Kole market regularly.
>
> (Indranil Mazumder, ACCESS Representative, interview)

5. Market operations

5.1 Market and procurement linkages

In the early years, between 2012 and 2015, marketing the farm produce was a major challenge as neither the farmers nor ACCESS was fully aware of customers' preferences and possible retail outlets. A large market survey was undertaken to understand consumer preferences and expected commodity prices. Gradually, BVPCL got a sense of the rates in different markets and how much they could expect for the produce. On the basis of consumer feedback, BVPCL also started growing different crops such as another variety of chilli, exotic vegetables, and the like. They have also experimented with exports of limited quantities of chilli, tomato, beans, and bitter gourd to countries like Singapore and Saudi Arabia through an intermediate agency and plan to procure an exports license soon. The producer company has also tied up with the Government of West Bengal to secure a platform to sell fresh F&V at the seven municipal corporation markets in Kolkata, where products are sold in wholesale quantities. Usually, an FPO cannot get access to such a platform due to immense pressure from the trader's lobby. However, the BVPCL got membership of the Trader's Association, which allows it to sell its produce in corporation markets.

There is a huge opportunity for in-house marketing among the FPOs/FPCs themselves since they are the producers of some commodities but consumers of other commodities. In order to tap this opportunity, ACCESS has promoted an apex-level FPC (Samayoga Agro Farmers Producers Company Limited), which facilitates inter-FPC market linkages. This FPC provides support to each of the member FPCs in marketing their produce to the other FPC within a well-framed policy, taking care of fair-trade practices and facilitating better price realisation. Some of the initiatives where Bhangar has played an important role are as follows:

- Pineapples from Sonar Bangla FPC (Darjeeling district) to Bhangar FPC (South 24 Parganas district)
- Gobindobhog rice (aromatic) from Mukundaram FPC (Purba Burdhaman district) to Bhangar FPC (South 24 Parganas district)
- Onions from Rise & Shine FPC (Purba Burdhaman district) to Bhangar FPC (South 24 Parganas district)

5.2 Innovative institutional arrangements – market access through Sufal Bangla

Nearly 75–80% of BVPCL's produce is sold through the mobile and static outlets of SB, which is a RKVY-supported direct marketing project under Paschimbanga Agri Marketing Corporation Ltd. of the Department of Agricultural Marketing, West Bengal. The total sales through these outlets are to the tune of Rs. 4.5–5.0 million per month. SB first came into existence as a mechanism to curb the price of potatoes in 2014–15, when the department of agri-marketing decided to subsidise the price of potatoes directly from wholesale markets and recruit FPCs to sell them at various locations while allowing the FPOs Rs. 2 margin for travel, labour, and loading/unloading charges. This allowed FPCs like BVPCL to earn some steady, if not large, profit due to assured supply and demand. Later, SB expanded to liaison exclusively with farmer groups by providing them access to mobile and retail outlets, along with accessories such as crates, weighing machines, billing machines, and so on. They also took on the role of releasing a daily price list for various commodities, thus reducing an FPC's work of finding the right price through informal market networks. In return, SB charges an FPC 1–2% royalty on total revenue earned. FPCs are provided the right to sell their produce at selected outlets through a two-stage bidding involving technical compliance and financial tenders. The FPC providing the highest royalty is given the sales rights. SB is also selling non-perishable items such as oil, grains, pulses, and processed products such as honey, ghee, and so on, the production of which is being supported by State Agriculture Universities (SAUs) such as Bidhan Chandra Krishi Viswavidyalaya and Uttar Banga Krishi Vishwavidyalaya in terms of providing seeds to farmers, milling and de-husking centres, and so on. Additionally, FPCs handling SB retail stores are given a 10% commission on the sale of these non-perishables. These arrangements have mostly helped FPCs like BVPCL develop effective market linkage and get associated with a brand such as SB. On the flip side, after gaining market exposure and experience in the sale of produce, BVPCL is now contemplating starting independent stores under the brand of Bhangar to save on the 2% commission being given to SB currently. The commission averages to roughly Rs. 0.2 million each month. A broad organisation and linkage structure of SB are explained in Figure 4.2.

5.3 Everyday business operations

The process of procuring the vegetables starts as early as 4 a.m. After the produce is harvested from the fields, these are taken to a grading and packaging centre where they are first washed and then packed into nylon carry units of 250 g, 500 g, and 1 kg with stickers that mention the weight. The vegetables are graded into three categories – A, B, and C. The vegetables that appear very fresh and green are put into Grade A, the rest are organised into Grades B and C. The company predominantly sells off-season and exotic vegetables for which they charge a premium along with the regular supply of vegetables required on a daily basis. The emphasis is on meeting consumer expectations in terms of product quality and variety.

The company has three such centres where the sorted, graded, and packed vegetables are loaded onto TATA Ace Trucks. Currently, more than 15–20 tons of vegetables are being supplied to the city on a daily basis. The vehicles reach different supply centres (74 mobile outlets, eight static outlets, and two government canteens) in Kolkata by 7 a.m. to unload the entire supply. Additionally, they also sell some produce to a few hotels on a contract basis. Vegetables are sold usually between 8 a.m. to 10 a.m. Unsold stock is taken back and sold to the markets that prefer Grade B and Grade C products at a wholesale price. Overall, about 10% of produce goes waste in the entire process. Computerised bills and payment receipts are created. The staff looks after all the stocks and the accounts. As per the discussions held, around 138 staff members have been hired, resulting in a monthly expense of Rs. 0.35 million (approx.). These employees are mostly the sons of farmer members working in the company handling various roles (driver, office personnel, labourers, sales, and so on) on a contract basis,

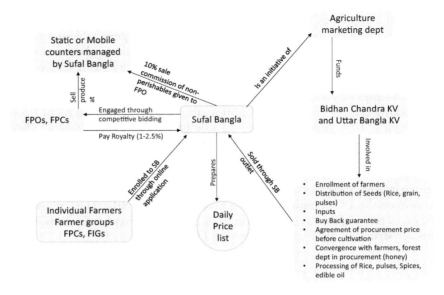

Figure 4.2 Various linkages initiated and supported through Sufal Bangla

and the additional income generated for the farmer members through such involvement has been well appreciated. The CEO tallies the account on Sunday every week. Cash is not kept at hand and is deposited in the bank every two days.

The supply chain is highly consumer sensitive and supplies only those vegetables that are in demand during a particular season. BVPCL monitors and supervises the entire chain very closely and efficiently. It can estimate the daily demand of a particular vegetable and can increase/decrease its supply within 2 to 3 days. It has also developed a sense of the maximum sale that can happen at particular outlets along with regional preferences, and they are able to customise the delivery accordingly. Jabbar explained that familiarising himself with these processes wasn't easy, and he just decided to persevere despite initial failures.

> We initially had to supply to 110 Mother Dairy booths all over.
> . . . Just two days before we started, we had received 400 crates
> from Malda; overnight, 40 to 50 labourers were employed to do the
> packaging thing. I still remember 500 kg of chilli was packed into
> 100 grams pack. So, it was a massive job, it was done with a few
> unskilled labourers and farmers. They were not used to it. This kind
> of difficulty was there . . . even after packing, we could not reach
> the market on time, and within a week we incurred a loss of nearly

0.1 million rupees. Members said we cannot continue like this. Then Indranil said we would try something else. I talked to the farmers to give it another try.

(Jabbar Khan, Chairperson, BVPCL, interview)

5.4 Pandemic and beyond

During the pandemic, a disrupted supply chain from distant producers turned into an advantage for BVPCL as they became a major supplier owing to the proximity to the city. As Jabbar explained,

Due to Covid, produce from Bankura, Asansol, Purulia, Bardhaman could not reach Kolkata market, but our products have reached Kolkata market regularly. The government has helped us a lot by giving us "On Govt Duty" labels for our trucks, so the police did not stop us. We tied up with many big apartment complexes to deliver them vegetables directly. . . . They are now our regular customers.

In terms of profit margins, they make the most profit out of fruits and exotic vegetables, much of which they may not be growing locally. So, depending on the demand, they actively procure produce from other FPCs, the initial linkage having been facilitated by ACCESS.

Shahid, the CEO, commented,

During festival time, like Christmas, Diwali, Id, Durga puja, during this time, there is a good demand of fruits; we are trying to get hold of that supply. Near Tarakeswar (Hooghly district), we have farmers cultivating vegetables, mainly potatoes. Similarly, in Kalna, that falls under Purba Burdhaman district, that side they produce Onion mainly. Monsoon Onion, which is harvested during September, October . . . generally Onion, cannot be cultivated, at this time, so when they sell this Onion, they get good price for this. We also got Onion from Nasik during Lockdown when there was a problem, we were not getting Onion; it was highly-priced, so we directly procured 25 tonnes of Onion from them. Like that we got pineapples from Sonar Bangla FPC in Siliguri.

(Shahid, CEO, BVPCL)

6. Financial performance

As of December 2020, the total share capital of BVPCL was Rs. 1.486 million, and they have received the matching equity grant of Rs. 0.743 million from SFAC. They have dabbled with exports and plan to obtain licenses to venture in this export business more systematically.

BVPCL has grown exponentially during the last three years with a proportional increase in profit. Their salary expenses have increased to 178% in the last FY due to an increase in operations and thereby their revenues from income. Their loans outstanding have increased from Rs. 2.935 million to Rs. 3.977 million from FY 2015–16 to FY 2019–20, respectively (26% increase) along with interest on loans from Rs. 0.049 million to Rs. 0.209 million during the same period. The SB initiative of the Department of Agriculture-Marketing, Government of West Bengal has not only augmented their financial figures but also helped grow their confidence in order to manage their operations and interact with individuals across different levels. Their reserves and surplus have grown 16.26 times from Rs. 0.125 million to Rs. 2.164 million from FY 2013–14 to FY 2019–20 (details in Table 4.2).

7. Looking back and moving forward

Bhangar was one of the earliest FPCs to be promoted by SFAC and ACCESS in West Bengal. Thus, Bhangar's relative success in part can be attributed to its first-mover advantage, wherein it could leverage the schemes and funds allocated for promotion of FPCs. Over the years, it has been awarded financial support to the tune of 60 million and used the funds to accumulate considerable assets such as poly-houses, shade nets, power tillers, and transport vehicles. Recently, BVPCL applied for permission to establish a modern pack-house for the grading, sorting, and packaging of vegetables. They have got part of a government facility for these operations. They also applied for the purchase of six refrigerated carts of 6 m capacity (2.4 million each) using their share capital, surpluses, and credit from financial institutions. Additionally, they plan to build cold-storage warehouses and a training centre in 2024. Most FPOs are unable to navigate the processes and access such schemes to good effect. However, it is not entirely clear if asset utilisation has been done effectively, or there are ways in which additional income might have been earned through renting the equipment and the like.

The uniformity of the religious and socio-economic backgrounds of the farmers seems to have played a role in enabling relatively easy collective decision-making, sharing of land, resources, and so on for installing the poly-houses. The proximity of the FPO from a major metropolitan city has also been a distinct advantage to create and operate a dynamic supply chain. The interventions created by SB have played a major role in contributing to the stability of the FPO, even if the commission charged by them has been a pain point for the FPO, especially when they feel that they might earn more by operating independently.

The high dependence on inputs and infrastructure to grow exotic, off-season vegetables enables them to get a premium for the vegetables but also creates a dependency and vulnerability that is expected to increase with

Table 4.2 Financial performance of Bhangar over the years (in INR)

Particulars	2013–14	2014–15	2015–16	2016–17	2017–18	2018–19	2019–20	2020–21
Total Revenue	2,785,770	5,536,480	10,125,234	19,651,754	8,175,775	33,371,706	75,529,060	134,036,052
Total Expenses	2,665,360	5,330,338	9,994,197	18,944,864	8,101,204	32,920,295	74,792,696	132,874,642.84
Profit Before Tax	120,410	206,142	131,037	706,890	74,571	451,411	736,364	1,161,409.16
Profit After Tax	120,410	206,142	131,037	706,890	767,073	451,411	555,802	891,276.11
Share Capital	725,000	743,300	743,300	743,300	1,486,600	1,486,600	1,486,600	1,486,600.00
Reserves and Surplus	125,401	244,850	375,617	450,188	1,157,078	1,608,489	2,164,291	3,055,566.84
Fixed Assets Including Investments	0	0	0	2,128,834	1,877,172	2,681,951	4,370,625	3,828,926.54
Current Liabilities	868,379	1,096,582	5,672,040	796,787	594,241	1,296,707	828,446	998871
Current Assets	826,613	1,068,738	1,775,982	1,649,901	2,188,324	3,546,345	3,840,206	5044490.25

erratic weather. The loss of all the poly-houses during the Amphan cyclone is a testimony to the problem. How to incorporate principles of sustainability and resilience, while chasing market goals is an open question for Bhangar.

Bhangar's steady growth is also largely a function of dynamic and strong leadership exhibited by Jabbar Khan, the current chairperson of the company. Being well respected and trusted in the community has allowed him to mobilise farmers and take risky decisions in ways that would have been difficult otherwise. However, this also has the associated danger of the company becoming person-centred rather than process-dependent. Creating reliable managers and decision-makers from within the community is ongoing work and can't be guaranteed in the absence of policies or programmes for such capacity building. As Indranil commented,

> The Govt has no such policies when the FPO is being promoted – how to sustain FPO in future, how the management of this FPO will take place. Who will work for such meagre salaries? No Agro business graduate will work with this amount. Circumstances allowed us to create Bhangar and we were lucky to have people like Jabbar, Ishmail and Shahid . . . it took years of effort to help them gain confidence . . . how to do such things consistently?
>
> (Indranil, ACCESS Representative, Interview)

Note

1 A case study by ACCESS, Global Learning Alliance, and IIRR covers the initial years of Bhangar in some depth. The case was written by Indranil Banerjee, Varun Prakash Dhanda, and Ram Narayan Ghatak in 2016.

References

Balaji, M & Arshinder, K (2016). Modelling the causes of food wastage in Indian perishable food supply chain. *Resources, Conservation and Recycling, 114*, 153–167.

Das, R & Mandal, S (2021). Determinants of smallholders' participation in farmer producer companies – Insights from West Bengal, India. *Decision, 48*(3), 327–342.

PCS (2017, October 28). Horticulture of West Bengal. *West Bengal PCS Exam Notes*. Retrieved from https://westbengal.pscnotes.com/geography-wbpsc/horticulture-west-bengal/

5

CONNECTING TRIBAL WOMEN TO MARKETS THROUGH PROMOTION OF SUSTAINABLE AGRICULTURE

The case of Ram Rahim Pragati Producer Company Ltd

Abhishek Saxena, Rajat Tomar,
and Animesh Mondal

1. Understanding the context

The tribal-dominated region of Bagli *tehsil* in Dewas district is one of the most neglected, under-developed (ranked 263 in human development having a Human Development Index (HDI) of 0.540) (Ranjan, 2016), and water-scarce regions of Madhya Pradesh (Wani et al., 2002). The major crops cultivated in the region are soybean, maize, sorghum (*jowar*) and red gram (*toor*) in kharif and wheat and chickpea (*chana*) in rabi. A majority of the farmers are *adivasis* and small and marginal; thus, they lack the resources necessary to access fair markets. When Samaj Pragati Sahyog (SPS) started its work on produce aggregation, the closest *mandi* (farmers' market regulated by Agricultural Produce Marketing Committee) for the sale of agricultural produce was located over 80–90 km away in Indore, making it inaccessible to these small farmers.

SPS is one of the pioneers in working on non-pesticide management (NPM) of crops as a pathway to sustainable agriculture. The idea of the NPM movement is to encourage farmers to grow crops without any chemical synthetic pesticides, create an identity for their produce, and link the small producers to markets. NPM agriculture emphasises building up soil fertility through appropriate management practices (such as composting and recycling of agricultural residues, use of farmyard manure, cattle urine, green manure crops like *Gliricidia*, and application of tank silt) with a gradual phasing out of chemical fertilisers.

Currently, over 7,600 farmers practise NPM agriculture across 6,700 hectares in the region. Agriculture extension poses a critical challenge to

DOI: 10.4324/9781003308034-5

the uptake of sustainable practices as identified by the extension personnel at SPS.

2. Samaj Pragati Sahyog – the bedrock of RRPPCL

SPS has been working for poverty alleviation in the backward regions of Dewas district since 1990s. The focus of their work has been a search for alternative paths to development. Since the region was water scarce, cultivation only used to happen in the monsoon season. For the rest of the year the villagers used to go and work as labourers in Indore. However, most of the money that the farmers earned from their monsoon crop went to the traders, middlemen, and money lenders. This had perpetuated a debt trap for the farmers of the region since input traders sold at exploitative prices and offered credit to farmers for input purchase at very high interest rates. SPS began its work with watershed management which resulted in farmers cultivating in *rabi* also.

SPS's core approach has been the development of livelihoods based on good agricultural practices with judicious use of natural resources. Its focus on NPM and its work in watershed and participatory irrigation management has resulted in *rabi* crops becoming common in the region. Prior to these interventions, the only cropping season was that of monsoon in this rain-fed region. Even in *kharif* crops, the interventions have led to drought proofing as the dependence on rain is reduced. However, unlike other instances, SPS believes that water conservation efforts only succeed if the end use is judicious. That is why it focuses on introducing diverse crops in the region that are native and can be cultivated with optimal water through NPM agriculture. Day-to-day responsibility rests with the 25-member core team of experienced professionals who work full-time at headquarters, leading the team of 225 SPS activists.

This philosophy of SPS has been the bedrock on which RRPPCL has been incubated and promoted. Thus, even though RRPPCL aspires to be financially stable and contribute to poverty reduction among its members, it never compromises on NPM and judicious resource usage. Also, SPS started working with women and organised them in SHGs since it realised that women cultivators spent more time working on the farm and were also keener to learn about NPM cultivation and other practices related to safe agriculture.

One of the most important tasks of the SPS agricultural team is education, awareness, and motivating farmers to take up NPM agriculture, grow crops suited to local agro-ecology, and practise mixed/multi-cropping. SPS has a demonstration farm and holds night meetings to discuss these issues with farmers. They also get the soil tested at regular intervals in the villages. The results of these tests are discussed with them, and corrective measures/ alternatives are suggested.

3. Empowering the women through collective action – precursors to RRPPCL

The women SHG-bank linkage programme of SPS began in 2002 with initial help from Dhan Foundation. This was to promote savings and seek formal credit, freeing farmers from money lenders and middlemen. NPM agriculture allowed lower dependence on market inputs and thus paved the way for farmers to come out of the debt trap. Post formation of the SHGs and with help from the agriculture programme of the organisation, interventions on the market side began in 2006–07. The initial focus was on aggregation and storage of soybean as it was a major crop being grown by the farmers. SHGs began by becoming a seller of aggregated produce at the Indore *mandi*, thus taking care of the information asymmetry regarding price and the malpractices that existed in the *mandi*. Soybean market prices were volatile and used to rise only 2–3 months later, so it was a good strategy to store the soybean and leverage it for loan against warehouse receipt (WHR). This provided the much-needed working capital and was used to pay the farmers. However, as the operations grew in scale, for ease of handling tasks, aggregation started happening at the *samiti* or cluster level at Udainagar and Kantaphod.

In 2011–12 the *samitis* aggregated and sold 1,000 MT wheat and 500–600 MT soybean. This success brought SPS in direct conflict with the local traders as the former cut into their share of farmer produce, and the farmers started negotiating for better price. Following a complaint from the traders to the Agricultural Produce Marketing Committee (APMC) about women (not legally farmers due to landholding-based definition) aggregating farm produce and indulging in trade. After a few rounds of arguments and justifications SPS was advised to take a legal route and register the SHG federation as a producer company since the former was a non-profit and registered under the Madhya Pradesh Societies Registration Act and could not engage in business activities, even though they had a *mandi* license. Thus, RRPPCL got registered on 12 April 2012, growing organically out of the interventions of SPS, representing 120 SHGs constituted by ~1,800 women members contributing an equity capital of Rs. 650,000 and is based in Bagli *tehsil* of Dewas district in Madhya Pradesh (see Table 5.1 for a timeline of RRPPCL).

4. Ram Rahim Pragati Producer Company – what it does and how

4.1 The evolution of a women's collective – experimenting with different business strategies

RRPPCL began as an alternative to the middlemen in the *mandi*. Being a member-owned enterprise, it helped the women get a fair price at the market for its produce of soybean, wheat, and chickpea. At one point of time, it

Table 5.1 A timeline of Ram Rahim Pragati Producer Company (blank spaces do not mean no operations; instead it means no change in the status from previous)

Year	Milestone	Major Stakeholders		Other Partners
		Banks/NBFCs	Market Channels/Forward Partners	
2002–06	SHGs promoted			Dhan Foundation, SPS
2006–08	Soybean aggregation at SHG level to raise capital through WHR while waiting for price to rise		Indore APMC	Panchayat office, SPS
2008–09	Soybean aggregation at samiti level (Udainanagar and Kantaphod samiti) and selling in *mandi* using capital raised through WHR		Indore APMC	Panchayat office, SPS
2011–12	10,000 MT of wheat and ~8,000 MT of soybean sold		Indore APMC	Panchayat office, SPS
	Issues with local traders and complaint with APMC		Indore APMC	Traders, panchayat office, SPS
2012–13	Ram Rahim Pragati Producer Co registered, started with input sales and aggregation of produce	IDBI Bank, Bank of India	Godrej Agrovet, Olam Agri Ltd., Reliance Industries, Ruchi soya, Safe Harvest, APMC	RoC office, licensing authorities, SPS
2013–14	Seed production for soybean and wheat aggregation and sales	Friends of the Women's World Banking (FWWB)		Certification authority, SPS
2014	Decentralised collection of produce	FWWB		SPS
	Registered with NCDEX and soybean trading	FWWB	NCDEX and others	SPS

2015–17	Soybean trading	FWWB	NCDEX and others	SPS
2016–17	Consolidation of operations: pulled out of soybean production and trading, bio-pesticides sales, animal feed sales, and so on.	FWWB	Safe Harvest	SPS
2017–18 onwards	Shareholder in Safe Harvest forward contract involving job work	FWWB, Avanti Finance, NABKISAN	Safe Harvest, Kasyap Sweetner, Urban SHGs located in Dewas and Khargone District, Ramesh Trader (Indore APMC), farmers (input supply – seed) Godrej Big Basket (for job work at Bagli WH Machines)	SPS, Avantee Mega Food Park, Sinhal Enterprise for pulses (kabuli chana and red gram) milling job work, Asha Industries for wheat flour making job work

boasted of several buyers such as Ruchi Soya, Reliance, Godrej Agrovet, Olam Agro, and Safe Harvest Private Limited (SHPL). The FPC also sold the member produce at the APMC. The first year of operations in which around 3,000 quintals of soybean and maize were aggregated and sold to Ruchi Soya and Godrej Agrovet was a great start, heralding a new beginning in the *Ghat Neeche* area of Dewas. Over 1,000 women came together to decide rates, date, and place of aggregation. The company was able to procure loans against WHR in which secured loans were obtained against hypothecated farm produce to the extent of 70% of market value of the produce. The members chose to wait for the payment of remaining 30% until the produce was sold after which full payment was made. The prevailing local market rates were at least Rs. 600 lower than the price at the Indore *mandi* in 2012 due to which the company could procure comfortably at spreads which allowed for the company to operationally break even.

Linking farmers to market simply by eliminating the middlemen was not doing much good to the FPC since the costs involved in procurement, storage, participation in *mandi*, and so on were still much more for the FPC and in turn for the farmers. If the member farmers relinquish the control of their produce just after selling it to the FPC, there are little gains to be realised.

The advantages the traders had in terms of low cost of operation and their ability to avoid *mandi* tax (2%) and entry tax for oil seeds (1%) by disguising as farmers were soon a barrier RRPPCL could not break through. Besides, unlike the first year, *mandi* prices were volatile, and a higher price was no guarantee. The year saw a 25% crash in the chickpea (*chana*) market prices in 2012–13. Thus, RRPPCL had to think beyond the APMC *mandi*.

Another basic change brought in was to decentralise the sorting and grading processes and bring them to the farm. This helped reduce the costs of RRPPCL in the long term. In the process of tackling the challenges that it faced, RRPPCL pioneered many such initiatives.

Some of those interventions mentioned earlier were engaging in numerous businesses such as soybean seed production and selling certified seeds of soybean to the members, maize-based animal feed, neem oil, and neem cakes as they had better margins as inputs. In 2014, RRPPCL advocated for FPCs to get listed on NCDEX and itself got registered on the forward market platform of NCDEX, a major first for the company.

4.2 *Governing a mammoth spread across 100 villages*

The corpus of ten interested SHGs (each contributing Rs. 10,000) was used as the initial share capital for the producer company, and thus they became the initial shareholders. The board of directors (BoD) initially had representatives from these SHGs, thus consisting of ten members in the board (five promoters + five directors). The membership has increased to 364 SHGs, and the majority of these SHGs are about 5–6 years old and have accounts with banks. The SHG undertakes collective purchase of household items including food items. This clearly reflects the overall quality of the SHG and its maturity level.

The BoD consists of six women who are representing the federations composed of clusters of women SHGs. Board meetings take place on a quarterly basis, and an annual general meeting (AGM) is organised once a year where all the members are expected to participate. The structure of the company is depicted in figure 5.1.

Apart from these, bimonthly SHG meetings keep taking place in villages. There are challenges in governing such a large collective of 5,000 women farmers organised in 364 SHGs spread over more than 100 villages. This is where SPS's clustering of SHGs and further clustering as *samitis* helps in choosing representatives and providing ease of reaching out to the agricultural team of SPS and the *mithaans* who are the community-level resource persons.

4.3 *RRPPCL's tryst with NCDEX*

In 2014 when RRPPCL registered for soybean trading on NCDEX, it became one of the pioneering FPCs to do so. However, RRPPCL engaged in futures trading only for two years 2015–16 and 2016–17 (Chatterjee et al., 2019), involving just 205 farmers out of more than 2,000 women members at that time aggregating approximately 180 quintals of soybean from them and selling 7,800 quintals from the previous stock in 2015–16. In 2016–17,

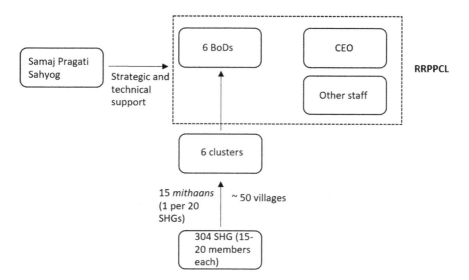

Figure 5.1 Organisational structure of RRPPCL

there was no aggregation from members and approximately 156 quintals were sold to the *mandi* and another 4,800 quintals to NCDEX. Thus, it appears that NCDEX registration of RRPPCL came about largely due to the efforts of the then CEO towards disposing the building stocks of soybean in the stores (approximately 12,600 quintals). After the stocks of soybean were cleared, the FPC, realising that futures trading was a complex endeavour and soybean prices were volatile, stopped trading soybean at NCDEX.

It was seen as a major breakthrough with several reports being written about the move. Today, however, a representative of SPS who has seen RRPPCL being formed and grow terms futures trading on NCDEX as a "mistake" and is of the opinion that there are too many complexities involved and an enterprise of small farmers is not well suited to futures trading.

4.4 The course-correction phase

RRPPCL moved out of several initiatives that they started between 2013 and 2017 including bio-pesticides sales, seed production, and hedging their soybean produce at NCDEX. The agricultural extension programme of SPS helped RRPPCL to discourage soybean cultivation among members as it was a risky crop with very volatile prices and incompatible with the core values of NPM agriculture promoted by SPS and moved to native crops like red gram (*toor*), chickpea varieties (*chana*), wheat, *jowar*, and so on.

Costs have also reduced due to less wastage since quality has gone up. A major decision taken by the management and the board was to do away with centralised grading of produce and introduce spiral graders that use gravity to grade the produce, are low cost (Rs. 6,000), and can be easily operated by women and children. This, along with decentralised collection centres, has been a major reason for bringing the costs down for the company.

This "course-correction" by RRPPCL has resulted in promotion of native crops, agro-ecological practices, and price correction in the market due to higher prices being offered by the FPC. Such practices have resulted in better profits and although the FPC is still not in a state to pay out bonuses, it gives incentives in the form of discounts on input prices and premium on output aggregation.

4.5 A glimpse of the processes involved in RRPPCL's business

RRPPCL focuses on agricultural extension, NPM cultivation and aggregation, and primary and secondary processing. Beyond that is the forte of SHPL or other buyers. The least risky method to take advantage of this arrangement is to have a forward contract with the buyer based on jobwork arrangement to process and pack for the forward partner.

On the input side of the business, that is the bread and butter of the operations of RRPPCL, the FPC sells seeds from companies such as Syngenta, Hytech, Balram seeds, and so on, and bio-pesticides. The FPC is helped by community resource persons called *mithaans* and the agricultural extension team of SPS for introducing better varieties of the commodities, namely wheat, chickpea, *jowar*, red gram, and so on. The women farmers are organised as SHGs and formed into clusters and federation. Each *mithaan* is responsible for 19–20 SHGs comprising around 350 women farmers. Farmers cultivating NPM crop are known to the FPC and SPS, and aggregation of produce happens from such women farmers at the collection centres. Farmers are motivated to do the primary cleaning, grading, and drying of the produce in order to get higher prices. The *mithaans*, aided by the collection centre supervisor, check the samples provided by the farmers for moisture content and other quality parameters before accepting the lot. Farmers whose produce is accepted for procurement based on physical parameters are asked to aggregate. Samples are picked up from the aggregated lot and sent to TUV India laboratory in Bengaluru to test for more than 120 pesticide compounds as per Jaivik Bharat standards laid down by Food Safety and Standards Authority of India (FSSAI). The prices paid to the farmers are dependent upon the quality of the aggregated lot and the quality parameters.

There are six crops that the FPC deals in, namely wheat, chickpea (Bengal gram and *Kabuli* chana), pigeon pea (*toor* or red gram), maize, *jowar*, and mung bean. The most important crops are wheat, chickpea, red gram, and maize. The actual process of deciding the price involves *mithaans*, collection centre supervisor, and BoD members. Information is gathered on the market prices and those being offered by the other traders. The prices are discussed every day in the procurement season and finalised by the CEO by factoring in the previous years' prices, the costs involved in logistics, production levels in the season, prices offered by the traders, and the minimum support price (MSP) offered by the government.

This does not mean that the women farmers are passive price takers. They are aware of the market prices and those being offered by the traders and negotiate well to get the best price for their produce. In an instance, a farmer simply told the CEO and the collection centre supervisor that she will only sell her chana to the FPC if they offer something above Rs. 4,800/quintal as that was the rate in the market. The deal was closed at Rs. 5,000/quintal!

The Avantee Mega Food Park[1] (MFP) is where the processing and packaging for wheat used to take place. RRPPCL has leased a facility that can process up to 80–120 MT/day of wheat or pulses and package 6–10 MT/day depending upon the SKU size. The unit processes and packs *daliya*, *urad* dal, whole *urad*, Bengal gram, chana dal, Kabuli chana, and so on. However, RRPPCL had to recently move their wheat milling operations to Asha Industries Ltd., Ujjain, since the wheat milling plant at Avantee has been leased to ITC for a year. The milling of chickpea and red gram to make dal takes place at Snehal Enterprises, Ujjain. The MFP facility is used only for storing processed flour and pulses to be packed and transported.

The procured commodities are sorted using colour Sortex, a facility available at Avantee after being manually checked for external material, farm waste, and so on. The RRPPCL facility at Avantee has hermetic cocoons for storage of processed flour. Manual packaging is done according to the demand of the key forward partner SHPL[2] (Anil, 2019) for their Delhi-NCR, Hyderabad, Bengaluru, Pune, Mumbai, and Chennai markets. However, the bags are sealed and stamped using machines. RRPPCL has warehouses in Bagli and Dewas of 500 MT capacity each and has leased a chamber in the cold storage in the Mega Food Park. The chamber capacity is 1,100 MT capacity for storing unprocessed pulses and wheat. Also, a 1,000 m² space in being leased in Avantee Food Park since volumes to be handled per day will increase from 100 MT to 200 MT.

The handholding support necessary to run the facility is being provided by SHPL, and the company has placed a professional who supervises on a daily basis. The SPS staff consists of Ms Sushmita who is the quality supervisor and manages a team of 19–20 workers, a majority of whom are women and are members of a SHG promoted by SPS.

RRPPCL's procurement of farmers' produce varies with the demand from SHPL and other buyers and supply from the producers. Thus, while for some crops like red gram RRPPCL buys 100% of the member produce, for wheat and chickpea, usually 65–70% is procured. RRPPCL is also keen on tapping into the demand for essential commodities from its SHG members who are based in peri-urban areas. For instance in FY 2020–21, RRPPCL sold 172 MT of wheat to Dewas and Barwaha SHG federations; 120 MT of wheat flour to SHGs in Dewas district; and close to 32 MT of *toor* dal to Dewas, Kantaphod, and Maheshwar SHG federations.

Though there are other forward partners of RRPPCL, apart from SHPL, such as Kasyap Sweeteners Ltd. and the urban SHG federations mentioned earlier, SHPL's role is much more than a buyer. Interaction with the SHPL operations manager revealed that SHPL is involved in capacity building efforts through handholding and exposure visits to Hyderabad, where SHPL is headquartered. SHPL also impacts business planning and strategising since it is the key buyer, and RRPPCL has stake in SHPL through shareholdings.

5. Financial performance, funding and costs involved

RRPPCL has been a profit-making enterprise since 2015–16. As mentioned earlier, the team at SPS and RRPPCL stopped dealing in soybean and consolidated their operations to few but less risky crops and took the forward contract route with SHPL that involved job-work model with RRPPCL procuring, processing, and selling for SHPL. This has reduced the costs involved and has added to the profits (Table 5.2).

Financial ratios especially the net profit margin and the debt-to-equity ratio that measures the liabilities of the company vis-à-vis its shareholders equity show that the company is not very profitable; in fact, loans for working capital have constantly added to its liabilities; thus, most of its earnings are spent in repaying the loans. Also, the costs involved have been very high leading to a very low profitability (Table 5.2).

Over the years SHPL has emerged as the main contributor to RRPPCL's revenue second only to the input sales to farmer members. While in 2016–17 the farmers contributed 67.5% to the revenue, SHPL contributed 27.8%. In 2019–20, input sales to farmers contributed 55.7% while SHPL's share increased to 41.8% (analysis done by the author using data provided by SPS).

SPS has invested in RRPPCL to reduce its costs through fixed asset purchase such as graders, sorters, warehouses, and hermetic storage cocoons. SPS has also been meeting some of the operational expenses of the company in its setting-up phase such as salaries, travel, and cost of storage of aggregated produce. These are visualised as essential support to the company till such a time as it can fully take care of its expenses.

SPS's share in the total operational costs of the company reached a maximum of 12% in 2017–18 but has come down to 6.2% by 2019–20 and is expected to fall further to 5.5% in 2020–21. This is partly a result of RRPPCL being able to take care of some of the operational expenses hitherto taken up by SPS, such as salaries, travel, and administrative expense. The other part of this reduction is due to the expansion in the scale of operations of the company. While the scale expanded, the actual contribution of SPS has remained in the vicinity of Rs. 3.8–4.0 million per year. This will go down in absolute terms as the profits earned by the company improve (Vijay Shankar, n.d.).

6. Challenges faced by RRPPCL

Arranging working capital is still a challenge. The model followed by RRPPCL is still a low-profit margin model. The FPC does not earn enough to take care of its operational costs completely. Thus, working capital loan has to be arranged every harvest season. CEO and the staff accountant talked about the challenges of seeking working capital from banks. Most banks still take FPOs and farmer collectives to be risky customers with very low credit worthiness. NBFCs provide loans but at a relatively high interest rate (12–16%) that might be too much for an FPC. Currently, RRPPCL engages with FWWB and NAB-KISAN regularly for working capital loans. This year, RRPPCL is trying for loan against WHR from SBI or some other banks.

Table 5.2 Revenue, expenses, and profit (loss) for all the years

Year	2012–13	2013–14	2014–15	2015–16	2016–17	2017–18	2018–19	2019–20	2020–21
Revenue (Rs.)	22,048,307	21,505,695	37,959,724	14,847,008	17,771,190	26,823,379	51,812,776	52,189,377	85,347,394
Expenses (Rs.)	22,091,681	24,138,547	39,195,855	14,825,237	17,460,123	25,350,615	51,692,334	51,159,640	82,057,288
Profit (loss) (Rs.)	−47,208	−2,638,562	−1,230,447	24,732	253,884	1,201,478	120,442	1,029,737	3,293,074
Debt to equity	3.20	15.61	5.57	4.21	3.12	4.41	4.43	3.49	3.61
Net profit margin	−0.002	−0.109	−0.032	0.001	0.018	0.058	0.002	0.020	0.039

Table 5.3 Working capital loans over the years (in Rs.)

	Bank of India (Loan against WHR)	FWWB @14% for 12 Months	NABKISAN @11% for 12 Months	Avanti Finance @14% for 12 Months	Total
2016–17	0	12,500,000	0	0	12,500,000
2017–18	0	8,500,000	10,000,000	0	18,500,000
2018–19	0	0	22,000,000	14,000,000	36,000,000
2019–20	0	5,000,000	10,000,000	0	15,000,000
2020–21	0	10,000,000	20,000,000	0	30,000,000

The requirement of working capital means that RRPPCL has to approach banks and NBFCs every aggregation season, especially when harvesting the rabi crop. Some of the major partners of RRPPCL have been FWWB and NAB-KISAN (Table 5.3). In the current year, the CEO is busy approaching SBI, ICICI Bank, and Yes Bank for loans against WHR and a cash credit facility.

Other than financial challenges, both Animesh Mondal (SPS representative) and Rajat (CEO) agree that acquiring professional human resource and their training and capacity building was the next big challenge. Currently, there are 8–9 employees, out of which five are on the rolls of RRPPCL while the rest are on SPS rolls; the latter includes Rajat. Animesh informed that a separate team is being built for training and capacity building, and a dedicated personnel has been hired for the same (as on September 2021, the 'dedicated personnel' had left). For RRPPCL the main challenges involve building a skilled team, especially when it comes to quality assessment. Currently, the staff deputed at Avantee Food Park facility is trained and hand-held by SHPL.

In December 2021, NABARD had sanctioned a Rs. 30 million working capital loan, and also due to meetings with other stakeholders, Avantee MFP had agreed, in principle, to provide space to RRPPCL for flour making. This has important implications on cost reduction since wheat milling operations can be shifted from Asha Industries Ltd. Ujjain to the MFP, practically 'next door' to the storage and packaging operations.

7. Perspectives from the field

Rajat, when asked how he ended up being the CEO of a FPC, says that he was supposed to join a start-up which ended up being a non-starter. He came to know about the CEO position at RRPPCL through a friend at SHPL and was motivated by the CEO of SHPL to join the organisation. He has no regrets joining RRPPCL, but there are a lot of challenges that are to be tackled to make the organisation sustainable. He mentioned that although in theory FPCs and collectives are seen as tools for connecting farmers to the formal credit system and banks, but in reality, FPCs are themselves not seen as credit worthy by the banks.

Animesh, the SPS representative, rants (a bit frustrated at the high interest rates of NBFC loans),

> Has ITC ever done business while accessing loans at interest rates as high as 14%? Neither Reliance nor TATA pay[s] those high interests. A multinational company gets all kinds of subsidies on water, electricity, taxes etc. from the government. There are so many barriers for FPOs from all sides and yet they expect FPOs to do business and be self-sufficient. How is that possible with such high rates of interest?
>
> (Animesh Mondal, Samaj Pragati Sahyog)

He claims RRPPCL can grow better by doing more business if the interest rates are brought down.

Animesh also has views on the general route that FPC policy should take in the country. He says that what MYRADA did for SHGs and the way government supported them should be the way forward for FPCs too. He is not very hopeful about the current top-down implementation of the 10,000 FPO programme by the government. Animesh is wary of state federations and private players like ITC and Ruchi Soya since in his view, collaborating with them dilutes the NPM focus of RRPPCL.

The operations manager of SHPL responsible for providing handholding support to RRPPCL at the Avantee Mega Food Park facility, feels that the FPC is doing something unique. It is working on inputs, helping in adoption of bio-inputs, popularising NPM and providing a market linkage. Being an IRMA graduate himself, he too shares his view on capitalisation issues of FPOs, importance of capacity building for BoD members and staff, and so on.

Meerabai Kambde of Ratatalai village is a BoD member, and she explains the work of SPS and her own SHG (Manglashree) that was formed in 2002. There are 18 members in the SHG now, and they have come a long way from the ten-member group formed in 2002 with Rs. 25/month saving per member. Though Meerabai has 25 *bighas* of land, she shared that most farmers in the village had <5 *bighas*. Most of the crops the farmers grow are sold to RRPPCL after saving for self-consumption. Some farmers grow soybean which is sold in the Indore *mandi*. She shows us the land she has bought adjacent to her *kuccha* house and boasts of her *pucca makaan* that she is keen on building in the next year. Her son goes to the village school and helps his mother with work related to the SHG and RRPPCL.

Farmers like Champabai Pathor of Ratatalai village, also a member of the Manglashree SHG, explain other initiatives of the SHG in collaboration with the panchayat, namely roads and infrastructure, nutrition, alcohol regulation and de-addiction, and so on. She also told that the SHG has a general store in the village where they sell groceries at rates better than other shop keepers. However, Covid has impacted this initiative since it is difficult to procure the entire basket of consumption of the village household. She explained how SPS's initiatives have weaned away the farmers from chemical inputs to *paanch patti kadha*, dung-based manure, and so on. Punibai and Tarabai of Godna village were associated with Dhanlaxmi SHG and had similar observations and opinions about SPS and RRPPCL's work. They explained the benefits to the members due to mixed cropping and the use of NPM agriculture.

A few other women farmers also put forward their aspirations from RRP-PCL. They mentioned about bonus and incentives. They aspire to see RRP-PCL selling products under its own brand with some details about them and how they grow their crop.

8. Impact of the FPO on the markets and the member farmers

SPS's work in Natural Resource Management (NRM) has resulted in the villagers growing a *rabi* crop in the region. Earlier, this was the dry season, and most of the men and women left to work on the larger farms as farm labour. RRPPCL has brought positive changes in the market too. Due to a competitive yardstick function, other traders have started offering higher prices to the farmers, and there has been a reduction in fraudulent practices. RRPPCL has been able to provide competitive prices to member farmers. Especially in chickpea (black gram) RRPPCL has been consistently buying at rates above the *mandi* and the MSP price. RRPPCL has also been able to buy wheat and maize at prices very near, even if lower to *mandi* or MSP. Since the farmers are saved from the drudgery of arranging for transportation and also can save on costs, they sell to RRPPCL even if the FPC is paying slightly lower than the *mandi* or MSP. Due to the FPC's interventions, women farmers in the region have become aware of market prices and do not let even RRPPCL become the price giver. They actively negotiate. The women who were interviewed had started other activities in their villages such as *kirana shops*, campaign against alcohol abuse, and so on with the savings of the SHG. Some of them have built *pucca* houses and have started taking part in the local self-governance at the village level. They have aspirations beyond just marketing through partners such as SHPL. Many of them want to have RRPPCL's own brand with their name and the village name declaring the origin of the produce!

Notes

1 The Avantee Mega Food Park is located in Dewas, Madhya Pradesh. The Mega Food Park is one of the 22 all over the country and is a public-private partnership between the Ministry of Food Processing Industries and Ruchi Soya Industries Ltd

with funding support from NABARD. It began its operations in 2019 and provides facilities such as cold storage, grain processing infrastructure, warehouse, and "plug and play" facilities for MSMEs. The Mega Food Park is one of the two in Madhya Pradesh and is still not completely operational. The silo capacity at Avantee is 16,000 MT, the cold storage capacity is 2,000 MT, the two warehouses are of capacity 2,500 MT and 5,000 MT, and a grain processing set-up of 18 MT per hour.

2 Safe Harvest Private Limited (SHPL) aims to make safe and natural food products accessible to all. This they achieve by advocating crops grown using non-pesticide management (NPM). SHPL actively partners with farmer producer organisations (FPOs) across ten states to achieve their aim; in the process benefitting farmers realise better incomes. SHPL deals in 53 products across five categories of cereals, pulses, spices, flavourings, and millets.

References

Anil, RK (2019). Linking farmer producers and urban consumers for pesticide free and safe food: Safe harvest private limited. In A Kanitkar & CS Prasad (Eds.), *Farming futures: Emerging social enterprises in India* (pp. 358–393). London: Authors UpFront.

Chatterjee, T, Raghunathan, R & Gulati, A (2019). *Linking farmers to futures market in India* (Working Paper). New Delhi: Indian Council for Research on International Economic Relations.

Ranjan, A (2016). Human development in Madhya Pradesh: Evidence from 2011 population census. In BP Singh, BK Singh & A Ranjan (Eds.), *India 2015: Population and human development* (p. 188). Bavla: MLC Foundation "Shyam" Institute.

Vijay Shankar, PS (n.d.). *Towards sustainability of producer institutions.* Bagli: Ram Rahim Pragati Producer Company Limited.

Wani, SP, Rego, TJ & Pathak, P (2002). *Executive summary of project launching and planning workshops. Tata-ICRISAT-ICAR Project: Combating land degradation and increasing productivity in Madhya Pradesh an Eastern Rajasthan* (p. 66). Patancheruvu: International Crop Research Institute for Semi-Arid Tropics.

6

SUSTAINING VALUE CHAINS OF NON-TIMBER FOREST PRODUCE

The Mahanadi Producer Company in Chhattisgarh

Niraj U. Joshi and Nikhila Shastry

1. Introduction

Kanker, an aspirational district located in the state of Chhattisgarh (erstwhile Bastar), is often dubbed as a red corridor region owing to Naxalism. According to Chhattisgarh's last Human Development Report (2006),[1] Kanker ranks very low among all the districts in the state on most social and economic indicators. In all the indices, the district ranks below the state average except education index. The district is at the seventh position in the case of education index with a value of 0.758 as against the state average of 0.711. The health index and income index of the district are 0.280 and 0.152 as against the state average of 0.392 and 0.310, respectively. More than 60% of the population is tribal and dependent on rain-fed, subsistence agriculture with low incomes and stagnant productivity.

1.1 Abundance of NTFP

Like most tribal-dominated districts, Kanker too has rich forested areas with abundant non-timber forest produce (NTFP) that forms a major seasonal source of income for the people. NTFPs such as local fruits (including custard apple, blackberries, mango, and tamarind) as well as economically important plants such as mahua and Terminalia species are found in large numbers. However, due to inappropriate harvesting methods, lack of value addition, and poor market negotiation skills, NTFP sales used to fetch very low and unviable rates for local tribal farmers. Vrutti – a not-for-profit organisation formed in 2002 has been working in Madhya Pradesh and Chhattisgarh among other states to improve livelihoods of disadvantaged communities (also see Section 6.2). In 2013, it was awarded a grant by the World Bank under its development marketplace scheme for improving farmers' livelihoods in Chhattisgarh. The grant's objectives were to identify and

DOI: 10.4324/9781003308034-6

support field testing of innovative, early-stage ideas that have potential for high development impact.

In 2014, the local district office of National Bank for Agricultural and Rural Development (NABARD) too approached Vrutti for promoting farmer producer organisations (FPOs) in its work area in Kanker. Both the World Bank grant and NABARD request gave the initial push and required resources for the formation of Mahanadi Farmer Producer Company Limited (henceforth MFPCL). Though Vrutti's initial support to MFPCL focused on improving agriculture productivity, the potential of value addition to the abundant NTFPs soon presented an opportunity which was then tapped by Vrutti to promote a custard apple value chain.

The rest of this chapter is organised as follows. In Section 6.2, Vrutti's role as an agribusiness incubator is explained briefly followed by Section 6.3 which gives a broad chronology of major events in MFPCL's journey especially its custard apple value-chain development. Sections 6.4 and 6.5 present the financial and governance overview followed by some broad outcomes in Section 6.6. In Section 6.7 we conclude by seeking to understand if MFPCL should diversify into new value-added products such as custard apple powder. How does it take over the current services provided by Vrutti in fund raising, business development, and value addition?

2. Incubation by Vrutti

Vrutti has been playing a crucial supporting role to MFPCL through its three-fold model[2] which provides integrated services and diversified options (value addition, farm, allied, and off-farm) appropriate to the farmers. The three-fold model is about *"building wealthy, resilient and responsible farmers – making them successful entrepreneurs, and sustained job creators, having their income increased by three times"* (as mentioned on their website). Vrutti began with top-down support where agri-extension services were provided to farmers. An evaluation study conducted later by Catalyst Management Services (CMS) made Vrutti realise that interventions for the farming communities were generally geared towards improving crop productivity and not profitability for the farmer. This led to a paradigm shift in Vrutti's approach where farming is now viewed as an enterprise and farmer as an entrepreneur. A three-fold model centred around individual, producer, ecosystem, and national levels was born to collectivise farmers and develop a marketplace for the farmers.

Its Business Acceleration Unit (BAU) thus played a crucial role in providing MFPCL with ecosystem enabling services such as backward linkages and forward linkages, accounts maintenance systems, and financial linkages. To comply with these needs, MFPCL with Vrutti facilitated the training of 'Activators'. Activators are field-level staff who coordinate the activities of MFPCL with BAU for smooth conduct of the operations. Demand aggregation of produce is done by these activators, one activator taking responsibility of five villages. Activators further actively engage with farmers providing guidance on crops to be grown, better agronomic practices, market information, and other farming-related information at the village level.

Further, Vrutti was instrumental in engaging with key players in the ecosystem of MFPCL including business partners, input suppliers, processors, financing institutions, and research and training institutions. The relations established with the support of BAU enabled the MFPCL to overcome some initial technological and funding hurdles. The critical support from Azim Premji Philanthropic Initiatives (APPI) and NABARD to Vrutti also helped tide over the initial operational and capacity development expenses of MFPCL (also see Section 6.4 and Table 6.2).

3. MFPCL's journey

3.1 The early phase of provision of extension services (2013–16)

In the initial years MFPCL with Vrutti support focused on providing extension services, agri-input supply and capacity building, as well as allied off-farm activities such as piggery and poultry. Farmers interest groups (FIGs) were formed in each village first, following which crop demonstrations and crop advisories were shared. Furthermore, small microenterprise support too was given including for piggery, bio-pesticides, poultry, and mushroom cultivation. Access to affordable and quality inputs such as seeds, fertilisers, pesticides, and so on was also a big challenge which needed to be addressed as these were being sold at very high rates at the time and also were of inferior quality.

The most important service provided to MFPCL's members was that of doorstep delivery of agricultural package of services which continues till date. Table 6.1 lists some of the extension methods used initially by MFPCL.

Table 6.1 Type and range of extension methods used from 2013 to 2016 by MFPCL

Serial Number	Type of Extension Events	Number of Events Organised	Number of Participants	
			Male	Female
1	Peer learning sessions	27	32	18
2	Training sessions	75	48	27
3	Farmer field school	72	47	25
4	Technical support for poultry-rearing and other allied activities	5		5
5	Village-level procurement centres	12	60	60

A dedicated team of field cadres called *krishak mitras*[3] engage with the farmer members and provide round-the-clock extension support; conduct peer learning between farmer members; organise regular training during the agricultural season; plan for procurement before the cropping season; maintain input materials outlet at their homes and provide input services to farmer members. All of these led to improved agronomic practices such as transplanting (replacing broadcasting) as well as adoption of system of root intensification (SRI) for paddy and new crops like maize. Paddy production has risen considerably from six to eight quintals per acre to 15–20 quintals per acre presently with those tribal farmers doing SRI producing up to 35–40 quintals/acre.

The tipping point began with understanding the market potential of wild custard apple fruit that is abundantly available in the forests. On recognising the huge potential of custard apple as an income source albeit seasonal, it was brought to the attention of the then (2014) Kanker district collector. It did not take long to convince her of the economic potential of the abundant wild custard apple population considering its high value in the market. The collector then spearheaded the efforts (see Table 6.2) of conducting a survey to estimate the population of custard apple trees and fruits in the region which revealed that at least 30,000 metric tons of custard apple production annually occur in Kanker district alone.

Coupling with building awareness of the tribals on the market potential of the product led to successful mobilisation of tribals into forming a for-profit producer company for and by the farmers of the region. To further develop this huge potential of custard apple fruit as well as its by-products in the market, the MFPCL directors, shareholders, and representatives of Vrutti were then sent on an exposure visit by the district government to Udaipur where they also got hands-on training in manufacturing of custard apple pulp. The district government also funded exposures to Rajsamand and Pali, Chittorgarh Krishi Vigyan Kendras for women's involvement in harvesting, grading, processing, and new variety grafting pruning processes (see Table 6.2 for a timeline). Thus began MFPCL's journey into custard apple fruit and pulp business. The initial year saw custard apple pulp production of 165 kg which has now risen to 25 tonnes.

3.2 Value chain and making of the Bastar Fresh brand with convergence efforts (2016 onwards)

The financial investments were then made by ATMA as well as the DMF and Vrutti. Further support came from APPI that provided funds for meeting the cost of professional management of MFPCL. A part of the funds was also used for capacity building of the BoD. The MFPCL thus began its custard apple value-chain development in late 2016. The various activities undertaken by MFPCL included the following.

Table 6.2 Timeline and key events in MFPCL's journey from 2013 to 2021

Time Period	Stage	Key Milestones/ Challenges	Support System/Remarks
2012–13	Ideation of concept	Mobilisation through SHG, FIG formation	Vrutti through World Bank market development marketplace
2013–14	Pre-FPC stage	Exposures and trainings on FPC formation, vision building for farmers, and BoDs	Exposure visits to Vrutti-promoted/supported FPOs, BIRD Lucknow, Raipur, West Bengal-Bankura, Pune
2014–15	Registration	Registered MFPCL as a producer company, business plan	Vrutti/NABARD
2015–16	Linkage and convergence with local government	Survey for estimating NTFP production potential; capacity building for NTFP value addition; first custard apple pulping machine purchased	District Administration, Agricultural technology Management Agency (ATMA) and District Mineral Foundation (DMF)
2016–19	Value-chain development of custard apple	Eleven more pulping units purchased along with deep freezer and hardener; SHGs trained in procurement, processing, and sales	ATMA grant for buying ten pulping units; further support by APPI[4] and NABARD[5] through Vrutti
2020–21	Crippling blow by pandemic	Stocks of unsold fruit and fruit pulp resulted in losses and high cost of hiring deep freezer in Raipur	The stock of custard apple pulp of 2019–20 expired in the deep freezer units with the SHGs; close to 43 quintals of pulp left unsold

3.2.1 *Promotion of proper harvesting technique and establishment of community-managed procurement centres*

MFPCL leveraged the existing social capital present in the form of the SHGs promoted by State Rural Livelihood Mission. Along with Vrutti, MFPCL trained these women SHGs initially from 23 villages (now from 50 villages) in the procurement and processing of custard apples. During the custard apple season (mid-September to December), fruit procurement, grading, and pulp production remain an all-women activity. It was ensured that the harvesting of fruit was done with the stalk which prolonged the shelf life of custard apples. Women from one SHG per village then pool in their money to procure all the custard apples from their village, sort, and grade the custard apples based on their size and other quality parameters. Grade A (the best quality) fruits are then sold in the local and regional market by MFPCL. While some Grade B and Grade C fruits are also sold as fruit, the rest are processed into pulp and supplied to buyers in Raipur, Indore, and elsewhere. The pulp is then sold for use in custard apple milk/fruit shake as well as ice cream preparation. Procurement centres scaled up from just 12 in 2016 to as many as 23 in 2020. The spaces for these centres were all donated by the village panchayats and managed by the community seasonally to collect, weigh, grade, store, and transport the fruits. The local panchayat of Lakhanpuri, as a show of support, has also donated 10,000 square feet of land to Mahanadi for lifetime – an invaluable asset for MFPCL when its operations expand (IRMA & Vrutti, 2018: 40).

3.2.2 Establishment of pulping units

In October 2015, Mahanadi established its first storage and processing unit at its field office in Lakhanpuri village. This unit has a storage capacity to accommodate 10 tons of fruit and space for processing pulp. In addition, two deep freezer refrigerators were bought and are being used for storing custard apple, blackberry, and mango pulp.[6] These efforts have enhanced Mahanadi's processing capacities over time and helped to expand the market reach of Mahanadi FPC. Initially the pulp was branded as Kanker valley fresh, but as the procurement areas grew to include larger areas from other parts of the district the branding was changed to reflect this and is now known as Bastar Fresh.[7] The main source of income of MFPCL is from the custard apple pulp sales followed by blackberry and mango pulp. Blackberry was even sold to Big Basket in 2019. MFPCL has been instrumental in establishing 12 pulp-processing units of which two have been purchased by the MFPCL and the remaining ten through the convergence with government schemes supported by the ATMA and DMF funds. The DMF has been a source of critical support in the initial setting-up stages of the MFPCL's pulp-processing units. Pulp production which began with 165 kg in 2016 now stands at a huge 25 tons annually and is growing.

3.2.3 Establishment and operation of "Bastar Fresh" brand for marketing custard apple

"Bastar Fresh" is the brand name under which Mahanadi farmers' produce is marketed. The brand is primarily targeted at local markets within 250 km covering Raipur, Bilaspur, and adjoining regions (IRMA & Vrutti, 2018: 40). According to the chief executive officer (CEO), MFPCL Ms Nagina:

For marketing the custard apple pulp, MFPCL had to build a brand and advertise in forums where bulk suppliers are usually sought, like Indiamart, JustDial, Alibaba, Yellow Pages etc. Participation in major trade exhibitions is also necessary to meet bulk buyers. Since MFPCL is looking mainly at Business-to-Business (B2B) marketing, it needed to have a brand name that is clear and communicates our identity – which is supplying Agricultural Food items and our key differentiating factor – which is natural, organic and healthy pulp.

(interview)

MFPCL's participation in farmer fairs, bazaars, and food festivals has helped in achieving expansion of the brand, in both rural and urban areas (especially among the customer base associated with juice shops and ice cream shops). MFPCL has begun focusing on better customer engagement practices (for instance, free samples to visitors during farmer fairs) and paying attention to different customer segments (small packet buyers) to expand their market reach. Moreover, MFPCL holds all relevant licenses for carrying out input business and marketing operations.

MFPCL has also established procedures for testing the product for shelf life, taste, and other features before launching in the market. While custard apple pulp constitutes the bulk of its portfolio, MFPCL has ventured into the "fresh on the move segments" like small packets of custard apple juice.[8] Sales have been driven largely by "customer pull" as they perceive that MFPCL provides a quality-assured product at an affordable price. Custard apple juice, a niche product, has helped MFPCL to position itself in this segment. The fruit's juice sells at a premium price of Rs. 80 per 300 ml. As the demand for this product is beyond and across other districts and states, efforts are being made to increase production and meet demands of local[9] and outside markets (Pune and Nagpur in Maharashtra). Although consistent focus has been given on marketing and branding of the products, "Bastar Fresh" brand is still a small player in terms of annual turnover.

In addition to custard apple, procurement and turnover from sales of tamarind and blackberries too have scaled up over the years as is evident from Figure 6.1. Indeed, collection and sales of tamarind have even surpassed those of custard apple in more recent years. MFPCL also trades in agricultural produce such as paddy, minor millets, maize, and livestock including goats, pigs, and poultry.

3.3 Business model

MFPCL, as of year 2021, primarily generates revenue through farmers and market. While farmers pay membership and service fees, markets generate revenue through NTFP (about 50%) and agricultural produce/livestock sales. The services provided by Mahanadi to producer members cover all activities, from procurement to processing to marketing, in the value-chain spectrum. MFPCL initially raised funds through equity contribution

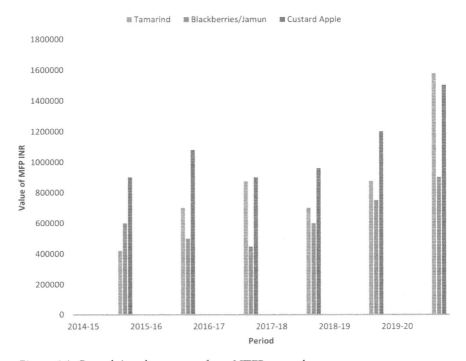

Figure 6.1 Growth in sales revenue from NTFPs over the years

from its shareholders/farmer members, who contributed one lakh rupees towards the enterprise. Authorised share capital of the company is Rs. 1 million with 100,000 equity shares of Rs. 10 each. Salary of the CEO is still paid by Vrutti as the FPC is unable to bear this cost internally. However, given its relatively positive financial performance in the initial three years it was able to access a loan worth Rs. 600,000 towards working capital from Bank of India (BoI), the lead bank in the region. The loan has been paid up entirely.

MFPCL has entered into several partnerships with wholesalers, retailers (forward linkages), as well as SHGs, local government departments, public sector banks, and input suppliers (backward linkages) to further its objectives. Its backward linkage with SHGs has been particularly beneficial in terms of scaling-up procurement, processing, as well as marketing of custard apple, blackberry, and mango pulp. The close relationships with input suppliers IFFCO,[10] Bayer, and so on have helped in ensuring quality input supply to its members. These relations have helped it to build a business network as, for example, one of the SHGs (Laxmi SHG) provides bio-pesticides to MFPCL. MFPCL packages, brands, and markets the bio-pesticide to the producer members and non-members in the area. IFFCO supplies seeds, fertilisers, and pesticides to MFPCL. Furthermore, MFPCL has also been recognised as a 'start-up,[11] by Government of Chhattisgarh, thus giving it tax- and compliance-related concessions from the state government.

4. Financial overview

A quick look at the balance sheet (see Table 6.3) indicates MFPCL's struggle with meeting working capital requirements to finance its high sales revenue.

Given that the collective had barely completed four years of custard apple value-chain development when the pandemic struck, operations and finances have taken a further beating in financial years 2019–20 and 2020–21. Share capital has shown a steady rise indicating sustained interest in MFPCL by local producers as well as ploughing back of dividends earned in the period. Furthermore, MFPCL is facing challenges of shortage of skilled human resources owing to its location being remote and Naxal-affected. Hiring such talent for an FPC becomes challenging due to financial and other resource constraints.

Table 6.3 Financial performance of MFPCL in INR from years 2015–16 to 2020–21

Particulars	2015–16	2016–17	2017–18	2018–19	2019–20	2020–21
Total Revenue	423,425	180,888	1,482,481	6,207,379	2,732,802	6,839,349
Total Expenses	529,889	94,602	1,407,449	6,072,250	2,680,992	6,823,168
Profit Before Tax	(106,464)	86,286	75,031	135,129	51,810	16,480
Profit After Tax	(106,464)	58,527	60,227	92,429	33,349	12,195
Share Capital	153,100	183,100	250,100	317,100	342,100	443,100
Reserves and Surplus	(106,464)	(47,937)	12,291	104,720	138,069	150,264
Long-Term Borrowings	60700	60,700				
Fixed Assets Including Investments	–	12,071	166,455	254,976	220,094	190,103
Current Liabilities	82,064	125,823	955,630	1,399,831	1,566,139	1,463,956
Current Assets	146,300	236,515	911,467	1,359,574	1,346,046	1,273,853

Source: MFPCL records, audited financial statements

In addition to working capital, MFPCL managed to get small loans from nationalised banks, but currently it requires a big funding support to have its own warehouse as well as a cold storage unit to preserve pulp of custard apple, blackberry, and mango. It also needs human resources to develop a viable business plan for next three to five years and access funding support.

5. Governance

The MFPCL governance structure includes the BoD, CEO, subcommittees, and membership all of which give strategic direction to MFPCL.

5.1 Membership

A core group of farmer members (lead farmers) who, from the initial days, were associated with Vrutti in Kanker played an important role in mobilising farmers for Mahanadi. These lead members (who also acted as promoters of the FPO), one from each of the 11 villages, were selected for mobilising members in their village. These lead members acted as volunteers in mobilising the members for the FPO. Motivation for collectivisation was achieved through conceptual seeding at initial stage for creating awareness about benefits of collectivisation among farmers. Furthermore, two factors helped to mobilise farmers for Mahanadi: first, the efforts to showcase value chain of custard apple and, second, the ease of accessibility to Vrutti and MFPCL team's physical presence in the same block. Farmer mobilisation for MFPCL happened directly at the village level without forming farmer clubs or any sub-group although some attempts were made to form FIGs initially. Lead farmers rallied for mobilising farmers for the company, motivating them to join the company by buying its shares.

5.2 BoD and CEO

MFPCL has 11 directors nominated from as many villages including one woman director. The BoD has two nominated members (apart from the directors); a chief executive officer (CEO who executes all the decisions of the board and manages the overall administration of MFPCL) and an office bearer of Vrutti, Kanker office. Satendra Lihare who was the first CEO has now left. The current CEO is Ms Nagina Netam who has been working with the MFPCL since 2015.

The term of the board is for three years, and every three years elections are conducted to elect new representatives. The BoD meets every month to review the reports of the previous month's activities and finances, collectively approve the budget proposals, and make other related decisions for the current month. Furthermore, the BoD is divided into two sub-committees which look after procurement and marketing, and each has a director as a member. These sub-committees meet every week to plan and review their activities. Strong focus is given on maintaining documents, and all relevant records are maintained in hard and soft copy formats.

An annual general meeting (AGM) is held every September to enable all farmer members to review and approve the annual financial statements. The AGM presents an opportunity for members to participate and discuss the future plan of the enterprise. These transparent and participatory processes have encouraged the farmer members to take collective responsibility for managing their enterprise and earn profits for it. Several capacity building measures have been undertaken by the MFPCL for its CEO and directors including the following: Custard apple procurement, farming – end to end, FPO management and leadership training, SHG member trainings on bookkeeping, pulping, mushroom cultivation, poultry, and piggery.

MFPCL has strongly believed in developing the capacities of the local cadre in running the FPC rather than getting young professionals from outside to run the FPO as a CEO. This was based on the belief that the local people remain committed to the company while also providing employment in their own region. This process has in turn helped to develop capacity and confidence of the directors; for instance, the business deal for hiring a cold storage in Raipur was negotiated and finalised by the directors with minimal facilitation by Vrutti staff.

Nagina Netam, the current CEO of MFPCL, initially joined Vrutti as a field-level resource person and then got promoted to a field coordinator position where she continued to work for four years before becoming the CEO of MFPCL. Realising her passion and commitment, the BoD unanimously elected her as a CEO in 2019. She holds a master's degree in political science.

6. Impact

Up until MFPCL was formed, the farming of custard apple was not commercialised. Farmers in Charama block, Kanker, had to personally transport their produce and custard apple to the local *mandi* (market) and accept the price being offered without any negotiation. On average one basket/crate of 20 kg would fetch only a price of Rs. 50 earlier. Thus, tribal farmers collected the fruits from the forested areas and sold it either on road side or in nearby markets at very low prices. Furthermore, as they harvested the fruits at improper maturity and using inappropriate method, more than 50% fruits either failed to ripen or over-ripened and got wasted. Pulp extraction was also a challenge, and only manual pulping was practised. This not just consumed more labour but also made the product uneconomical. Furthermore, the manually extracted pulp was unhygienic and not available throughout the year due to storage problems. However, MFPCL changed this purchase procedure and ensured that the producers and primary collectors get fair or higher price for their produce. This was achieved by adopting the following measures:

- The produce is weighed by the farmer members themselves, enabling them to verify the weights.
- The produce is purchased by MFPCL at the farm gate, so farmers save on transportation expenses.
- MFPCL buys at ten times the earlier rate so per kg each farmer gets Rs. 20 at least instead of Rs. 2 to Rs. 2.5 that they earned earlier. This price is much higher than the price offered by local traders and middlemen. Value of custard apple has thus gone up substantially, and now each crate of 20 kg is bought by MFPCL at a rate of Rs. 400 at least.
- Farmers are now much more aware about the market value of custard apple
- Farmers are now able to grade and sell their produce with good bargaining power and get good returns on sales of custard apple

Furthermore, pulp of custard apple is sold at Rs. 200 per kg. Thus, a quick price spread analysis reveals that each member earns at least Rs. 120 per kg of fruit and pulp sold as opposed to approximately Rs. 2/3 prior to joining MFPCL. These benefits offered to members are in addition to the extension services offered by MFPCL. Socially and economically the women are much more empowered now. Much investment in building women's and women SHGs' skills in procurement, processing pulp, marketing, banking, and negotiating with traders has contributed towards this social and economic empowerment.

Women get to keep the income from custard apple fruit and pulp sales and decide how they spend that money. Furthermore, women are able to grade fruits and negotiate prices of produce much better than before MFPCL began work. Finally the tribal women who had never ventured out of their villages are also now competent to train and build capacity of other women in all of the above skills.

The interventions by MFPCL also have had a good impact on environment as farmers now use the seed and leaves of custard apple for making bio-pesticides which have helped reduce the use of chemical pesticides. Custard apple seeds are dried and sold at Rs. 80/kg for use by nurseries and also to make bio-pesticides from the oil extracted from seeds. This oil is used as a key ingredient in making insecticides. The skin of custard apple is also used for making organic manure which helps reduce the use of inorganic fertilisers on the farms. Due to reduction in use of chemical pesticides, cost of fertiliser use has come down from Rs. 1,250 to Rs. 350 per acre per farmer thus helping save Rs. 900 per acre per farmer.

Some other sustainable initiatives include procurement of only wild/ naturally growing custard apple – plantations not promoted – which is more sustainable as no inputs are required.

- SRI promoted to conserve water;
- maize introduced in addition to SRI to reduce water consumption. Further, rabi/winter paddy cultivation is discouraged by MFPCL by promoting alternate crops to save water such as vegetables, sunflower, maize, and pulses;
- soil conservation measures like land levelling and farm bunds promoted to conserve soil and retain moisture.

7. Conclusion

Mahanadi Farmer Producer Company Limited happens to be located in a particularly challenging geography which makes it all the more difficult to get quick results. Though Kanker is also Naxal-affected, fortunately it has not had any adverse effect on MFPCL's growth, save perhaps the availability of local skilled human resources. MFPCL is highly dependent on Vrutti for sustaining the NTFP value chain and building upon it. The incubation and business advisory support from Vrutti have been critical. Given that the FPO needs to be run by a socially and economically marginalised tribal community with its limited entrepreneurial and managerial skills as well as the perishable nature of the NTFPs in general and custard apple in particular it is understandable that MFPCL would require handholding for several more years before it can become more independent in handling its own businesses. How closely its fortunes are linked to Vrutti support can be gauged from the fact that leadership turnover and funding struggles in Vrutti also affected the performance of MFPCL in the last three years despite scaling up custard apple procurement and pulp production.

The funding support from Vrutti to the MFPCL lasted for four years post which the FPC has been struggling to meet its working capital costs as well as the need for infrastructure to store custard apple pulp and stocks of other minor forest produce. With insufficient funds, it has become difficult to pay the salaries as well thereby resulting in staff being reduced to half, currently supporting only the BAU Head of Vrutti and CEO of MFPCL. The investments in storage infrastructure as well as working capital and product diversification thus had to take a back seat. The onset of Covid further impacted the operations of MFPCL and SHGs. The stock of custard apple pulp of 2019–20 was lying unsold at the time of writing this chapter and expired in the deep freezer units with the SHGs. The SHGs could not process pulp in early 2021 as the previous year pulp remained unsold, and there was no space to store the new pulp.

While the custard apple value-chain development has helped improve incomes of shareholders, it has also underlined the risk and importance of having alternatives when trading in perishables sans infrastructure.

Despite these challenges, MFPCL has done relatively better in building local capacity, developing a value chain and local markets in NTFPs such as custard apple, which did not exist a few years ago. MFPCL has also leveraged the extant social capital of the SHG movement in Chhattisgarh to its advantage by skilling them in procurement, processing, and marketing in a relatively short period of four years. Given the highly perishable nature of custard apple – both fruit and pulp – it begs the question, why alternate value chains have not been developed for NTFPs such as tamarind? Tamarind is abundantly available, of very good quality; also has high value, good markets (both domestic and export); and has a longer shelf life compared to custard apple. It could have served as a good buffer during the pandemic when custard apple pulp stocks were piled up and attracted a high cost including losses.

Possibly MFPCL could also have diversified into making custard apple powder which has better shelf life besides having significant export value. Both or either of these could have helped the FPC cope better with the pandemic and similar unforeseen emergencies.

7.1 Way ahead

With the lockdown restrictions easing in July 2021, markets opened in Raipur, and the MFPCL started its planning for procurement and processing in October 2021. MFPCL also hopes to receive funds from NABARD under its PRODUCE grant hopefully to develop the custard apple powder value chain. The future looks good as demand for custard apple in fruit, pulp, and powder form (as well as other NTFPs) is high and growing both domestically and overseas.

Indeed, MFPCL has to its credit demonstrated that harnessing and developing value chains of locally abundant NTFP are possible and can be sustained in challenging geographies to deliver supplementary income to tribals. MFPCL has also demonstrated encouraging progress on the three objectives of institutional sustainability, that is, member centrality (NTFPs being relevant to members' livelihoods as agricultural incomes are inadequate), patronage centrality (NTFPs being a critical sector of local business-forested landscapes), and domain centrality (contributing significantly to local economy).

Notes

1 Retrieved from https://www.im4change.org/docs/chhat_chap6-189-198.pdf
2 See https://vruttiimpactcatalysts.org/our-core-impact-model/
3 *Krishak mitras* means 'farmer friends'. They are persons who look after farmer members from a specific village. Each village has one *krishak mitra* appointed from Mahanadi FPC side.

4 Azim Premji Philanthropic Initiative (APPI).

5 National Bank for Agriculture and Rural Development (NABARD).

6 Custard apple pulp has very short life. It needs deep freezing at –18 degrees Celsius.

7 An article detailing the process of brand creation can be read at https://www. smallfarmincomes.in/post/bastar-fresh-the-making-of-a-wild-custard-apple-brand-by-the-tribal-women-of-chhattisgarh

8 They cater to passers-by on the National Highway number 27, that is in the vicinity of their office. Fresh custard apple juice is sold to the customers who usually stop for quick refreshments.

9 CEO of Mahanadi says, "There is huge demand even in the local market of Raipur and Bilaspur. We have demands from far off cities like Nagpur and Pune. At present we have limited production capacity. We have to increase production to meet all these demands."

10 Indian Farmers and Fertilizer Cooperative (IFFCO).

11 Department of Industrial Policy and Promotion, Government of Chhattisgarh, has recognized Mahanadi as a start-up company for duration of 7 years. It'll get investment and regulatory support from the government.

Reference

IRMA, & Vrutti. (2018). A Systematic multi-method synthesis on Farmer Producer Organizations (FPOs). Unpublished report submitted by the Institute of Rural Management Anand and Vrutti to the International Initiative for Impact Evaluations (3IE), New Delhi.

7

MARKETS THAT EMPOWER WOMEN FARMERS' COLLECTIVES

Vaibhav Bhamoriya and Anita Paul

1. Context

The interface between man and nature is a necessary condition for survival of mountain farming systems, which depends upon adequate flow of a stream, biomass supplies from the forest support area in terms of tree leaf-fodder and tree leaf-litter for organic compost.

The degradation of forests has impacted the availability of these critical ecosystem services which has in turn impacted negatively on traditional food security. Lack of opportunities for gainful employment had resulted in outmigration of men to supplement family incomes leading to feminisation of hill agriculture. Alongside, climate change vulnerabilities are posing new challenges for securing sustainable livelihoods, here and now, and for future generations.

Making markets work in the face of rampant migration and in the absence of profitable employment or avocation for a large part of the population is literally an uphill task as markets rarely come to the mountains. Lack of tradable quantities, poor logistics, lack of affordable finance, and poor infrastructure make it challenging for women to gainfully engage in economic activities as producers and entrepreneurs.

2. Pan Himalayan Grassroots Development Foundation: where it all began

The Pan Himalayan Grassroots Development Foundation (henceforth Grassroots) is a voluntary organisation engaged in spearheading community-driven holistic mountain development programmes in the Indian Himalayan Region since 1992. Founders of Grassroots were initiated into community development processes as spearhead team members in the farmers organisation division of the National Dairy Development Board and, therefore, have conviction in power of collectives as a tool for linking small and marginal farmers to distant markets for economic empowerment.

                    DOI: 10.4324/9781003308034-7

Due to the lack of any formal employment opportunities, daily wage labour such as head loading materials at construction sites and other rarely available odd jobs were the only options available for women to maintain their homes and hearths. Rapid appraisals and dialogues with communities strengthened the belief that interventions based on strengths and weaknesses of the region along with market assessments were a critical need. Forming a collective was the only option available to women farmers, most of whom were managing their lives alone.

To find a fresh balance in the quality of lives for such marginalised farming communities, Grassroots promoted Umang as an ethical producer-owned company in the year 2009 with women as the primary stakeholder. Value chains based on surplus farm produce such as temperate soft fruits like apricots, plums, apples, and pears along with other cereals, lentils, millets, and spices formed the basis for on-farm interventions. To further strengthen livelihood opportunities off-farm initiative of hand-knitted woollens was adopted to address the needs. Ethical business practices based on deep respect for ecology and non-polluting production processes, focus on agrobiodiversity and seed sovereignty along with complete ownership by communities were some core values adopted right at the time of conception.

In the initial years focus was on local markets as mountain communities themselves are also consumers of goods and services and are dependent for these supplies from downstream markets in neighbouring urban areas. In situ production for local consumption was, therefore, attempted initially, and pilots for production of daily-use items such as clothes and school bags and intra-basin trade of farm surpluses were attempted as the first steps in this direction. This assisted in building confidence and skill enhancement. However, this strategy had to be dropped due to hyper-competitive prices of cheap goods from the plains flooding hill markets. With spread of public distribution system infrastructure in the region, intra-basin trade of food surpluses also took a hit, which led the team to rethink the entire process. Focus then shifted to adopting hand-knits for urban consumers as an avenue for home-based livelihood opportunity to augment agriculture incomes.

It was evident that urban markets had to be accessed which led to the adoption of value-chain approach linking farm gates to consumers. Urban middle-class families were the targeted market segment for the high-quality niche products such as natural honey, jams, jellies pickles, millets, lentils, spices, cereals, walnuts, and herbal teas. Building institutional capacities and adopting an appropriate form of organisation for sustainability were the next challenge. With the orientation of the promoters to the existing model of vertically integrated milk producers' collectives popularly known as the Anand Pattern, the foundations for building community-owned enterprise were laid. 'For the people, by the people based on Fair Trade and not aid' was the new norm guiding these actions. Considerable energy was spent on doing feasibility exercises and finalising production processes to develop standard operating procedures which could be understood and adopted by the community members. Building capacities of local youth as changemakers to lead this enterprise was also another challenge that had to be addressed at the same time.

3. In the company of mountain women farmers

Umang started as a voluntary organisation in the year 2001 when women spearhead team members of Grassroots hived out and formed an independent entity called Mahila Umang Samiti. Mandate of the organisation was to establish a collective of self-help groups (SGHs) as the base for engaging in building upon the capacities of women to engage in appropriate livelihood improvement initiatives and to provide the necessary ecosystem support for them to play a larger role in participative democracy. Due to changes in the policy of the government guiding the operations of voluntary organisations, it metamorphosed into a farmer producer company (FPC). Mahila Umang Producers Company was then promoted as a collective of SHGs and individual producer members engaged in promoting sustainable livelihoods opportunities through establishment of micro enterprises in order to improve their quality of life. It was formally registered on 9 January 2009 under Section 9A of the Companies Act 1956.

Umang is located in a tiny hamlet Naini, up at 6,000 feet, 9 km outside Ranikhet town, in Almora district of Uttarakhand, with its own processing and administrative offices along with a showroom for sale of its products. This showroom accounts for over 20% of its sales due to tourist traffic. The primary objective of Umang is to promote enterprises, directly controlled by producer members, based on the principles of fair trade. Umang is guided by triple concerns of ecology, economics, and equity. The organisation strives to work towards economic and social empowerment of its members by building on their entrepreneurial and leadership spirit,

Umang is guided and governed by an all-women board selected from among producer members and led by a team of professionals from the region with the aim to transfer maximum share of consumers rupee to shareholders. Efforts over the past decade have led to the consolidation of this network engaged with various viable business activities, which provide small yet significant incomes on a sustainable basis. Each business activity is directly controlled by the producer-group, all assets are owned by them, and all are equal shareholders of the business. By adopting a value-chain approach, Umang has been able to set up business verticals based on the strengths of the area and link farm gates, weavers, and artisans to distant markets.

Owned by local women farmers and producers, Umang is a marketplace for handmade knitwear, organic jams, jellies, pickles, honey, and various cereals, pulses, spices, and much more. The spirit of Umang is best expressed in the words of one of its key managers, Suneeta, "I am everything due to Umang, and I'm also nothing on my own. That's how Umang is, for every single woman. We come together and collectively impact our lives" (interview).

3.1 SHGs as the bedrock

Umang has consolidated its operations with 160 SHGs with 2,300 women in 100-plus villages of Almora, Nainital, Bageshwar districts of Uttarakhand, and Sirmaur district of Himachal Pradesh. These SHGs form the bedrock of all change, development, and village-level operations. However, currently only 110 SHGs consisting of 1,000 women are the shareholders of this community-owned enterprise.

The churning at the SHG level facilitates the process for maintaining a balance between the twin objectives of social and financial value. It is viewed as the platform that facilitates the organisational processes of maintaining its social mission and the required ecosystem that enables the active participation of women farmers as entrepreneurs. With a focus on sustainability and ecological security as a cornerstone for farming systems, Umang encourages its members to engage on issues of "*Jal-Jungle-Jameen*" through its network of SHGs. Staff members of Umang service this larger platform of SHGs as facilitators because of the critical support that it provides as a catalyst for their engagement as entrepreneurs.

Socio-economic profile of members surveyed in 2021 as detailed in Table 7.1 reveals that over 40% of the members are below the poverty line classification as defined by the Government of India; 70% of the members have been engaged with the organisation since inception. Keeping the organisation young is a stated strategy, and 45% of its members are under the age of 45 years; 14% of its membership are single-women-headed households and as such they are the main bread-earners of the family.

Table 7.1 Socio-economic profile of members

Particulars of the members' socio-economic background	%
Below Poverty Line (BPL)	41
Above Poverty Line (APL)	59
Participation in Panchayati Raj institutions	9
Women headed households (HHs)	14
Age category	
<25 years	1.41
<35 years	12.30
<45 years	31.26
<55 years	32.67
<65 years	14.17
65 and above	4.92

Building on the strengths of the region and the tradition of *Bara anaaj* (which is a traditional method of intercropping 12 or more rain-fed crops in Uttarakhand), Umang evolved the following three value chains as the way forward:

- Fruit growers are involved with adding value to local soft fruits like apricots and plums through production and marketing of natural fruit preserves, chutneys, and pickles, and beekeepers are involved with processing and sale of their honey. All these value-added products are sold under the brand name of Kumaoni. Fruits are collected at the village level by the SHGs and transported to the main processing centre of Umang by its staff incharge for value addition and packaging as per the required food processing guidelines of the Government of India.
- Farm surpluses in terms of millets, cereals, pulses, spices, walnuts, and herbal teas are processed and sold under the brand name of Himkhadaya. Primary processing in terms of drying, cleaning, and sorting is done by the concerned member at the household level. On a pre-appointed day the concerned Umang vertical staff aided by the SHG/cluster leaders would aggregate and transport the produce to Umang store for further processing and packaging.

In order to add to its basket of farm produce for consumers and also to build economies of scale, Umang has formed a collective of 30 walnut growers as its shareholders in Sirmaur district of Himachal Pradesh. Processing of walnuts is done there itself in rented premises equipped with vacuum packaging machines, de-humidifiers, and other necessary equipment. The activities of this centre are coordinated by a local woman team member whose capacities have been built overtime. She handles the entire processing of walnuts, vacuum packaging, and also distribution for sales as per the orders received from the central office in Uttarakhand.

Over 500 members from 50-plus villages are the shareholders for the above on farm verticals of Umang.

- Besides the above two on farm initiatives members are also involved with the production and sale of hand-knitted woollen and cotton garments as an off-farm activity branded as Umang Handknits. This is a home-based production activity based on the skills, interest, and aptitude of the knitters. Cluster approach is adopted, and activities are coordinated by a cluster leader with necessary knitting skills who is tasked with the responsibility of guiding the de-centralised production processes in her area. Initial quality control is her responsibility, and she is the conduit for distribution of raw material, production briefs, collection of finished products, and delivery to the central store of Umang. Raw materials are centrally procured and distributed by the Handknits

118

vertical incharge and production done as per the annual plans. Another 500 shareholders from 50 villages in and around Umang headquarters are engaged in this off-farm vertical.

Each shareholder has a unique identification number, and individual ledgers are maintained for all the activities on the basis of which patronage bonus is calculated at the end of the financial year. SHG and cluster leaders/ area incharge play a critical role for which a fixed percentage of the total value of production in her area of operation is paid to her as an honorarium for her time.

Along with streamlining production processes attention was also laid to necessary certification processes. Umang is a member of Fair -Trade Forum India and initiated organic certification through farmer pledge and peer-review process known as participatory guarantee system as opposed to third-party certification in order to keep the pride of the farmer alive and also draw consumers as a stakeholder in this process.

Umang has its own online shop (*www.umang-himalaya.com*). It is Umang's belief that those who purchase these products are directly assisting resource-poor households through 'trade and not aid'.

4. Business at a glance

Over its decade-long journey Umang as a community-owned social enterprise has been balancing its twin objectives of social and entrepreneurship as two sides of the same coin. Building insights and channelising them towards action with business at the heart of it have been the process to engage its members. Growth, innovativeness, competition, market relevance, and consumer connect are some parameters that are analysed regularly. Maintaining value to its shareholders is a pursuit which is at the core of annual plans and its governance mechanisms. Seasonal procurement plans and purchase price, costing and pricing, and sales are shared and discussed at length by the board of governors.

Overview of the business generated by this collective over the years is as detailed in Table 7.2. On an average sale has been close to 15 million rupees. HimKhadya, which is the brand for safe foods from the Himalaya, contributes 31% of the total turnover followed by Kumaoni – value-added fruit preserves and pickles at 20% and honey at 11%. Hand-knits/weaves have been added as an off-farm activity and account for the remaining 40%.

Maximising the return of the consumers' share of the rupee to producers has been a principal concern for this community-owned enterprise. As described in Table 7.3, shareholder earnings as percentage of sales reflect over 50% of the sales revenue as direct earnings by the producers. Salaries and other expenses of the organisation are also met out of the sales generated.

Table 7.2 Overview of business (Rs. in millions)

Year	Gross sale (Rs.)	Net Sale (Rs.)	Sales Tax Paid (Rs.)	Net Sale after Tax (Rs.)
2010–11	11,642,757	8,902,257	125,000	8,777,257
2011–12	10,927,305	9,042,746	125,428	8,917,318
2012–13	15,677,694	13,887,587	347,584	13,540,003
2013–14	13,273,732	11,113,944	215,528	10,898,416
2014–15	15,566,981	13,481,387	301,580	13,179,807
2015–16	16,293,245	14,536,045	303,562	14,232,483
2016–17	16,198,100	14,502,340	385,190	14,117,150
2017–18	15,984,667	14,677,356	738,869	13,938,487
2018–19	16,400,419	14,433,655	458,927	13,974,728
2019–20	16,397,900	14,525,095	531,133	13,993,962
2020–21	14,030,936	11,981,386	388,417	11,592,969
Totals	162,393,736	141,083,798	3,921,218	137,162,580

Table 7.3 Overview of shareholder earnings as percentage of sale

Year	Villages	No. of Participating Members	Earnings from 4 Verticals (INR)	Earnings as % of Sale
2009–10	70	1,259	3,180,656	61
2010–11	70	1,059	2,827,000	48
2011–12	96	1,221	3,670,065	57
2012–13	133	1,327	4,715,741	45
2013–14	127	1,340	4,770,235	58
2014–15	139	1,419	5,412,669	54
2015–16	146	1,284	8,381,304	72
2016–17	124	1,050	6,202,793	62
2017–18	127	1,169	6,272,053	62
2018–19	95	878	4,594,045	51
2019–20	101	862	5,600,500	57
2020–21	88	830	4,064,323	52
	Total		59,691,384	

Over the years, while the sales have been stable, it also seems to be pla-teauing. This is a concern for the management. Drops in farm outputs due to ecological degradation, climate emergencies, man-animal conflicts are some threats that the shareholders are facing. Change in inter-generational aspirations is a challenge too. Geographical challenges and migration of younger generations are a reality. In Umang's area of operations 43% of households have members who have migrated for livelihoods, and another 10% have shifted temporarily for education purposes. These external factors have been impacting the performance of business and necessitate the process of consolidation of membership from time to time. Currently, Umang has been reviewing its shareholder engagements which revealed that drop in farm surpluses has led to an increase in non-performing shareholders leading to initiating the process of share transfers to active farmers. There has been a decline in active engagement of members year on year, and team Umang is currently engaged in consolidating its outreach by strengthening the farming practices through trainings on agro-ecological principles and securing remunerative prices for its produce.

Umang provides a range of on- and off-farm options so that together shareholders can have a stable source of livelihoods. With an average farm holding of an acre majority members are marginal farmers with low volumes of farm outputs. Only surpluses are being aggregated with due consideration for household food and nutrition security kept intact. This sentiment is well reflected by a BoD member Indira Kabadwal of village Kafra, Dusad cluster, who reiterates that "only surpluses should be aggregated and the rates for the farm produce that the BoD decides should be such so that the farmers are not tempted to sell the entire produce leading to negative impacts on household nutrition security and cultural exchange of farm produce with friends and neighbours" (interview).

5. Markets don't come to the mountains!

From subsistence mountain farmers to becoming an active player in the market economy was and still is a challenge which is further aggravated by the fact that markets don't come to the mountains. Building managerial capacities of women's collectives to strengthen market access has been a long process involving enhancement of skills and knowledge at every stage of the value chain. Developing clusters, identifying cluster leaders as the first ladder for operations and quality check, exposure to markets, customer interactions and feedbacks, innovations to meet market requirements, consistency in quality and recipes, legal compliances are some of the components that are a part and parcel of on-the-job learning for team Umang.

With a basket of goods Umang has had to adopt a multi-pronged approach as its marketing strategy. B2B and B2C partnerships with e-commerce platforms such as Jaypore and existing retailers, exhibitions, dialogues with chefs in new organic restaurants to popularise traditional millets in modern-day living, production for pre-orders for existing market players for its woollen range such as Fabindia, online sales, and self-owned retail outlets are some of the measures adopted. Partnerships have been developed with over 40 existing retailers in different metro cities and within Uttarakhand. Over the years, Umang has developed its own customer data base of close to 1,000 and counting. There is a dedicated person to service the shops in the markets close to its headquarters and a dedicated team to handle all e-commerce sales. The sales team works in close connection with the respective vertical heads which in turn do the final quality test, packaging, and invoicing.

Each avenue of sales is serviced with a different skill set, and clear responsibility centres have been created in house for this purpose. With the mantras of 'Buy Fresh Buy Local' and 'Promote Fair Trade Not Aid', the Umang team is striving to meet the challenges and make use of the current opportunities of increasing consumer awareness for the aforementioned values. However, striking a right balance in terms of costing and pricing and seeking a fair price for its premium products produced ethically remain a challenge.

6. The changemakers

Building on local human capital as changemakers has been the strategy that has been adopted right from the start. Recruiting a suitable team from the region and moulding them into professionals were largely done by selecting leaders with promise from the communities and providing on-the-job training. Roles of SHG leaders at the village level and cluster managers at cluster level provided the opportunity for developing leadership and the much-needed opportunity for members with spark for upward mobility and fulfilling personal ambitions.

Experiential learning through cross visits to other producer groups and interactions with resource persons/institutions, short-term courses, subject-specific training modules, upgradation of skills and knowledge, experience in marketing and sales through participation of leaders and producers in exhibitions enabled direct interactions with consumers and all aided the growth of manpower over time. Knowledge of various legal compliances and implications of non-compliance by vertical heads, financial literacy, and the role of management information systems as a business tool were some areas of concern that had to be addressed.

Team building and a suitable organisational structure are perhaps a challenge that FPCs would have to reckon with. Managers versus leaders, inter-personal conflicts, reporting, communication, hierarchies, and such paradigms that may be a normal human resource policy may not be a normal for FPC realities. Umang chose to develop an organisational structure which is like a hub-and-spoke model, wherein all spokes are equal, and the hub is operated on a rotational basis. The rotation of leadership at the group level in every village has ensured the fundamentals of rotational leadership run strong and deep in the structure and members.

Rotational leadership at Umang is a natural extension of the leadership system at the village and SHG level where members take collective ownership and support the leader by taking care of her animals and even family in her absence when she is out for a meeting. This helps to naturally broaden the leadership base at the bottom of the organisation and allows a leader to grow through the ranks as a SHG leader, area/cluster head, and finally a member of the board. Many members of team Umang have also been selected through this process of upward mobility.

Each business vertical is manged by a manger who is responsible for the entire value chain along with her team. Shadow team leaders are appointed as and when required for ensuring continuity and keeping knowledge systems alive. Members of the board also play a critical role in their areas of operation as a focal point for operations, procurement, conflict resolution, market intelligence, and spokesperson for the collective. Today, Umang is managed by a team of 13 full-time professionals and assisted by part-time workers as and when required for processing. This team is led by a woman managing director, and 70% of her team members are also women who in their own rights were the main bread-earners for their households. This gender-inclusive strategy is an important feature for eliciting and strengthening the participation of women members. To promote and recognise excellence and quality of produce, awards have been instituted for all the core business activities. This motivates the women to perform much better resulting in pursuit of excellence. These awards are distributed to the winners at the annual general meeting of all its shareholders held annually at the end of every financial year.

Umang has been governed by an elected board of governors selected and appointed by its 1,000 shareholders who constitute the general body of this FPC. Currently it has seven women farmers as its board that changes as per the memorandum of association adopted at the time of registration. The organogram of Umang is given in Figure 7.1.

7. Financial overview

Umang has evolved from grants-driven pilots by the promoting organisation to a revenue-generating social enterprise as the driver for creating sustainable livelihood opportunities for its shareholders. Investments to the tune of Rs. 8 million were mobilised by Grassroots as the promoting organisation in the form of a grant for creating the necessary infrastructure, tools, equipment, working capital, and meeting basic expenses for a couple of years in the year 2009. This investment has in turn led to revenue generation on an average to the tune of Rs. 15 million annually.

Umang has been operating as a self-sufficient unit and distributing patronage bonus to its shareholders for the past five years. As stated earlier individual ledgers are maintained for each participating member to track her contribution to the business generated across all the business verticals. Profit and loss statements are maintained separately for each activity and bonuses declared as per the performance of the brand and bonus disbursed as per individual shareholder contribution in terms of fruits, food, and knits produced. This keeps the competitive spirit alive and aids in adding to the feeling of ownership and allegiance to the organisation.

The unutilised savings deposits held by the SHGs were utilised to fund the activities of Umang as and when needed. Short-term loans from SHGs have been mobilised in the past essentially for tiding over working capital crunch. Detailed financials are described in Table 7.4.

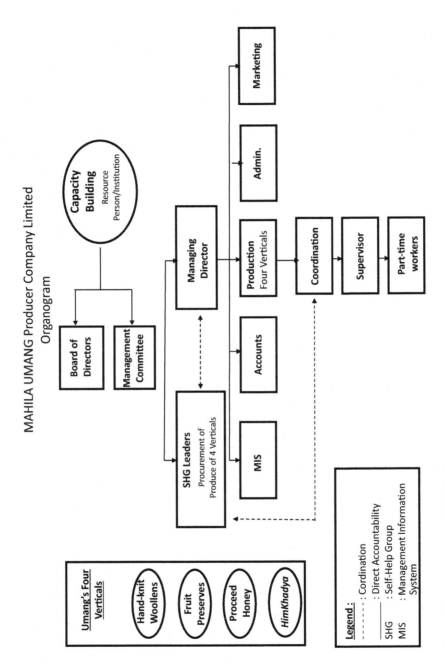

MAHILA UMANG Producer Company Limited
Organogram

Capacity Building
Resource Person/Institution

Board of Directors

Management Committee

Managing Director

SHG Leaders
Procurement of Produce of 4 Verticals

Accounts

MIS

Production
Four Verticals

Marketing

Admin.

Coordination

Supervisor

Part-time workers

Umang's Four Verticals
- Hand-knit Woollens
- Fruit Preserves
- Proceed Honey
- HimKhadya

Legend :
- - - - - : Cordination
———— : Direct Accountability
SHG : Self-Help Group
MIS : Management Information System

Figure 7.1 Organogram of Mahila Umang

124

Table 7.4 Details of financial performance of Umang

Particulars	2009–10	2010–11	2011–12	2012–13	2013–14	2014–15	2015–16	2016–17	2017–18	2018–19	2019–20	2020–21
Gross Sale	7,843,804	9,211,067	9,128,331	13,761,702	11,190,413	13,595,431	14,564,110	14,509,449	14,350,602	13,744,959	14,109,186	11,444,933
Member Earnings	3,180,656	2,827,000	3,670,065	4,715,741	4,770,235	5,412,669	8,381,304	6,202,793	6,272,053	4,594,045	5,600,500	4,064,323
Total Expenses	7,734,720	9,103,463	8,969,557	13,572,395	10,930,437	13,333,901	14,349,803	14,333,376	14,315,143	13,708,822	14,037,076	11,332,550
Profit Before Tax	109,084	107,604	158,774	189,307	259,976	261,530	214,306	176,073	35,459	36,137	72,109	112,383
Income Tax Paid	35,333	36,443	61,846	58,496	70,099	91,081	64,590	62,689	20,575	9,000	18,748	30,073
Profit After Tax	73,751	71,161	96,928	130,811	189,877	170,449	149,716	113,384	14,884	27,137	53,361	82,310
Share Capital	167,780	170,800	170,800	170,800	215,880	215,880	215,880	215,880	215,880	215,880	215,880	215,880
Reserves and Surplus	1,700,471	1,844,112	3,004,540	3,167,402	3,343,648	3,514,097	3,659,948	3,773,332	3,788,216	3,815,353	3,868,715	3,951,025
Long-Term Liabilities	–	–	–	–	–	–	–	–	–	–	–	–
Debt from SHGs	253,000	235,140	–	–	–	–	–	–	–	–	–	–
Fixed Assets and Investments	532,237	1,036,399	917,887	772,087	794,693	656,004	540,798	613,300	327,102	264,003	231,301	559,089
Current Liabilities	2,067,150	3,288,025	2,306,997	2,146,423	2,143,751	2,314,281	3,536,763	3,689,499	4,336,587	3,456,495	3,670,968	3,231,121
Current Assets	3,664,247	4,504,504	4,561,950	4,710,038	4,874,867	5,381,754	6,810,445	6,996,241	7,945,266	7,140,997	7,440,015	6,433,791
PBT/Revenue	1.39	1.17	1.74	1.38	2.32	1.92	1.47	1.21	0.25	0.26	0.51	0.98
Debt-Equity Ratio	0.14	0.12	N.A	N.A	N.A	N.A	N.A	N.A	N.A	N.A	N.A	N.A
Debt to Asset Ratio	0.06	0.04	N.A	N.A	N.A	N.A	N.A	N.A	N.A	N.A	N.A	N.A
Current Ratio (Current Assets/ Current Liabilities)	1.77	1.37	1.98	2.19	2.27	2.33	1.93	1.90	1.83	2.07	2.03	1.99

The major challenge for Umang in times to come would be to increase the gross sales while maintaining the earnings to sales ratio to deliver benefit and utility to a larger number of members. This would also necessitate creation of a larger reserve for funding resilience activities in the expectation of extreme weather events such as floods and droughts. In October 2021, just about when the Covid situation was easing, the rainfall and floods ravaged the area, and the damage was widespread leading to a major setback to the Umang and its members.

8. Dignity is everything

Umang has a stated mission of empowering mountain women through provision of sustainable livelihoods options to improve their quality of life. Umang as an example of gender-inclusive social enterprise has encouraged and enabled self-reliance, courage, and independence. Over the years, members have started to value their lives, and almost 40% have opted for life insurance coverage for themselves and their families. Dialogues with visitors, exposure visits, and market interactions have led the members to go beyond Umang and connect with the larger ecosystem in a more meaningful manner.

Women have traditionally been more confined to home and farms, and slowly Umang became the new home to enable their engagement with market, organisation's office, training centres, SHG meeting spaces, banks leading to the creation of a new identity as a Umang shareholder as these gendered spaces allow her engagement and evolution. Umang's product line has been developed in order to create value out of what they could do by building their professional skills which in turn has enabled for them to build an identify for themselves with such work

As Talat, an employee of Umang, states, "institutions don't push you to do something, they only create the environment that enables action towards a particular goal."

Some sentiments of empowerment, as viewed by those who are impacted, point towards the centrality of collectives as a necessary ecosystem support for impacting quality of life. Change in self-perception is a transformation experienced due to this collective strength. Almost 10% of its members are playing a leadership role in different ongoing development programmes in their respective villages/areas. With awareness comes the feeling of self- reliance too as echoed by Bimla and Jyoti:

> Earlier we hesitated. For our own work we had to depend on others. Sometimes I would give the paperwork for my pension to the Pradhan. They would say we will do it tomorrow and it wouldn't get done. Now we are highly aware, and we do the work ourselves. If we go ourselves and do the work, the work happens quickly.

Bimla was also elected as the village Pradhan, and she acknowledges the support of her group. She said, "Through the group I became the Pradhan as well. The members told me that I can do it." Today there are nine other members currently playing the role of Gram Pradhans, and 68 others are engaged in different roles in Panchayati raj institutions and other social development programmes of the state government.

Fatima who lives in a semi-urban area near Ranikhet said that while she used to go out earlier as well, going out to do SHG-related work has given her new confidence.

Shabnam's children admire their working mother because she is the only woman in their family and extended family who works outside the home boundaries. This sense of pride in the coming generations creates hope for changes in the patriarchal society. Radha takes care of her parents and in-laws after her husband's death. In the society where there is a preference for male child, Radha is the new son. She is breaking certain myths by taking all responsibilities.

Munni Devi said that after associating with Umang she gained multiple perspectives about what is right or wrong. During this process, she developed a friendly relationship with her daughter. She ensured her quality education and later fulfilled her daughter's desire to marry the boy of her choice. It is the 'power within' that led her to consider herself right and entitled to make that decision. Daughter of Durgeshwari Devi from village Damtola has given wings to her ambitions and is an accomplished nurse today. Another cluster leader related her son's desire to be like his mother as she was the bread-earner in the family.

All these experiences indicate that women use their agency to rework their power relations. As one of the members suggests 'dignity is everything'. Opportunity and capability to be able to take decisions that matter in their lives are empowerment as expressed by many others.

Umang as a community-owned enterprise with a people-centric approach as active partners and not beneficiaries, valuing their knowledge and ground realities, has been instrumental in building the foundations. Team Umang is actively engaging in sharing its experiences with other stakeholders within the state and in other parts of the Indian Himalayan region wanting to set up producer organisations. Providing opportunities for study tours and mentoring women leaders through Training of Trainers programmes is an ongoing process now. Seeing is believing and a critical learning tool for women farmers wanting to form collectives for economic empowerment.

8

KRISHI BAGWANI SWAWLAMBI SAHAKARI SAMITI LIMITED

Adaptive management and convergence in an all-women tribal collective

Gautam Prateek, Pranamesh Kar, and Debanjan Ghatak

1. Introduction

Krishi Bagwani Swawlambi Sahakari Samiti Limited (KBSSSL) is located in the tribal-dominated, forested, and mineral-rich, but relatively underdeveloped[1] Gumla district in southwest Jharkhand. Forests cover roughly 25.6% of the total available land (NIC-Gumla, 2021), and the scheduled tribes constitute around 68% of the total population in Gumla (Census, 2011). Gumla is predominantly rural (95%) and is home to larger tribal groups such as *Oraons* (47%), *Mundas* (21%), and *Khariyas* (16%), as well as particularly vulnerable tribal groups (PVTGs) like *Asur*, *Korva*, and *Birijia*, among others (Chatterjee et al., 2016; PRADAN, 2017).

In the colonial era, this region engendered active participation in the independence movement, mostly around the rights of the natives to the land and forests in the region. Importantly, the creation of the state of Jharkhand in 2000 (from Bihar) was majorly built on the demands for greater recognition of culture, customs, and traditions of the native tribes inhabiting Jharkhand.

Livelihoods in Gumla comprise agriculture (including livestock), daily wages, mining, and collection of forest produce (Chatterjee et al., 2016; PRADAN, n.d.). Subsistence rain-fed agriculture[2] is predominant, where paddy, wheat, and maize are the main cereal crops, while *arhar* and *urad* in pulses, and groundnut, linseed, and mustard in oilseeds are majorly cultivated in this region. With significant forest cover, rural livelihoods in Gumla also include considerable use of diverse forest produce, for both subsistence and sale (NABARD, 2017).[3]

A major livelihood challenge in this tribal-dominated district is posed by low productivity and returns from rain-fed agriculture, considered as one of

DOI: 10.4324/9781003308034-8

the drivers of out-migration to other states and districts within the state of Jharkhand (Census, 2011; PRADAN, n.d.). On the brighter side, the agro-climatic conditions in Gumla are considered suitable for horticultural crops, like mango, guava, and litchi among the fruits and a variety of vegetable crops (NABARD, 2017).

Professional Assistance for Development Action (PRADAN) had been working on watershed development and livelihood promotion through live-stock management since the late 1990s, and it was keen to form a cooperative in the area (Tiwary, 2010). Although the community had an adverse experience of collectives due to financial fraud in the "chit-fund groups," the mentorship by PRADAN executives, particularly the initial exposure trips to other cooperatives, significantly assuaged the reluctance.

Established in 2003, KBSSSL covers villages from Raidih, Gumla, Palkot, and Ghaghra blocks of Gumla district. The cooperative is connected to the community *via* a three-tier structure, with women federations, or Mahila Vikas Mandals (MVMs), at the apex, the village-level organisations (VOs) in the middle, and the women self-help groups (WSHGs) at the community level. Currently, the major activities performed by KBSSSL are agricultural input supply, output marketing, crop-planning and extension services, as well as grooming of entrepreneurs at the community level (agri-entrepreneurs[4]). Paddy, millets, and pulses in cereals; brinjal, tomato, cabbage, and cauliflower in vegetables; and fruits like watermelon and mango are the major commodities that the collective deals with.

This chapter attempts to highlight the evolution of KBSSSL in the past 19 years, marking a shift from subsistence agriculture to engagement in the dynamic agri-commodity markets. Broadly, we have attempted to capture the incubation process, especially the role played by the promoting organisation. Further, we highlight the role of two critical factors, namely convergence with other development interventions, and adaptations towards sustained engagement with the community. Also, we hope that this chapter will offer insights on tackling some of the challenges faced by a women's collective.

2. Need-based genesis to self-reliance

Through previous livelihood interventions in and around Gumla, the PRADAN team had identified low production of cereals (mainly paddy) and pulses, and a lack of other remunerative livelihood options, as the major determinants of seasonal, distress-induced out-migration in the community (PRADAN, 2017). Besides agriculture, livelihoods in the community comprised wage labour, selling of firewood, and the collection of non-timber forest produce (NTFP) majorly.

In a group meeting, the community members revealed that before the establishment of the collective, most of the households were food sufficient for only half the year due to low crop production.[5] In addition, they also highlighted that the farming households, who had a marketing surplus, were being exploited by the local traders. Consequently, the financial condition of tribal households constrained adequate nutrition, and even the regular schooling of children was a challenge.

In this context, the collective was conceptualised to focus on increasing productivity in agriculture by better extension services and good-quality agri-inputs. Support in the marketing of produce was also planned but kept as a future option in the initial days. The current PRADAN team revealed that to arrive at these interventions, they had consulted the experts and conducted multiple meetings with the community. Market surveys were also conducted to find out the marketing channels for crop inputs and outputs (see Table 8.1 for a timeline of major milestones).

In 2002, the PRADAN team started motivating the women farmers of Palkot to form a collective. Importantly, around two hundred SHGs were already working on financial inclusion (group saving and group lending activity) in the Gumla-Palkot region. Hence, it is from these SHGs that the members of the collective were chosen. Interestingly, the formal registration of the SHG federation happened after the formal registration of KBSSSL.

The initial intervention, via the collective, was planned around the widely cultivated but low-yielding paddy variety. The increase in its production was achievable. Hence, a different high-yielding paddy breed (Lalat) from Odisha was introduced and promoted in the community. Arrangements for better quality and relatively cheaper agri-inputs (seeds, fertilisers, and pesticides, cheaper due to bulk buying) were made concurrently.

In 2003, KBSSSL was registered under the Jharkhand Self-supporting Cooperative Societies Act, 1996. This Act allows more autonomy to the cooperatives by decreasing the role of the state in the appointments and other functions of the collective. The women from the community were elected as the office bearers (president, secretary, and board of directors) to manage the collective. Hence, PRADAN had to work on the initial capacity building of the board members, and they also placed a paid professional as chief executive officer (CEO) of KBSSSL. Till 2011–12, PRADAN supported the CEO's salary, but the lack of funds prevented this appointment in the following years, only to be revived in 2019.

Considering the community's impression of groups (chit fund scams), KBSSSL decided to set up its office campus to increase visibility in the region. The corpus fund of KBSSSL was used for buying the land, and PRADAN provided a grant of Rs. 0.2 million for setting up the campus. After the establishment of the campus in 2006, monthly meetings of board of directors (BoDs) members started taking place within its premises.

The first members of the BoD of KBSSSL are of the opinion that the establishment of a physical campus for the collective contributed towards

Table 8.1 Timeline of major milestones in KBSSSL's journey

Phase	Year	Milestone/Major Event
Inception to Take-Off	**1997 to 2006**	
	1997	PRADAN starts work in Gumla;
	2002	Mobilisation of SHG members for the formal collective;
	2003	KBSSSL established under Jharkhand Self-Supporting Cooperative Societies Act, 1996 with 243 members;
	2003	Input sales to member farmers, and other community members focus on paddy;
	2006	Campus of KBSSSL established in Palkot block and tomato cultivation promotion starts;
Sustained Growth Phase	**2007 to 2013**	
	2009	Convergence with Agricultural Produce Clusters for horticultural products marketing (SGSY);
	2010	Output marketing starts with tomatoes and mangoes;
	2008–13	Phase of growth in profits;
	2013	Funding for CEO withdrawn and profits begin to fall till 2017–18;
Back on Trajectory and More Diversification	**2014 to Present**	
	2016	Kitchen garden under Poshan Vari;
	2017	Solar lift irrigation convergence;
	2018	Funding resumed and profits regained;
	2019	Watermelon cultivation and marketing;
	2020	Funding from Merryl Lynch and Bank of America, application for membership increment;
	2021	Membership at 3,000 (+8,000 likely), turnover at 12 million and net profit 0.94 million.

increasing its credibility in the community. They further mentioned that the major discussions in the BoD meetings in the initial days revolved around saving, lending, agricultural input procurement, and crop planning.

Gradually, PRADAN started supporting KBSSSL with market linkages for the farm produce. This was accomplished by connecting the collective with vendors from Ranchi (90 km), Gaya (220 km), and Bokaro (200 km) in Jharkhand and Bhubaneswar (500 km) and Rourkela (135 km) in Odisha for direct marketing of the farm produce at a better price. Although transportation is a challenge, given the distance, availability of transport, and the road conditions, the aggregation of farm produce, and thus the trading in higher volumes, has attracted vendors/traders. In this model, the PRADAN team explained that member farmers have realised better prices for their produce, and the monopoly of specific traders has decreased.

3. Governance and management

The governance structure of KBSSSL, like any producers' cooperative, comprises the democratically elected BoDs at the apex of decision-making. Further, the operational structure of KBSSSL has been built on its functioning in the initial days, when the cooperative was predominantly dealing with aggregation of demand and distribution of agricultural inputs and package of practices (PoPs).

Any major decision taken by KBSSSL is first discussed among the BoDs. Then, it is passed to the MVM and further relayed to the VO leaders, SHGs, and finally the community. Similarly, from the bottom-up, there is one supervisor for hundred farmers, responsible for consolidating the demands from the community and help KBSSSL in placing orders for agricultural inputs. Once the order is ready with KBSSSL, the supervisors help in doorstep delivery of the inputs and demonstrate its usage and related recommendations (see Figure 8.1).

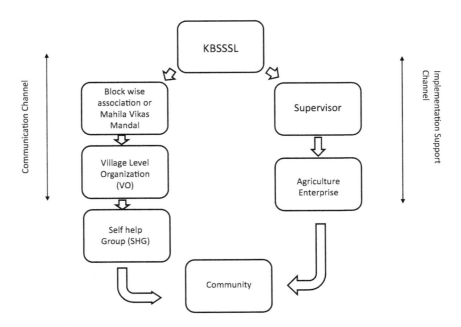

Figure 8.1 Illustrating the flow of communication at KBSSSL

BoD meetings are held once every month or as per the urgency of the matter. These meetings are crucial due to the participation of the BoDs, who act as leaders of their locality and are also members of their respective VOs and SHGs. Decisions on member addition, crop planning, fund mobilisation, purchase and procurement of inputs (seeds, fertilisers, pesticides), subsidy distribution, convergence work, and membership contribution usually take place in these meetings.

Mrs Sukarmuni Dhanwar (current president of KBSSSL) shared, meetings are usually held when they need to buy inputs like seeds, fertilisers, or insecticides. She also emphasised that meetings are held proactively around the time of audits. Further, these meetings are not restricted to exclusive discussions on crop agriculture – the core operation of KBSSSL. Rather, discussions on contingent matters affecting the broader socio-economic well-being also occur. For instance, a BoD member suggested a discussion at KBSSSL around the sale of forest resources in the context of the pandemic-triggered lockdown.

> Last year during the COVID-19 induced lockdown, we discussed how to sell the sal leaf, mahua, char, and sal seeds collected by communities at a remunerative price (if not MSP) and avoid exploitation by local traders.
>
> (BoD member, interview)

The annual general body meeting (AGM) invites all the shareholders to the KBSSSL campus every year to discuss the current status of the cooperative. Suggestions on improving operations and achieving new targets in upcoming times are usually sought in these meetings. In the AGM, all the expenditures and incomes, and the net profit or loss are reported to all the member shareholders. In the last AGM, they decided that the application for increasing formal membership of the collective from around 3,000 to 8,000 will be pursued with the registrar. Accordingly, the application has been made as well.

For the AGM, PRADAN contributes by arranging logistics for members, inviting government officials and elected representatives to the AGM, and demonstrating the field experiences and recommendations to the AGM to follow in future times. Currently, KBSSSL has appointed three office bearers (president, secretary, and treasurer), three production managers, three stock managers, one office assistant, and 45 supervisors for smooth functioning and achieving the vision, mission, and goal of the cooperative.

The rotational leadership for BoD followed in KBSSSL is fairly recent. PRADAN team members put forward three reasons for the same: change of BoDs is a compliance by registrar of cooperative (RoC); it is done to avoid corruption in the cooperative; and, the new BoD is elected so that the women farmer members get the opportunity to play a leadership role in the collective. Presently, the fourth generation of BoDs is serving the collective, but the first set of BoDs had served for a longer time period than required under the rules presently. Once the new BoD member joins, their training on general office management, financial management, operational modalities, and so on is done. Currently, efforts are on towards making a standard operating procedure (SOP) for operations as well as the financial management at KBSSSL.

4. Business model of KBSSSL

Over the years, KBSSSL has procured the required licenses for selling seeds, fertilisers, and insecticides from the government. It provides a PoP to the community members through supervisors (community resource persons – CRPs). The PoP contains seeds, fertiliser, insecticide, and a manual of use. This helps farmers to remember when to apply what ingredient and in what quantity, along with access to the recommended ingredients. The supervisor not only delivers the PoP but also demonstrates its usage to the community members.

In addition, services like storing, sorting, grading, cleaning, ripening, and marketing of mango, watermelon, peanut, ginger, and tomato are also being done by KBSSSL. At present, around 198 villages in Palkot, Basia, and Kamda block are serviced by the collective. Over the years, KBSSSL has attempted to intervene across the entire value chain: starting from timely supply of agri-inputs initially in 2003 to buying/selling the farmer's produce at fair prices starting in 2010–11.

The current PRADAN team maintains that ensuring member farmers about certain benefits from the collective is paramount in sustaining collective action. Following the same, KBSSSL attempts to assure 40,000–50,000 (INR) per year farm income for the members, if the recommended practices are followed in 60 decimals of land (Sutar and Ghatak, 2013). Back of the envelope calculations in a meeting at Gudma village also revealed Rs. 40,000 per year as income (and Rs. 12,000 as cost) under specific conditions, namely access to two acres of land so that 0.24 hectare could be spared for horticultural crops; three crops in the year; and average market and weather conditions for the crops grown.

Illustrative examples of two crops might help elucidate this a bit. In the case of watermelon, in 0.04 hectare land, watermelon is cultivated. In that case, around 10 gm seeds, 1 ton of vermicompost, nitrogen-phosphorus-potash (NPK), Ektara, Trichoderma, farmyard manure (FYM), di-ammonium phosphate (DAP), and urea is required. KBSSSL sells the PoP kit of watermelon at a price point of Rs. 4,000 to farmers. This package helps in the safe and quality harvest of 6 kg/plant from 1,000 plants in 0.04 hectares of land. The minimum market price of the watermelon harvest is Rs. 28,000, which farmers receive once the traders receive the watermelon.

Similarly, in the case of tomato cultivation in 0.12 hectare of land, the agricultural input package (POP) costs Rs. 12,000 to farmers. When cultivated following the advised timeline under the guidance of a community resource person, or the agricultural entrepreneur, tomato gives a rough profit of around Rs. 48,000, which is four times the initial investment done (omitting labour cost).

Also, there are persons at the village level, who receive an honorarium to train and handhold the farmers. These village resource persons, or agricultural entrepreneurs, support crop planning, agricultural input demand planning, weeding, harvesting, and other activities. After the crop planning is done, a PoP is given to agriculture entrepreneurs. She facilitates raising nursery beds, transplantation of saplings, weeding, and the application of fungicides, insecticides, and necessary fertilisers. Even the member farmers work in groups, helping each other to follow the recommended practices. The supervisors monitor the work of agriculture entrepreneurs and finally help in bulk sales of the harvests at the farm gate (see Figure 8.2).

When the revenue from a harvest is accrued, a part of the amount earned is used for rotation for other seasonal crop farming in the village to ensure that every member farmer of the community gets a chance to earn from farming and understands the improved agronomic practices. Thus, the land is cultivated round the year to ensure continuous income generation.

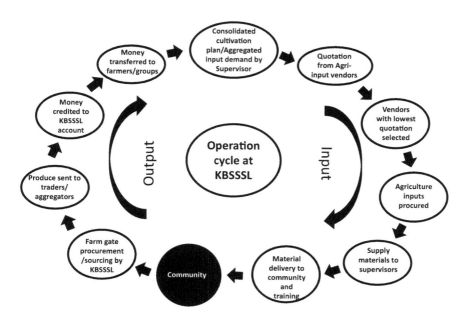

Figure 8.2 Illustrating the operational model for agri-inputs and outputs at KBSSSL

Perhaps, this is the "theory of change" followed by PRADAN, where the members grow cereals (increased productivity) along with horticultural crops (high value and productivity) following the recommended agronomic practices round the year (Sutar and Ghatak, 2013). This diversification, supported by increased productivity, is assumed to generate viable income under normal market conditions.

4.1 Agricultural input and output dynamics at KBSSSL

KBSSSL majorly deals with agricultural input sales, technical support, and marketing of farm produce of the community. As per the latest available data, a total turnover of 12 million (INR) was realised, of which the output sales amounted to roughly 23%, while the rest came from input sales. This translated into a gross profit of 1.65 million (INR) and a net profit of 0.94 million (INR). The cooperative has set up a full-fledged agricultural input store on its campus, comprising good quality seeds, fertilisers, insecticides, pesticides, fungicides, and farm mechanisation devices like sprayers. These products are sold to farmers (both members and non-members) at lower prices (relative to market price), and guidance/training is given on its usage in the field.

KBSSSL, with support from PRADAN, distributes the PoP of different crops through a channel that ensures sowing of seeds at the right time and the tilling, application of fertilisers, and spraying of insecticide at the right intervals. This ensures an estimated harvest, and then farmers can choose from among the following three options for sale of produce: (1) sale at the farm gate (pre-decided price), instant direct payment by vendor decided by KBSSSL; (2) sale at farm gate (pre-decided price) to local vendor decided by KBSSSL, and payment via KBSSSL after 3–4 days; and (3) produce sent to vendor via KBSSSL, and vendor pays after selling the produce. The third option is usually the case when there is glut in the market (Sutar and Ghatak, 2013). The following quote from a KBSSSL member illustrates the point.

> We get seeds, fertilizer, insecticides, and technical inputs . . . output is sent to traders from the farm gate itself, and money is either credited to our accounts, or we are instantly paid at the farm gate.
>
> (Gitni Kumari, member farmer
> from Gudma village, interview).

The drop in profits after 2012–13, nearly by 93.12% in 2013–14, was attributed to the lack of a full-time CEO to manage the collective. At the same time, this downfall cannot be completely attributed to the withdrawal of the CEO but the input market too. Previously, quality agricultural input unavailability in the region was a major issue, but later on the local market has seen the entry of private local players. Also, the demand for output marketing of

Table 8.2 illustrating the financials of KBSSSL

KBSSSL Financial Details

S. No.	Particulars	2012–13	2013–14	2014–15	2015–16	2016–17	2017–18	2018–19	2019–20	2020–21
1	Total revenue	1,161,453.5	4,124,552.8	3,800,742.7	6,704,536	4,519,066	2,058,857	3,588,960	11,683,441.2	16,716,037.4
2	Total expense	7,786,725.2	3,104,741	3,086,062	5,834,469	3,823,699	1,151,309	2,576,810	8,843,377.71	11,767,957.4
3	Profit before tax	901,662.5	49,687.5	148,652.5	258,118.8	181,188	139,404	482,022	–289,430.89	1,283,834.1
4	Profit after tax	982,936.3	49,687.5	148,652.5	258,118.8	181,188	139,404	482,022	–289,430.8	1,283,834.1
5	Share capital	213,200	215,500	220,700	231,800	233,200	233,200	239,800	245,500	245,400
6	Reserve surplus	2,123,570.4	2,173,257.9	2,321,910.4	2,580,029.3	2,751,582	2,890,986	3,361,849	3,362,349.2	6,187,725.2
7	Fixed asset incl. investment	575,723.8	556,544.5	542,359.1	518,691.4	598,419	574,480	556,677	540,920.1	552,963.8
8	Current liabilities	51,624.5	225,823.5	102,408	73,433	163,753	233,094	54,160	186,203	45,556.2
9	Current assets	1,747,610.2	1,777,018.7	2,069,065.7	2,046,936.1	1,358,155	1,855,819	1,812,136	536,372.1	301,797.6

agricultural produce increased during that period to which KBSSSL could not accommodate with lack of committed leadership for a few years.

However, the financial statements also show a sustained rise in net profits after the financial year 2017–18. The rebound in profits was not possible until a professional CEO was appointed again to look after the business operations at KBSSSL in 2017–18 by PRADAN. With the latest data compared to the base year of 2007–08, the profit figures have risen by 1,017% (or roughly ten times).

5. Ecosystem and role of PRADAN

The ecosystem around the community shows the actors connected with the member farmers at KBSSSL and PRADAN as the central connecting node. Beginning with input and output dealers to academic and research institutions, and various government agencies, PRADAN has attempted to link these with the community to benefit member farmers. Even the linkage with banks *via* the SHGs that takes care of the financial needs of the collective has been an outcome of mobilisation by PRADAN.

PRADAN has a plan to withdraw at a point where the community earns 80,000–90,000 (INR) per year from farming. SHGs and VOs are the instruments of KBSSSL to communicate and implement activities in the community. The funds required by KBSSSL for its operations have been mobilised from the State Rural Livelihood Mission (SRLM) promoting SHGs, VOs, and CLFs as loans. These funds are the community institution development fund (CIF) and the revolving fund (RF). Through rotation of funds, the community funds earn interest and grow faster too.

Recently, in partnership with the KVK, a newly grafted tomato variety has been purchased by KBSSSL. This variety is suitable for the agro-ecological region and is high yielding and climate-resilient as well. The technology costs 10,000 (INR) and 2% of the sale value of the harvest per year. Also, improved seeds for groundnut and watermelon from National Seed

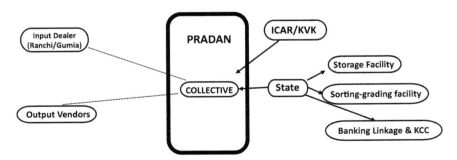

Figure 8.3 Illustrating the ecosystem evolving around KBSSSL

Corporation (NSC) have been procured periodically due to their suitability and high yielding traits.

The supply of mango in the market was observed to be less in the district market through market survey, so the PRADAN team contacted subject matter experts and found out that less supply was due to less interest of the community in mango plantation. Further, when the community was asked about low production, reasons like the difficulty in the timely spray of fungicides, the workload at the household level, and lack of financial capital emerged. Thereafter, multiple group meetings were organised around whether a cooperative could be a solution for the problems. Through a participatory process, the community members were convinced about the scope of improved agronomic practices in mango cultivation.

In 2007, KBSSSL started Amrapali mango farming, and 2011 was the first year of mango marketing by KBSSSL. Furthermore, the PRADAN team shared, mango is cultivated in around 1,800 acres in Palkot and Basia blocks. Around 2,500 MT of mangoes are produced, and one acre on average gives 60,000 to 80,000 (INR) to the farmers, subject to normal weather and market rates. KBSSSL sells around 20% of the produce and earned around 60,000 (INR) from the mango sales this year.

In 2020, PRADAN's research team found out that the watermelons could be cultivated in the land of Palkot, which has a substantial demand during Eid-ul-Fitr. Upon discussion with KBSSSL and the community, watermelon cultivation was executed on a commercial scale. This strategic move was profitable as the cultivating community earned a relatively better income within a shorter interval of time than other crops.

Through an annual general meeting (AGM) in 2020, the BoDs got approval for membership addition of up to 8,000 from the registrar of cooperatives (ROC), Gumla. Due to constraints on the kind of relations that non-members can have with the collective as per the Jharkhand Self-Supporting Cooperative Societies Act, expanding the membership will be instrumental in offering complete services to the more interested community members.

6. Convergence of interventions

PRADAN has attempted different convergence activities at KBSSSL to promote and support livelihoods in the community. It manages two types of convergence activity: one, within PRADAN; and two, convergence with government line departments. Through the former, the members have obtained individual and community-managed poultry and goat farms, which have created a diversified portfolio of livelihood for a significant number of community members. Essentially, PRADAN has attempted to merge many of its livelihood interventions (namely overlapping membership in poultry cooperative, lift-irrigation pumps) into this collective. In this context, it is vital to note that the substantial success of a poultry cooperative in the same region, with a significant overlap of membership with KBSSSL, is also contributing towards livelihood augmentation and, consequently, risk minimisation for the members. PRADAN established the Gumla Gramin Poultry Co-operative Society Ltd. (GGPCS) in 2002, covering Palkot, Raidih, and Gharha block, and with a membership of 795 drawn from 17 villages. Similar to KBSSSL, the members of this poultry collective come from the existing SHGs that PRADAN had been supporting for decades now. The cooperative deals with broiler poultry and has its own feed plant. A federation of ten such poultry cooperatives has been established, called the Jharkhand Women's Poultry Self-Supporting Co-operative Federation Ltd. This federation now captures 20% of the market share of live birds in Jharkhand and recently achieved a net profit of Rs. 79 million.

Likewise, through convergence with government line departments, individual household, and community-managed solar and motor-pump-based irrigation systems, vegetable sorting and grading centres, storage houses, fencing, and other construction materials, watershed management structures, concession on electricity usage, new types of seeds/saplings, and so on. have been made possible.

Recently, KBSSSL has received 1,000 vegetable stocking crates, weeders, and spraying tools at a subsidised price from NABARD. Indian Council of Agriculture Research (ICAR) Ranchi unit has been helping in new variety agro-horticultural plant innovation. KBSSSL has worked with different governmental departments like Department of Agriculture; Animal Husbandry & Co-operative; Department of Drinking Water and Sanitation; Department of Forest, Environment & Climate Change; Department of Women, Child Development & Social Security; Department of Water Resources; Department of Scheduled Tribe, Scheduled Caste, Minority; and Backward Class Welfare. Being a prominent cooperative in Palkot, district administration recognises and considers the submissions and plea of KBSSSL for the well-being of the community.

7. Impacts

The region had a different identity ten years ago, but now, the collective members claim that the area is well known for vegetables and mangoes in the local markets. To illustrate, there is a special mango fair of mangoes (*Aam ka mela, Aam ki shaadi*) that is being observed by the local community regularly since the increase in mango production in the past few years. Basanti Tete (member farmer from Gudma village), pointing at a fruiting mango tree, says:

> This is my pension tree . . . even if my children and grandchildren do not take care of me in old age . . . this plant will pay me through its good fruits.
>
> (interview)

A similar change can be observed in tomato and paddy cultivation due to improved agronomic practices and fair returns via better market linkages. That during the rainy season, tomatoes do not grow was a myth in the village, as per the community members. Timely seed delivery and farming training have allowed multiple villages to produce tomatoes for subsistence as well as cash income. The following quote by a community member illustrates the same.

> Earlier, through 40 kg of paddy we used to obtain 5–6 bags of paddy (each 40 kg), and now we get 10–15 bags from only 1 kg of paddy. During July-August we never used to even see tomatoes, leave alone cultivating it. Now, we have tomatoes almost round the year. Isn't this a benefit of creating a cooperative?
>
> Radha Devi, member farmer from Gudma village (interview)

Adopting new techniques of agriculture is also observed in the collective members. For example, *Machaan-kheti* (three-tier farming), popular with farmers in West Bengal, is gradually being adopted by the farmers in Gumla. Another change has been seen in terms of the consumption pattern of the community. Previously, they used to have rice and finger millet as staple food, but now there is a diversity of vegetables on their platter. A quote from a community member brings this out clearly, as given here.

> Earlier we would rarely have meals with vegetables. It was only the rice broth, or at the most one vegetable. These days, we have some disposable income, so we can afford two vegetables in our meals often.
>
> Teresa Kerketa, member farmer from Gudma village (interview)

Also, the women of the community, who earlier had a minor role in household decision-making, are now participating in the significant decisions of the households, especially decisions around where to farm, what to cultivate, and where to sell. The office bearers of the collective shared in a group discussion that when the women started contributing to household income, the family members also started to accept them as decision-makers. Some resistance from the older-generation male and female members, especially mothers-in-law, was encountered. Nevertheless, seeing the trend of more extensive participation of women at the community level, changes began to emerge.

> Men used to run the household earlier, but now the women are doing it . . . through us, income is coming from crop agriculture as well as poultry . . . in this sense, women are the head-of-the-household nowadays.
>
> Teresa Kerketa, member farmer from Gudma village (interview)

The rise in collective action at the community level was apparent in the Gudma village, where Sunita Dungdung shared that they never do farming alone. Instead, the members of the cooperative contribute collectively to the labour demanded in each other's land. The ownership of the produce remains with the landowner, but the group helps with labour and technical inputs.

Currently, the KBSSSL has a campus with a sorting-grading facility, a storage hall, a meeting hall, an office-cum-agri-input sales centre in its Palkot campus near the block office. It has hired one full-time accountant, stock manager, and contractual supervisor for the smooth functioning of the works.

Also, when a significant social structure emerged under KBSSSL, the village women members of Gudma proudly shared their experience about how they thwarted the production and consumption of *handia* (local liquor), which negatively affected their village. After the SHG members intruded and warned two of the villagers who used to indulge in country liquor processing and selling, the activity stopped.

8. Concluding thoughts

The experiences garnered in mobilising and training women members for active participation and leadership roles in the collective need academic and policy attention. In this context, both the PRADAN team and community members concurred that increasing participation and nurturing leadership have not been easy. Crucially, it has entailed co-opting male members in the community as opposed to alienating them. Woven in gender relations, these transformations call for changes in values, norms, and beliefs. Put broadly, a cultural shift is needed, which takes time and solidarity of all the stakeholders. Moreover, the way this has been achieved to a reasonable extent in this collective, as evident in the confident BoDs, is through a mix of persuasion and confrontation without alienating the males.

The business turnover of KBSSSL was 10.54 million (INR), and it obtained 1.04 million (INR) as net profit in the year 2019–20, which was thrice the previous year. In 2020–21, the cooperative's turnover was 13.5 million (INR) in 2020–21, where roughly 75% of the amount is from input sales. Now, what does this high reliance on input sales, including chemical inputs, mean for both the financial and ecological sustainability is a critical question.

In 2020, a sum of 2.5 million (INR) was approved to be spent on KBSSSL by PRADAN. This support is for the first time given by the funding agencies, namely, Merryl Lynch & Bank of America to revive the operations of KBSSSL. A significant development that KBSSSL is planning involves creating a permanent cadre of paid professionals who will act as an interface between the PRADAN team and the community members. There are plans to extend the solar water-pump-based irrigation in every village through convergence with the "Jharkhand Opportunities for Harnessing Rural Growth Project (JOHAR)," a World Bank–funded programme through the Water Resource Development Department.

Till the recent past, KBSSSL had not received any financial support from the government, but the local government has helped with storage facilities, and convergence with various schemes meant for agriculture and development has been crucial. Since inception, PRADAN has been supporting the capacity building of BoDs and member farmers, while also helping in creation of linkages with markets, financial institutions, government, academic institutions, and other stakeholders. In order to facilitate bookkeeping and the simple transfer of fertiliser payments to farmers, it has also introduced accounting software Tally, and 'fertiliser DBT' software, respectively. Although the present BoDs are the fourth generation and expressed confidence in the ongoing work, it remains to be seen how sustainable the collective will be after PRADAN's exit.

Notes

1 Rich in minerals, the district struggles in case of human development with a poverty ratio at 74.75%, literacy at 64%, and the infant mortality and the maternal mortality rate are 18 per thousand and 3.8 per thousand respectively (NIC-Gumla, 2021).
2 Net irrigated area as percent of net cultivated area is 6.7% (NIC-Gumla, 2021).
3 See https://www.nabard.org/demo/auth/writereaddata/tender/2110161402JHA_Gumla.3-7.pdf
4 Agri Entrepreneur (AE): one AE per 4–5 gram panchayats works like a vendor to KBSSSL. Mostly, the AE raises nursery beds for various agricultural and horticultural crops. An AE earns a remuneration of 20 paisa per sapling from KBSSSL. Both male and female progressive farmers are engaged as AEs in the regions.
5 See Chatterjee et al. (2016).

References

Bhattacharya, S, Kerketta, P & Dangi, H (2018). Achieving sustainable livelihood promotion through strategic stakeholders' engagement: A case study of Gumla Gramin Poultry Co-operative Society Ltd. *Vilakshan: The XIMB Journal of Management*, 15(1), 89–104.
Census of India (2011). *Village and town-wise primary census abstract (PCA) Vol (XII-B)*. Gumla: Directorate of Census Operations.
Chatterjee, K, Sinha, RK, Kundu, AK, Shankar, D, Gope, R, Nair, N & Tripathy, PK (2016). Social determinants of inequities in under-nutrition (weight-for-age) among under-5 children: A cross sectional study in Gumla district of Jharkhand, India. *International Journal for Equity in Health*, 15(1), 1–9.
IIAB-ICAR (n.d.). *Small input – Large gain intervention in tribal village*. Retrieved from https://iiab.icar.gov.in/icar_highlights/small-input-large-gain-intervention-in-tribal-village/
Manoharlal, M (1972). *The nagbanshis and the cheros*. New Delhi: Oxford Printcraft India Pvt Ltd. Retrieved from https://archive.org/stream/in.ernet.dli.2015.119550/2015.119550.The-Nagbanshis-And-The-Cheros_djvu.txt

National Bank for Agriculture and Rural Development (NABARD) (2017). *Executive summary: PLP 2016–17 – Gumla*. Retrieved from https://www.nabard.org/demo/auth/writereaddata/tender/2110161402JHA_Gumla.3-7.pdf

National Informatics Centre-Government of Jharkhand (2021). *About District Gumla*. Retrieved from https://gumla.nic.in/

PRADAN (2017). *South chhotanagpur development cluster (SDCC)*. Retrieved from https://www.pradan.net/wp-content/uploads/2017/02/South-Chhotanagpur-Development-Cluster-SCDC.pdf

PRADAN (n.d.). Goat rearing: A livelihood opportunity for rural women in Jharkhand. *Power-Point Slides*. Retrieved from http://www.sapplpp.org/files-repository/information-hub/bhubaneswar-regional-workshop-presentations/rp-pradan-gumla/at_download/file

Sutar, NC & Ghatak, D (2013). *Agriculture production cluster: Breaking the market hegemony in Gumla*. Retrieved from https://www.pradan.net/sampark/wp-content/uploads/2019/07/Agriculture-Production-Cluster-Breaking-the-Market-Hegemony-in-Gumla-.pdf

Tiwary, R (2010). *Community lift irrigation systems in Gumla District, Jharkhand*. Retrieved from https://www.pradan.net/sampark/wp-content/uploads/2019/08/Community-Lift-Irrigation-Systems-in-Gumla-District-Jharkhand.pdf

9

IS THE AMUL MODEL POSSIBLE IN PULSES? THE CASE OF HASNABAD FARMERS SERVICES PRODUCER COMPANY LIMITED

Ajit Kanitkar and C. Shambu Prasad

1. Beginning of the HFSPC: promotional grant from SFAC to ALC India in 2011

Access Livelihoods Consulting (ALC) India was founded by alumni of the Institute of Rural Management Anand (IRMA) Krishna Gopal and Satya Dev in 2005. They were later joined by fellow alumni Madhu Murthy and Sarat Kumar, all of them had worked in different development organisations such as Mulkanoor Dairy, Cooperative Development Foundation (CDF), and Society for Elimination of Rural Poverty in erstwhile Andhra Pradesh (now in Telangana). Blending technical and managerial expertise, ALC aims to assist the economically marginalised communities through building livelihoods that are more stable, rewarding, and sustainable. In 2011, ALC responded to the Expression of Interest (EOI) of the Small Farmers' Agribusiness Consortium (SFAC) of the Department of Agriculture of the Government of India and was empanelled as an agency for the promotion of FPCs for the states of Andhra Pradesh (now Telangana and Andhra Pradesh), Karnataka, Maharashtra, Kerala, and Tamil Nadu.

In Telangana's Kodangal Mandal of Vikarabad district, ALC proposed to promote three all-women farmer producer companies (FPCs) namely Kodangal, Angadi Raichur, and Hasnabad Farmers Services Producer Company Limited. The promotional grant support for the formation of the producer company was finalised by SFAC at Rs. 1,800 per farmer for 2.5 years under National Food Security Mission-Accelerated Pulses Production Programme (NFSM-A3P). Each FPC was designed to have a membership base of 1,500 members, going by ALC's criterion, even though SFAC's guidelines recommended 1,000 members. At about 1,500 women farmer members from eight to ten contiguous villages, the total promotional cost per FPC sanctioned by SFAC amounted to about Rs. 1.4 million a year.

DOI: 10.4324/9781003308034-9

1.1 HFSPC: women-owned FPC in rain-fed subsistence agriculture region

HFSPC was one of the three FPCs in the Kodangal areas that ALC proposed to SFAC. Kodangal, in Vikarabad district, is 114 km from Hyderabad, and the entire region is rain-fed. The predominantly small and marginal farmers have rocky landholdings, the actual farmed land less than the landholdings. Red gram has been traditionally grown as a monocrop rather than as part of a mixed cropping system. Productivity is stagnant, and the rampant use of chemical fertilisers on poor soils has resulted in decreasing land productivity recently. Hasnabad is about 7 km from Kodangal and 30 km from Tandur, a major trading centre for pulses. While SFAC's contract letter was sent to ALC India in June 2011 and a diagnostic study report submitted in July, ALC received the first instalment of the promotional grant support unfortunately after the cropping season in December 2011. The intensive promotional efforts from January 2012 till March 2013 included recruitment of field staff, awareness camps on promotion of FPOs in villages, exposure visits to successful cooperatives and producer collectives in Telangana and Maharashtra, good agricultural practices training, and so on. Farmer Affinity Groups (FAGs) were mobilised, and capacity building programmes were conducted on institution development and productivity enhancement. Promoters were identified among the women members, and a share capital mobilisation drive was launched. Hasnabad Farmers Services Producer Company Limited (HFSPC) was registered on 27h March 2013 with the Registrar of Companies (RoC) office in Hyderabad. ALC consciously proposed to the SFAC that it will form all-women FPC in the region given its mission to work for inclusive development. Using the promotional grant received from SFAC, its team initiated several capacity development programmes for the members of the FPC. This was considered necessary to establish a feeling of ownership among the members of the newly promoted HFSPC.

ALC established a project office in Kodangal and deployed five of its professional staff for promotion of the three producer companies. All necessary compliances needed for the FPC registration were completed. It did extensive mobilisation and preparation in the first two years of the formation of the FPC. In 2013, the promotion phase continued with training of board members and exposure visits to the International Crops Research Institute for the Semi-Arid Tropics (ICRISAT) and the Mulkanoor cooperative. Various licenses to trade and registration with the *mandi* were obtained. The rationale of ALC was that there was a great opportunity that the FPC had to tap. The plans were ambitious, and the ALC aimed to get the FPC to provide a complete bouquet of services for the women farmers at their doorstep. These included soil testing and productivity enhancement through improvements in soil moisture content and soil organic content, both of which are crucial for crop productivity.

2. The three-year business plan: trying various business models

ALC also prepared an elaborate three-year business plan for the HFSPC. The business plan preparation process included a detailed study to understand the value chain and overall business of red gram (*toor*). The study comprised administering a structured questionnaire to 300 women farmers, focused group discussions (FGD) with farmers and village leaders, and talking to the APMC (*mandi*) traders and dal millers. The business plan was discussed with the community leaders. The premise for the business model was

1   Producer-to-consumer (P2C) model is always safer as in trading there are many millers and traders on whom dependency is there. There was risk of payment defaults too.
2   Processing red gram into dal and packaging and selling in retail outlets was more remunerative for the members.
3   Dal being an essential commodity, there is sufficient end market existing in Mahbubnagar and in Hyderabad that could be tapped.

The initial business plan had planned an investment of Rs. 17.8 million towards a dal mill and a warehouse. The turnover for the first year was projected to be Rs. 19.1 million, and by the third year it was projected to be Rs. 87 million with an accrued surplus of Rs. 9.6 million. The business plan also calculated benefits to the farmers. The benefits were owing to reduction in the cost of selling for the farmers, due to efficient procurement and simultaneous enhancement in the share of value to producer, through processing red gram into dal. The translation of the plan on the ground though was significantly different.

2.1 Input aggregation

The board of directors (BoD) decided to start their agri-input shop. In 2014, based on the information collected, they bought the pesticides and fertilisers in demand. In the first three years, the HFSPC made conscious efforts to offer a range of services starting with collective procurement of inputs for agriculture as also collective marketing of red gram. The FPC provided 1,300 bags of di-ammonium phosphate (DAP) in 2015–16, up from 300 bags in 2014–15. The total value of inputs increased to Rs. 1.3 million from Rs. 0.3 million in 2013–14.

The BoD also decided to experiment with bio-pesticides, which they made available at lower prices compared to chemical pesticides. While these services were useful to the farmers, in value terms, financially they did not contribute much to the revenues of the FPC. That year Hasnabad and Angadi Raichur together did Rs. 0.105 million of bio-pesticide business. Due to the drought situation in 2014, chemical pesticides used that year did not show any remarkable results, and the farmers who used bio-pesticides fared better and reduced their costs as well. In 2015, despite adverse climatic conditions, the FPC sold Rs. 0.31 million worth of bio-pesticides.

Another initiative in the first two years was to provide timely information to farmers. Through *Krishidoot*, a mobile-based agricultural knowledge service extended by Reuters Market Light (RML), engaged by SFAC, farmers got 3–5 messages per day on their mobiles on aspects like production, markets, general agricultural news, and so on. The farmers also could call on a toll-free number that provided answers to specific queries. The pilot, however, did not continue.

2.2 Marketing of pulses

The FPC realised the need to be involved in marketing from the beginning. The first year was promising due to participation in the minimum support prices (MSP) procurement. HFSPC was able to procure 1,514 quintals of red gram valued at Rs. 6.2 million and 1,635 quintals of groundnut at Rs. 6.5 million in 2013–14. It was a useful experience for the organisation to interact with the market. Business-wise, it was an unusual year. The Government of India had announced a MSP of Rs. 4,300 per quintal for red gram whereas the open-market price that the traders were offering at the end of harvest in November–December was just about Rs. 3,800–4,000. In such a scenario, members found it beneficial to transact with HFSPC. Besides, another 500 quintals were procured at an open-market price and got processed into dal. HFSPC hired a state-run cooperative (District Cooperative Marketing Society (DCMS)) dal mill in Tandur, about 30 km from Hasnabad to process the red gram. It got the work done in May 2014, paying Rs. 3.50/kg as the processing charges. Processed dal was sold to Hyderabad Agricultural Co-operative Association Ltd and a large trader in May and June 2014. The FPC also dealt with 2,000 quintals of groundnut. It was procured at MSP of Rs. 3,600/quintal whereas open-market price was only Rs. 2,500/quintal. In total, HFSPC had done a business of Rs. 13.543 million (Rs. 6.51 million of red gram and Rs. 7.03 million of groundnut) with SFAC.

Organising MSP activity was the first experience for the HFSPC leadership, its board, and the staff of ALC. There were inordinate delays in ensuring that the MSP operations began in the field with appropriate logistical support for receipt of the commodity, weighing, checking for quality control, packing, and despatch to the warehouses involving coordination with several agencies. ALC professionals and FPC board members took up this burden to ensure better prices for the farmers and in return also earn a commission for the FPC on the entire procurement operations. The buying was done on behalf of the procurement agency hence the financial transactions were not recorded in the books of accounts of the HFSPC (except commission received for this work).

The subsequent year the FPC marketed 714 quintals of red gram (valued at Rs. 3.7 million) for processing at a local dal mill, and this came down to 626 quintals. Interestingly though the value was higher at Rs. 6 million as the price of dal had increased from Rs. 4,300 per quintal in 2013–14 to Rs. 5,225 and Rs. 9,665 in subsequent years. The FPC sold some of the produce and stored the remaining stock at the warehouse hoping to make profits by waiting a little more.

2.3 Unpredictability in MSP operations

Marketing of aggregated commodity like red gram had its challenges. While the MSP procurement of earlier years boosted the morale of the FPC that it can undertake a meaningful intervention on behalf of its members, the situation drastically changed in 2014–15. It became evident in the first three years that HFSPC could *not* plan its business assuming that MSP operations will happen and that its members will need those services. This was largely due to the huge price difference each year in the market price and the MSP announced. In 2013–14, the MSP for red gram was Rs. 4,300/quintal, and the prevailing market price was Rs. 3,800. Farmers wanted the MSP procurement to be organised. The following year, in 2014–15, the situation was reversed, MSP was at Rs. 4,500, and the open market at Rs. 5,200. Farmers preferred to sell in the Tandur APMC market. In 2015–16, the MSP was Rs. 4,800; however, there was a huge surge in both the commodity price and the price for dal in retail, and the market price of red gram at Rs. 11,000 and for processed red gram (dal) was being sold in retail at Rs. 200 a kilogram (Rs. 20,000 /quintal). Table 9.1 indicates the fluctuating prices of red gram in the region over the years.

The market price at the time of the arrival of the new harvest (at an average of Rs. 5,700/quintal) was higher than that of the MSP (Rs. 4,500/quintal).

Table 9.1 MSP, APMC price (Tandur), and retail market price (Hyderabad) for red gram

	Year	Red Gram MSP (Rs./kg)	Red Gram APMC Price (Rs./kg)	Red Gram Retail Market Price (Rs./kg)
1	2012	38.50	40.88	66.91
2	2013	43.00	34.60	68.75
3	2014	43.50	36.28	77.50
4	2015	46.25	82.55	131.66
5	2016	50.50	97.58	109.25
6	2017	54.50	59.25	69.16
7	2018	56.75	59.22	72.16

Source: Discussions during field interactions with the FPC staff

Farmers were thus not interested in MSP procurement of their produce. HFSPC agreed to supply red gram to a miller (Farmer Pulses Private Limited) in Bidar, a decision affected by the lack of availability of working capital and growing interest of the members due to timely payments the previous year. Payments for the first few consignments were paid in full, the trader/miller making online payment when the stock was received.

However, after about a month or so, the post-dated cheque given by the same trader/miller was dishonoured by the bank as there was no adequate balance in his account. Unfortunately, the stocks were already dispatched. The HFSPC thus was caught in a situation that its stock sold worth over Rs. 5.7 million with a threat of almost Rs. 3 million potentially turning into bad debts. After almost three months of follow-up and visit by ALC and HFSPC board to Bidar, this money due to the HFSPC was recovered without interest.

2.4 Direct sales to consumers

In 2015–16, the HFSPC sold one truckload of red gram to Safe Harvest Private Limited (SHPL), a Bengaluru-based private marketing company that promoted zero-pesticide products procured from farmers in the dryland regions. SHPL placed an order worth Rs. 1.9 million for the bio-pesticide-sprayed processed red gram, at the highest market rate then prevalent. SHPL had given 50% advance towards procurement and made the payment within 15 days of delivery. It placed a repeat order for one more truck load. However, due to the consignment failing to meet the SHPL standards (prescribed chemical residue limits), it returned the entire consignment. HFSPC had no option but to take back the stock from the SHPL dealer in Hyderabad. However, an opportunity to store red gram in a warehouse, financed through a warehouse receipt loan, came to HFSPC. In April 2016, the producer company had a stock of 30 tons in the warehouse pledged to the Ratnakar Bank Limited.

The first three years are the foundation years of any business enterprise. The progress made in these three years subsequently can become a launching pad for that enterprise to achieve its vision and objectives. The converse is also true. Any setbacks might create huge obstacles for the business to recover in time. Unfortunately, despite the concerted promotional efforts and plans to tap opportunities, the performance of the HFSPC was not encouraging as reflected in the profit and loss statements and the balance sheets for the financials of the FPC since its inception presented in Table 9.2.

The promotional grant that SFAC gave was drying up. ALC was forced to withdraw five of its professionals placed in Kodangal project area, responsible for the promotion of three FPCs. Mr Vaseem, field staff of ALC and a resident of the area, was the lone supervisor responsible for supporting the three FPCs. The three HFSPC women staff were just beginning to understand

Table 9.2 Financial performance of HFSPC over the years

Particulars	2012–13	2013–14	2014–15	2015–16	2016–17	2017–18	2018–19	2019–20	2020–21
Total Revenue	8,149	342,144	166,595	8,799,992	72,651,776	3,567,056	1,460,082	1,457,000	34,612
Total Expenses	5,320	308,458	165,595	8,868,609	71,675,707	4,022,901	3,468,365	1,793,391	1,374,062
Profit Before Tax	2,829	7,686	5,399	(75,208)	(1,524,897)	(973,676)	(2,008,904)	(496,698)	(1,349,450)
Profit After Tax	2,829	7,686	5,399	(75,208)	(1,524,897)	(973,676)	(2,008,904)	(496,698)	(1,349,450)
Share Capital	179,500	431,500	432,500	1,210,500	1,266,500	1,266,500	1,266,500	1,457,500	1,457,000
Reserves and Surplus	2,829	10,515	7,515	(164,513)	(1,689,410)	(2,596,443)	(4,605,347)	(4,266,422)	(5,603,682)
Fixed Assets Including Investments	0	25,000	44,460	397,472	398,026	429,223	417,025	407,000	28,051
Current Liabilities	146,940	0	1,632,060	5,183,122	12,920,149	235,845	122,032	2,474,000	908,750
Current Assets	329,269	2,550,015	2,062,535	5,831,627	14,521,149	6,705,053	4,083,085	2,892,530	1,952,000

the business operations and record-keeping but were not yet ready to manage the complexities of the commodity business. The ALC team was under increasing pressure from members to do something more.

3. Struggle in accessing working capital

In the first three years, another bottleneck was to mobilise working capital for conducting the business. Commercial banks were reluctant to advance working capital that was necessary to operate a commodity business. As a result, the ALC team had to run from pillar to post to mobilise working capital for each financial year. The professionals had to spend considerable time in approaching the funding agencies. Each had its own requirements. Table 9.3 shows the overview of the working capital loan mobilised by ALC India for the HFSPC.

In the first year, since the procurement was tied up with SFAC and NCDEX, this marketing arrangement substantially reduced the need for the working capital since the payment to farmers was made by NCDEX within seven days of the procurement of the red gram. The payment was directly deposited in the accounts of the farmers. Another issue was the non-payment of the overdue amount. Red gram worth Rs. 2.1 million was sold to Raghavendra

Table 9.3 Working capital raised by HSFPC in the first three years (2013–16)

Year	Source of Working Capital Raised	Amount in Rupees Million (Interest Rate in %)	Purpose of Working Capital and Comments
2013–14	ALDF (ALC India-promoted entity Access Livelihoods Development Finance LLP)	1.05 (16%)	Input and red gram procurement
2014–15	FWWB-I and NABFIN	2.5 (14%)	Loan route was FWWB-I to ALC India to HFSPC; NABFIN for repaying Ratnakar Bank Limited and for red gram processing
2015–16	Rang De, Ratnakar Bank	1 million and 1.6 million, respectively (12%)	For providing micro loans to farmers (micro loans at Rs. 6,000 per member to 346 members for six months); Ratnakar Bank for warehouse receipt

Source: Interactions with management team and HFSPC records

Trading Company, Hyderabad, of which Rs. 1.1 million was received. The post-dated cheques given by the traders were dishonoured when presented to the bank. HFSPC filed a legal case against the buyer. After three years the case was closed after the balance amount was paid. The trader did not pay interest amount on delayed payment. HFSPC had to bear these losses. To manage the cash flow resulting from these challenges was a continuous task.

In 2015–16, 2.475 acres of land was purchased at a price of Rs. 0.35 million. However, the deal ran into some difficulty. The previous owner had given General Power of Attorney (GPA) to some other party. The land was registered in the name of that party with the FPC management in the dark about this deal. When the FPC decided to convert land from agriculture to non-agriculture purposes, the *tehsildar* told that there is an issue of GPA in another person's name. A subsequent agreement was done with the land-holder to settle the issue. Subsequently the registration issue was resolved, but it consumed a lot of time of the management.

4. Members' ownership and patronage for services

ALC was determined to promote all-women FPC that is also managed by women board members. The challenges were manifold: to enrol women members who often do not have any land and/or other assets on their names in spite of them taking the maximum burden of working on fields, mobilise equity, sustain their participation in business (procurement) and govern-ance (meetings), and also ensure that the board is empowered to take criti-cal decisions in spite of limited formal educational qualifications of them. Members' participation is a critical indicator of the functioning of the FPC. During field interactions in 2016, we observed that there was a decline in the number of members using the services of the FPC. Table 9.4 provides details of the patronage of the FPC by its members that gives a sense of the number of active members.

The annual general body meetings (AGMs) were held regularly. The FPC had a board comprising nine directors, all women. All board members were 10th pass or below, as far as educational qualifications go.

Table 9.4 Membership profile of FPC services used and participation in meeting

Year	Members Availing Input Services	Members Availing Output/ Marketing Services	Minimum Amount per Member for Input Aggregation	Maximum Amount per Member for Market Aggregation	Attendance in the AGM
2013–14	200	350	Rs. 1,500	Rs. 36,600	89
2014–15	350	130	Rs. 1,630	Rs. 28,700	103
2015–16	500	90	Rs. 2,400	Rs. 67,200	375

5. Challenges in running the FPC

5.1 Implementing MSP during and after demonetisation

A significant challenge faced on completion of the project (when the SFAC grant support was over) was the unexpected demonetisation announced in November 2016. It squeezed banks for cash and significantly affected agricultural operations. During the MSP procurement, the volume of business was large, over Rs. 60 million. Farmers who had supplied red gram were getting impatient for not receiving payments. Banks had long queues of customers, cheque books were in short supply, and online money transfer was taking too much time. On top of it, in one single cheque amount released by the bank, multiple payments of farmers were clubbed. The FPC did not have a trained accountant since the very start, and at such a chaotic time, the pressure of work in the field combined with inaccurate record-keeping resulted in some farmers receiving payments twice. The issue of double payment became a huge headache for the FPC leadership and management for the subsequent four years. The amount thus locked in was Rs. 1.25 million. HFSPC had to spend enormous time and money to recover that money from the farmers.

5.2 MSP again in red gram

In 2016–17 notwithstanding the challenges posed as a result of demonetisation, with the support of SFAC funding, it did a procurement business of red gram for Rs. 64,978,000. HFSPC obtained a 1.5% commission charge for facilitating the procurement operations. Unlike the previous year, this time the entire procurement amount was recorded in the books of accounts of the HFSPC. Money was paid to the HFSPC account and from there was credited to the accounts of individual farmers.

In 2017–18, the input business continued with 692 farmers with turnover of Rs. 2,096,000 of which Rs. 1.3 million worth of inputs were sold on credit to 649 members. HFSPC members began savings to mobilise working capital. Five hundred and ten members contributed Rs. 224,000 that was saved in the bank account of the FPC. New shareholders were added with the shareholder base increasing to 1,004 members, each new member contributing a share capital of Rs. 1,000. A warehouse was taken on lease for starting a groundnut oil mill with the lease amount of Rs. 180,000 for five years. This business was not a part of the FPC operation but an initiative of one of the promoters who wanted to build on his previous experience in the family business of groundnut oil mill.

Red gram procurement of Rs. 20.3 million was done on behalf of the state marketing federation (MARKFED). Despite repeated demands by the FPC board and CEO, the government delayed the procurement of the red gram till almost the end of the season. The members put pressure on the elected state functionaries including the minister in the state government. The state government then suddenly decided to close the procurement as it had exhausted the budget for MSP payment. The decision left the remaining farmers disenchanted. The entire facilitation was done by the team of FPC, and the 1% commission that they are entitled to is yet to be received. Only 273 members could participate in the short procurement window.

5.3 Paddy procurement for state federation

Paddy procurement for DCMS was also done on behalf of 126 members. HFSPC did paddy procurement for three seasons on behalf of the DCMS. As luck would have it, this business activity did not improve the financial viability of the enterprise. The agreement was to procure and send the stock to rice millers for processing. The entire transaction though facilitated by the FPC was not routed through the books of accounts of the organisation. Farmers were to be directly paid by DCMS after the procurement was done. The FPC for its procurement efforts was to receive 1% commission charges and reimbursement of expenses such as transportation and loading and unloading charges.

Transporters went on a nationwide indefinite strike from 20 July 2017 to protest against the constant increase in diesel prices, toll expenses, practical problems with e-way bills, and so on. This coincided with the procurement time. To add to the woes of farmers, there were unseasonal rains, and the entire paddy procured got wet and could not be transported for many days. As a result, most of it got damaged, and some even started germinating. The rice miller refused to accept the stocks. Farmers were paid, but FPC did not have any addition to its revenue. The FPC is yet to receive about Rs. 0.4 million. The operation resulted in another setback for the organisation.

6. Efforts to turn around the FPC

6.1 Merger of three FPCs

In 2018–19, the HFSPC continued its input business with the service extended to 250 members and a total value of Rs. 1.2 million and paddy procurement of Rs. 1.6 million. To increase operational efficiency, a resolution for the merger of three producer companies was passed in the AGM of 2018–19 to achieve economies of scale and ease of management. Though passed in the AGM, the merger process is not yet complete due to completion of audit that also got delayed during the time of pandemic.

6.2 Covid's impact on business operations

The year 2020–21 began with the Covid-19 pandemic. HFSPC made some efforts to respond to the crisis. Grocery retail services were started to support farmers during the lockdown. A women manager of the HFSPC who had worked for seven years resigned accepting the mistake of making double payments during the red gram procurement in the post-demonetisation months. In both 2020–21 and 2021–22, no business activities were taken up by the FPC except one staff member who was tasked to recover loans of about Rs. 1 million. In 2021–22, procurement of red gram was undertaken by the two other FPCs promoted by ALC for a private processor (miller). The market prices were between Rs. 6,500 to Rs. 6,700 above the MSP of Rs. 6,300.

With the general appreciation in the property prices, the land purchased by the FPC, about 7 km inside the main road, was likely to fetch Rs. 0.025 million/acre in just about five years after it was purchased. The board after a lot of deliberation decided to sell the land. Unfortunately, as luck would have been, the buyer paid some advance, but the transaction could not be completed as a result of the restrictions on movement imposed by the pandemic. The payment was made in the subsequent year, 2019–20.

6.3 Human resources for managing HFSPC

In the initial years, HFSPC had two full-time staff on its role. Mrs Nisha (name changed) was with the organisation since its registration. She was an administrative manager and supported by an ALC-trained person in accounting and book-keeping. Mr Vaseem Yousef supervised the two-member staff and was paid by ALC India. He had the responsibility of supervising two other producer companies in the same region. He belonged to the area where all three FPCs were located and knew the context well. During the procurement season, two more contractual staff were appointed at the procurement centres. The BoD of HFSPC took the responsibility of supervising the centre, assisted by the contractual staff. Each centre has two board members in charge of quality control and two staff. When the SFAC grant ended in 2014, ALC continued its relationship with the FPCs though on reduced human resource support. From 2013 November till 2015 March, ALC supported HFSPC through its earnings and entered an agreement with HFSPC for payment of services given to the FPC at a fixed amount of Rs. 5,000 per month (later increased to Rs. 7,500) and subsequently 1.5% of the business turnover of the FPC as a variable component. The search for grant funds to support FPC continued. In 2019–20, Axis Bank Foundation came forward to support the HR costs of ALC. While ALC as an organisation continued to invest a lot of time and energy in ensuring that the FPC is strengthened, operationally one experienced a lot of movement of professionals who were associated with the day-to-day functioning of the organisation. Mr Vaseem continues to assist the FPC even now.

6.4 *Down but not defeated: HFSFC ready for the long haul*

Mr Krishna Gopal and Mr Sarat reflected on their journey of the company and also the declining patronage of members.

> While we had good experience in mobilising women farmers and we also knew the appropriate processes that we needed to deploy, in retrospect, we feel that we did not create a strong foundation for this FPC. The SFAC project had tight deadlines and critical milestones. We realised that we were compelled to short circuit processes that actually needed longer time. We enrolled women farmers as members once they just filled in a membership form (of Rs. 50) and not necessarily after contributing share capital of Rs. 1000 per member.
>
> It has been a continuous challenge for us to mobilise working capital for the business in general and marketing of the produce in particular. We need at least Rs. 50 million each year to run this business and we ended up getting just about Rs. 5 million to 10 million. We did receive loans after a lot of running around but most of the time the disbursements were so late and untimely, that the loans were practically of no use to the members of the FPC. Members need inputs well before the time of sowing. If the working capital is available after rains are over what is the use of that loan?
>
> (interview)

In the initial years, the FPC did attract positive press as a result of its persistent efforts in making MSP work for women farmers. Despite the financial struggles, NDTV, ETV and DD1 approached the producer company and featured the case study. A news story in the name of "Mahilalu Maharanulu" was published in the local newspaper *Eenadu*. *Economic Times* awarded "Krishi Vikas" award for the best business management done by the producer company in the year 2016–17.

Mr Sarat continued,

> We are still struggling to maintain a balance. It is balancing the viability of the FPC and while doing that also to ensure that we as ALC India are in a position to give them the services and hence our viability as a promotional institution. While we as ALC needed grant support to sustain our staff in the field to promote FPC, we also needed to build local human resources to continue to manage operations after we leave the area.
>
> (interview)

ALC in later years did make attempts to increase both the membership base and also the share capital per member. However, in any given year, the

157

number of active members contributing to the business of the HFSPC was not more than 400 to 450, the rest being passive or dormant in terms of patronage to the business operations.

Have the members and ALC staff lost hope on the revival of the FPC? When confronted with the question they were optimistic. "We have given ourselves two years for the turnaround. We are confident that we can turnaround the situation." Another member of the ALC team responsible for the turnaround was cautiously optimistic.

> The members have lost interest; some of them are angry with us. They had high hopes from this institution. They feel that the institution did not come up as per their expectations. However, the same members and the Board is with us when it comes to discussing the turnaround plan. It is this engagement of theirs and their genuine interest that we are banking upon in our journey and are hoping to achieve sustainability of this FPC.

Having observed HFSPC's functioning for several years, the journey of Hasnabad FPC has a lot of learnings to offer to both the policymakers and the practitioners. The policymakers often have the vision of transforming the agricultural value chains with AMUL as the iconic model for the country. The practitioners too are motivated by this vision. There are many challenges in reality as observed in this chapter translating this vision. These are finalising a robust business model amidst a volatile external environment, identifying a long-term partner for financial resources to back a business model, building capacities among the women board members while being committed to gender and inclusion goals and remain responsive to the aspirations of members. The road in building AMUL model in commodities is indeed a long and tiring journey. Corona pandemic of 2020 and 2021 added to more challenges to the functioning of the FPC. In both the years, there were no significant business activities undertaken by the HFSPC. Having gone through a rollercoaster ride in the nine years, promoting, nurturing, and strengthening such FPCs, poses many challenges that all the stakeholders need to collectively address.

10

TRADITIONAL TRIBAL GOAT-REARER WOMEN TAKING THE FPC WAY

The case of Pandhana PashuPalak Producer Company Limited, Madhya Pradesh

Shilpa Vasavada and Naveen Patidar

1. Introduction

1.1 Context

Goat rearing and backyard poultry are important livelihood options for the marginalised rural communities of the country. They require low investments and have low input costs for feeding, veterinary care, and so on, thus also making them an important risk mitigation strategy for rain-fed farming families as compared to large animals. Both are highly liquid assets which can be sold anytime during distress periods, besides being important sources for food and nutrition for rural population. Large numbers of rural women are directly engaged in these sectors and can potentially benefit from further development of these sectors.

As against a national growth rate of 10.14% in goat population at the national level during the period 2012–18, the growth rate in Madhya Pradesh of goat population was over 38% and backyard poultry 45.78%, reflecting both goat rearing and poultry to be viable livelihood activities for the rural households. Small livestock and backyard poultry, however, have remained neglected sectors with very little investment gone into them. These sectors remain largely unorganised, and ecosystem needed for strengthening these livelihoods such as preventive veterinary care, availability of good-quality chicks and goats, good shelters, better feeds, and fair market rates is mostly absent from remote tribal regions of the country restricting development of these sectors.

Pandhana PashuPalak Producer Company Limited (PPPCL) is tribal women-owned and -managed producer company based in Pandhana block of Khandwa district (Madhya Pradesh). It deals with not only these dual products of small livestock – goats and poultry – but indigenous and

DOI: 10.4324/9781003308034-10

improved breeds of the two – having better taste, fast weight growth, high nutrition, fetching a better price, and being climate resilient. A combination of the unique producers and the products offered by the company makes the FPO different than other goat-based or poultry-based FPOs in a rain-fed tribal set-up.

2. Introduction to AKRSP(I)

PPPCL is promoted by a non-denominational, non-government development organisation, Aga Khan Rural Support Programme (India). AKRSP(I) aims at the empowerment of rural communities, particularly the underprivileged and women through collectivisation, and extends direct support to local communities. Active in over 2,700 villages of Gujarat, Madhya Pradesh, and Bihar, it has impacted lives of over 2 million people from marginalised sections of society, 60% of which are women. It is a pioneer in participatory development approaches in the country in natural resource development and has won various national and international accolades. Its core area of work involves natural resources management, sustainable agriculture, water and sanitation, education and rural youth development. Over the period around, 85,000 hectares of land has been brought under irrigation, 8,000 hectares of forest land has been rehabilitated, 110,000 women have accessed financial services and productive assets, and 75,000 citizens have received entitlements through improved grassroots governance. Women empowerment, improved rural governance, and climate change mitigation and adaptation are cross-cutting objectives of all AKRSP(I) programmes, which have led to substantial gains for the communities as well as overall improvement in the natural resources. Building on this, AKRSP(I) is now facilitating market linkages of these communities through promotion of FPOs and has mobilised over 20,000 farmers in 28 FPOs.

2.1 Promotional efforts by promoting institution

AKRSP(I)'s work in the tribal, rain-fed block of Pandhana from late 2004 to 2016, where the focus had been on natural resource development, was the foundation of the formation of PPPCL. On request of women from SHGs to start goat rearing as an income-generating activity, AKRSP(I) had supplied a goat unit of four goats and a buck each to 100 landless families in 2011. A large number of these goats however died due to diseases, and it was realised that supply of goats was not the right strategy to promote goat rearing.

On invite of AKRSP(I) to the area in 2012, the experts of the Goat Trust suggested to promote an integrated programme of veterinary care, shelters, feeds; and promoting local and not external breeds, if AKRSP(I) wanted to establish this as a sector in the region. That was the beginning of a systematic programme on goat rearing by AKRSP(I) with multiple components of trainings to community on livestock management practices; creating a cadre of women para-veterinarians known as Pashu Sakhis; introducing low-cost shelters and better feed management.

By the year 2016, AKRSP(I) had already organised large numbers of women into SHGs for financial inclusion, better agriculture, and livestock practices. Exercise of gender analysis in small livestock highlighted the contradiction of high contribution of women in small livestock care, but little involvement in decision-making, or in access to technical skills, new knowledge, or marketing. That made AKRSP(I) change its strategy from mixed-gender PashuPalak Samuh to formation of exclusive women's PPS. This coincided with formation time of FPO in 2016. By this time, efforts of 12 Pashu Sakhis, who had been trained to provide various preventive veterinary care services to small livestock in ten villages, had started yielding results: mortality rates in goats had reduced from over 30% to less than 5%.

3. Main story of PPPCL

Pashu Sakhis, however, were directly accountable to AKRSP(I) professionals and worked under their guidance. A need was felt to reorganise and expand the programme in order to bring sustainability to interventions, while reducing dependency on the organisation. NABARD provided that opportunity in 2016. Women from PashuPalak Samuhs (PPS) in ten villages were encouraged and mobilised to form and register PPPCL as an enterprise with local tribal women farmers as its shareholders and directors on 4 February 2016 with twin objectives:

- To strive towards doubling income of members from goat and poultry rearing through:
  - reduction in mortality and increase in body weight by offering timely availability of livestock feed and healthcare facilities at village level;
  - fetching better price for small livestock producers and ensuring timely payment for the livestock sold, by taking advantage of economies of scale through collectivisation and cooperation.
- To facilitate local women livestock rearers' institution, and thus give visibility and create their identity, while leading towards local sustainability of the intervention.

3.1 Timeline of PPPCL

Journey of PPPCL is reflected briefly in the timeline in Table 10.1.

It is evident that the FPO has a gradual evolution of services and products, as also institutional arrangements at the ground level.

Table 10.1 Major milestones in PPPCL journey

Year	Major Milestones
2014	• First batch of ten Pashu Sakhis trained to provide preventive veterinary care services in goats
2014 to 2016	• Mixed-gender goat-rearing groups (GRGs) with nominal membership fees promoted in selective villages
	• Meetings of GRGs conducted by Pashu Sakhis in addition to providing preventive veterinary care services to group members
2016	• Project for promotion of livestock FPO approved by NABARD
	• PPPCL got registered; Pashu Sakhis became promoter directors; and membership fee collected in GRGs became initial share capital
	• Village institutional form changed to PPS of exclusive women instead of mixed-gender GRGs
	• PPPCL's first product: production of salt bricks for goats
	• Beginning of services for backyard poultry by Pashu Sakhis
2017	• Mineral mixture for livestock launched by FPO
	• 'Muskan' developed as brand name for PPPCL products
	• Initiation of sales of feeders and drinkers for poultry birds
2018	• Started bulk procurement of poultry feed and onward sales to members
	• Beginning of bulk procurement of day-old *satpuda desi* chicks and sales to members
	• Women BoD explored buck trading at whole sale market of Indore
2019	• Beginning of production for poultry feed
	• PPPCL awarded as best FPO in Madhya Pradesh by NABARD regional office, Madhya Pradesh
2020	• Change of institutional structure: work of PPPCL started directly with SHGs instead of separate platform of PashuPalak Samuh to avoid multiple livelihood groups on ground
2021	• Reached coverage of FPO to 28 villages of Pandhana block; cadre of 30 Pashu Sakhis

4. Activities and services of PPPCL

Activities of PPPCL can be broadly categorised into three sets: production services, market linkages, and financial services, as referred in Table 10.2.

4.1 Pashu Sakhi Services: The backbone of PPPCL

Pashu Sakhis, who deliver last-mile services to FPO members; and who are crucial link between the organisational leadership and its members, are critical part of PPPCL. Board of directors (BoDs) of the FPO have also emerged from this cadre. They charge a fixed commission decided time to time by the FPO leadership for the services they offer to the FPO members. Household reach of services extended by Pashu Sakhis over a period is in Table 10.3.

Table 10.2 Activity details of PPPCL

Activities	Details of Activities
Livestock Production Services	• Capacity building of livestock-rearing households on improved management practices for goat and poultry rearing. • Providing preventive veterinary care services and basic curative treatments to small livestock of FPO members and non-members at village level • Accessing vaccines, de-wormers, and related items from local block government veterinary department • Producing and selling of various feeds such as goat feed, mineral mixture, salt bricks, and poultry feed • Supplying day-old chicks, poultry feeders and drinkers, and so on • Providing material for improved shelters for goats and poultry, such as iron mesh.
Market Linkages	• Facilitation of marketing of birds and goats to traders, where transactions take place directly between members and traders • Direct whole sale marketing of goats • Creating linkages with suppliers of various materials such as day-old chicks, feeders, drinkers, and so on • Creating distribution network for PPPCL-manufactured products outside core geographies • Piloting retail shops of goat meat in the core geographies for value addition purpose
Financial Services	• Credit linkages with bank and onward lending to members

Table 10.3 Household reach of Pashu Sakhi services in Pandhana block

Activity	2016	2017	2018	2019	2020
Vaccination in Poultry Birds	81	90	233	18	165
Deworming of Goats	785	785	1303	485	971
Goat Vaccination (ET)	200	750	1,200	370	1,238
Goat Vaccination (PPR)	277	758	1,300	255	1,485
Treatment of Goats	923	805	948	1,007	1,006
Salt Bricks Sales	15	50	55	105	396
Mineral Mixture Sales	10	25	20	54	180
Poultry Feed Sales	0	0	0	25	125

Pashu Sakhis are intensively trained by AKRSP(I) on technical aspects. A five-day technical training is followed by several rounds of additional or refresher trainings, and exposure visits to build their capacities. Over the period, Pashu Sakhis and the FPO leadership have gone for exposure visits to Indian Veterinary Research Institute and the Goat Trust, UP; Amul

Dairy, Gujarat; SRLM, Maharashtra; and PRADAN, MP, to ensure that they develop sound technical background around livestock sector with a broad vision for the company.

4.2 Trainings of members on better management practices

Training on better management practices of members through SHGs is a focus area for the FPO. It has set training calendar based on seasonal needs. These trainings are mostly facilitated by Pashu Sakhis with intensive hand-holding from AKRSP(I) professionals. FPO is slowly taking over the planning and execution of training programmes on ground.

4.3 Production of livestock feeds

Community in FPO villages hardly used feed supplements needed for better nutrition and health of small livestock. The increased use of feed supplements by villagers, thanks to trainings and awareness created by FPO, motivated PPPCL to shift their strategy from merely supplying these items from market to manufacturing them themselves. PPPCL now possess manufacturing and packaging machines for mineral bricks and poultry feed. Under the brand name 'Muskan', PPPCL has got into manufacturing of salt bricks for goats since 2016, mineral mixture since 2017, poultry feed since 2019, and goat feed since 2021. These products are sold in the catchment of PPPCL and also externally. Product details are given in Table 10.4.

4.4 Supply of day-old chicks

From the very beginning, PPPCL has got orders for day-old chicks of *satpuda desi* variety and has sold over 50,000 chicks to the members so far, sourcing from Bhusaval (Maharashtra), 130 km from the FPO location.

Table 10.4 Products manufactured by PPPCL

Product Name	Usage (Type of Animals)	Weight (kg)	Cost of Production (Rupees)	Selling Rate (Rupees)
Muskan Pashu Amrut Aahar	Goats and cattle	1	53	70
Muskan Pashu Mineral Mixture	Goats and cattle	1	65	100
Muskan Poultry Feed	Poultry birds	50	1,470	1,700
Muskan Goat Feed	Goats	5	141	200

4.5 Sales of fully grown bucks and poultry birds with fair practices

Normally goats and poultry birds are either sold in local weekly markets or purchased directly from rural households by local traders, where rates are decided without weighing the animals. Indigenous poultry birds still fetch satisfactory rates in weekly markets as demand for this variety is high round the year. However, marketing of goat is an issue.

PPPCL is promoting the practice of weighing animals before they are sold so that members can negotiate better rates with traders. Members inform the FPO via Pashu Sakhis for surplus poultry birds when available, who coordinate with traders to go directly to villages and purchase, making direct payments to the women sellers. While Pashu Sakhis get a nominal commission per animal for facilitating this work, members get buyers at their doorstep whenever needed, who offer competitive prices, as they are contacted by PPPCL.

Goat marketing is still an evolving business vertical for PPPCL. The FPO has initiated its efforts of wholesale marketing of bucks around Id festival to the Indore wholesale goat market since 2017. Thirty to 50 bucks weighing roughly 40–50 kg each are taken in each trip for the last three continuous years. This initiative has helped fetching a good profit for the FPO with an average of Rs. 500/goat in the first two years. In 2019, however, due to low turnout of traders from outside Indore owing to heavy rains, prices in the market remained very low and PPPCL incurred huge losses. Indore wholesale goat market was closed in both 2020 and 2021 due to Covid-19 pandemic.

Indore wholesale goat market is a night market held from 21.00 p.m. to 4.00 a.m. It was impossible for women BoD to move freely and negotiate in this completely men-dominated market in their very first visit in 2017. While the FPO continues to sell goats during Id to Indore market, women do not accompany any more.

As per discussion with members, the combined gain for members due to the marketing efforts is estimated to be about 10% value gain (Rs. 1,000 to Rs. 2,000 per member per annum) in comparison to what they would have received otherwise.

4.6 Processing and selling of goat meat at local village market level

The vacuum of fresh mutton shop in weekly village markets compels villagers to go all the way to Pandhana, the block headquarter to buy mutton. With few traders in Pandhana market, the mutton is priced high and sold stale. However, with no other option, villagers have to accept this going all the way to Pandhana or curtail their own meat consumption.

In order to avail more profit while ensuring supply of fresh processed goat at the doorstep, PPPCL ventured into processed meat and set up a mutton shop in Pandhana town in March 2020. Fearing business loss, existing mutton sellers resisted this move and threatened the CEO of PPPCL, claiming their exclusive rights to this role. The shop had to be closed in 3 weeks.

As an alternative, the FPO leadership explored the weekly village markets instead of the one at Pandhana block and set up shops in two village weekly markets. The shops are supervised by a local woman member. PPPCL person procures goats as per the demand collectedly by him/her in the morning of the weekly market, processes, and supplies fresh mutton in the noon for villagers to cook in the evening. Started in March 2020, this decentralised, local market system had to be stopped soon after Covid-19 lockdown but has restarted since June 2021. The local market of processed meat has given PPPCL almost 80–100% more profit margin, Rs. 1,000/goat than selling goat at the wholesale market.

Being closer to villages has also ensured higher footfall of women as consumers. According to women of SHGs, normally it is the men who purchase from mutton shop of Pandhana town. Now women have direct access and are getting into decision-making for purchase. Proximity and women's part in decision-making have led to increased consumption at the household level, enhancing their nutritional diversity. Fresh availability and hence better health and savings of transportation cost are additional benefits.

4.7 Facilitation for credit and government schemes

While large numbers of women avail livelihood loans from their respective SHGs, PPPCL also piloted credit service once. It availed a loan of Rs. 0.5 million from Madhya Pradesh Grameen Bank in the year 2018–19, part of which was invested in feed packaging, and Rs. 40,000 were extended as credit to four members for purchase of goats. The FPO repaid entire bank loan by year 2020–21. However, instead of the FPO, the Grameen Bank had shown this loan in the personal accounts of BoDs. This, along with delayed repayment from members, discouraged the BoDs to go ahead in this. With an increased demand from members for credit services to buy animals, the FPO leadership is again actively considering starting this.

The FPO closely coordinates with local government veterinary department to avail government schemes and procures vaccines, de-wormers, and other medicines free of cost, apart from gaining the department's regular technical guidance as and when needed.

4.8 Capturing the catchment of other FPOs of the area

Of the eight FPOs promoted by promoter organisation AKRSP(I) in Khandwa, Burhanpur, Badwani, and Dhar districts of MP, only two companies are livestock based, and six FPOs are crop based. PPPCL is the only company which is into manufacturing of goat and poultry feed products. Since goat and poultry rearing is common in most tribal households, PPPCL has expanded its market base of 'Muskan' brand products through other AKRSP(I)-promoted FPOs. Two per cent of the turnover in 2019–20 and 3.3% of its turnover in 2020–21, worth Rs. 94,122, were occurred through this strategy.

5. Financial analysis of PPPCL

5.1 Shareholding

As of 31 March 2021, FPO has the share capital of Rs. 282,700 from 552 shareholders while Rs. 18,250 is pending for allocation to shareholders. Shareholders are all women. While the share fee is Rs. 1,000, there is flexibility, and instalments are allowed considering women's lesser access and control over money. Except for 198, all shareholders have paid between Rs. 500 and Rs. 1,000 as share capital as on 31 March 2021. BoDs are considering standardisation of the multiple slabs created due to flexibility of payment, which, at times, acts as a barrier.

5.2 Financial support received by the FPO

Initiated with the initial support of Rs. 0.9 million from NABARD in the year 2016, of which Rs. 0.5 million was direct support to FPO and Rs. 0.4 million for the promotional efforts, PPPCL has also received direct and indirect support worth Rs. 1.67 million for business development and administration costs over the period, details of which are provided in Table 10.5.

Table 10.5 Support received by PPPCL over the period

Source	Amount (million)	Year of Support	Purpose
NABARD	0.5	2016–17	Initial office establishment cost and partial administration cost for three years
AKRSP(I) through APPI grant	0.72	2017–18 to 2019–20	Working capital and administration cost
AKRSP(I) through BRLF grant	0.14	2018–19	Poultry feed manufacturing machine (not funds were given)
SFAC	0.3	2021–22	Equity grant
Total	1.67		

5.3 Business performance of the FPO

FPO revenue was on an upward curve till 2019–20, where exceptional losses of Rs. 0.46 million were incurred in business operations in goat marketing. While FPO had done this successfully for the first two years, heavy rains and floods slashed the turnout of traders in the market, leading to disposal of stock at exceptionally low rates. Fortunately, FPO could recover from this shock in subsequent year 2020–21 due to robust demand for feed inputs, partly due to Covid-19 relief work undertaken by AKRSP(I). Resilience and determination of FPO leadership were a key to this bounce back.

Performance of FPO on various business indicators is in Table 10.6.

5.4 Source of revenue

Major revenue sources for the FPO are inputs for production system and marketing of live goats and poultry birds. The revenue stream of FPO's own manufactured input products such as salt bricks, goat feed, poultry feed, and mineral mixture is consistent. Revenue from goat marketing was significant for couple of years before the Covid crisis hit the livestock markets which are closed since March 2020, leading to significant revenue loss for the PPPCL, which otherwise could have availed much larger revenue than what has been possible.

It might be worthwhile to note that while veterinary care services extended by Pashu Sakhis are critical part of FPO business model, there is no revenue

Table 10.6 Business performance of PPPCL

Indicator	FY 2016–17	FY 2017–18	FY 2018–19	FY 2019–20	FY 2020–21
Total Revenue	278,175	1,064,756	2,479,615	2,196,764	2,995,488
Total Expenses	275,710	1,032,795	2,471,950	2,658,435	2,208,152
Profit Before Tax	2,464	31,960	7,664	−461,671	787,335
Profit After Tax	1,719	23,650	5,671	−461,671	787,335
Share Capital	100,000	100,000	282,700	282,700	300,950
Reserves and Surplus	1,719	25,370	31,041	−430,630	356,705
Long-Term Borrowings	0	0	0	495,708	0
Fixed Assets	0	0	137,598	182,520	267,205
Current Liabilities	174,145	387,872	4,448,347	272,192	233,348
Current Assets	275,864	588,992	624,489	453,951	623,798

Table 10.7 Share of input and output in revenue of FPO

Year	Total Revenue	Revenue From Inputs (Feed, Chicks, and so on) (%)	Revenue From Outputs (Buck and Fully-Grown Poultry Birds)
FY 2016–17	278,175	100.0	0.0
FY 2017–18	1,064,756	51.7	48.3
FY 2018–19	2,479,615	40.4	59.6
FY 2019–20	2,196,764	20.5	79.5
FY 2020–21	2,995,488	98.1	1.9

on books of accounts for this as medicines are provided free by government department to the FPO, and Pashu Sakhis charge a nominal service-fee from members, but there is no corresponding revenue for the FPO itself from this critical service. Similarly, facilitation of marketing of live animals through traders by FPO at village level does not have financial transactions in the books of account of the FPO.

Share of revenue from input and output services is provided in Table 10.7.

Table 10.7 reflects that share of outputs (due to goat marketing) in total revenue was consistently increasing but came down drastically during the year 2020–21 primarily due to closure of animal trading markets in Covid-19 times.

6. Governance and leadership

Though SHGs are institutional base of this producer company, shareholding of the company is of individual women and not of SHGs. All (100%) of 552 shareholders of PPPCL are members of SHGs, possess an average landholding of 1–2 acres, and are thus small and marginal women farmers. As per conversation with CEO of the company, most members are active and conduct regular business with the FPO for some or the other activity.

At the time of registration, it was decided to have five BoDs and five promoters in order to accommodate for the expenses incurred to get the paperwork done and based on the availability of documents required for registration with women. The company, in its formative years, functioned in ten villages. One woman leader was decided by the SHG women from each of these ten villages: five women as BoD, five women leaders as promoters of FPC.

All BoDs and promoters are also Pashu Sakhis. Logic for this, according to the AKRSP(I) staff, was that at the time of formation of FPCs in 2016, Pashu Sakhis were more aware of the technicalities and were the only ones possessing documents required for registration. Members of SHGs were also quite familiar with them.

This works well because they are constantly connected with the constituents/shareholders by virtue of their daily routine, and they are able to convey all the necessary information and notices effectively. By virtue of being Pashu Sakhis they are de facto leaders in their own villages particularly in matters related to animal husbandry.

There are no external expert directors on the board of the FPO. BoD members have a tenure of three years. The first term got over in 2019 when the general body decided to continue with the previous BoDs in the general body meeting (GBM). Replacement for one of the BoDs who has left village in 2020 is pending due to documentation requirement of digital identity number (DIN), PAN card, and so on, though resolution has been made for new board member. BoDs meet monthly to discharge routine works. In terms of decision-making, it was reported that the BoDs take all the decisions, while the CEO and AKRSP(I) staff play a facilitative role. Administrative, management, and financial capacity building of the office bearers of the FPO is an important strategy of the FPO. BoDs are given periodical training on accounting, business negotiation skills, and market handling.

GBMs of PPPCL have been held every year in September since its formation, regularly at the block headquarter Pandhana, as that's the closet central location for all. Average attendance is 50–60% of the shareholders, though non-member women are also encouraged to attend GBMs to understand the functioning of PPPCL and get motivated to become members of PPPCL. In 2020, due to Covid-19, the attendance was restricted to 200.

The company has hired a CEO, an accountant, and off late, in July 2021, a marketing person. CEO's main role is to execute decisions taken by BoDs and shareholders. He had worked as para-veterinarian with AKRSP(I) for four years before joining PPPCL as CEO. He has done a diploma course in livestock and thus possess a technical background, which is crucial, according to BoDs, for this FPO. He has been the CEO since inception of PPPCL and looks after all operations and marketing activities of the company. Being in its nascent stage, and with two new staff joining only recently, the FPO doesn't yet have an HR system and is in the process of coming up with its HR policy and HR manual.

7. Impact of the FPO

PPPCL works with *tribal women* in a highly *unorganised sector* of small livestock. Keeping its objectives in mind, its impact hence can be seen from three perspectives:

- Productivity and income gains for tribal farmers who are engaged in goat rearing and backyard poultry in the region
- Its efforts to organise a highly unorganised sector
- Empowerment of women from highly marginalised tribal communities

Productivity improvement services have the biggest impact on the FPO members. Preventive veterinary care services through Pashu Sakhis, trainings on better management practices, improved feeding practices, and provisions for improved shelters have all led to substantial gain for the members. Biggest gain is observed in terms of reduced mortality rates in goats as well as poultry birds. A couple of baseline studies of projects implemented by AKRSP(I) revealed that mortality in goats was above 35% while in poultry birds it was more than 55% prior to preventive veterinary care services. It is now less than 5% in goats while less than 8% in poultry birds. Thus, it is a huge gain which ultimately translates into increased income for the members. An impact evaluation study (NAVIK project final evaluation, 2020) of a project also highlighted increasing contribution of these sectors in the overall income of families. In year 2020, income from goat rearing is around Rs. 14,000 per annum while income from poultry is around 9,000 per annum for the PPPCL members. Income from these livelihood sources continues to act as risk mitigation against crop failures due to weather shocks.

PPPCL is trying to organise the entire sector value chain – from inputs to market linkages of final output from small livestock activities. It has created a set of locally produced products and locally delivered services which are completely new to target communities. Production of mineral bricks, goat feed and poultry feed has given PPPCL not only the business opportunity to sell these products but also visibility to PPPCL among its key stakeholders. State-level award from NABARD helped increasing visibility of this enterprise. Experimentation around next stage ideas such as entering goat meat market has led to effective completion of value chain right from inputs to market side.

The most noteworthy among all impacts is the empowerment of tribal women because of this collective enterprise. Traditionally, women's involvement within livestock sector is limited to only rearing practices while having no access to income from these activities. This sector is heavily dominated by men, particularly in the veterinary care services, marketing of animals, and income-related activities. PPPCL is slowly changing these equations by bringing in women at the centre of whole business operation. Tribal women not only got the chance to own a collective enterprise but are also actively running the enterprise. This is a significant breakaway from the traditional norms of local community. FPO BoD have gained significant knowledge and skills around the whole sector of small livestock, thanks to the continuous trainings and exposure opportunities provided by promoting institution. Participating in markets has helped to enhance their level of confidence for negotiating with the local traders in districts of Khandwa and Burhanpur. "First time we didn't know how to make deals. But now we know very well," said one of BoDs during the interactions. PPPCL makes all payments directly to women members, again recognises women as producers, and makes them feel more confident due to increased control over the income from the livestock-rearing activities –"Money has come to my account." Increased production of poultry birds, eggs, and goats has also led to increased nutritional diversity at household level in some of the households, as outlined during discussions with the community members.

8. Current situation and plan ahead

FPO continues to provide vital services to its members. Covid-19 pandemic and related supply chain disruptions have hampered some of the plans of the FPO. FPO mostly suffered due to closure of animal markets during this period. There are also difficulties in sourcing important inputs such as day-old chicks from the suppliers. AKRSP(I) plans to further invest in this FPO to improve its services and product portfolio. Currently FPO is actively considering setting up a hatchery for local production of chicks. BoDs think that it would not only meet the demand base of the area at reduced transportation cost but also help reduce the time lag between the advance money paid to company at Bhusaval (1–2 months right now) and reduce the mortality rate of getting it from a place which is 130 km away. This will reduce price of day-old chicks, making it more affordable to members. This is expected to give major boost to FPO business in near future. FPO is also in the process of finalising a leased land in Pandhana town. FPO plans to set up integrated facility at this place including office, hatchery unit, warehouse, and a shelter for aggregating goats for marketing purpose. PPPCL is also exploring business opportunity in desi-eggs market. Credit services for members are also on the cards learning from past experience around this.

PPPCL wishes to expand its membership to 1,000, doubling the existing number in the next five years by setting up sub-outlets in nearby blocks, where network of trained Pashu Sakhis already exists. At the governance level, while the same BoDs have been elected again in year 2019, they have realised the need for having an executive committee of members apart from Pashu Sakhis, covering all functional villages of PPPCL. This would help Pashu Sakhis being accountable to the BoDs and executive committee and focus more on interests of the members than Pashu Sakhis, strengthening the case of PPPCL.

9. Conclusion and author's analysis

PPPCL is a unique collective enterprise from the point of view that it seeks to empower most marginalised population of the country – the tribal women. It works in rain-fed tribal region, and it works with small livestock-rearing community which is further at margins. FPO is owned by tribal women who hardly have any control over productive assets and income. Hence it is of great importance from gender-equality perspective. Within a short span of five years, it has experienced both successes and failures in business operations. Improvement in productivity and hence income levels of its members is the key achievement of the FPO. Output marketing of live goats and poultry birds seems like started on a bright note. However, Covid-19 has put a break on this important revenue stream for the FPO. It remains to be seen how quickly FPO can regain this main revenue stream. On governance side, FPO needs to do much more to look beyond Pashu Sakhi cadre for broadening the leadership base. There are many more women leaders already in the region due to widespread SHG network. Hence, it should not be a big issue to identify and institutionalise processes leading to more tribal women coming forward to lead this institution. Livestock development needs technical expertise which is currently being provided by AKRSP(I) as the promoting institution. It would be worthwhile for the FPO to plan and improve its own technical capacity, independent of AKRSP(I), to become self-sustainable in the coming future.

The case also makes it abundantly clear that promoting FPO of this nature is not a short-term process, and it requires long-term engagement with community and other stakeholders. It is also clear that the investment needed for promoting such FPOs is much more than what was initially invested through government scheme. Promoting institution in this case could leverage investment from several sources which kept FPO floating over the period. The FPO received grants from several agencies plus time and cost of AKRSP(I) in building the social capital, and still the FPC is struggling. Conclusion is that if one has to build an inclusive FPO for difficult regions, it is a long-drawn journey of patiently building social and financial capital.

If PPPCL succeeds in its mission, it will create newer pathways and hopes to empower most marginalised tribal women of our society.

11

MARKET-FIRST APPROACH OF A COMMUNITY INSTITUTION

The case of Kazhani Farmer Producer
Company in Tamil Nadu

Parthasarathy T., Pallavi G. L., and Balakrishnan S.

1. Introduction – building upon the foundation of strong SHG network

Located in Gobichettipalayam, the Kazhani Farmer Producer Company Limited (henceforth Kazhani) was started in 2016 by Mysore Resettlement and Development Agency's (MYRADA) Krishi Vigyan Kendra (KVK). MYRADA is a leading NGO from the southern states, credited with pioneering the SHG movement in the country in the 1980s.

Gobichettipalayam is in Tamil Nādu's Erode district, through which the River Bhavani flows. The major crops in the region are paddy, banana, and sugarcane. Adjoining the block is the Sathya Mangalam forest area, where the major crop is millets. The farmer producer company (FPC) currently has 1,000 shareholders and spreads across 32 villages of Gobichettipalayam and neighbouring TN Palayam and Andiyur blocks. The geographic spread of the FPC is wide as the farmers were mobilised from the villages where MYRADA had promoted SHGs and farmers groups.

It is reasonable to say that while Kazhani was formed in 2016, the foundation for the FPC was laid much before it was registered. MYRADA's Community Managed Resource Centre (CMRC), an institution for strengthening SHGs, was formed in the area in 2004. MYRADA itself has been working in Erode district since the 1980s, mainly in the hilly Sathya Mangalam region. Its inroads into the plain area began with the establishment of the KVK (partnership of MYRADA and Indian Council of Agricultural Research (ICAR)) in 1992. MYRADA had good experience in farmers' mobilisation and farmers interest group (FIG) formation. Kazhani's formation coincides with MYRADA's strategy of expanding its focus areas from mobilisation of self-help group (SHGs) initially to watershed development and enterprise promotion through FPCs.

In 2011, MYRADA KVK was focused on production practices, organic farming, and sustainable agriculture. In 2012, discussions started on secondary

174

DOI: 10.4324/9781003308034-11

agriculture in which interventions across the agriculture value chain were explored. KVK started working on contract farming model in addition to exploring dairy, poultry, and other subsidiary activities. At that time, the idea of establishing FPCs began to emerge. The KVK, with support from the state government, Small Farmers Agribusiness Consortium (SFAC), National Bank for Agriculture and Rural Development (NABARD) together established eight FPCs, of which one is Kazhani. Formed with NABARD support, Kazhani received technical and managerial support continuously from KVK, while CMRC provided the foundation and support for the formation of FPC.

KVK supported Kazhani in extension, business development, capacity building, identifying the crops and varieties for the district based on its extensive experience. In the initial one or two years it also provided logistics support to the FPC. Innovations such as precision agriculture, pilot project of NABARD and KVK for vegetable and fruits ripening, processing and value addition activities were introduced in the later years.

One of the key initiatives undertaken by the CMRC prior to Kazhani's registration was exposure visits to successful FPCs. The visits helped farmers associated with the CMRC to understand the concept of FPCs, the scope for value addition and marketing in the main commodities, especially banana, which is widely grown in the region. Other farmer-centric initiatives such as introducing paddy transplanter to improve mechanisation, enabling access to government schemes and subsidies were helpful. Apart from this, the CMRC formed joint liability groups (JLG) and organised entrepreneurship development trainings with support from KVK and other agencies like Coconut Board on various enterprises such as poultry feed production, bee keeping, goat rearing, food processing, and use of mechanical coconut tree climber, among others.

2. Evolution of Kazhani's business model

The initial business model was built upon the foundation that CMRC created for Kazhani FPC. It started with marketing of products such as honey, goat milk soaps, organic toothpaste, and so on, produced by the entrepreneurs trained earlier. Building upon this, Kazhani started introducing different services to its members.

2.1 Initial success – crop insurance

Kazhani's initial success came from an unexpected twist of fate. It was through the introduction of crop insurance under the Pradhan Mantri Fasal Bima Yojana (PMFBY) scheme in partnership with Agriculture Insurance Company of India Ltd (AIC) in 2017. During NABARD training, Kazhani's chief executive officer (CEO) Kavitha met with an agent of AIC, who was appointing sub-dealers. Kazhani became the sub-dealer for Erode district and not only started enrolling farmers from Kazhani but partnered with other FPCs in Erode to enrol their farmers as well, especially those FPCs promoted by MYRADA. Around 200 farmers from Kazhani were enrolled for crop insurance.

That year, the water that was being released from Bhavani Sagar dam in the initial field preparation for paddy had to be stopped at the time of transplanting due to water shortage. This led to severe losses for the farmers who much to their frustration watched their fields dry up. In this difficult situation, the insurance claim came as a silver lining to all those farmers who had opted for insurance. Each farmer received around Rs. 4,000–5,000 per acre, which covered the costs they had incurred. For the entire Erode district, the FPC managed to get claims of nearly 8 million that year. Kazhani helped farmers in preparing the documents and did the data entry on the website, and the money was credited directly to the farmers' accounts. Though these transactions do not reflect in the FPC's books, it helped create a positive impression about the FPC among the farmers and gave confidence to Kavitha and her team about the benefits of registering as an FPC.

2.2 Initial setbacks – collective marketing of rice

The very first product to be launched by Kazhani was unpolished, hand-pounded rice, which it initially tried to sell to its own members. It seemed like a good business to start with since paddy was the major crop in the area and rice is the staple food. This business activity was initiated as soon as the FPC had enrolled about 250 members and had just registered itself and started filing GST. The FPC tried to sell unpolished rice under the 'Kazhani' brand name to both FPC members and non-members, through its SHG networks. But it didn't work as well as expected, as the market practices were well established. As a new entrant with limited capital Kazhani followed a cash-and-carry model and could not offer credit to customers.

2.3 Learning from failure – sale of grocery items

Rather than withdraw from its strategy, Kazhani decided to learn and improve. The next business idea that Kazhani experimented with was sale of grocery items (including rice) through the FPC. Kavitha was inspired by the work of other FPCs in Tamil Nadu, which retailed groceries through their extensive SHG network. Kazhani decided to try and implement the idea. Kazhani started procuring produce like pulses, spices, and so on, from various FPCs, and in turn supplied unpolished rice to those FPCs.

Later on, though the idea of FPC supplying these items through SHGs was discontinued, the business improved to the extent that Kazhani decided to open three outlets to sell these products. Kazhani has also tied up with about 80 retailers, which includes FPCs in the adjoining three districts to market Kazhani's products. They continue to stock produce from local entrepreneurs, and these are now packaged with the 'Kazhani FPCL' brand name and supplied to retailers that the FPC has tied up with. It has started direct sales to consumers in Mangalore through a tie-up with Mangalore-based company, Smart Cache.

2.4 Forays into bulk marketing of banana

In 2017, Kazhani received an order for supply of banana to Chennai through WayCool, an agri-products distribution start-up company. The order was a part of a one-year corporate social responsibility (CSR) programme, and the bananas were to be used for the mid-day meal scheme for school children. Though this programme did not continue post the one-year duration, Kazhani carried on with the banana business by supplying banana to traders in Chennai's Koyambedu market but found it difficult as the margins were wafer thin, and getting payments from traders was a challenge. Undeterred, Kazhani decided to expand its work on banana and explored other avenues like supplying to corporate buyers in Chennai. Two years later, in February 2020 it tied up with a banana exporter to supply banana for export markets, which is currently a major focus area for the FPC.

2.5 Value addition – millet processing

Since its early days Kazhani has been selling millet products produced by its entrepreneurs. To scale up production, in 2020, it received machinery for millet processing and value addition from the state government. It is in trial stage, and the company is currently producing millet cookies, health mixes, millet flours, and flour mixes, and trying out new packaging, new markets, and so on. Kazhani procures millets from farmers across the Erode district and not just its members. Also, it procures from other FPCs especially those promoted by MYRADA.

2.6 Overview of Kazhani's business

Of the 11 million turnover in 2020–21, 57% is from sale of value-added produce, 20% from sale of banana, 15% from input sales, others from drip equipment and seeds. Overall, Kazhani is a diversified FPC, which offers a range of services from insurance, inputs business to value addition and output marketing, even groceries. It works across commodities from paddy, banana to millets. It works with members and non-members and sources products from individual entrepreneurs and FPCs mainly but also from the market at times. The unifying theme in Kazhani's diversified approach seems to be a single-minded focus on business growth and viability of the FPC.

3. Key business strategies

Kazhani has experimented with various businesses depending on the capital and capability. With each experiment, the business model has evolved and currently Kazhani has three main product lines.

- Millets, where it is involved in value addition and processing;
- Paddy, where there is no procurement from members, but the FPC is involved in trading, but there are future plans for expanding paddy seed processing; and
- Banana, where the focus is on exports.

3.1 Millets

There is a growing interest in reviving millets in the country. Difficulty in processing millets is a major challenge that hinders upscaling potential for minor millets. The lack of suitable processing units close to millet fields means that local producers have to take their produce to distant places, which causes price increases across the value chain, including for consumers who have to pay higher rates for millet-based products as compared to paddy and wheat products. In this regard, it is interesting to note that the establishment of millet processing units by Kazhani FPCL is having a very positive effect on increasing demand for millets, by shortening the value chain and favouring local and regional consumption through affordable products.

Kazhani is involved in the procurement, primary processing of millets (destoning, de-hulling, and de-husking) and value addition into millet flour mixes, cookies, bread and rusk, noodles and pasta, and marketing of millet rice varieties and other value-added products.

The company wants to be able to provide the entire range of millet value-added products in the near future. It is working closely with the farming members to achieve this goal. FPC is planning to undertake a complete range of millet processing activities and market it under its own 'Kazhani' brand. It is also planning to establish an information kiosk on the national highway and establish separate display units at leading department stores to promote millets.

While Kazhani has an established market for millet value-added products, external factors like price fluctuations of the raw materials and availability of produce could be challenges. Also, it faces tough competition from established companies and well-funded newer start-ups that have entered the market selling millet-based products. Kazhani has enough funds currently to cater to the needs of the proposed millet processing activity. However, Kazhani's continued efforts to enter into new businesses may cause a scarcity of funds for the proposed business activities.

3.2 Paddy

Paddy occupies a large proportion of cultivated area in Erode district. Kazhani FPCL is located in the irrigated area of Erode district which covers more than 5,000 hectare area and has a production potential of 30,000 tonnes. Farmers in these regions cultivate paddy two times a year with all the major paddy varieties.

Nearly all the paddy grown by farmers is procured by the government at minimum support price (MSP). In this situation, Kazhani decided not to venture into procuring paddy – either for direct sale or for milling. Their initial venture of selling unpolished rice did not yield desirable results. The main reason being, the normal practice in the region was to purchase rice on credit, while Kazhani was not able to offer credit to customers. At present, it procures rice from a shareholder who is also a rice mill owner and repackages and sells under Kazhani's own brand. The FPC also sells traditional varieties of rice.

Apart from rice marketing, Kazhani is involved in the supply of paddy seeds, development of nurseries, and paddy transplantation. The seed requirement for raising the crop is quite less, and its cost is also less compared to other inputs, but the potential income a farmer gets depends upon the quality of the small quantity of seed they use. Kazhani procured quality seeds from reputed universities and research centres and distributed them to the farmers. Encouraged by the results, Kazhani plans to expand its paddy seed business. The construction of a seed processing and storage unit is underway. The plan is to procure seeds locally and sell locally and later venture into foundation seeds.

3.3 Banana

Banana and mango are two major fruit crops grown in the district. The economic importance of banana is increasing on account of increased demand in both domestic and international markets. Kazhani has been focusing on banana business and developing it in stages.[1]

Kazhani FPCL started the banana output business in March 2018. It aggregated and supplied bananas to corporates in Chennai under a contracting arrangement. So far Kazhani has supplied around 100 tonnes of banana varieties. It also registered as a vendor with WayCool for supplying banana varieties.

It established a market tie-up with Green Agro Products for export to Europe starting from January 2021 and started demand-based cultivation of Banana varieties. Initially, Kazhani supplied one consignment of G-9 bananas to Singapore and four sample consignments of red banana to Italy. The results of the test marketing were encouraging – the product received positive response from consumers.

In addition to learning the ropes of export market, Kazhani has been working steadily to develop backward linkages required for exports.

Demand-based banana cultivation started in August 2020 and by July 2021 covered 150 acres. The area under particular banana variety is decided by the FPC in consultation with the exporter, and the area of the plantation will be within the FPC's working area. To ensure remunerative income for the farmers Kazhani arranges for adequate and timely supply of inputs. It provides high-yielding hybrid varieties, timely financial assistance, guidance on pest-control measures, and better market linkages.

Banana crop cultivation involves a total cost of Rs. 0.15 million per acre, right from preparation of land till harvesting of the crop. Tissue culture planting material provided by Kazhani to the farmers has the following advantages over suckers – it ensures pest and disease-free seedlings, uniform growth, increased yield, and early maturing that provides for better land utilisation, and two successive rotations are possible in a short duration which minimises the cost of cultivation.

To ensure uniform quality, the company selected farmers, supplied them with all the inputs on credit (through tie-up with Jaikisan, a fintech start-up), and provided technical trainings through MYRADA KVK. The organic bananas are certified by Tamil Nadu Organic Certification Department (TNOCD). Kazhani applied blockchain technology from Madurai Agribusiness Incubation Forum (MABIF) to enable traceability of the farmers and the cultivation process. With blockchain technology, the FPC can put relevant information regarding each step in the cycle of agricultural events onto blockchain to enable farmers to get access to transparent and trusted source of information. Farmers can get instant data related to the seed quality, soil moisture, climate- and environment-related data, payments, demand and sale price, and so on, all at one platform. Blockchain can also help in establishing direct link between farmers and consumers/retailers.

However, the business has not taken off as per plan due to pandemic-related disruptions, shortage of refrigerated containers, and so on. Kazhani did not have a back-up plan to sell locally, and the farmers sold the produce on their own. That said, the CEO and the farmers are encouraged by the acceptance of the produce and are looking forward to a better season next time around. Despite initial setbacks and Covid disruptions, Kazhani wants to get into direct export of Banana after understanding the export business, which members estimate could take them another 3–4 years. The plan is clear among the stakeholders associated with Kazhani.

3.4 Financial performance

There has been a clear focus on the FPC sustaining itself through its revenues. Kazhani ventured into procuring value-added products made by local entrepreneurs like spices, spice powders, masala mixes, cold-pressed oils, honey, and so on. The sale of packaged grains (particularly rice) and pulses is a reliable source of revenue. Millet products in retail packaging have been rolled out for urban markets with an aim to generate consistent revenues.

The company was started with a project funding of Rs. 0.91 million from NABARD. The company has been able to achieve steady growth in business turnover from Rs. 3.43 million in (2017–18) to Rs. 7.97 million (2019–20) to 13.49 million in 2020–21. For the last three years, Kazhani has booked small annual profits between 0.1 million and 0.2 million. It is yet to pay any dividend to its shareholders.

It currently has 11 full-time staff, including the CEO, whose salaries are covered by the FPC from its revenues. In its fifth year now, the FPC receives only a small component (25%) of CEO salary from NABARD. A summary of its financial performance is given in Table 11.1.

- The total revenue of the FPC increased from Rs. 3.4 million in 2017 to Rs. 13.49 million in 2020.
- FPC also reported increased expenses over the years from Rs. 3.28 million in 2017 to Rs. 13.3 million in 2020. It implies that the total expenses of the company increased in proportion to the total revenue earned.
- Profit Before Tax (PBT) ranged between Rs. 66,000 and Rs. 0.22 million during the past four years (2016–17 to 2020–21).
- Profit After Tax (PAT) ranged between Rs. 15,000 and Rs. 0.1 million during the past four years (2016–17 to 2020–21).
- Share capital increased over the years from Rs. 1 million to Rs. 1.99 million which includes SFAC equity grant.
- Current assets in 2020–21 increased by nearly 15 times of the initial year 2016–17.
- FPC does not have any borrowings.

Out of the total Rs. 1.98 million share capital, Rs. 1 million is from paid-up capital, and the remaining is from SFAC equity grant. Funds for working

Table 11.1 Financial performance of Kazhani during 2016–21 (Rs. in million)

Particulars	2016–17	2017–18	2018–19	2019–20	2020–21
Total Revenue	0	3.43	5.87	7.97	13.49
Total Expenses	0.02	3.28	5.65	7.84	13.32
Profit Before Tax	(0.02)	0.14	0.22	0.07	0.09
Profit After Tax	(0.02)	0.11	0.11	0.02	0.03
Share Capital	0	1.00	1.00	1.99	1.99
Reserves and Surplus	0.95	0.06	0.18	1.21	6.82
Fixed Assets Including Investments	0	0.32	0.36	2.10	5.90
Current Liabilities	0.02	3.40	1.37	5.51	10.32
Current Assets	0.91	1.09	2.23	6.75	14.89

Table 11.2 Sources of capital for infrastructure development of millet processing unit

S. No	Source	Amount (Rs. in million)
1	Bank balance of FPC	1.10
2	Additional contribution by FPC (SBI loan)	1.30
3	Grant/subsidy available	3.00
4	Any other source (liquid stock value)	1.50

capital are a key constraint for the growth of the FPC. Says a director, "Considering the potential in banana business or even paddy procurement, we need a working capital of at least 25 million, but we are managing with only about 2 million capital so far."

The company received its share of SFAC's equity grant and a loan of 0.5 million from Sanghamithra Rural Financial Services (at 6%, term loan) in 2018–19. In the same year, it received a loan of 4.7 million from SBI under SFAC's credit guarantee scheme.

For its millets processing business, Kazhani invested around 1.8 million for infrastructure. The project cost was Rs. 4.8 million including working capital requirement of Rs. 1.05 million; Kazhani received grant of Rs. 3 million under Tamil Nadu Irrigated Agriculture Modernization Program (TNIAMP) of state government. Kazhani has mobilised funds required for infrastructure development and working capital from the sources mentioned in Table 11.2. The proposed business activity of establishing a complete range of millet products is going to generate a turnover of Rs. 15 million to 20 million for the financial year 2021–22 with a net profit of Rs. 0.92 million in the first year of operation.

Thus, the FPC which started with its financial source as share capital has been able to access government grants, loans, infrastructure support, and is looking to sustain its business through profits from the business.

4. Shareholder outreach and governance

An estimated 600 members receive at least one form of service from the company; they either purchase grocery, farm inputs, or sell their farm produce or value-added produce. Paddy/banana is procured from local farmers but also from non-members when the need arises. Millets are procured from non-members in hilly regions, where another FPC promoted by MYRADA operates.

The board is aware of the challenges in engaging shareholders, as a director puts it succinctly,

Fulfilling shareholder expectations is very challenging for the FPC. A farmer sees the FPC as a Government body and expects benefits like grants or loans to the tune of 0.5 million each, otherwise they don't show much interest in the FPC activities.

In that sense, developing a shared vision among farmers, directors, and key stakeholders is a critical need and is important for the institutional sustainability of the FPC, which might become dependent on individuals otherwise.

4.1 The 'core' team of the FPC

Sustained growth and development of FPCs depend on the cooperation and coordination of different stakeholders involved in its operations. Kazhani has 12 board of directors (BoDs) and Kavitha, the CEO, has more than eight years of field experience in working with farmers through CMRC. Her previous experience in mobilising, capacity building, and identification of farmers' needs helped in the collectivisation, formation, and promotion of Kazhani. She has also played a significant role in the development of marketing and financial linkages for the FPC. She has participated in various training programmes organised by NABARD, Coconut Development Board, Coir Board, and various central and state government agencies and is also involved in conducting training for directors and farmers of state government-promoted FPCs and farmer collectives.

Kavitha's transition from CMRC manager to Kazhani's CEO is interesting. She attended the exposure visits to successful FPCs organised by NABARD and the concept of FPC. She then started canvassing the concept of FPC among farmers. She was involved with the share collection for Kazhani even before it got its name. Incidentally, it was initially planned to be registered as a society with the name of the CMRC, Thenkoodu Farmers Service Centre.

Kavitha recounts farmers asking, when handing over the share money to her, as to who would handle the money and build the FPC, which was still a concept then. Narrating her mental state at that time, Kavitha says,

> When I used to collect the Rs. 1,000 from farmers, I did it with fear and excitement. I knew the value of the money that the farmers were giving me, and it developed in me a sense of personal responsibility, in addition to the belief in MYRADA's work with farmers.

In 2019, MYRADA decided to let the CMRCs be run by the community itself and stopped supporting CMRC managers. Kavitha got the option to shift to another district to join a project or join Kazhani as its CEO. She chose the latter and has been its CEO since then.

The current directors of Kazhani are progressive farmers from the farmers groups, who actively participated in KVK trainings and exposure visits to successful FPCs, organised by NABARD. Four of the directors of the company come to the office almost every day. Among these, the chairperson is a retired schoolteacher, two of the directors have the responsibility of marketing FPC's products, and one director is responsible for accounts and financial management.

Few of the directors have experience in working with CMRC, and it has instilled a sense of ownership and commitment in the minds of directors to work for the growth of FPC. The company holds BoD meetings every month, on the 25th of every month, and emergency meetings as and when required. Though no agenda is circulated before the meeting a formal presentation is made on financial status and operational decisions to be taken. All the discussions are verbal, and minutes are recorded. Generally, each meeting has the participation of more than ten BoDs and the FPC conducts more than 12 meetings in a year.

Kavitha says,

> Each director represents a group of farmers and communication of day-to-day activities to farmers happens through BoDs. BoDs come to the office daily, they spend at least a half-day in the company and inform the discussion to members through an informal meeting.

Mr Gokulnathan, one of the BoDs, says, "Farmers' cooperation is very good with the FPC which is the result of transparent governance."

5. Leveraging support from the ecosystem

One of the things that stand out in this FPC is the manner in which it has leveraged several government schemes to obtain capital assets. The FPC received millets primary processing equipment and value addition unit from the state government under various schemes. It has also received seed processing and storage unit and a transport vehicle. The total value of these grants is about 10 million. The company has committed 20–30% of the project value from its own resources for obtaining these grants.

The company has worked with MABIF, Tamil Nadu Agriculture University (TNAU), National Banana Board apart from KVK, which is also the promoting agency. MYRADA KVK had earlier promoted producer associations with a reasonable degree of success, and the idea behind promoting Kazhani FPC was to explore institutional means for promotion of secondary agriculture. Funding was obtained from NABARD's Producer Organization Development Fund (PODF) initiative.

6. The road ahead

Kazhani has its task cut out. It has identified its key business lines, as explained in the previous sections. Looking ahead, it would like to become a complete end-to-end solution for farmers, first by setting up a hub for the complete set of value-added products from millets; second, a seed processing unit; and third getting into coconut procurement and value addition; and finally, paddy procurement and processing.

6.1 Proposed activities and goals for the next five years

6.1.1 Focus on sustainable agriculture

Having the passion to grow organic products, Kazhani is promoting the use of organic inputs among the farming community. During the field visits, members of Kazhani shared excitedly about their experiments with organic farming and were encouraged by the decrease in input costs and no decrease in yields.

The FPC is also planning to cultivate organic vegetables in 100 to 200 acres in the current year with a focus on reduced input costs for farmers. Implementation of drip irrigation with government subsidies aimed at judicious use of water and other resources is one of the ecological concerns of Kazhani.

6.1.2 A Model FPC

In the long run, all stakeholders aim to develop Kazhani as a model FPC. They see Kazhani as having the opportunity to explore partnerships with private players and state agencies for agriculture value-chain development at the regional/local, national, and international levels.

6.1.3 Big on tech

Information and Communication Technologies (ICTs) have become an important tool in promoting agricultural value-chain efficiency. Kazhani is already working on blockchain technology to improve traceability in its banana business. In 2019, Kavitha attended a week-long seminar in Germany on use of traceability technology in organic banana and is looking to implement the learnings.

7. Summing up

To sum up, in a short span of five years since its establishment, Kazhani has explored various ventures. Some have worked and others didn't. There have been delays as well – Kazhani's plan for seed processing unit has been delayed, the plan was to start seed procurement in the current season, but there is a delay in completing construction due to pandemic-related disruptions.

But rather than withdraw from its strategy when things don't go as planned, it has learnt from each setback and grown stronger from its experience. Kazhani's unique aspects are the ability to learn quickly and network extensively and a focus on execution (learning by doing).

Another distinctive quality is to think and act like an entrepreneur (as opposed to an NGO working on grants or a researcher trying to analyse/learn) at each step during its journey – be it attending trainings or meetings or interacting with various stakeholders. Each interaction is an opportunity to "learn and do" something new, which seems to be the need of the hour for the FPC. Kazhani has been good at this learning by doing approach.

As an organisation with a huge farmer base and a professionally run company, an FPC has the potential to attract government schemes and programmes to build its capital and develop infrastructure. However, this does not happen by default. Not every FPC is able to successfully work with government agencies. It requires networking skills and programme implementation capabilities, such as reporting progress at government review meetings, managing visits, inspections, and dealing with the expectations and demands of government officers.

Kazhani has been able to constantly interact with buyers, sellers, manufacturers, government institutions, and their own farmers and look for new opportunities. Taking up such large amounts of grants and investments also requires an appetite for taking risks. As a sustainable FPC, Kazhani is poised to grow exponentially. It has not been easy getting here, and it has several challenges up its sleeve as well. It will be interesting to see how it evolves from here.

Note

1 A blog written by the authors on Kazhani's banana business can be accessed at https://www.smallfarmincomes.in/post/venturing-in-market-going-bananas-experiences-of-kazhani-farmers-producers-company-limited

12

BRIDGING SMALLHOLDER FRUIT FARMERS AND CONSUMERS

The case of Navyug Kisan Producer Company Ltd

Gouri Krishna and Rajesh Verma

1. Introduction

Navyug Kisan Producer Company Ltd. (NYPCL) is a collective of mango-growing farmers promoted under the Sodic Land Reclamation Project by the Government of Uttar Pradesh. The Uttar Pradesh Bhumi Sudhar Nigam (UPBSN), an autonomous institute of the Government of Uttar Pradesh, was established in 1978 with the mission of preserving the health and productivity of land resources sustainably and to protect, rehabilitate, and regenerate all potentially cultivable lands in the state affected with sodicity. (Sodicity is caused by the presence of sodium attached to clay in the soil. A soil is considered sodic when the sodium reaches a concentration where it starts to affect soil structure.)

UPBSN implemented the Sodic Land Reclamation Project in 29 districts through 20 project management units in the state in three phases from 1993 to 2018. The long-term project included several activities which could have a favourable impact on agriculture and socio-economic aspects of the districts falling under the project at the individual project activity level. The third phase from 2009 to 2018 envisaged greater market linkages, and as part of the project implementation, it was planned to hire the services of a specialised agency. The agency was assigned with the task of providing support to the farmers for accessing larger markets and improving the profitability of the project beneficiaries sustainably.

In the year 2011, UPBSN selected Bhartiya Samruddhi Investments and Consulting Ltd (BASIX) for promotion and nurturing 100 FPCs in 29 districts in the state as a business support organisation for institutional strengthening and capacity building for market access of farmers in these districts. The duration of the project was for three years up to December 2014 but subsequently the project was extended up to December 2018. Additional

DOI: 10.4324/9781003308034-12

FPC formation and more tasks were added for the extended period.[1] While initially the existing sodic farmer's groups were to be federated into FPCs, the PA was asked to form new producer groups (PGs) in the same area.

At the end of the seven years, BASIX had incorporated 120 FPCs from 4,484 PGs with a total membership of 102,563 farmers as shareholders across 1,035 villages covering 29 districts in Uttar Pradesh (UP).

1.1 Navyug Kisan Farmer's Producer Company Ltd.

NYPCL is one of the five FPCs promoted by the promoting agency (PA) in the district of Lucknow. It has its headquarters at Kaji Khera village. Kaji Khera is a small village/hamlet in Malihabad Block in Lucknow district of UP. NYPCL is one of the early FPCs formed by the PA.

UP has 14 designated mango belts. Four million tonnes of mangoes are produced in UP, and that counts for 23% of India's total mango collection (GoI, 2018). Lucknow division is the main mango-growing belt producing 28% of the total production of UP. The largest of 14 mango belts in UP, Malihabad has 30,000 hectares of land under cultivation. It accounts for nearly 12.5% of the mangoes produced from UP.[2] Hundreds of mango varieties are grown here, including the Chausa, Langda, Safeda, and most famously the Dasheri, which is one of the kinds of mangoes exported from India.

Malihabad region is famous for the cultivation of mango which is a major source of livelihood. Several factors such as changing pest and disease dynamics, lack of processing industry and organised marketing network in the region, and predominance of middlemen in the trading network contributed to the reduced profitability of mango production system, particularly for small and marginal farmers.

Kaji Khera has the largest number of sodic farmers which was one of the reasons for the PA to select the village in the catchment area of the FPC. Most of the members of FPC are small and marginal farmers with an average holding of 1.7 acres.

2. Services by the PA

2.1 Institution development services

BASIX is the holding company of BASIX Social Enterprise Group. It is engaged in the promotion of livelihoods of the rural poor, women, and marginalised communities for over two decades in India and other developing countries in the world. As a livelihood promoting institute, BASIX evolved a comprehensive livelihood TRIAD model (Datta et al., 2014) to work with vulnerable and poor families living in rural and urban slum areas. Financial inclusion, institutional building, action research and policy advocacy are the core areas of BASIX's work.

BASIX initiated its field activities in Mallihabad block by identifying five progressive farmers in the villages from the catchment area of NYPCL. The benefits of the collectivisation process were discussed in detail with these farmers. Over the next three-month period the BASIX's team along with the UPBSN team and the five farmers who subsequently became the promoter directors held a series of meetings with the farmers to seed the idea of the farmer's collective. Day-long workshops were conducted for small groups of farmers in catchment villages. Three of the promoter directors visited Hardoi Agriculture Marketing and Producer Company Pvt Ltd in Madhya Pradesh which helped in sharing the vision of the collective with fellow farmers. Navyug Kisan Producer Company Ltd (NYPCL) was thus incorporated on 20 January 2014.

BASIX developed a set of six training modules and training kits to build awareness among the members on the basic characteristics of FPC and its functioning. Around 250 farmer members were trained using the modules. Apart from basic training on FPC concept and operation, a few specialised training programmes were also conducted which included leadership and enterprise promotion for the board members; books and accounts and statutory compliances for CEO and selected board members; and so on.

To provide NYPCL with the latest technology update on crop production, productivity, and managing risk to optimise profit, BASIX helped NYPCL in establishing linkage with research institutions, universities, companies, and technology providers. Some of such initiatives undertaken were demonstration plots for high-yielding varieties of wheat, onion organised through KVKs, and animal health improvement programmes on the use of effective microorganisms for improving animal health.

2.2 Business development services

BASIX encouraged NYPCL to cater to the needs of the members for the input requirement and facilitated mango sales through private traders in the initial years. The centralised network of agri-input suppliers, technology providers, and buyers that BASIX had built over several years helped in catering to the needs of the New Age collectives of farmers. Over the years, through several collaborations, NYPCL could strengthen its relationship with various input suppliers and established an input centre to cater to the needs of the members for seed, fertilisers, and pesticides. IFFCO made NYPCL its authorised dealer for Urea and DAP. Table 12.1 refers to collaborations built for input and output activities.

On the output marketing, NYPCL has consistently supported members in the sale of their wheat production over the years. As for the sale of mango, the FPC faced a setback in the initial years due to non-receipt of payment from the buyers which lead to huge losses. This resulted in the FPC taking a back step for mango marketing.

Table 12.1 Tie-ups facilitated for NYPCL

S No.	Particulars	Company Name/Institution
	A. Input	
1	Seed	
a	Paddy	Nuziveedu, Bio-seed, Ganga Kaveri
b	Wheat	UPBSN, Kumar seed Pilibhit
2	Urea	IFFCO, Chambal, IPL
3	DAP and NPK	IFFCO, IPL
4	Sulphur	IFFCO, Dayal Fertilizer
5	Zinc	IFFCO
6	Micronutrient	Khandelwal Industries
7	Pesticide	Awadh Lucknow & Ahmad Pesticide
8	Weedicide	Awadh Lucknow & Ahmad Pesticide
9	Agro-chemical	Buyers, PI, HPM
10	Bio Fertiliser	Maple Agri Ltd, Cedilla, Margosa
	B. Output	
1	Mango	Private Traders
2	Wheat and paddy	Government MSP centre
3	Potato	ITC

2.3 Financial services

Raising working capital was a major constraint for NYPCL. Initially, it used the share capital fund and contribution from the board members to meet its working capital needs. BASIX had helped the FPC explore various avenues to overcome the challenge to a certain extent. NYPCL received Community Investment Fund (CIF) of Rs. 0.45 million from UPBSN, borrowed Rs. 0.30 million from Bhartiya Samruddhi Finance Limited (BSFL), the microfinance arm of BASIX through its members it received an equity grant of Rs. 0.50 million from Small Farmers Agribusiness Consortium (SFAC).

3. Governance of NYPCL

3.1 Board of directors

NYPCL has a five-member board that is very active. In the year 2020, the board inducted a representative of Uttar Pradesh Kisan Producer Company Ltd (UPPRO) as an expert advisor to help NYPCL in commodity marketing. UPPRO helped the FPC in mango sales under its brand name 'Umang'.

In addition to the mandatory quarterly board meetings, the directors of NYPCL meet more frequently to discuss the operational issues of the company. Each board member interacts with members of the village of their residence on regular basis. Minutes of the board meetings and annual general body meetings are maintained. Annual budgets are prepared. The board has one women member as director. The CEO and the chairman have adequate knowledge of the statutory compliances required to be performed by the company and fulfil the same with the support of the chartered accountant.

3.2 *Catering to members and non-members*

On average 600 small and marginal farmer members and 200–300 non-members benefit from NYPCL activities. Figure 12.1 shows the number of shareholders and non-shareholder beneficiaries serviced by NYPCL over the years. The FPC was successful in increasing the number of shareholders over years.

> We offer services to non-members also. We procured from non-members during difficult times too. We did not discriminate on the selling price of inputs or procurement price of output between members and non-members to earn goodwill. We endeavour to enrol them and attract more members in the future.
>
> (Chairman of NYPCL Mr Vasu Deo
> Singh divulged his strategy)

Ninety-eight per cent of the shareholders of NYPCL are small farmers. Only 13 farmers are marginal and four large farmers. According to the chairman of NYPCL, the large farmers support the growth of the FPC. A few farmers have provided financial assistance when working capital loans were channelised through them.

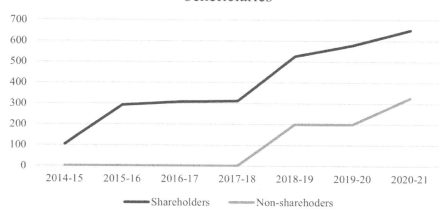

Figure 12.1 Graph showing members and non-members serviced by FPC

NYPCL has only 12 women members. The backwardness of the area and cultural practices and lack of active efforts by the board and CEO to encourage enrolment of women were the reasons for low women participation. The board has one woman member whose participation in the board deliberations was minimal. A few of the women members are also members of self-help groups (SHGs) in the area. The chairman admitted that efforts were lacking and assured that the board will consciously work to increase women's participation in the future. He has indicated a plan to work with SHG women for their support in producing value-added products by NYPCL.

4. Growth of NYPCL

Between 2017 and 2021, NYPCL has increased its members from 350 to 1,005 members. Most members are small farmers with less than two acres of land with an average of 1.7 acres. Eighty per cent of the members are mango growers. The other crops grown include wheat and vegetables. Potato is the major crop among vegetables followed by chilli, brinjal, ladyfinger, cucumber, pumpkin, tomato, ginger, coriander, and radish.

Input linkages to member farmers were well established by NYPCL over the years. Accessibility, availability, and price advantage are the features that helped NYPCL to establish itself in this area of business. It had also successfully established market linkages for output. Tie-up with corporate buyers led to price realisation up to 40–80% higher than the market price to both the FPC and its members. The company traded mango through institution tie-ups with corporate buyers and B2C sales using online transactions through secured payment gateway during the pandemic year. NYPCL is actively exploring the export market for mangoes. Awareness creation among members to adopt best practices to cater to the export market is one of the priorities in the agenda of NYPCL. Tie-up with Mother Dairy is actively being pursued to supply vegetables. The success in mango marketing and opening of new avenues of marketing formed a stepping stone for NYPCL for focusing on mango marketing for the benefit of its members.

4.1 Mobilisation and membership increase (2014–15; 2015–16; 2016–17)

For a period of three years since its inception in 2014, NYPCL focused on increasing membership in the FPC in the initial years of its formation. The dynamism of promoter directors played an important role in achieving this substantially. Around 350 farmers were enrolled by the end of the financial year 2017. The share capital from members increased from Rs. 0.10 million at inception to Rs. 0.62 million.

Table 12.2 Commodity sales

Year-wise Sale Facilitation				
S. No.	*Year*	*Crop*	*Total Quantity (in Quintals)*	*Amount (Rs. in Million)*
1	2015–16	Mango	315	0.63
2		Wheat	475	0.71
3	2016–17	Wheat	300	0.48

There was no business operation during the year 2014–15. Input sales formed the major chunk of business turnover during 2015–16 and 2016–17. Members sourced fertilisers, pesticides, and seeds from the FPC. FPC acquired licenses for input and output sales despite prevailing challenging protocols for obtaining license in the state of UP.[3] Members got a price advantage of Rs. 20–30 per 45 kg bag of urea (average market rate during the period was Rs. 330 per bag) and Rs. 10–15 on 50 kg bag of DAP (average market during the period was Rs, 1,050 per bag) which was an attractive incentive for the members to purchase from the FPC and more members to join.

The FPC initiated procurement of wheat from its members which it undertook consistently in all the years. Mango sales were taken up in the first year of its business operation. Table 12.2 indicates commodity sales in the initial years.

Working capital was a major constraint for the FPC. The FPC utilised CIF of Rs. 0.45 million received from UPBSN and loan from BSFL, the microfinance arm of BASIX through members for its operations.

The turnover of the company increased from Rs. 1.50 million at the end of 2016 to Rs. 6.20 million as of 31 March 2017.

4.2 Asset acquisition (2017–18; 2018–19)

During the two years between 2017 and 2019, NYPCL focused on the acquisition of assets. The FPC received CIF from UPBSN as a part of the project grant for warehouse construction. The FPC leveraged the government farm machinery scheme and received a subsidy for the purchase of a tractor and other agriculture equipment. The total grant received was Rs. 1.05 million.

NYPCL purchased land measuring 4,050 sq. ft. and constructed an input centre with storage space and office space. Part of the unconstructed area with a roof is left for procurement and aggregation of commodities for output sales. NYPCL has assets worth Rs. 2.72 million. While 50% of the cost of assets was covered by the grant, the balance was met through long-term borrowings.

The PA, BASIX withdrew in December 2018 after the project closure with UPBSN. With an increased focus on asset acquisition, the business operations suffered during this phase. The income fell to Rs. 4.50 million as of 31 March 2018 and to Rs. 2.20 million as of 31 March 2019.

4.3 Exploring alternate market channels (2019–20; 2020–21)

During the year 2020, and the subsequent part of the pandemic year, the FPC sought the support of the state-level producer company, namely UPPRO. UPPRO has a membership of 40 farmer producer organisations (FPO) in UP.

With its headquarters at Lucknow, UPPRO supports its members with an emphasis on output and value addition which is the primary objective of collectives, that is, to achieve better returns to its member's produce. With support from UPPRO to find a market for mango sales, NYPCL encouraged the members to sell mangoes through FPC. The tie-up with corporate buyers and B2C sales helped in better-than-market price realisation to its members.

During the year 2019–20, NYPCL witnessed two important outcomes from its sustained efforts. One was the receipt of a matching equity grant of Rs. 0.50 million from the SFAC after a prolonged process to complete the required documentation for availing the grant. Second, there is an increase in the turnover from Rs. 2.20 million in 2019 to Rs. 5.20 million in 2020, and Rs. 5.40 million by the end of 2021 with intervention of UPPRO and mango sales through alternate channels.

5. Changed approach of output marketing

NYPCL is engaged in input sales largely with the bulk of its revenue coming from fertiliser sales. On commodity sales, the company consistently facilitated wheat sales through *mandis* after cleaning and grading. While mango sales were taken up in the initial years, this was subsequently stopped because of heavy losses incurred by NYPCL owing to default from the buyers and non-remunerative prices. With the intervention of UPPRO, NYPCL has once again embarked on mango sales providing remunerative prices to the members.

UPPRO is a state-level producer company (SLPC) which is a federation of FPCs of small and marginal farmers operational in different districts of UP. Forty FPCs in UP are at present enrolled as members in the SLPC, and the membership is growing. UPPRO offers advisory services to its members for production enhancement and builds a marketing network to facilitate output marketing. It supports in leveraging government schemes by FPCs and enables financial linkages with banks and other financial institutes. Its mission is to provide end-to-end services in agriculture and allied products to improve the profitability of small and marginal farmers. UPPRO markets its members' produce under the brand name 'Umang'.

NYPCL became a member of UPPRO in 2020. With their support, NYPCL adopted a market-oriented approach for output marketing, especially for mangoes. Over the years, UPPRO established relationships with a variety of organisations for supporting FPCs for leveraging technology, markets, and finances. It has identified institutional buyers for mangoes and facilitated mango sales for NYPCL.

5.1 Institutional tie-ups

NYPCL was able to sell 6,200 kg of mango during the pandemic through a tie-up with Reliance Fresh (4,900 kg) and Big Basket (1,300 kg) with support from UPPRO. This gave huge encouragement to NYPCL to restart the mango procurement and sales which it stopped in the year 2015. The profitability from these institutional sales was considerable compared to market price. The members received Rs. 10–12 per kg higher price than the market rate. The selling price to institutions ranged from Rs. 35 per kg of mangoes at the beginning of the season to Rs. 45 per kg at the end of the season when the prevailing market rate was Rs. 25–35 per kg.

As it was a first-time transaction with NYPCL, Reliance Fresh agreed to pay 50% advance and balance after receipt of the consignment. Big Basket sent a representative to verify the quality of the product and paid 100% before delivery. NYPCL sees the potential to increase this type of transaction in the future.

5.2 B2C sales

UPPRO also facilitated online sales directly to the customers, which was a new avenue of commodity sale for NYPCL. Approximately 3,600 kg of mangoes were sold online during the lockdown period in 2020 due to the pandemic. Instamojo payment gateway was set up by UPPRO for online transactions for B2C sales. A total of 158 customers purchased online in three days. The success of online sales was overwhelming for NYPCL as they have not expected large demand for online sales. The customer feedback was positive in terms of the quality of the product and timely delivery.

6. Financial performance

Table 12.3 gives a summary of the financial performance of NYPCL over the years on key parameters. The company had achieved the highest turnover in the third year after inception – which was the second year after it had initiated the business transactions (NYPCL was registered on 20 January 2014 and didn't undertake business during the year 2014–15). The total

Table 12.3 Financial performance of NYPCL (amount in rupees)

Particulars	2014–15	2015–16	2016–17	2017–18	2018–19	2019–20	2020–21
Total Revenue	–	1,556,415	6,218,339	4,545,888	2,247,960	5,214,227	5,359,636
Total Expenses	11,000	1,585,737	6,206,810	4,712,611	2,221,244	5,193,786	5,316,623
Profit Before Tax	(11,000)	(29,322)	11,529	(166,723)	26,176	20,441	43,013
Profit After Tax	(11,000)	(29,322)	7,966	11,529	26,716	12,357	38,089
Share Capital	100,000	310,000	620,000	620,000	800,400	1,313,000	1,313,000
Reserves and Surplus	(11,000)	(40,322)	(32,356)	(196,521)	(169,805)	(142,234)	(104,145)
Long-Term Borrowings				1,008,188	239,727	687,675	521,897
Fixed Assets Including Investments			420,000	1,425,702	1,962,049	1,206,820	1,135,995
Current Liabilities	5,000	6,000	875,193	227,655	134,460	389,581	789,604
Current Assets	70,000	480,902	1,574,807	634,625	368,185	1,280,291	1,528,373

Figure 12.2 Graph showing the financial performance of the company

turnover as of 31 March 2020 is Rs. 5.21 million and for the year 2021 is Rs. 5.40 million.

As shown in Figure 12.2, NYPCL has increased its revenue from Rs. 1.50 million to Rs. 5.40 million in 2021. It generated profit in four out of seven years of its existence which ranged from Rs. 8,000 in 2016–17 to Rs, 40,000 in 2020–21.

NYPCL acquired several assets over the years which include 4,050 sq. ft. of land which has been declared as commercial property for which they are likely to receive a subsidy on the cost of purchase. Under the agriculture farm machinery scheme, NYPCL purchased a tractor, a thresher, a seed drill, and other agriculture tools.

NYPCL has a cash credit limit of Rs. 0.50 million with Indian Overseas Bank to meet the working capital requirement of its business operations. Owing to the inadequacy of the limit, NYPCL has approached the bank for increasing the limit. They have also applied to Ananya Finance for a working capital loan.

7. Benefits to the members

The members perceive a twofold benefit from the activities of NYPCL: first, the accessibility of quality inputs from the input centre of the FPC and timely availability. This reduces the travel time to the block headquarters for the purchase of inputs. Second, the cost advantage is due to the lower price of the inputs than the market price.

On the output front, there is a clear advantage of supplying to FPC as against the market. The FPC makes payment to the total quantity procured from the farmer unlike the trader who would deduct a certain quantity of any commodity supplied before making the payment. This applies to both wheat and mango supplied by members.

> I source my fertilizer requirement from the input Centre of Navyug. Without the Centre, I have to travel eight kilometres to Malihabad market. On average, Urea is Rs. 5–10 less than the market rate and DAP is Rs. 15–20 lesser. Sometimes, the difference is as high as Rs. 15–20 on Urea and Rs. 20–30 on DAP. I save on transportation also.
>
> (Mr Vineet Shukla, a member of NYPCL)

The other benefits members accrue from the FPC are the renting of the farm machinery. The seed drill specifically contributes to the reduction of time, drudgery, and cost of cultivation. The FPC provides the machinery at lower rental charges than the market. Easy availability at a cheaper cost is considered beneficial by the members. Members get a benefit of Rs. 50–100 per hour on the rental charges than hiring from the market.

NYPCL proved to be a saviour not only to members but also to the non-members during the pandemic time. The timely intervention helped the farmers to find an avenue to sell their products which otherwise could have affected their income and sustenance.

Some of the intangible benefits most members expressed were that proximity and accessibility of the inputs save them time. Before NYPCL came into existence farmers travelled on an average of 5–6 km to buy input from local traders.

Quality of inputs is another benefit perceived. The major challenge for mango growers is the pest attack. The farmers have 50–60% of the land under mango orchards and pesticide is used liberally as part of orchard management. While many traders deal in pesticides, there is a danger of spurious products which are hazardous to the orchids. Members depend on the FPC for the genuineness of the quality at a justified price that is lower than the market.

> For the past six years, I am selling wheat to Navyug. Earlier I used to sell at Malihabad market. The arathiya would deduct 5 kg from the quantity I offered to sell and made the payment only for the balance. He would say that he has to pay big traders for taking produce from him. Now I don't lose that 5 kg. I get paid for the total quantity I sell to Navyug.
>
> (Mr Shivam, member of NYPCL)

8. Future plans

With the benefit accrued from a tie-up with Big Basket and Reliance Fresh for institutional sales, NYPCL is exploring similar buyers for mango sales. The market for online sales was another avenue NYPCL is ready to cater considering the payment gateway in place and the good customer feedback it had received. NYPCL plans to increase its mango procurement by 400–500 quintals. It proposes to sell 50% online, 30% institutional sales, and 20% export.

Usage of excessive pesticides is one of the biggest hurdles for producing export-quality mangoes. NYPCL with support from Bayer Crop Sciences, a network partner of UPPRO, proposes to educate the farmer members in restricted usage of pesticides to produce export quality output that can help in increasing the revenues of the farmers. Talks were initiated with mango packhouse, an entity of the horticulture department that oversees the exports.

NYPCL has applied for grant funding of Rs. 6.00 million under the Decentralized Rural Infrastructure and Seed Technology Initiatives, a joint scheme of the Government of India and the state government. The grant is provided for the establishment of a seed processing unit and godown. A total area of 6,500 sq. ft. is required for this purpose. NYPCL proposes to utilise 50% of the unconstructed area available out of 4,050 sq. ft. of its land. Additional land of 4,500 sq. ft. adjacent to this land was acquired on a long-term lease from the members.

NYPCL is an authorised seller of seed corporation of UP and proposes to encourage farmers to multiply the foundation seed, buy back the produce, process and sell to the seed corporation, and also direct sale to members.

With the support of UPPRO, NYPCL has initiated the digitisation of its books of records. For this purpose, NYPCL has recruited Mr Pappu Kumar who is being trained by UPPRO through its network partner Centre for Digitization of Financial Inclusion (CDFI). UPPRO is offering financial support for the training and cost of the individual during the training period. The training will continue for six months. NYPCL has procured the required hardware for the implementation of digitisation after the training is completed. NYPCL signed a MoU to participate in MeitY project of Government of India under Ministry of Electronics and IT. The project goal is to digitise all the transactions with the farmer members.

9. Conclusion

With nearly 900 FPOs (upshaktifpo.com), UP stands second to the state of Maharashtra in the number of FPOs promoted in India. In a state where cooperatives have failed, the success of farmer collectives under FPO promotion schemes is a welcome change. The state government has also been encouraging the FPO movement by allowing FPOs to leverage government schemes by getting them linked to various government departments under convergence mode to help the FPOs get direct benefits from the various government schemes. It claims to be the first state to have launched the FPO portal in the country.

The story of NYPCL shows that commitment of the founding members greatly contributed to its success. Consistent growth since its inception showcases it as a potential collective for growth. The active role played by the governing body and support rendered to the management helped in achieving this. The growth phases of NYPCL indicate a goal-oriented approach. The management has initially focused on increasing the membership which is crucial for the collective to grow. It then created assets for the FPC that enhanced its reputation among members and created visibility.

In providing services, it catered to the access and affordability needs of members for inputs initially. The management had surmounted the challenges of obtaining licenses for the input and output transactions by actively seeking external support in achieving its goal.

The strategy to leverage all possible government programmes and schemes available for farmers through FPC paid off to the benefit of members and the organisation. NYPCL has benefitted from the farm machinery scheme of the agriculture department which proved as an income-generating activity for the FPC. It is planning to establish infrastructural facilities under the joint scheme of central and state governments.

The strategic decisions concerning the output marketing were oriented for members' benefit. The decision to explore new markets and tech-enabled platforms for mango marketing depicts the zeal to tread an unknown path for benefit of farmers. The FPC also had taken the prudent decision of not including vegetables in its product portfolio where it was evident aggregation would not bring value addition.

On the HR front, NYPCL had the benefit of a trained CEO at the helm of affairs who has been recruited and trained by the PA which provided handholding support until it exited. The continuance of the CEO since its inception helped in the standardisation of systems, processes, and timely compliances. The working relationship between board and the CEO supported achieving the objective of the collective.

A purposeful and coordinated engagement among the founding members, board of directors, and the CEO of the FPC proved an important ingredient to the consistent growth of NYPCL over the years. The continuity of the CEO is another aspect that helped in the strategic decision-making process. Openness to explore new avenues that benefit the organisation and its members, reaching out for external support, and sharing benefits with non-members are contributors to the mission of the organisation to support smallholder farmers.

> We sold 100 quintals of mango in a pandemic year, and this is the product of 100 farmer members. Consider a ten-fold increase when all the members contribute, and we can cater to customers all over the world. This is our goal.
>
> (Mr Vasu Deo Singh, Chairman of NYPCL)

Notes

1 For details of the challenges in promoting FPOs in Uttar Pradesh, see https://www.smallfarmincomes.in/post/a-100-difficult-dreams-tracing-a-development-profes-sional-s-journey-of-incubating-FPCs

2 On Malihabad's history of growing mangos, see https://www.hindustantimes.com/brunch/malihabad-in-the-land-of-famous-dussehri-mangoes/story-eK976k3RH-Wo4HSeLjTLrAL.html

3 For details on the overall environment for promoting FPOs in UP, see https://www.smallfarmincomes.in/post/learning-to-work-at-scale-the-elusive-ease-of-doing-business-in-rural-india

References

Datta, S, Kandarpa, R & Mahajan, V (2014). *Resource book for livelihood promotion* (4th edition). Hyderabad: Institute of Livelihood Research and Training.

GoI (2018). *Horticultural statistics at a glance 2018*. New Delhi: Ministry of Agriculture & Farmers' Welfare.

13

SUSTAINING LIVELIHOODS AND SECURING SOVEREIGNTY

Tracing the journey of Desi Seed Producer Company Limited, Mysore, Karnataka

Tara Nair and Hareesh Belawadi

1. Introduction

Desi Seed Producer Company Limited, Mysore, Karnataka, owes its origins to Sahaja Samrudha, a movement started in the early 2000s in Karnataka by a small group of organic farmers to spread the message of diverse and sustainable agriculture. Steered by N R Shetty, a telecom engineer, and G Krishna Prasad, trained in environmental engineering – both passionate about organic farming – Sahaja Samrudha spawned many institutions over the years working collectively towards promoting ecological agriculture through revival of indigenous seeds and traditional crops.

Sahaja Samrudha's genesis coincided broadly with the period when Karnataka state was reeling under a serious agrarian crisis. As per the official data between 1996 and 2000 about 11,000 persons engaged in farming and agricultural activity in the state died by suicide (Menon, 2004). This had set the state to thinking of innovative strategies to help the farming sector rid of costly practices that result in increased cost of cultivation and indebtedness of farm households. Promotion of organic agriculture was identified as one such strategy. Organic farming, it was thought, would eventually free farmers from the vicious circle of high input costs, increasing indebtedness, and poverty.

Also, it was around the 2000s that organic farming started receiving overt attention in the policy debates globally and in India. The Food and Agricultural Organisation (FAO) set up the Inter-Departmental Working Group on Organic Agriculture (IDWG/OA) in late 1999 and began to support efforts across countries to explore how organic agriculture reinforces the drive towards sustainable agriculture, biodiversity, and food/nutrition security (FAO, 2003). By 2002 many countries had introduced legislations, institutional arrangements, and standards to promote organic farming. In India the 10th Five Year Plan (2002–07) included promotion of organic farming

DOI: 10.4324/9781003308034-13

as one of its thrust areas. Following the recommendations of the Task Force on Organic of Farming (2001),[1] the plan approach endorsed the need to convert farm waste and municipal solid waste into good-quality organic manure mainly to correct the increasing micronutrient deficiency of soil. The National Programme for Organic Production (NPOP) was also launched in 2001 as an institutional mechanism for accreditation and certification of organic farming processes.[2] These developments formed the backdrop for the introduction by the Karnataka state of its Organic Farming Policy 2004, one of the first such policies to have been formulated by any state.

In such an enabling environment, the informal association of Sahaja Samrudha decided to register itself as a pubic charitable trust in 2006. It promotes the cause of saving indigenous crop varieties and farm practices in collaboration with farmers, breeders, and seed savers from across Karnataka and through campaigns and networks. Many of its campaigns have been instrumental in pushing the organic farming frontier in the state. *Save Our Rice* campaign, for instance, was an impactful one in that it brought 1,500 rice conservers and farmer-breeders, who have collectively conserved more than 1,000 varieties of scented, medicinal, deep-water, saline-tolerant, and dry land rice over the years. The campaign carried out in collaboration with the Millet Network of India (MINI) for the revival and promotion of millet diversity has led to the formation of the Millet Network of Karnataka. The seed repository of Sahaja Samrudha consists of around 800 varieties of rice and 120 types of millets apart from several types of cotton, cereals, pulses, vegetables, and fruits.[3]

Importantly, the leadership of Sahaja Samrudha realised right at the beginning that their efforts cannot be limited only to strengthening solidarity among seed savers and farmers. Market linkages must be developed eventually to incentivise farmers to take to seed farming to improve their livelihoods while ensuring faster dissemination of indigenous varieties. Realising the opportunity to nurture the market focus of organic farming, the Sahaja Samrudha Organic Producer Company Limited (Sahaja Organics hereafter) was incorporated in 2010 as a marketing arm of the association. The company has been formed with the mission of helping organic farmers explore markets for their produce and also to inform the general public of the importance of consuming indigenous food crops. The crops produced by the members of the company are sold to food processors, health centres, retail outlets, and direct customers under the brand name 'Sahaja Organics'. Sahaja Organics has grown to be the largest wholesaler of organic grains in Karnataka with an operational income of Rs. 88.5 million and profit of Rs. 1.56 million in 2019–20.

As the business of marketing organic produce started growing steadily, the scope for another business opportunity became evident: of production and marketing of organic seeds. Thus, three years after the incorporation of

Sahaja Organics an exclusive entity to focus on seed business was launched. Desi Seed Producer Company Limited (Desi Seed hereafter) was incorporated in 2013 at Bengaluru with ten promoters. The company started operations with an authorised capital of Rs. 100,000 divided into 10,000 equity shares of Rs. 10 each and six directors. Two of the founder directors – G. Krishna Prasad and Anand Teertha Pyati – were also founders of the marketing company. The registered office was located in Bangalore until it was shifted to Mysore in 2019.

2. The nature of business

The seed industry in India is made up of both private – domestic and multinational – companies and public sector enterprises. Some degree of specialisation has evolved between private companies and public sector establishments with respect to the type of seeds produced by each. The public sector system (including the National Seed Association of India, State Farms Corporation of India, and the different state-level seed corporations) mainly supplies high volume, open pollinated varieties as certified seeds, while the private companies (such as Mahyco, JK Seeds, Kalash seeds among many others) focus on the production of high-value hybrid seeds and varietal seeds as Truthfully Labelled (TL) seeds (NSAI, n.d.). Since the self-pollinated seeds or farm-saved seeds can be produced directly from crops by farmers and reused, they have a lower replacement rate. However, such reuse is not possible with hybrid seeds as that would lead to dilution of genetic purity. Hence, hybrid seeds have a higher replacement rate. This is an important factor that drives the growth of commercial seed industry in the country (NSAI, n.d.).

It may be noted that farm-saved seed production activities are not covered in the commercial seed industry in India. This segment usually involves informal exchange of seeds between farmers. This is a highly fragmented process without any coordination between breeders, savers, and users. The community seed banks to a large extent have helped maintain seeds for local use (Vernooy et al., 2015). Desi Seed has entered this 'non-commercial' realm with a clear commercial interest and market vision as a community-owned collective enterprise. The company is involved in the production of seeds of a variety of crops – vegetables, field crops like millets and rice, fruits and flowers, and herbs – under a certified organic system. The process of growing crops for seeds demands longer time commitment on the part of the farmer as compared to conventional farming. The crop has to remain in the farm for a longer time – almost double the usual duration – so that the seed has the required maturity. The seeds are produced without taking recourse to genetic modification, irradiation, sewage sludge, or synthetic agrochemicals. Seed farms are kept separate from other farms and are typically below 2.5 acres. The seeds are open-pollinated which means that the saved seed will breed true type and the farmers have direct access and control of their seed supply. The locally governed community seed banks are also used to store and maintain seeds for use by local farmers and also to meet excess demand from the outside market.

3. Production planning, quality control, and marketing

The farmers use their own seeds and also seeds from the seed banks. The production manager of the company regularly visits the seed farms and monitors the germination process. Once seeds are ready, the company gets them collected, cleaned, and transported to Mysore. They then undergo germination test at the seed-testing laboratory of the College of Horticulture of the University of Horticultural Sciences, Bagalkot. The company also randomly does germination checks. The seeds that pass the germination quality checks are packed as per order in airtight pouches and packets to be sold.

The true seeds are sold in their brand name 'Sahaja Seeds' to farmers, home gardeners, urban farmers, professionals who have taken up farming (see Box 13.1 later), and NGOs/farmers organisations and also supplied to various institutions like the International Institute of Millets Research, Hyderabad, and State Seed Departments of Kerala and Karnataka. Small-sized packs are also sold through exhibitions/fares. Desi Seed has remained a major supplier of seeds and technical advice under the Organic Village Programme of the Karnataka government and to state-level programmes like Kudumbashree of Kerala. The Seeds Savers Network established by the company is promoting and sourcing the seeds across the country. Through this process the company has preserved more than 1,500 varieties of seeds. With the help of grant assistance from NABARD routed through Nab Kisan Finance Limited, Desi Seed have published a Seeds Calendar to popularise seed diversity and seed knowledge to farmers (NKFL, 2019).

The company has chosen not to sell its seeds through stores or retail outlets. More than 50% of Desi Seed's turnover is generated from direct sales through online and social media apps whereas about 30% from local farmers. The company follows a simple system to sell seeds against direct orders. Buyers can order seeds over phone, email, or WhatsApp. The seed order forms are available on the company's website. Once an order is placed and availability confirmed, customers pay for the purchases in advance. Payment can be made through different modes like bank transfer and various payment apps. The seeds are then packed in required quantities and despatched to the buyers either by India Post or through a private courier service. Local farmers can buy seeds either from the company's office in Mysuru or from the select stores including those of Sahaja Organics where Desi Seed has kept 'seed racks'.

The company's market is mainly concentrated in southern India, Karnataka being the largest market (51% as of March 2021), followed by Andhra

Pradesh and Tamil Nadu. Rajasthan and Telangana are at the fourth and fifth positions. These five states together account for 84% of the total operational income.

Marketing is the most critical constraint to commercialising organic products in general and seeds in particular. Further, the organic seed farmers find it difficult to compete with their counterparts who produce hybrid seed for generic markets. Desi Seed helps them by entering into a buy-back arrangement and assures them of a market for their produce at a predetermined price. Local seed savers who reproduced seeds and helped in intergenerational transmission of genetically robust and nutritionally rich seeds form the core strength of the Desi Seed.

3.1 Shareholding structure and governance

As mentioned earlier the company was incorporated with ten individual promoters. The entire equity capital was subscribed to by them till 2017, three of them accounting for 60% of the total shares in the company. The shareholding structure has changed significantly in recent years. While equity capital has increased about three and a half times from Rs. 100,000 to Rs. 346,850, that is, by close to three and half times, the percentage of promoters' equity declined to 24.5%. Farmer groups (or *sanghas*) have come to hold a quarter of the equity while the rest 51% is owned by individual seed farmers. The total number of shareholders in the company as of September 2021 is 502. They hail from 29 villages across nine districts. These include eight *sanghas* who collectively have 472 members. The group size ranges from 35 to 130. The company has not yet paid any dividend to the shareholders. However, it has paid Rs. 64,502 and Rs. 24,381 as withheld price in 2018–19 and 2019–20 respectively.

The company is governed by the board of directors (BoD) which currently has six members including one woman. The CEO reports to the BoD. The board usually meets once every three months while the annual general body meets every year. All policy decisions of the organisation are taken after consultations within the board. Such decisions include among other things inclusion of new members, appointment of staff, loan approvals, and investments. The board also decides on the production targets and price based on market demand and communicates it to the farmers and ensures that every seed farm and produce is NPOP compliant with the help of approved government and independent certification agencies. Decisions relating to the price to be paid to the producers, the quantum of price to be withheld,[4] and the mode of paying the withheld price subsequently are also taken by the BoD.

The management and administrative team is small and consists of the chief executive officer (CEO) who is responsible for the overall operations, production and accounts managers, administration executive, packing and distribution executive, and technology and media assistant. The CEO, Ravi K Magal, was earlier holding senior management positions in the manufacturing industry sector. The company has recently recruited a young professional to steer its marketing activities.

BoD and management team communicate regularly. Team meetings are held every month to assess progress and to plan work. Efforts are currently under way to upgrade the technological capability of the company especially in producer tracking, product labelling, and so on.

3.2 Business performance

During the year 2020–21 Desi Seed earned Rs. 5.59 million from its operations, a 45% increase compared to 2019–20. Interestingly, monthly sales spiked during the first pandemic-lockdown phase between March and July 2020. The company earned close to Rs. 4.2 million in revenue during this period. The two months when it witnessed income peaks were in March and June 2020 – Rs. 1.3 million each. Much of the demand appears to have come from urban farmers who got locked in work-from-home arrangements.

Overall, as shown in Table 13.1 Desi Seed has improved its earnings consistently in absolute terms since 2016–17. The revenue from seed sales, the only business operations the company is involved in, increased about four times between 2016–17 and 2020–21. Operational expenses too have increased over the period

In terms of profitability, the company faced a grave crisis in 2016–17 when it suffered a loss of close to Rs. 400,000, and the net operating margin dipped to –25%. It has recovered since and has made positive profits net of taxes and interest in 2017–18 and 2019–20, though there was a marginal

Table 13.1 Major performance indicators

Year	Equity (Paid-Up capital) (Rs.)	Sales (Rs.)	Profit Before Tax (Rs.)	Net Profit (Rs.)	Gross Margin (Rs.)	Total Liabilities (Rs.	Total Fixed Costs (Rs.)
2013–14	100,000	108,970	–82,634	–82,634	52,676	106,514	24,000
2014–15	100,000	1,444,092	125,060	125,060	71,973	545,355	171,302
2015–16	100,000	4.108,625	57,309	57,309	890,278	1,621,329	665,810
2016–17	100,000	1,548,063	–389,441	–389,441	570,221	564,149	639,403
2017–18	233,850	2.977,112	288,304	288,304	1,216,530	659,534	453,828
2018–19	291,850	3,733,450	–4,183	–4,183	898,131	1,199,997	832,565
2019–20	291,850	3,900,207	301,892	301,892	1,563,080	2,436,256	887,640
2020–21	346,850	5,836,101	652,194	652,194	NA	1,889,733	1,060,207

Source: Audited financial statements of the company.

Note: Gross margin or contribution = Sales cost of goods sold

207

Table 13.2 Structure of expenditure

Year	Salaries and Benefits (Rs.)	Other Expenses (Rs.)	Value of Sales (Rs.)	Personnel Cost/Value of Sales (%)	Other Costs/ Value of Sales (%)
2013–14	24,000	37,712	108,970	22.02	34.61
2014–15	167,280	137,044	1,444,092	11.58	9.49
2015–16	589,744	413,671	4,108,625	14.35	10.07
2016–17	558,977	327,889	1,548,063	36.11	21.18
2017–18	258,641	638,769	2,977,112	8.69	21.46
2018–19	593,796	839,484	3,733,450	15.90	22.49
2019–20	722,503	1,049,507	3,900,207	18.11	26.30
2020–21	999,882	1,105,800	5,836,101	17.13	18.95

Source: Same as Table 13.1.

loss in 2018–19. Every year 25% of the net income is transferred to the general reserves of the company.

A closer look at the expenses reported by the company reveals greater variations in the cost of manpower since 2013–14 (Table 13.2). Other administrative expenses, on the other hand, have been growing steadily since 2015–16. Two heads that registered greater increase are rent and travel. Withheld price paid to the farmers is the other item of expenditure. In 2018–19 Rs. 64,502 was paid as withheld price which came down to Rs. 24,381 in 2019–10.

4. Impact on seed farmers: a case study

Periyapatna in Mysore district has been a tobacco-growing area for several decades. Farmers are known to have been in debt for generations. Struggling to cope with mounting debts many had taken their lives. Kalappa, the seed farmer whom we met in Periyapatna too, was a tobacco farmer once. When he realised that long years of tobacco farming had significantly harmed his land, he stopped the cultivation completely. For about a decade now he and his wife Manjula have been following organic farming practices in their 2.5 acre farm. "I took to organic cultivation to take care of my health and the health of this soil." He been associated with Desi Seed for the last six years.

Kalappa grows around 100 varieties of vegetables exclusively for the production of seeds. He also cultivates paddy and millets mainly for the family's consumption in the two acres of land that he has inherited from his father. There was ginger, *amaranthus*, spinach, chillies, radish, and tomato standing in the field when we visited him in September 2021. Some seeds were in the process of getting ready. Seeds of many vegetables were seen conserved inside dried fruits, while some others were being dried in seed trays. He also maintains a small personal seed bank at home.

According to Kalappa, organic seed farming is quite remunerative. Apart from the cost incurred in certification, the cost of cultivation is practically zero. However, this cost too has come down drastically for him as Desi Seed helped them get group certification. Under this, multiple landowners are certified under one organic certificate. Kalappa's group has 70 farmers who have divided the total initial certification cost of about Rs. 360,000 equally among themselves.

He makes bio-fertilisers and pesticides by himself by mixing locally available leaves and grains with cow urine known locally as 'poochi marunthu' and 'panchagavya'. His wife and daughters provide the labour along with him. The income cycle generally starts after about three months. He makes up to Rs. 100,000 from seed sales every three months. Kalappa also acts as a trainer in programmes organised by Sahaja Samrudha.

5. Enabling factors

5.1 Desi seed and Sahaja Samrudha: organic linkages

Desi Seed's location within the larger Sahaja Samrudha family and the organic movement that it spearheads evidently bestows the company certain critical privileges. Sahaja Organics and Desi Seed together constitute a mutually reinforcing organisational setting that effectively supports the realisation of a collective business vision as they operate as part of a nested structure. The farmers who work within the Sahaja ecosystem can draw upon the multiple resources offered by the different institutional arrangements for sourcing seeds/inputs, receiving training and capacity building support, accessing market for their organic produce, and also sell seeds.

Sahaja organics sometimes has to purchase seeds from Desi Seed to be supplied to farmers. The latter often procures consulting services from the former. The ideological moorings of Sahaja Samrudha are deeply embedded in all aspects of the functioning of Desi Seed company. In our interaction with the staff members, it was often difficult to associate them with just the business of seed. They are wedded to the wholesome philosophy of organic cultivation that Sahaja Samrudha represents.

5.2 Role of leadership

The contribution of G Krishna Prasad, the founder and director, in shaping Desi Seed needs to be acknowledged. He is known as the 'native seed man' of rural Karnataka. He was elected to the Ashoka Fellowship in 2010. He has also been a trainer-motivator for many organisations and networks across India. He is passionately driven by the dream of creating a market for organic farming in India by leveraging the knowledge and networks of existing farmers. He believes that an assured supply of good-quality organic seeds is the first step towards incentivising farmers towards preserving traditional varieties of seeds.

Born in a family of farmers and inspired by Masanobu Fukuoka's seminal work *One Straw Revolution* he took to the idea of natural farming quite early. He was particularly concerned about the extinction of local food varieties. Krishna Prasad started working with the GREEN (Genetic Resource, Ecology, Energy and Nutrition) Foundation, a non-profit initiative set up in the mid-1990s to empower local communities by enriching biodiversity and ensuring nutritional security through seed conservation. He has been engaged since then in activities like building farmer networks, creating community seed banks, and writing and publishing on matters related to seeds.[5]

He left the Foundation in 2006 after working with it for 12 years and became part of Sahaja Samrudha to pursue his vision further. By that time, he was convinced of the necessity of linking organic farmers with the market if the movement has to sustain its steam. The idea found fruition in the setting up of Sahaja Organics, the producer company of organic farmers that markets their produce. That seemed a partial solution. Ensuring sustained supply of good-quality organic seed still remained a key constraint. This led Krishna Prasad to be part of the founding team that set up Desi Seed in 2013. Currently, Krishna Prasad devotes his attention almost exclusively to growing the business of Desi Seed.

Box 13.1 New champions of ecological agriculture

The new crop of agri-preneurs emerged in India over the last decade holds great promise to the organic farming sector. We met one such weekend agri-preneur during our field visit. He was visiting Desi Seed office in Mysore to buy seeds. He cultivates paddy, millets, vegetables, and some tree crops in his four-acre farm. A working professional with the IT sector, he started doing farming a few years ago. He is a complete believer in the idea of zero-budget natural farming of Subhash Palekar. He has been buying Sahaja Seeds regularly. According to him natural farming is cost-efficient for farmers and affordable to customers. He also drew our attention to the difference between 'organic' and 'natural' cultivation and suggested the need for both practices to move closer to make farming less capital-intensive and farm produce affordable to price-sensitive customers. He believes that "[p]eople are coming to agriculture as they are frustrated with urban life. Now people prefer to stay closer to nature and work at busy places like Bangalore." He was referring to an emerging shift in the lifestyle of urban India which augurs well for natural farmers.

5.3 The role of the state

As mentioned earlier, Karnataka was one of the pioneers in introducing a separate policy for organic farming in 2004. This policy tried to address the various concerns raised by experts about the lack of sustainability of conventional farming in the state due mainly to the over dependency of farmers on chemical fertilisers and the resultant soil degradation. There was strong advocacy favouring alternative approaches for reclaiming soil fertility and productivity. The 2004 policy emphasised on the need to follow an integrated approach to farming by sustaining soil fertility and productivity, promoting judicious use and proper care of water, integration of animal husbandry with farms, and preservation and enhancement of traditional and indigenous farming knowledge besides seeds and crop variety. The organic farming policy was soon integrated within the state's agricultural policy introduced in 2006. The 'panch sutra' concept was used to describe the philosophy of organic farming – protecting and improving soil, conserving natural resource, providing credit in time, integrating post harvesting with production process, and transferring farm technology from lab to land (Shannikodi, 2013).

The state has also started allocating resources for the development of organic farming since 2007. The Organic Farming Project (2006–09), the Organic Agricultural Mission (2009–10), and the Organic Farming Mission (2011) were some of the initiatives introduced in the initial phase. The Savayava Bhagya Yojane (SBY) launched in 2013–14 was meant to facilitate not-for-profit organisations to form associations of organic farmers and federate them at regional level into cooperative organisations. As per the data provided by the Department of Agriculture, Government of Karnataka, there are 14 regional-level federations of organic farmer associations in the state.[6] The federations are expected to take up activities like collection, grading, value addition, processing, packing, brand development, and also wholesale and retail marketing of organic produce. There are other schemes like market-based crop-specific organic cluster development and Paramparagat Krishi Vikas Yojana (PKVY) aimed at promoting organic production systems. Raitha Siri Scheme is another scheme that provides cash incentive to organic millet producers. These schemes and programmes have helped develop an ideological environment within the state that is conducive to the spread of organic cultivation and steadily though slowly expand the area under organic crops.

The state has revised in 2017 the earlier organic farming policy of 2004. The Karnataka Organic Farming Policy 2017 emphasises the importance of organic production systems in promoting sustainable agriculture and developing value-chain linkages between producers and consumers. It is envisaged that by 2022 at least 10% of the cultivable area in the state will turn organic. This is a tall order given that organic area accounts for only 1.1%

of the net sown area even as of 2019. Many other states like Chhattisgarh, Odisha, and Uttarakhand also have recognised organic farming as key to building a sustainable farm sector. Even in states like Gujarat farmers are attracted by the idea of organic and natural farming. Such an environment offers significant growth opportunity to Desi Seed in the years to come.

6. Constraints and prospects

The regulatory provisions with respect to commercial production and sales of organic seeds were not very clear when Desi Seed started its activities. There was no organic business worth its name in Karnataka then. Only a small number of farmers were confident about following organic practices as they considered hybrid seeds and chemical fertilisers as essential ingredients for assured and better yield. The concept of organic farming also looked shrouded in uncertainty despite the presence of the state policy that enabled its dissemination. All these factors added to the fear and hesitation of farmers. Moreover, the organic farming movement in general was more focused on consumers and their expectations.

The above context has considerably changed since then. The organic produce market, including the market for seeds, now appears poised for growth provided some of the distinct structural bottlenecks are effectively addressed and the available opportunities efficiently exploited. It is true that the commercial hybrid seed segment has registered high growth rates (15–20% over the 2010s according to market intelligence agencies) and is looked upon by the state as a prospective high-growth industry of the future. At the same time, agro-ecological agriculture is also gaining greater visibility, policy attention, and consumer's patronage over the last couple of decades as a way to progress towards a sustainable future. Particularly, legislative provisions initiated under the Protection of Plant Varieties and Farmers' Rights Act, 2001, and the Geographical Indications of Goods (Registration and Protection) Act 1999 aim at enabling farmers to protect their traditional varieties. But studies have noted that farmers have limited awareness of these provisions (Blakeney et al., 2020).

The lack of a market mechanism that coordinates the activities of seed breeders, seed savers, and seed banks makes collectivisation of seed producers a challenging proposition, especially when the purpose is to build a viable collective business.

The other critical bottleneck is certification, which is compulsory for the marketing of organic produce through retail stores. The products marketed to end consumers through direct sales by the small original producers or producer organisations are exempted from the certification requirement (FSSAI, 2021). The organic certificate[7] is usually issued for a year by any agency accredited by APEDA. The cost of certification usually varies between Rs. 15,000 and Rs. 50,000 per farmer. The normal window of waiting for the certificate is six months to one year for those who already follow organic practices. For farmers newly engaged in the cultivation of perennial crops the waiting period to get a certificate is three years, whereas those who grow annual crops have to wait for two years. The Paramparagat Krishi Vikas Yojana (PKVY), a scheme to encourage traditional farmers, allows group of farmers to apply for certification under what is known as the participatory guarantee system (PGS). This is a peer-review system wherein farmers themselves review the fields during sowing and harvesting times and once in between. The cost and the time-consuming processes of inspection as well as record keeping may act as deterrents to the development of viable business models in the organic seed sector. Initiatives that work on promoting organic and agro-ecological farming need to learn from the strategies employed by hybrid seed producers like aggressive farmer education and extension support.

Over the past seven years Desi Seed has developed a market for organic seeds and mobilised a community of market-focused seed farmers into a collective business by keeping the rules of the game simple and community driven. The company has so far been able to maintain a low-cost structure due to its leaders like Krishna Prasad who travels widely interacting with seed farmers and organic agriculturists in Karnataka and other states and helps exchange local seed varieties for wider use. But constraints do remain. Technologies like greenhouses are not affordable to smaller farmers. Dearth of adequate cold storage facilities is another lacuna. More importantly, convincing banks to finance organic ventures is near impossible. NABKISAN, the subsidiary of NABARD, is the only formal financial institution that Desi Seed has ever borrowed from (Rs. 1.02 million in 2019–20). According to its leadership NABARD's presence is a boon to the sector as it plays a very critical promotional role.

7. Conclusion

Initiatives to develop viable business models around organic agriculture, and that too organic seeds, are not many. The dependence of organic production on local agronomic conditions and the resultant variation in productivity and cost gains, fragmented distribution of seed farmers and seed users, irregular production, and popular perception about low productivity of organic seeds seem to be some factors that prevent commercialisation of organic seeds. Desi Seed's small and steadily growing business strives to transcend these constraints by leveraging the conditions favourable to the wider dissemination of organic agriculture specific to the state. For instance, as previous research has pointed out the interest of the farmers in the state is keener to reduce cost of cultivation given the financial risk and distress they have been facing (Patil et al., 2014). In other words, the dominant motivation to shift to the organic mode of cultivation is not maximising profits but saving on financial costs of inputs. The other important factor has been the good work done by the Sahaja movement in the state since the mid-1990s in terms of mobilisation of farmers around the ideas of seed sovereignty, and adoption of organic cultivation practices appears to have created a community of market-ready seed farmers across the state. The leadership of Desi Seed has been able to maintain a low-cost structure as at current levels of production seeds do not require large storage, processing, or retail facilities. The company is also very cautious in expanding the farmer base as the land conversion and certification processes are lengthy and cumbersome and demand high levels of commitment and integrity from the members. Any setback during the inspection of farms would mean loss of credibility for the business.

Desi Seed company was set up with the vision of extending the organic farming value chain backwards to the supply of authentic organic seeds so that the farmers can benefit from the emerging market opportunities and improve their livelihood security and economic well-being. By promoting organic cultivation practices in regions already experiencing considerable degradation of soil quality, thanks to their dependence for decades on input-intensive agriculture, it also envisioned to deliver on the goals of conservation of local biodiversity and nutritional security by blending the logics of market and civic action.

> We believe that seeds belong to the communities, and not any individual or a company. Our seeds reflect this, and therefore they are organic, open pollinated[8] and open source. Our seed producers are located across different agro-climatic regions collectively produce regionally adaptable varieties conserved by farmers for its flavour, taste, colour, adaptability and health benefits, that are unparalleled for over generations. We seek to bring back the tradition of seed saving amongst us by collecting, propagating, and exchanging indigenous and rare varieties. We seek sustainable living and a more self-reliant lifestyle.[9]

Notes

1 Constituted by the Department of Agriculture and Cooperation, Government of India.
2 The Agricultural and Processed Food Products Export Development Authority (APEDA) under the Ministry of Commerce and Industry oversees the implementation of NPOP.
3 For more information on Sahaja Samrudha, see https://www.equatorinitiative. org/2020/04/24/solution11329/
4 Withheld pricing is a mechanism allowed under the relevant law for members of producer companies to gain monetary benefits restricted to the value of pooled resources of products and production. It is the responsibility and discretion of the

BoD of companies. Withheld pricing can be disbursed either in cash or in kind (through equity share allotment). The amount of the latter is determined in proportion or equal to the quantity of production in a single financial year. As per the articles of association of the Desi Seed company, the members will receive only a part of the value of produce they supply as determined by BoD. The part of the value withheld could be disbursed later in the form of cash, kind, or equity shares.

5 Krishna Prasad: Social Entrepreneur and Seed Revolutionary, https://bangalore. explocity.com/article/krishna-prasad-social-entrepreneur-and-seed-revolutionary/, 11 October 2019.

6 Karnataka's organic and millet policy initiatives can be explored at http://organics-millets.in/index.php

7 Seed certification is voluntary and is done by state-level certification agencies in most cases. The seed certificate is valid for 9 months.

8 Or it is pollinated by natural mechanisms like birds, insects, wind, and humans which cause genetic diversity. As opposed to this hybrid pollination is a method wherein the pollen of different species of varieties is crossed through human intermediation.

9 Response to the questionnaire mailed on 5 August 2021.

References

Blakeney, M, Krishnankutty, J, Raju, RK & Siddique, KHM (2020). Agricultural innovation and the protection of traditional rice varieties: Kerala a case study. *Frontiers in Sustainable Food Systems*, 3, Article 116.

Food and Agriculture Organization (2003). *Organic agriculture*. Rome: FAO.

Food Safety and Standards Authority of India (2021). *Food safety and standards (Organic foods) regulation, 2017: Chapter I*. New Delhi: FSSAI.

Menon, P (2004, November 19). An Agrarian crisis. *The Frontline*. Retrieved from https://frontline.thehindu.com/other/article30225418.ece

Nabkisan Finance Limited (2019). *Farmer producer organisations: Emerging aggregators*. Mumbai: KFL.

National Board for Organic Farming Mooted (2001, November 29). Retrieved from https://archive.pib.gov.in/archive/releases98/lyr2001/rnov2001/29112001/r2911200120.html

NSAI (n.d.). *Note of information for National Seed Association of India's proposal on capacity building program initiatives for Indian seed industry as part of Atmanirbhar Bharat Program submitted to NABARD*. Retrieved from http://nsai.co.in/storage/app/media/uploaded-files/Detailed%20note%20for%20NABARD.pdf

Patil, S, Reidsma, P, Shah, P, Purushothaman, S & Wolf, J (2014). Comparing conventional and organic agriculture in Karnataka, India: Where and when can organic farming be sustainable? *Land Use Policy*, 37, 40–51.

Vernooy, R, Shrestha, P & Sthapit, B (2015). The rich but little known chronicles of community seed banks. In V Ronnie, S Pitambar & S Bhuwon (Eds.), *Community seed banks: Origins, evolution and prospects* (pp. 1–7). Oxon: Routledge.

14

FEDERATING FOR RAPID (MAHA) GROWTH

The MAHA Farmers Producer Company in Maharashtra

Ajit Kanitkar

1. Introduction

Maharashtra has a long history and a vibrant cooperative movement with a dense network of village-level and district cooperatives in both rural and semi-urban areas. While the cooperatives flourished in the first thirty years after 1947, their coverage remained largely in rural western Maharashtra and that too focusing only on a few commodities such as sugarcane and milk. Over the years, the true spirit of cooperation dwindled and the movement became highly politicised often leading to a bitter rivalry and one-upmanship among leaders often neglecting the real needs of the small farmers. Like in other parts of the country, with the amendments to the company's act, many individuals and organisations began exploring possibilities of promoting FPCs under the amended act.

1.1 Rationale for federating FPCs

Yogesh Thorat and the initial team of promoters of MAHA Farmers Producer Company Ltd. (henceforth referred in the text as MAHAFPC) were trying to conceptualise the role of an apex organisation based on interactions with organisation like the Small Farmers Agribusiness Consortium (SFAC) and National Cooperative Development Corporation (NCDC). Yogesh, an agriculture graduate and a post-graduate from National Institute of Agricultural Extension Management, known as MANAGE (formerly National Centre for Management of Agricultural Extension) in agribusiness management, worked for a year in the (then) Planning Commission in Delhi. Later, in his village in Ahmednagar district, he promoted an FPC around *jowar* and other minor millets. Dr Hanumant Wadekar, another promoter of MAHAFPC is a value-chain expert and a PhD in bio-technology. In his village on the outskirts of Pune, having tried his hands in running

DOI: 10.4324/9781003308034-14

a vegetable FPC with the help of about 30 graduate youths, he soon realised that an individual FPC cannot have the wherewithal of engaging with the market. The economies of scale that a federation can potentially offer was beyond the reach of an individual FPC.

As recounted by Dr Wadekar,

> I and my team worked from 4 am till 11 pm for over 3.5 years. We opened a retail outlet for vegetables, had three transportation vehicles and even had our brand and supplied fresh vegetables to Pune. We had developed an App that time, ahead of others. However, when large corporates entered the space, we had no way of competing with them in the market. The FPC is closed now, being run by a few farmers as individual business.

The process got further acceleration as a result of the World Bank–supported Maharashtra Agriculture Competitive Project (MACP) that began in early 2010. MACP was implemented with the objective to "increase productivity, profitability and market access of the farming community in Maharashtra." In a workshop in March 2014 titled "Development and sustainability of FPOs" organised by MANAGE at Hyderabad, 45 representatives of FPCs across Maharashtra deliberated on the need for forming an apex federation. These members including the current Chairman and Managing Director Mr Yogesh Thorat had experiences of organising FPCs. However, all of them felt a need for federating to attain economies of scale. After a couple of rounds of discussion, the registration of MAHAFPC was done on 3 September 2014.

Table 14.1 traces the journey of MAHAFPC from the beginning year till 2021. While the first three years were more as foundation years to stabilise the business model, there was manifold growth in the turnover of the federation after 2017 onwards.

As activities of the federation began to expand all over the state, in 2020, for better coordination and supervision of business operations, MAHAFPC set up offices in Amravati for the Vidarbha and in Latur for the Marathwada region. Both Amaravati and Latur offices play an important role in the business of pulses and soybean whereas the Pune office has proximity to FPCs specialising in onion and other commodities in the western region. In 2020–21, it decided to reduce the number of board members from 11 to 7. Mr Yogesh Thorat is the chairman and managing director; the remaining six are non-executive directors, one each for Ahmednagar, Aurangabad, Nashik, Amravati, and two from the Latur region. They are chairpersons of the FPC located in that region. There are no women members on the board. The seven members represented the three regions of western Maharashtra, Vidarbha, and Marathwada. The board has three sub-committees for shareholders, audit and remuneration (of farmers/staff/BoD) each headed by a

Table 14.1 Milestones in the journey of MAHAFPC

Year	Key Events
2014	45 FPC representatives meet to discuss formation of the apex federation in state-level workshop in March
	11 FPCs join as initial promoters of the federation
	MAHAFPC Registration in September 2014
2015	25 members join Federation by March 2015
	The first (pilot) procurement of pulses and onions under the price stabilisation scheme (PSS) of the central government
2016	MAHAFPC declared nodal agency for procurement of pulses in the state
	33,000 metric ton pulses procured from 147 procurement centres of member FPCs
2017 and 2018	In addition to business with the government, 638 metric tons of soybean business with private sector for the first time of Rs. 22.70 million
2019	MAHAFPC appointed as official state facilitator along with NAFED and FCI for procurement of onion, *tur* dal, chana, soybean, and maize
	The first public-private partnership (PPP) in the country between MAHAFPC and NAFED (Mahaonion) for developing infrastructure for procurement and storage of onion
2020	Mahaonion project inaugurated by the chief minister of Maharashtra in October, capacity 6,000 metric tons
	Under PSS of the government, record 120,000 metric ton procurement done despite pandemic
	A retail and online outlet for member FPCs for marketing opened in Pune as NAFED E Kisan Mandi
2021	NCDC and NABARD select MAHAFPC as cluster-based business organisation (CBBO), in 11 clusters in March 2021. MANAGE and MAHAFPC organise entrepreneurship programme for agriculture graduates to train them in management of FPCs.

Source: MAHAFPC records

separate board member. In 2020–21, the board met for seven meetings. Except the managing director, other board members are not compensated.

Table 14.2 shows the growth in the membership of FPCs over the years. While the membership has grown, staff strength has remained steady.

2. Business model and member centrality in a federation

The promoters decided that the new federating entity should be a 'for-profit' entity and not registered like a society run on charity and grant support. MAHAPFC board felt there were many pre-existing interventions on the input provision side. The federation should do the role of 'business facilitation without conflict of interests' with its members and should be focusing

Table 14.2 Membership over the years

S. No.	Year	No. of FPC	Board Members	Staff Strength
1	2014–15	11	11	1
2	2015–16	25	11	1
3	2016–17	48	11	1
4	2017–18	147	11	5
5	2018–19	247	11	5
6	2019–20	541	11	7
7	2020–21	604	7	19

Source: MAHAFPC records

on market linkages (for output) and building infrastructure for its farmer members to better deal with output markets. This strategy was in response to persisting deficits in market information, lack of warehousing, and thus holding capacities for commodities closer to the farming locations. Another feature of the strategy was to focus on commodity clusters and build on the member FPC's strengths vis-à-vis commodities that farmers produce in the clusters. It therefore chose to work with farmers cultivating onions (largely in western Maharashtra) and soybean, *tur* (pulses), and *chana* (gram) mostly in the Vidarbha and Marathwada regions.

While this thinking was going on, operationalising the strategy in practice was not an easy task. A workable business model was yet to emerge. The initial share capital for member FPCs was fixed at Rs. 11,000 (Rs. 10,000 towards equity capital plus Rs. 1,000 as membership fees). Initially 11 members became the signatories and the founding directors of MAHAFPC. MAHAFPC did not have its own office for the first three years. It operated from the office of a member FPC from Narayangaon, about 50 km from Pune. It started with one employee who was performing all functions ranging from the CEO to a peon, a clerk, and an accountant. The federation did not have any tangible assets. In the absence of professional and dedicated staff for the federation, membership remained limited and the functioning almost dormant.

The third annual general meeting (AGM) in 2016 was an important turning point. There was not much business activity happening in the earlier two years either for the MAHAFPC and or for its member FPCs. Many compliances such as finalisation, audit of financial statements, and GST returns were pending. The ecosystem was at a nascent stage; clarity on the business model for MAHAFPC was lacking too. The bank balance was just about Rs. 200,000! Thus, there were no significant resolutions to be passed in the AGM. There was a lot of discussion around the future road map of the federation. At the end of the discussion, a decision was taken that the organisation needed one full-time managing director with clear operational and management mandate to steer the performance. Mr Yogesh Thorat stepped

219

into that executive role. His responsibilities were two-fold: to work on the institutional development of the organisation and simultaneously on the business development aspects. Another important decision was to shift office from Narayangaon (outside of Pune) to the heart of the commercial centre, near Agricultural Produce Marketing Committee (APMC) in Pune, and in the neighbourhood many other offices of the state government engaged in agricultural development. Mr Prashant Pawar is the chief executive officer since 2017 while Mr Kunal Baset is the chief financial officer. Prashant is an agriculture graduate from Pune and later did his post-graduate management in agribusiness management. Together, they assist Mr Yogesh in strategy implementation.

3. Business with the central government

Being recognised as an official procurement agency for the minimum support price (MSP) intervention was a task that needed lots of patience and persistence. The newly formed MAHAFPC had no locus standi compared to the existing state-level marketing federation patronised over the years by both the state and central government departments and ministries. Yogesh and his team had to carefully and often cleverly manoeuvre the 'covert' resistance from these entrenched stakeholders. Applications to the government departments in Mumbai and personal follow-up meetings with officials and like-minded politicians were required. Yogesh and his team also had to resort to using the provisions of the Right to Information (RTI) Act. A writ petition was also filed in the court to seeking intervention of the court to enrol MAHAFPC as an official agency for public procurement.

3.1 Procurement agency for MSP interventions

NAFED procures pulses under two government schemes: price support scheme (PSS) and Price Stabilisation Fund (PSF). PSS, which is under the Agriculture Ministry, is operationalised when prices of agri-produce (pulses and 22 other commodities) fall below the MSP. The government then steps in and procures at the declared MSP. The food stock is used as a buffer and later supplied to the ration shops run under the public distribution scheme (PDS). The PSF is under the Ministry of Consumer Affairs; commodities (onions) are purchased for the buffer stock so as to ensure necessary market intervention when market prices fluctuate. The stocks are sold in open market by the government.

The salient feature of the business model was facilitating the public procurement on behalf of the central government agencies and earning commission (revenue) as a percentage of volume of business undertaken with these agencies. The service fees would thus be accrued to both the federation and the member FPCs participating in the procurement activities.

Mr Prashant Pawar has seen the operations of MAHAFPC expand over the years, in both size and complexity. He narrated his experiences and challenges in managing the operations of the federation.

Procurement for the government in 2017 was an important milestone for us. It was pulses procured under the PSF for the government. However next two years were "slack" years for us as the government did not procure. Officers in the government change, new officers have different perceptions. However, we continued to engage with the marketing institutions, albeit on a trial-and-error basis. We tried a pilot with NCDEX for 50 tons of maize marketing, did about 100 tons of sale for *haldi* (turmeric) for our members, connected with a private sector buyer for soybean and transacted 200 tons. In the process, we also obtained registration as a vendor for that company. Internally, we used this time to streamline our operations for compliances needed for example for GST. These efforts made us more knowledgeable about the market for our produce.

The appointment of MAHAFPC as a procurement agency for pulses in addition to the already existing two marketing federations – the state marketing federation and the Vidarbha Marketing Cooperative Federation – was another step in expanding the business in commodity-specific clusters. Since the existing two institutions did not reach many locations, the state government appointed MAHAFPC. Starting with a modest 1,000 tons in pulses, MAHAFPC expanded its business to 90,000 metric tons in spite of restrictions imposed by the lockdown in 2019–20 and 2020–21. It was given a target to open 125 centres (for procurement) but managed to make 87 of them functional.

3.2 Benefits of engaging in MSP procurement

While the government had policy announcements for MSP operations, commensurate actions for small farmers to participate in the MSP were seen sorely lacking at the ground level. Farmers often experienced delays in opening of centres of procurement; even if centres were opened, no 'actual' procurement was taking place in distant regions. There were long queues at the APMC centres, outputs from a large number of smallholders never reaching the market, and finally payments by the agencies who procured were delayed significantly. An efficient operation would lead to multiple benefits. Member FPCs will gain trust of farmers while learning the business of organising procurement, weighing, grading, and transporting. Earning trust of farmer members is critical in any intervention. Its role as a 'facilitator' and 'catalyst' ensured that in all marketing transactions, the payments are made directly into the accounts of individual members (farmers and not FPCs) while the FPCs are compensated appropriately for generating the business by payment of service fees in the transactions.

The experience gained in public procurement was seen as a learning ground that would help MAHAFPC and its members to diversify into business with the private sector. Learning to manage accounting and management systems for large-scale business operation, data and information flow from the market, quality control norms, and so on would be of immense use for other business. The MSP would be a practical training field for the staff to acquire management skills.

Another benefit was since the government was buying and payment was assured, there was almost no working capital requirement. Unlike private traders, procurement done by the government would ensure payment with zero default. While continuing to play the role of the aggregator, it would partner with state- and national-level institutions in both the government sector (B2G) and corporate sector (B2B).

3.3 Logistics in procurement

The number of FPCs that can participate in the procurement is a result of several factors. Initially, the procurement agency indicates an overall target for volumes as also the number of centres to be opened. Due diligence by MAHAFPC then determines the eligibility of its member FPC. Each FPC is generally allotted one centre that is at a central/convenient location for its members and has some storage facility. Also, to be noted is that 2020 (both *kharif* – October to December and *rabi* procurement – November to February) had severe restrictions as a result of the Corona outbreak all over the country. The following Table 14.3 for 2020–21 presents the number of active FPC members participating in procurement.

A positive spin-off of being a participant in the MSP operation was to ensure creation of local-level infrastructure at the member FPCs level,

Table 14.3 Active FPC members in 2020–21

Number of Active FPCs Participating in Procurement			Districts				
NAFED	FCI (Pulses)	Total	NAFED	FCI	Total	Year/Season	Commodity
1	0	1	1	0	1	2020 kharif	*Tur*
5	0	5	2	0	2	2020 kharif	Mung
165	3	168	17	1	18	2021 rabi	*Chana* (gram)
48	0	48	6	0	6	2021 rabi	Onion
219	3	222	26	1	27		

Source: MAHAFPC records

leveraging government promotional schemes for storage and value addition, thereby building leverage of its members to deal with the market.

Also, a direct benefit of local infrastructure and efficient implementation of the MSP operations was to ensure that the farmers receive assured price as stated in the policy measures. Even a 100-rupee price difference in the sale price of the commodity would result in significant additional income to a large number of small farmers.

Finally, MAHAFPC handling large volumes of commodities as an aggregator became visible at the policy level both in the state and at the national level. By emphasising economies of scale and transparency in operations as unique value proposition compared to other stakeholders, it wanted to project itself as a genuine stakeholder representing farmers' interest in the fluid political economy prevalent in the state.

3.4 Monitoring the operations

Both Mr Prashant and Mr Kunal showed how they can track procurement and payment right up to the level of individual farmers. The entire process can be monitored at MAHAFPC head office. There is a maximum ceiling on transactions up to Rs. 127,000 (imposed by the government for procurement) per farmer. Of course, a farmer with medium landholding can register additional family members to increase the number of transactions taking place at household level. The time taken for procurement to credit of the amount of transaction is 15 days, maximum. This is a clear example of direct benefit transfer (DBT). Payment to farmers is not routed via FPC account. The FPCs receive reimbursement of expenses/charges for packing, grading, and transportation in addition to 1% commission as income. However, Prashant observed that there have been delays close to one year or even more in releasing full payment to FPCs because the procurement agencies (NAFED and so on) delay the payment. There is exhaustive documentation including e-warehouse receipts, vouchers for transportation, reconciliation of accounting entries for rejection of the commodity procured, and disputes on quality of the material procured.

Mr Dasrao Patil, a board member, is the chairperson of Ranban FPC at Nilanga near Latur. The FPC has 1,500 members in 2021. He is a board member of MAHAFPC since 2019. He explained experiences of participating in procurement operations as a board member:

> When we formed the FPC in Nilanga in 2017, we had 500 plus members. MAHAFPC facilitation enabled FPCs in the region to increase their business. We did a business of pulse procurement of Rs. 30 million. The number of individual farmer members went up to 1,500 in two years. Simultaneously, we did a business of Rs. 3 million with the private sector. We have now more funds in the balance sheet as a result of large transactions.

4. The revenue model for the federation

As a result of the business facilitation, the federation derives its revenue from the commission it receives from the procurement agency of the government. It receives 2% commission per ton of which 1% is passed on to the member FPCs. Additional income for member FPCs over and above the 1% is about 0.50 to 0.75% for transportation, grading, sorting, and gunny bags. This is reimbursed by the procurement agency against submission of the expenses. Fifty per cent of it is paid immediately and the rest after scrutiny of bills.

4.1 Benefit to farmers in the member FPCs

A rough calculation of the net economic benefit to an individual farmer is visible in terms of the differential prices. For instance, when the MSP for *tur* dal was Rs. 6,000 per ton, the prevailing market price was in the range of Rs. 5,000 to Rs. 5,600. Farmers who participated in the MSP through their respective FPCs benefited with an additional price of at least Rs. 200 to Rs. 1,000 per ton, depending on the month of selling their commodity. A small farmer with a 10 ton produce thus gained additional Rs. 10,000 over and above savings in transportation and other associated costs. Similar trend is observed for *chana* (gram) procurement.

Beginning 2018–19, MAHAFPC began exploring opportunities of marketing soybean to the private sector players. It was a strategy to diversify and not to remain solely dependent on the MSP operations on behalf of the government for pulses and onions. Table 14.4 shows MAHAFPC's business (in soybean) with the private sector.

5. Financial performance of MAHAFPC

The decision to focus largely on implementing the MSP operations via member FPCs is directly reflected in the financial operations of the MAHAFPC. Its revenue from operations is therefore erratic, as the only source of revenue is 1% commission earned on the volume. Also, to be noted is that the MSP operations are recorded in the books of neither the MAHAFPC or its members. MAHAFPC acts as a procurement agency. Warehouse receipts are

Table 14.4 Business with the private sector

Year	Quantity (Metric Ton)	Value (Rs. in Million)
2018–19	638.1	22.70
2019–20	1,224	48.20
2020–21	4,592	206.30
2021–22	9,408	423.66

Source: Annual reports and data from the MAHAFPC

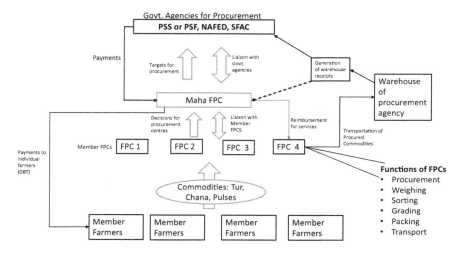

Figure 14.1 A graphical presentation of the flow of transactions among MAHAFPC, its member FPCs, and farmers

generated at the procurement centre, and payment is made by the government. Money is directly transferred as a DBT to saving accounts of members.

6. MAHAONION: a new initiative

While business in pulses and other commodities was stabilising, a recent initiative of the federation is in the marketing of onions. Maharashtra is the largest producer of onion in the country; however, small farmers have rarely benefitted from the cultivation of onions. Drastic price fluctuations in tomato, onion, and potato affect the farmers, the consumers, and the government! The consumers have experienced both glut and shortages in all the above three vegetables. In 2019 and 2020, onion prices in the retail market went as high as Rs. 150 a kilogram. MAHAFPC has plans to construct 25 warehouses, each of 1,000 tons storage capacity. Eighteen such warehouses are ready and operational. The infrastructure is to be built under the PPP model. The escalated total cost of each warehouse is approximately Rs. 10.15 million, of which about Rs. 4.4 million is given as subsidy by the central and the state governments under the Rashtriya Krishi Vikas Yojana – Remunerative Approaches for Agriculture and Allied Sectors Rejuvenation (RKVY-RAFTAAR) scheme of the Ministry of Agriculture and Farmers' Welfare. The infrastructure is built on principle of Public Private Partnership-Integrated Agriculture Development (PPPAID) project under RKVY. NAFED has contributed 26.2%, whereas MAHAFPC has contributed 5%, and FPC has contributed 21.2%. It would be 47.6% as public contribution

Table 14.5 Financial statements of MAHAFPC

Year	MAHA Farmer Producer Company Ltd. – Performance per Year						
	2014–15	2015–16	2016–17	2017–18	2018–19	2019–20	2020–21
Total Revenue	100,000	4,270,674	2,000,811	42,849,646	106,208,927	15,539,695	510,646,801
Total Expense	99,670	3,996,239	2,705,866	40,456,474	105,758,016	14,537,167	421,464,490
Profit Before Tax	330	274,435	–705,055	2,393,171	450,911	1,002,528	89,182,311
Profit After Tax	228	189,635	–708,932	1,941,456	352,659	741,383	88,639,097
Share Capital	100,000	100,000	100,000	1,530,000	2,000,000	2,320,000	3,860,000
Reserves and Surplus	228	189,863	–519,049	1,422,386	1,775,045	12,516,429	91,155,526
Fixed Assets Including Investments	–	–	107,253	97,334	124,746	249,113	6,277,039
Current Liabilities	1,054,030	1,266,780	302,079,469	22,556,522	34,148,625	349,771,235	949,299,491
Current Assets	1,054,030	1,266,780	302,079,466	22,556,522	34,148,625	349,771,235	949,299,491

Source: MAHAFPC records

226

in the form of subsidy of the total project cost. The FPC has to avail land on lease for the project. A part of the warehouse is used as a spot market for farmers to participate in the auction to sell the produce whereas the other remaining is used for procuring and storage of onions for NAFED, sold by NAFED on the instructions of ministry of consumer affairs at a later stage. The infrastructure is flexible in a sense that while onion storage is done between March and September, the same godown can be used for storage of soybean/maize and other horticultural crops (October to February) as the storage racks (for onions) can be dismantled and open space can be created for soybean storage.

One such warehousing facility is functional since 2020 at Vaishanavdham Parunde Farmers Producers Company (VPFPC) Limited at Eknathwadi, Savargaon, 90 km from Pune. It had a business turnover of about Rs. 15 million in 2019. In 2020, it increased to Rs. 35 million. The FPC acting as a procurement agency for NAFED bought onions and earned commission. In the first year, they managed to procure 259 tons. The volume increased to 2,500 tons in 2020. In addition to procuring for NAFED, it also conducted open auctions twice a week, where traders and farmers transacted business, facilitated by the FPC (Table 14.6).

7. e-Kisan Mandi

In September 2020, in collaboration with NAFED, MAHAFPC started Nafed e-Kisan Mandi in Pune. The objective of the initiative is to tap opportunities that will open up as a result of the new farm laws especially in the area of Agricultural Marketing Reforms in the country. Nafed e-Kisan Mandi is an electronic trading platform with physical infrastructure. This was set up in partnership with local FPOs (FPCs and cooperatives) to be integrated with a national-level digital marketing platform. It is a marketplace for more than 50 FPCs in and around Pune city for wholesaling and retailing of processed and unprocessed (whole grain)

Table 14.6 Business under MAHAONION initiative

Year	Under PSF		Retail Trade (Open Market)		Total	
	Quantity (MT)	Value (Rs. in Million)	Quantity (MT)	Value (Rs. in Million)	Quantity (MT)	Value (Rs. in Million)
2018–19	5,261	68.10	2405	19.30	7666	87.50
2019–20	24,773	295.5	0.015	3.00	24,773	298.50
2020–21	37,448	419.8	0.007	2.60	37,448	422.40

Source: Annual reports and data from the MAHAFPC

products. In February 2022, it organised a week-long rice festival in Pune. The idea was to directly connect farmers with the consumers in the city. Seven FPCs joined in the festival, marketing various varieties of rice produced by its members.

8. Challenges in institution building: views of stakeholders

MAHAFPC as a young federation is attempting to balance both the business and institution building dimension of its working. Five stakeholders explained the challenges and opportunities that are posed in this process. Mr Prashant Pawar explained the challenges in business expansion:

> Our job is to prepare a track and our member FPCs will run on these tracks. However, there are instances where member FPCs as also individual farmers become opportunistic. They don't like to follow the standard operating procedures (SOPs) we have developed. We have noticed that, sitting in Pune, some promoters have set up FPCs! There is no member connect, they do not have any storage infrastructure, no weighing-grading (minimal) facilities. We insist on adhering to three simple thumb rules before any FPC becomes a member and is enrolled under the MSP. We ask last year's audited balance sheet, a list of at least 250 members and names of board of directors. We keep a watch over such "dubious" boards and also member FPCs. There are surprise visits by me to FPCs when procurement operations are going. In one of the regions, even traders and *adatiyas* have registered new FPCs.

Kunal Baset is with the MAHAFPC for the last four years. He supervises and leads finance and accounting operations of the organisation. According to him, the biggest challenge is to work with farmers and convince them about the work processes. MAHAFPC has decided to focus on the younger generation of farmers in the age group of 30–45. They are tech-savvy, more educated, and literate. While their elder family members continue in farming (production), this group can learn to manage institutions and will be more market-savvy. Training of agricultural graduates with MANAGE was organised with this aim in mind.

Sudhir Kumar Goel is a renowned expert in the field of agriculture and FPC movement. During his tenure as a senior IAS officer and post-retirement, he has been a guide and mentor of the FPC movement in the country. He shared his perspectives on the journey of MAHAFPC so far.

> Formation of FPC is not an end in itself. For MAHAFPC, they need to plough back the learning of the MSP operations to strengthen

own capabilities as also those of their member FPCs. As they expand
business operations with the government, proportionate share with
the private sector organisations should also increase. They need
to see themselves as an aggregator and not a trader. They should
aspire to be a service provider for the entire value chain (similar
to GCMMF in Gujarat) for their members. When they begin to do
more business with private sector organisations, there will be more
stringent demands from them on issues of traceability, quality and
so on. If they have to be a bridge between both quality conscious
growers (farmers) and buyers (the private sector), their role will
become more challenging.

Sunil Kumar Singh is additional managing director of NAFED. As a
senior official from NAFED and SFAC earlier he has seen the growth of
MAHAFPC as an organisation since 2016. His perspectives on the journey
of MAHAFPC provide an interesting mirror.

The FPO model stands on three pillars: standardisation – aggregation and connection to the market. Local storage, generating local
employment, assuring quality storage and payment to farmers at
the doorstep eliminating the uncertainties they face in APMC, is
the value addition they bring to farmers. However, MAHAFPC
has to ensure that as their operations grow in size, their roots and
stems (the primary membership – FPCs) remain strong. Otherwise,
the tree can be healthy but with weak roots as has happened in
some cooperative federations. They have a young, tech-savvy and
dynamic team. They should inculcate mutual trust and build a sense
of ethics among their members, as they expand.

8.1 Finding the human resources to manage FPCs

Arunachalam Sankaran who is a consultant to MAHAFPC and who
earlier worked as a consultant for many years with the World Bank–
supported MACP projects in the state cites that the single most important challenge is that of finding the right people, the FPC leaders who
will show direction for the movement in the state. MAHAFPC is hiring
either consultants or staff where it lacks in adequate domain expertise.
Also on the anvil is the ambitious plan to build and enlarge a more
enabling ecosystem, inviting interns from IIM Ahmedabad, linking up
with agricultural colleges, offering students in the final year intern-
ship for agro industrial work experience, collaborating with MANAGE
Hyderabad for agri-entrepreneurship course, adding to network of chartered accountants (CAs) by appointing five more CAs, assigning them to
help FPC members in compliances and so on. Yogesh says, "What IRMA

did for AMUL and Operation Flood, MAHAFPC wants to do for FPCs in Maharashtra!"

9. A 'corporate cooperative' and remaining relevant in changing times

The vision of MAHAFPC as articulated in its annual report of 2019–20 states, "Our vision is to develop commodity centric clusters of FPCs with common business models for value addition through markets at farm gate level."

Yogesh Thorat elaborated further on this vision. He observed that the federation and the member FPCs should aspire to remain as a vibrant institution for next 10 to 20 years. The federation has to be meaningful and relevant for its member FPCs. For this to happen, he has set his eyes on overall system improvement, acquiring domain expertise in financial instruments, marketing, warehousing, and electronic trading platforms, data mining and other disciplines. Currently, the breadth of expertise is missing. He does not endorse the idea of FPCs seeking tax concessions, rebates, and favours. He strongly feels that MAHAFPC should be seen and functioning as a commercial and professional organisation. The role has to be reimagined as that of a 'corporate cooperative' and not a 'socialist era cooperative' of the 1970s and 1980s! According to him, a federation has to develop a business model that has assets with minimum liabilities (on its account books). For this to happen, commodity monetisation could be a strategy. Another role that he sees for MAHAFPC is to facilitate investments into member FPCs through special-purpose vehicles (SPVs). Mahaonion is one example. There is also a proposal under discussion to launch a Non-Bank Finance Company (NBFC). Investments for warehousing are being discussed.

Yogesh Thorat is articulate in explaining the likely challenges MAHAFPC might have to face as it expands its footprint across the state. He opines,

> Currently we have 650 FPC members, half of whom are active in a sense doing some business with the help of our facilitation. Adding more members is not a challenge for us. The challenge is what we are delivering to them and the reason for which members are joining. Thus, the what-how-why questions are critical to us.

10. Why federate: lessons for other emerging federations

The opportunities for MAHAFPC to expand its operations are manifold. As it expands its geographical footprint enrolling more members across the state, adding more commodities in the business facilitation model and diversifying into trade with the private sector, it is bound to attract both praise and criticism. The leadership of MAHAFPC is sensitive about the political economy challenges. As soon as MAHAFPC begins large-scale procurement, other stakeholders including the state marketing federation become slightly jittery. They feel somewhat challenged by a new entity that is offering a competition to hither though unstated monopoly of their operations. Already there are two other state-level federations that have been formed; one with less than six months of experience (and presumable some political backing) has been granted permission to procure under the MSP. In 2021, NABARD and NCDC has entrusted the responsibility as CBBO to build capacities of FPCs in 11 clusters in Maharashtra.

For a federation on a fast-growth trajectory, MAHAFPC has begun to occupy a critical space in marketing of select commodities as a result of its active participation in the public procurement schemes of the government. How it can build on the experiences of these operations, engage more with the private sector creating multiple options beyond uncertain public procurement, build a stable business model, develop a strong network of leadership at the members' level, remaining responsive to the needs of the members, staying relevant in the politically active environment of competing stakeholders in the state, will determine if it can truly attain the status of a new generation of 'corporate cooperative' as its leadership has aspired to be. It has taken baby steps to overcome the perennial capital inadequacy in farmer organisations by converging with the existing governmental schemes. These strategies may provide possible alternative solutions to many other FPCs. Experiences of MAHAFPC could also provide important lessons to other federations that are soon expected to emerge as the FPC movement spreads deeper in the country. The lessons learnt from the journey of MAHAFPC in the area of its business model, institutional development, governance, convergence, and policy advocacy are valuable to the entire sector and thus need to be disseminated widely.

15

SEEDING AN FPO MOVEMENT

The Madhya Bharat Consortium in Central India

C. Shambu Prasad and Abhishek Saxena

1. Madhya Pradesh: agricultural growth, small farmers, and markets

Unlike many other Indian states where the share of agriculture in total GDP has been declining over the last two decades, in the case of Madhya Pradesh (MP), it has consistently increased since 2011 and was a high of 40% in 2018–19. MP's agricultural GDP increased at 8.1% per annum during 2005–06 to 2016–17 and at 11.8% per annum in the three years since. In 2015–16, 75.5% of small and marginal farmers with a holding size of less than 2 hectares accounted for 48% of the total area operated. Short-term agricultural credit grew from Rs. 33.3 billion to Rs. 112.1 billion from 2006–7 to 2013–14 with interest rates having dropped from 7 to 0% (Gulati et al., 2021: 145–175).

Despite the creditable performance on agriculture, credit access to farmers has been through the Primary Agricultural Credit Societies (PACS). A former Secretary of Agriculture in the state remarked that there has been significant elite capture by large farmers in MP with membership of small and marginal farmers being as low as 11% in 2010 in PACS. Despite many efforts to broad-base PACS, extending credit to small farmers in MP has been low, and they have little voice in existing cooperative societies. The emerging alternative of producer companies seemed promising from a small farmer point of view if only they were mobilised appropriately and the positive experiences from the farmer producer organisations (FPOs) during the World Bank–supported MP District Poverty Initiative Project (MPDPIP) were leveraged to provide greater voice for small farmers.

Analysis of the Ministry of Corporate Affairs (MCA) database indicates that MP accounts for less than 6% of all FPOs in India as of March 2021. Yet FPOs from the state have won 16 of the 68 awards in the FPO Impact awards organised by Access Development Services from 2018 to 2021. Part of this success can be explained through the active involvement of non-governmental organisations (NGOs) such as Action of Social Advancement

DOI: 10.4324/9781003308034-15

(ASA) and Professional Assistance for Development Action (PRADAN) in creating some of the earliest FPCs in the country. The MPDPIP project that began in MP in 2001 had attracted agribusiness professionals to manage these fledgling institutions. Yogesh Dwivedi, who later became the CEO of the Madhya Bharat Consortium of Farmer Producers Company Limited (henceforth Madhya Bharat), was an integral part of the District Poverty Initiative Program (DPIP) pilots in the FPO space since 2005. A post-graduate in agriculture, he had experience of working with private seed companies earlier and was part of a seed collective Panchmahudiya Khedut Beej Utpadan evam Bechan Sangh Maryadit (Lunavada, Dahod, Gujarat).

2. Supportive ecosystem for FPO federation formation

The year 2006 was a watershed year in the FPO movement in India as for the first time 16 farmer producer companies (FPCs) were registered from a single state, MP. These FPCs were part of the MPDPIP. The FPO movement in MP had good support through proactive involvement of officers like Ravindra Pastor (the then DPIP project director) and Pravesh Sharma (agriculture secretary, MP government). In one of the earliest articles about FPCs, Yogesh Dwivedi and Arun Joshi (2007) remarked:

> The unexploited and underutilized market offers huge business potential for expansion and growth . . . the positive and proactive support from the Government of Madhya Pradesh has provided long term support by reforming 12 major policies in favour of strengthening these federations.

However, there was lull in MP after 2007 since most FPOs were promoted by NGOs that got busy with other projects in their agenda. Things changed in 2010 again when Pravesh Sharma went on to head the Small Farmers Agribusiness Consortium (SFAC) as the managing director and is credited with spearheading the FPO movement nationally. Experiences of MP have largely shaped later process guidelines of the department of agriculture and cooperation through the SFAC in 2013 that led to a national roll-out of formation of FPOs in the country. With FPCs growing in the state and good policy support, when the idea of a federation of FPOs was promoted by the SFAC in eight states, MP seemed ready for a state-level federation of FPOs. Madhya Bharat was incubated at the Action for Social Advancement (ASA) with initial support from the Rajya Ajeevika Forum (RAF) and an initial seed fund of Rs. 1 million from SFAC. A subsequent grant to ASA of Rs. 19 million from Rabo Bank helped Madhya Bharat in managing their capacity building and human resource requirements for two years. Its spacious office in Bhopal that has facilities for training has been a prominent space for many FPO conversations in the state ever since.

Table 15.1 Evolution and milestones of Madhya Bharat Consortium

Year	Event
2007	Yogesh Dwivedi and Arun Joshi write one of the earliest articles in the publication of LEISA India on producer companies as new-generation farmer institutions
2007	Department of Panchayat & Rural Development (DoPRD), Government of MP provides for HR, working capital, and infrastructure support to federation of self-help groups (SHGs) registered under FPCs for the first time in the country
2011	DoPRD provides support to consultants for FPCs to develop business plan and market linkages up to Rs. 0.5 million per year and administrative costs for five years up to Rs. 0.7 million
2012	Ministry of Agriculture & Cooperation, GoI, letter for extension of benefits to FPCs at par with cooperatives under all government schemes
2014	Order of State Marketing Federation to supply fertiliser to FPCs enabling FPCs to engage in input business
2014	MBCFPCL registered in September with seed capital of Rs. 1 million from SFAC
2015	MBCFPCL gets a 2,000 MT warehouse on lease from the State Marketing Board in Dewas district
2015	Rabobank supports MBCFPCL through ASA with a grant of Rs. 1.9 million
2017	MBCFPCL trades 80 MT soybean with NCDEX
2020	3,000 MT of wheat procured through MSP
2020	Options trade in commodity markets for the first time by MBCFPCL with a start-up Kamatan and Samunnati (NBFC)

Madhya Bharat was registered in September 2014, and Yogesh became the first CEO. Beginning with 34 members initially, the federation now has 137 FPO shareholders (134 FPCs and three cooperatives). The main objective of Madhya Bharat is to provide umbrella support to its member FPOs, particularly on marketing, financial linkages, brand development, value addition, policy advocacy, representation, extension, and insurance. With an equity base of Rs. 5.01 million Madhya Bharat today serves 175,000 small farmers of 52 districts from MP and Chhattisgarh. In 2020–21 its turnover was Rs. 293 million with a profit of Rs. 899,000. Table 15.1 presents a timeline of the early evolution and important milestones of the Madhya Bharat Consortium. It is evident that an enabling ecosystem for spread of FPCs was in place at MP unlike other states.

While the support system for FPCs was being shaped a consortium was a new institution and needed its own business model and support.

3. Business model of MBCFPCL

The initial years of Madhya Bharat were largely in establishing its identity as a new-generation producer collective, and it faced challenges on multiple fronts. Being seen as a legitimate yet independent entity of farmers was a challenge as *mandi* boards, and most government departments would only recognise cooperatives and not recognise FPOs. On the other hand, given its association with SHGs, the state rural livelihood mission was keen to see it as an extension of the government and wanted the consortium under its fold. Madhya Bharat though was keen to remain a people's institution. The other challenge interestingly arose from the success of dairy cooperatives in India and the design principles for a successful cooperative that emerged out of the famous "Anand pattern" of cooperatives. There were few success stories of producer collectives beyond milk and sugar, and the expectation was that perhaps like the Amul model, an apex FPO would work in other commodities too. While expectations were high there was not enough experience across the country that could guide Madhya Bharat or similar federations on which part of the agricultural value chain was more amenable for scaling up at an apex level.

How does a consortium of FPOs find regular business? Will it be in facilitation of inputs for its members, in procurement (including for the government), or in processing or marketing? These were many of the design challenges that Madhya Bharat had to address in its early years. The sheer diversity of member FPO produce added to the complexity. They were involved in 24 crops, and most member FPOs were dealing with at least three crops. Soybean was reported as the main crop by over 63% of FPOs though wheat was reported by most FPOs (95), and soybean and gram were reported by 80 FPOs.[1]

3.1 Innovations in agri-inputs: capturing certified seed market

Fortunately for the consortium, experiences of some FPOs started showing a direction, and they found certified seed business as a major opportunity. The Sironj Crop Producer Company in Vidisha, a member FPO of Madhya Bharat, promoted by PRADAN was the first seed collective registered as an FPC in 2005. Providing good seeds to farmers is something that Yogesh Dwivedi and Sanjay Pandya (Senior Manager, Production and Processing at Madhya Bharat) have been doing for over a decade, a journey that began with Yogesh's involvement in the Participatory Varietal Selection Program in 2005 and their active involvement in the MP-DPIP project. Among the early FPCs in the state the Samarth Kisan FPC, in Shajapur district, and its branded soya seeds were popular.

With good buy-in from a few state government officials in the seed corporation and department of agriculture, certified seed business became the mainstay of these few FPCs. Madhya Bharat capitalised on this opportunity taking it to scale and today has a good name in the state in all the 43 districts for the quality certified seeds of soybean, wheat, gram, pulses, and paddy. Unlike other FPOs that often focus on provision of agricultural inputs such as pesticides and fertilisers, Madhya Bharat and its members valued providing quality seeds at reasonable price to small and marginal farmers. Company records indicate that the gross profit from sale of seeds of Madhya Bharat consortium constitutes between 35 and 40% of its overall profit.

Following good cooperative principles Madhya Bharat does not compete in seeds or any other line of business with its members. The experience of members like Samarth Kisan or Sironj is taken to other districts and regions. Madhya Bharat realises that not all small and marginal farmers are suitable for seed production and recognises the risk in this business too, especially with climate-related risks in recent years. It is important to maintain quality and establish a good market share in the seed business, for which Madhya Bharat also procures seeds from non-members.

Madhya Bharat operates a 2,000 MT warehouse that has been leased by the State Marketing Board since 2015 in Dewas district. Sanjay Pandya oversees this important business line of Madhya Bharat, and the Board of Madhya Bharat also has Mr Bhatnagar with over three decades of experience in the seed sector who serves as an expert director.

3.2 Forays in output market: procurement for government and commodity trading

Beyond seeds, Madhya Bharat has always been keen to make a difference in the output markets. Madhya Bharat works with government agencies, private players, and financial institutions. The FPOs that are part of Madhya Bharat deal with multiple crops such as soybean, wheat, cotton, maize, and pulses. While wheat is the most important commodity in terms of quantities traded with 3,000 MT being traded in the last season (2020–21) through MSP, soybean is an important crop that is sold to private partners. The storage and value addition, if any, are the responsibilities of the member FPO, with Madhya Bharat as only facilitating linkages and taking commission on the deal, but the risk sharing is 50–50 in most cases. Farmers have benefitted since Madhya Bharat's procurement operations have been more efficient than that of government under minimum support price (MSP) scheme in red gram procurement. Maize and pulses sold to private players and government agencies though have added to the revenue but have been low on the profit side. Madhya Bharat has even faced issues of non-payment of dues while dealing with National Agricultural Cooperative Marketing Federation of India Ltd (NAFED) in 2018–19 and 2019–20.

Apart from crop marketing support and seed production Madhya Bharat does commodity trading. Madhya Bharat began trading with National Commodities and Derivatives Exchange (NCDEX) in 2017, mostly in soybean with commodity trading of 80 MT. This increased to 200 MT of soybean and 90 MT of Bengal gram in 2019 and to 1,450 MT overall in 2020. It traded over Rs. 140 million worth of soybean and other commodities with the NCDEX benefitting 3,600 farmers in 2020–21.

Futures trading is risky for individual FPOs. Corporates, including multi-national companies, constantly speculate and trade huge amounts of commodities as they have ready stocks in the warehouses to hedge in the market. They also have high risk-taking capacity. For FPOs (including Madhya Bharat) ready stock was only available in the first year (2017). If Madhya Bharat or the FPO hedges on behalf of the members, one assumes a normal yield. If the crop fails or yield is impacted in quality or quantity, they face rejection from NCDEX. Also, if the market price is down, NCDEX might offer them a lower price.

This is where "put" option is important. In a put option, once the price is set, even if the market price falls, the transaction will happen at the fixed price. This way, the FPO either will make profit or will at least recover costs but will not make losses. Also, a price risk buffer of Rs. 0.5 million (Rs. 100/quintal) was offered by Securities and Exchange Board of India (SEBI) in 2019-20 to FPOs and their federations towards promotion of trading on commodities exchanges. Trade with NCDEX has been a big contributor for Madhya Bharat's growth in recent years especially after SEBI in May 2019 reduced the regulatory fee on Stock Exchanges with respect to turnover in agricultural commodity derivatives for FPOs.

Samunnati facilitated the execution of the first "options" trade-in Soybean at NCDEX along with Madhya Bharat and Kamatan in 2020. In the options market, buyers have the right but are not compelled to buy or sell an asset at a fixed price on or before a given date. On the expiry day, it is the farmers'/FPO's wish to remain in the options or come out of the option and sell it at the market price.[2] However, recently (2021) the government banned the 'put' option upon reports from the various stakeholders that it was being used to artificially inflate the price of some commodities in the market.

Nevertheless, in April 2021, Madhya Bharat has been recognised for trading the highest volumes of soybean on NCDEX on behalf of the member farmers and their collectives. Madhya Bharat had also tried to enter the vegetables business but found risks high and difficulty to enter the market that is cartelised. They charge higher commission from the FPO. Infrastructure for storage is essential in case of perishables. Unless that happens, Madhya Bharat cannot deal with perishables. It currently only deals with onion and garlic and recently included ginger too. Madhya Bharat's own business in 2019 was Rs. 1540 million, and if its member FPOs are taken together the total revenue is Rs. 2560 million of business.

4. Governance of the consortium

Madhya Bharat serves 224,000 farmers both directly through its FPOs and indirectly through its services for seeds. The average membership of farmers in an FPO of Madhya Bharat is 1,007, and the largest FPO, Samarth

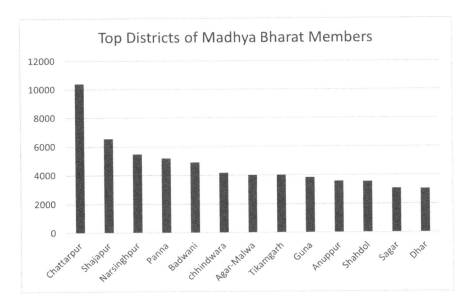

Figure 15.1 Top ten districts of MBCFPCL membership

Kisan Producer Company is having 6,552 members. Over 75% of Madhya Bharat's members were registered between 2012 and 2016. While Madhya Bharat has its presence across the state, 13 districts account for nearly 60% of its members as shown in Figure 15.1. Close to 45% of Madhya Bharat farmer members are from ten districts largely in the north-eastern MP and the Malwa belt in the East.

The governance of a complex organisation with a presence in 45 districts does pose a challenge. There are ten board of directors (BoD), including one woman, representing 13 districts of MP as seen in Figure 15.2. They belong to FPOs that have been registered between 2006 and 2016 indicating about 5–15 years of running an FPO. Currently, there is one expert director who is a retired seeds expert. His presence on the board helps the consortium in advisory and strategic support.

The share capital contribution was initially 5% of the potential member FPO's equity, but later it was fixed at Rs. 2,000. Multiple members from single households should not be part of the same FPO, and Madhya Bharat insists that the focus of its members should be on small and marginal farmers. Yogesh Dwivedi has been vocal in arguing that government representatives should not have voting rights in boards since that would dilute the ownership and decision-making at the board level. Other issues like representation of women have yet to be tackled since even after government mandate of 33% women to be part of FPOs, there

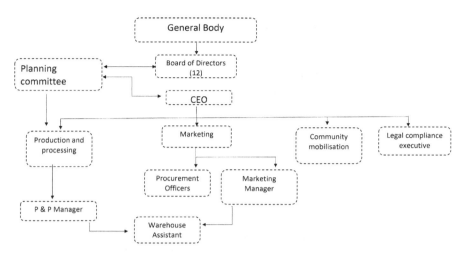

Figure 15.2 Organisational chart of MBCFPCL

are few women in many member FPOs. Part of the reason is that land is not in the name of women and that often presents problems during registration as a BoD.

Madhya Bharat is led by Yogesh as a CEO and has 16 staff. Madhya Bharat has a policy of giving preference in hiring to those who have worked with FPOs at ground level and is looking for greater responsibility and role in the FPO ecosystem. Many of their senior staff are those with significant agribusiness experience with FPOs at the grassroots. There are currently three verticals – seed production, marketing, and community mobilisation. The marketing unit is involved in working with the FPOs in the field, as well as with marketing outside the network in case of clearing surplus stocks. Having a full-time marketing unit is costly, and Madhya Bharat therefore works with contractual employees. For mobilisation of communities, Madhya Bharat chooses those with a background in social sciences. One employee looks after legal compliance. The CEO and the BoDs are also part of the planning committee that reviews and improves on business plans and takes strategic decisions from time to time.

Madhya Bharat holds an annual gathering, a state-level FPC *Sammelan*, where member FPOs and ecosystem players across MP and outside are invited to participate. These gatherings go beyond typical FPC annual general body meetings (AGM) and are curated to enable better FPO policies for the state. The last Sammlean on 29 February 2020, before the pandemic, had the objective of appraising the government about the progress of FPCs, and to get their attention on FPC's challenges. These challenges included long-term solution such as fertiliser allotment, provision of working capital, seed subsidies, infrastructure development grant, and the inclusion of FPOs in different government schemes like Food Park, Organic Promotion Scheme, Operation Green & MSP Procurement, and so on.

Overall, Madhya Bharat has appropriate infrastructure and committed manpower with capabilities to run the organisation successfully. There are no templates currently available for apex FPOs, and thus Madhya Bharat, like other federations, is learning by doing. Thus, while the governance structure is suited to the purpose of a consortium there are many challenges in handling such a complex and diverse group in 41 districts. Not all members are active and neither does the FPO federation have enough capital to engage with all the FPO members in commodity trading. Reaching out to distant members and making the board active and more inclusive (gender representation) are some of the challenges that Madhya Bharat faces. An even greater challenge is to raise both resources and capabilities that would enable Madhya Bharat to go to the next level by getting into value addition of products. With a growth in the organisation Madhya Bharat might need expert directors with expertise in value addition and marketing expertise and beyond seeds.

5. Financial overview

The summary of the finances of the consortium is shown in Table 15.2.

The share capital has increased in initial years but has become stable. Raising the next round of capital for the consortium from its members would be a challenge and is dependent on the health of individual FPOs. While revenue has grown significantly in the year 2018–19 to Rs. 1,540 million, largely due to MSP procurement, there has also been a fall the following year indicating the risky nature of business and lack of stability even after seven years of operation. The revenue and profit appear to rise and fall depending up on MSP sales. The profits of the FPO are modest and so too are the reserves and surpluses. The FPC is asset light but might need to explore means to raise resources either alone or in collaboration to make a bigger difference in farmers' lives. As its operations grew since 2015–16, Madhya Bharat has been raising working capital through loans from Ananya Finance, NABKISAN, loan against warehouse receipt (WHR loan) from IDBI Bank, Samunnati, Friends of the Women's World Bank (FWWB), and a cash credit (CC) limit loan.

6. Advocating 'ease of doing' business for FPOs

Madhya Bharat continues to engage in a dialogue with NAFED, state agricultural universities, department of agriculture, NABARD, and other agencies. It is also in touch with Samunnati for finance as well as for commodity trade (mainly

Table 15.2 Financial overview of MBCFCL

Amount in Rs/Year

	2014–15	2015–16	2016–17	2017–18	2018–19	2019–20	2020–21
Share capital	565,000	1,601,390	4,734,780	4,882,780	4,961,780	4,981,780	4,997,380
Reserves and surplus	1,466,444	972,917	617,222	694,062	813,142	1,459,229	2,003,815
Revenue	739,781	19,181,792	79,291,989	232,630,524	1,545,463,899	62,878,117	299,966,471
Profit (loss)	10,548	71,473	535,201	76,840	102,259	646,087	544,585

soybean) but would ideally like to have loans at much lower rates. The FPC treads cautiously and is suspicious of high growth figures and would like to avoid applying for risky loans from different organisations where often the terms are very exploitative.

Beyond its work for its members on inputs, and aggregation of produce, impressive by themselves, the most significant contribution of Madhya Bharat though is in building a vibrant FPO ecosystem in MP that benefits all the 510 or more FPCs in the state. Madhya Bharat supports its members by enabling credit linkages, assisting with statutory compliances, and building capacities of FPO functionaries to promote good governance. Not all FPOs can enter the seed business and yet need many other services to remain profitable. The Kalesindh Farmer Producer Company in Ujjain district (registered in 2016), for instance, does not deal with output marketing and has a membership of 1,500 members from 20 villages in the region. Apart from guidance on best practices on governance and management Madhya Bharat is working with the FPO to vision and plan for its future growth. With support from MBCFPCL, the FPC is linked to both NABKISAN and Samunnati for credit and applied for an equity grant from SFAC. The FPO has also purchased land from its members to set up a warehouse that would soon have a grading machine.[3] Madhya Bharat also facilitates farm machinery hiring through its custom hiring centres (CHCs).

Madhya Bharat helps FPOs like Kalesindh in building its asset through making government schemes more accessible to small and marginal farmers. Being the voice of farmers and FPOs is seen as an important task of Madhya Bharat and a significant value add for its members even though it does not necessarily translate into business for the consortium. Madhya Bharat also acts as a voice for FPOs in state-level discussions and works with government officials to provide FPOs linkage with different government schemes for agricultural infrastructure development. MP was the first state to have an FPO policy as early as 2007 and one of the few that created good support to FPOs through provision of working capital. Despite a government order in 2014 that enabled FPOs to supply fertilisers, operationalising these on the ground has been a continuous challenge. Table 15.3 indicates some of the successful advocacy efforts of Madhya Bharat in enabling 'ease of doing' business.

The strong lobbies of the agricultural marketing and credit infrastructure that were directed at large farmer-controlled cooperative societies prevented entry of FPCs in *mandis*, and they were often treated as private companies. Madhya Bharat worked hard to advocate the same benefits as cooperatives to these member-owned institutions through a government order in September 2017. This was followed by another order in May 2018 that declared Madhya Bharat as a registered entity that could take up MSP procurement for gram, pulses, and oilseeds. Later in the year Madhya Bharat worked further to get the State Agriculture Marketing Board to permit the FPCs to aggregate produce from their members even without any *mandi* license, at their

Table 15.3 Madhya Bharat's advocacy for ease of doing business for FPOs

2017	Department of Agriculture (DoA) passes an order declaring FPCs at par with cooperatives for all government schemes
2018	DoA declares Madhya Bharat as a state-level agency for MSP procurement under price support scheme for chana, *masur*, and *sarson*
2018	State Agriculture Marketing Board allows aggregation by FPCs from their members without any license at their collection centre
2018	DoA to make FPCs eligible for use of government infrastructures and reduce their monthly rent for FPCs for Agricultural Produce Marketing Committee (APMC) warehouse
2019	Order of State Agriculture Marketing Board allowing FPCs to obtain APMC Trading License and the simplification of the application process
2019	FPC representative included in creation of infrastructure under government scheme for farmers organisation and cooperatives

collection centres. According to the draft policy "Laghu Krishak Krishi Vyapar Protsahan Neeti 2018," prepared by Madhya Bharat, FPOs should be allowed to operate outside the APMC premises and the tax liability be shifted to the buyer. Once the *mandis* have been informed in the prescribed format of such an arrangement, the FPOs can sell directly to the buyers. There is also a proposal to simplify the APMC licensing in the same document. The APMC trade licence followed in 2019 and FPCs were made eligible for use of government infrastructure that helped them reduce their monthly rent for APMC warehouses. Warehouse rental charges (infrastructure or warehouses built by *mandi* board or APMCs) range from Rs. 2.5 to Rs. 1.5/quintal per month for FPOs. Earlier it was available only for government agencies/organisations. Madhya Bharat is also recognised as an FPC representative and part of the infrastructure creation under government schemes. MP is seen as a pioneer in developing FPO-specific guidelines to create an enabling ecosystem for FPOs, and Madhya Bharat has an important role in this. FPOs in MP tend to see Madhya Bharat Consortium as a single-window help centre to get solutions for problems related to business licences, marketing, or issues related with government departments.

Yogesh Dwivedi widely shares these government policy orders in national discussions to enable other states and federations to work towards enabling 'ease of doing' business for FPOs. Madhya Bharat is now called upon by many implementing agencies and has been nominated as a cluster-based business organisation (CBBO) in the new 10,000 FPO policy for the states of MP and Chhattisgarh with a target of promoting 34 FPOs in both the states, on behalf of SFAC, NABARD, and NCDC. Mentoring and forming newer CBBOs especially in Chhattisgarh is an opportunity for MBCPFCL to expand and share its learning on how to incubate new FPOs with a strong focus on small farmers.

7. Impact of the FPO

Madhya Bharat provided benefits to 45,000 farmers, where these farmers were made members of the federation directly for purchase of chickpea and red gram (*toor*). Due to the operations of Madhya Bharat, an estimated 70,000 member farmers got Rs. 1,000–1,500 per quintal extra income and on an average Rs. 1,500–15,000 per season extra income. Thousands of small farmers got access to government MSP in wheat, soybean, and pulses through their FPOs. With the use of better technology farmers got access to better crop management practices, and a 25–40% yield enhancement due to high-quality seeds. Member FPOs got 0.5 to 5% commission for all business with Madhya Bharat. Rs. 2.8 million was distributed among 28 FPO members in 2017.

The socio-economic conditions of farmers have improved through the FPO movement. The Samarth FPC in Agar, Neshkala FPC in Guna, and Rewa FPC in Sironj did seeds business of over Rs. 800 million where seeds-producing farmers realised additional income from Rs. 4,000–15,000 per season in 2018–19. The per-farmer gain of the Mandla FPC through seeds was Rs. 8000–16,000/season additionally, and the 130 farmers who sold the seeds to Madhya Bharat were doing subsistence agriculture a few years before. The Chindwara FPC at Junnardeo did a business of custard apple pulp for Rs. 10 million in a season benefitting farmers who got Rs. 5,000/farmer additional income. While many of the government schemes are still skimmed off by merchant groups, small and marginal farmers are more aware today of the market operations and are also beginning to think entrepreneurially. Maintaining consistency over the years in market operations is a challenge. FPOs do not have access to regular funds or professionals; the project support from NABARD or SFAC is only for three years.

8. Current situation and future plans

Many operations of FPOs were affected by Covid 19, and many of the efforts of Madhya Bharat were essentially to ensure that operations were not impacted too much, and Covid guidelines were followed and reliefs for essential commodities were utilised (Kanitkar, 2020). The revenue for the year 2020–21 increased from Rs. 60 million to Rs. 300 million. Much of this was from trading of commodities, mainly soybean and wheat and purchase and supply of onion to NAFED under the Price Stabilization Scheme of the Government of India. More than 1,000 farmers were benefitted from the direct purchase of onion from their field and received incentives ranging from Rs. 200 to Rs. 350/quintal. The seed business was around Rs. 25 million which was also affected to some extent as mobility in the field had been limited. During the second wave the price of wheat fell. Although they could sell it, profits were meagre and not the windfall that was imagined earlier.

9. Conclusion

FPOs continue to face major challenges, and the road is a long and winding one. Challenges that Madhya Bharat faces include shortage of skilled and experienced human resources in member FPOs, lack of working capital and infrastructure for processing, high interest rates for loans and lack of awareness and understanding about FPOs among government departments. Capacity and vision building of BoDs and their active participation are very important for their continued growth. FPOs and the consortium need to explore product differentiation for better market penetration. One such opportunity that Madhya Bharat is pursuing is aiming for third-party accredited quality certification such as Round Table on Responsible Soya (RTRS) in the soybean trade. Dwivedi is currently on the executive board of RTRS.

Reflecting on the journey ahead Yogesh Dwivedi remarked,

> We have reached 170,000 members; we want to make it five times in the next five years or so. We had a two-year set back in our seed business due to climatic and market variations. We have diversified our business activities from seeds production to trading a range of commodities like soybean, wheat, gram, maize and pulses and started aggregation and sales of vegetables like onion, garlic and ginger. We are also entering the processing and marketing of traditional scented rice grown by the farmers of our newly formed FPOs of Chhattisgarh state.
>
> As federations we need to further explore credit access. Also, we should be able to provide greater opportunities for processing and value addition. As it is very few FPOs can take the benefits of the schemes focused on processing and value addition. For FPOs which have poor members, it becomes difficult to get such infrastructure, as the subsequent volumes may not be enough to recover the cost of these infrastructure. We could bring together a few FPOs to set up processing units. Madhya Bharat can act as a facilitation agency on a not-for-profit basis. Market linkage can only be made possible at higher volumes, otherwise cost recovery is not possible, whether for transportation or processing.

The experience of Madhya Bharat highlights the need for an apex body of FPOs at the state level despite the myriad challenges that a federation of FPO faces. More than any other state, MP has been at the forefront of agricultural market reforms in recent years. During the debates on the new and contentious farm laws introduced by the Government of India, supporters of the farm laws invoked FPOs in general, and experiences in MP in particular, to indicate how farm laws could benefit farmers. The experience of producer collectives of MP then offers an alternative view of markets for small farmers beyond the polarising debates of the farm laws being seen as the '1991 moment in agriculture' by the proponents and 'corporate takeover' by those opposed to them. Madhya Bharat in its eight years of operation has tested the producer company model for a state-level consortium of FPOs and demonstrated its effectiveness for small farmers, provided there is a continuous engagement with stakeholders in the ecosystem and enabling policies are in place. There is guarded optimism in translating their vision of transforming agriculture of over a million small and marginal farmers by 2025, many of whom would realise a greater share of the consumer rupee.

Notes

1 Data collated from FPOs in Madhya Bharat's database of 109 members until financial year 2018–19.
2 See https://samunnati.com/options-in-goods-is-a-progress-in-price-realisation-for-farmers/ for details.
3 For more details, see https://www.smallfarmincomes.in/post/seeding-an-fpo-movement-madhya-bharat-consortium-s-million-farmer-mission

References

Gulati, A, Rajkhowa, P, Roy, R & Sharma, P (2021). Performance of agriculture in Madhya Pradesh. In A Gulati, R Roy & S Saini (Eds.), *Revitalizing Indian agriculture and boosting farmer incomes* (pp. 145–174). Springer Nature: Singapore.
Kanitkar, Ajit (2020, April 15). Farmer producer company bridges consumers and farmers during lockdown. *Village Square*. Retrieved from https://www.villagesquare.in/farmer-producer-company-bridges-consumers-and-farmers-during-lockdown/
Yogesh, D & Arun, J (2007). Producer company – A new generation farmers institution. *LEISA India*, 9(1).

16

FROM CIVIL SOCIETY ORIGINS TO AN INDEPENDENT MARKETING FEDERATION OF FARMER PRODUCER ORGANISATIONS

The case of Gujpro Agri-business Consortium

Sachin Oza and Abhishek Saxena

1. The FPO movement in Gujarat and the birth of Gujpro

1.1 Sajjata Sangh and the need for primary producer collectivisation

The Watershed Management programme launched by the Government of India in 1994 provided the non-government organisations (NGOs) in Gujarat an opportunity to intervene in Participatory Natural Resources Management (PNRM) on a large scale. The Development Support Centre (DSC), an NGO based in Ahmedabad, provided capacity building and hand-holding support to some of these NGOs on technical, institutional, and financial aspects. When the first phase of the watershed programme was nearing conclusion in 2000, the NGOs felt that they would continue to need such support for carrying out "Watershed Plus" activities, that is, for enhancing the livelihoods of farmers through promoting sustainable agriculture and market-related interventions. An informal committee of NGOs working on PNRM and sustainable agriculture was formed by DSC in 2000, and it was formally registered as a Network – "Sajjata Sangh" (SS) in 2002. The SS had 34-member NGOs at one point of time (Bikkina and Sarin, 2013) but currently has 25 NGO members located in different regions of the state.

Initially, SS and its member NGOs analysed the production and price risks faced by farmers in their respective regions and were involved in extension and capacity building of NGO staff and farmers on sustainable agriculture practices. They promoted practices such as Integrated Pest Management (IPM), Integrated Nutrient Management (INM), vermicomposting, and drip

DOI: 10.4324/9781003308034-16

irrigation and formed sub-village groups such as Kisan Clubs and SHGs. Sensing the need for market-based approach to livelihood enhancement the Kisan Clubs and SHGs were aggregated into FPOs at the cluster and block level by many NGOs in various parts of Gujarat. From 2009 to 2012, these FPOs were working on innovative models of agriculture input distribution and marketing of produce. While the input distribution model worked for most of the FPOs, value addition and marketing of produce remained a grey area.

The "FPO movement" in Gujarat started from the civil society, unlike in states like Maharashtra and Madhya Pradesh where state government and civil society partnered under specific programmes. The first few FPOs including the Avirat Farmer Producer Company Ltd and the Krushidhan Producer Company Ltd. (see Chapter 2) were registered in the year 2004–05 by NGOs who were members of the SS. Unlike in neighbouring states with FPO federations like Maharashtra and Madhya Pradesh where there has been significant growth, in Gujarat the growth has been moderate. As is evident from Table 16.1, despite an early start, over the last 15 years, only 316 FPCs have been registered in Gujarat, with more than half of them registered in 2019–20 and 2020–21.

1.2 Setting the stage for a state-level federation of FPOs

Kuldeep Solanki, the current CEO of Gujpro Agribusiness Consortium Producer Company Ltd. ((henceforth called Gujpro)), joined as the executive director of SS in 2012. In the same year, a state-level workshop was conducted by the SFAC, New Delhi, in collaboration with Friends of the Women's World

Table 16.1 Farmer producer companies in Gujarat over the years (data source: MCA website)

Year	No. of FPOs Registered	Percent of Total
2005–06	1	0.32
2006–07	1	0.32
2007–08	0	0.00
2008–09	2	0.63
2009–10	1	0.32
2010–11	0	0.00
2011–12	6	1.90
2012–13	5	1.58
2013–14	6	1.90
2014–15	9	2.85
2015–16	26	8.23
2016–17	41	12.97
2017–18	18	5.70
2018–19	30	9.49
2019–20	36	11.39
2020–21	134	42.41
total	316	100.00

Bank (FWWB), DSC, and SS. A state-level forum that could explore collective action in value addition, enable marketing of agriculture produce, build capacities through knowledge and information sharing about FPOs, and work towards policy reforms was proposed during the workshop.

After initial consultation with FPOs, promoting NGOs, experts, and other stakeholders from Gujarat, an informal forum of FPOs, the Gujarat Rajya Krushak Manch (GRKM) was formed on 27 November 2012 by SS. The forum had representatives from FPOs formed by NGOs and corporate social responsibility (CSR) foundations of SS and other FPOs in the state. One of the basic tasks of GRKM was to provide hand-holding support to the NGO staff for developing a business plan for the agriculture produce in their geographical area. GRKM also conducted regular meetings with the FPOs for knowledge and experience sharing. Capacity building programmes and exposure visits were also organised for FPOs, and representatives of NGOs engaged in promoting FPOs. Under the GRKM initiative in 2013, SS anchored the minimum support price (MSP) procurement of groundnut organised by SFAC. About 14,900 MT of groundnut worth Rs. 560 million was procured from farmers through its member FPOs. It was a confidence booster for GRKM and the member FPOs as it provided an opportunity for many FPOs to scale up their business. This experience also provided a major learning for SS, GRKM, and the FPOs in terms of the processes, logistics, and standard operating procedures (SOPs) including quality checks required for carrying out such large-scale trading of groundnut.

Realising the urgent need for marketing of agricultural produce to get better price, the FPOs decided to register the GRKM as a producer company. Hence, Gujpro was formed on 31 October 2014, and SFAC provided a grant of Rs. 1 million. Ten FPOs subscribed 100 shares of Rs. 100 each and provided the initial share capital of Rs. 100,000. The first Chairman of Gujpro was Mr Hemantkumar Naik, who represented the Amalsad Vibhag Vividh Karyakari Sahkari Khedut Mandali Ltd, one of the most successful farmer's cooperatives in Gujarat.

Member expectations and the pressure to scale up and provide new marketing/business opportunities for its members were high following the registration. Unlike in the past where a lot of emphasis was placed on capacity building of members, Gujpro was unable to focus much on institutional strengthening including governance, leadership, and bringing robustness within its member FPOs that increased from ten FPOs to 30 FPOs. While SS continued to provide support to Gujpro from 2014 to 2017, it was also short of funds and therefore could no longer afford to conduct regular training programmes for NGO staff for all FPO members of Gujpro. Since Kuldeep's interest was in enterprise development, it was felt that he should concentrate on strengthening and scaling up Gujpro as its CEO while the programme manager of SS, Mr Manoj Karayat, would take forward the activities of SS as its new executive director from 2017.

2. The journey of Gujpro (2014–21)

Since its inception in 2014, Gujpro has undertaken several activities with its member FPOs. Table 16.2 maps the key activities of Gujpro from 2014 to 2021. It also describes the changes that took place in terms of its membership and activities.

Figure 16.1 provides an overview of the year-wise growth of Gujpro in terms of membership and share capital. As seen from the figure, there has been a steady increase in the FPO membership and share capital of Gujpro since its inception in 2014. The membership has risen by three times from

Table 16.2 Key events of Gujpro from 2014 to 2021

Year	Key Events
2014	Gujpro registered in October with ten FPOs and a share capital of Rs. 1,00,000
	Grant support of Rs. 1.0 million by SFAC
2015–16	Initiates pilot of selling mangoes procured from FPOs in Saurashtra and Kachchh to Ahmedabad
2016–17	Procures 7,819.68 MT of groundnut worth Rs. 330 million from seven FPOs for NAFED and 2,700 MT of *toor* to SFAC from 8 FPOs
	Facilitated sale of 28 MT of groundnut pods worth Rs. 117.46 million to VNKC Agrocom Private Ltd
2017–18	A record sale of 33,985 MT of groundnut worth Rs. 1,613.11 million to NAFED
	Rented warehouses at Gandhidham block of Kachchh district to stock groundnut for NAFED procured under MSP programme
	Facilitated sale of 687 MT of certified groundnut pods to VNKC Agrocom Private Ltd.
2018–19	Sale of 4,405 MT gram worth Rs. 194.71 million and 8,290 MT of mustard worth Rs. 331.65 million to NAFED
	Sale of 990 MT of groundnut and groundnut kernel to VNKC Agrocom Private Ltd. Hired a groundnut processing unit in Savarkundla block of Amreli district
2019–20	Enters into an agreement with VNKC Agrocom Private Ltd, a leading exporter of peanuts for production and supply of blanched peanuts at their production facility in Dholka, Ahmedabad.
	Processing of groundnut at Una on job work basis
	Set up the "Satvik Grahak Bazaar," a retail shop in Ahmedabad
2020–21	Processing of groundnut at Keshod block of Junagadh district on job work basis
	Initiates trading in wheat and gram during Rabi 2020–21
	Initiates seed production in wheat crop
	Explores the fruit and vegetable market through sale of mangoes and coconut
2021–22	Initiates sale of hybrid maize seed, groundnut seeds, wheat, and gram seeds
	Starts trading of groundnut pods and soybean
	Collaborates with Samunnati Finance to scale up the business operations of partner FPOs.

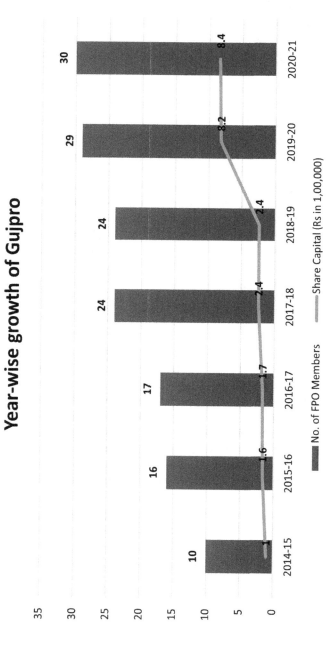

Figure 16.1 Year-wise growth of Gujpro

Table 16.3 Region-wise location of FPOs

Region	No. of FPOs	No. of FPOs
	2014	2021
North Gujarat	0	3
Eastern Tribal Belt and Central Gujarat	1	5
Saurashtra	3	12
Kachchh	5	7
South Gujarat	1	3
Total	10	30

10 to 30, and the share capital has risen by 8.4 times from Rs. 1,00,000 to Rs. 8,40,000.

Along with the steady growth in the FPO membership, their profile in terms the promoting agencies and location has also undergone a shift. While the number of FPOs promoted by member NGOs of SS has increased from 5 in 2014 to 11 in 2021, the percentage has marginally reduced from 50% in 2014 to 37% in 2021. Similarly, while the number of FPOs promoted by non-members of SS has increased from 4 in 2014 to 11 in 2021, the percentage of FPOs promoted by non-NGO members has marginally reduced from 40% in 2014 to 37% in 2021. However, the number of self-initiated FPOs (as members of Gujpro) has increased from 1 in 2014 to 5 in 2021, and their percentage in membership has increased from 10% in 2014 to 16% in 2021.

Table 16.3 provides a comparison of the change in the FPO membership profile of Gujpro as per their location. There has been a shift in the profile of the FPOs since the inception of Gujpro. In 2014, out of ten FPOs, half (5) belonged to Kachchh region, whereas in 2021, even with an increase in the absolute number of Kachchh FPOs, their representation as a fraction of the total 30, has gone down to less than a quarter (7), whereas the number of FPOs from Saurashtra has increased from 3 in 2014 to 12. The growth in the number of FPOs in Saurashtra also reflects the focus of Gujpro which is primarily on trading and value addition in groundnut.

3. Governance and leadership: member expectations and management systems

3.1 The composition of the board

There are seven board members (six men and one woman) in Gujpro at present, and Sureshbhai Gohil of the Bandhutva FPC is the chairman of Gujpro. The board members represent the FPOs located in different regions of Gujarat including three members from Saurashtra, two from

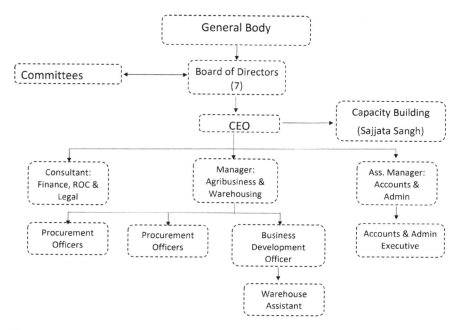

Figure 16.2 Organogram of Gujpro

North Gujarat and one member each from Kachchh and South Gujarat (see Figure 16.2).

The board members meet once every quarter for planning and review of activities to be undertaken during each season. The annual general body meeting is also conducted once a year wherein the balance sheet of the company is presented by the CEO and approved by the board. In the past, there have been expert directors on the board of Gujpro. Mohan Sharma, Executive Director, DSC, was the last one from 2016–18. Since then, there have been no expert directors.

The board members of Gujpro are proactive and well versed with the internal and external challenges faced by Gujpro. They support the CEO in exploring different business opportunities for Gujpro and have also made effort to recover the pending dues from the National Agricultural Marketing Cooperative Federation of India (NAFED) and VNKC Agrocom Pvt. Ltd. (discussed later in the next section on business). During the discussion, with the board members, newer aspects of risk management and risk sharing emerged. It was revealed that Gujpro's directors take risks for seeking credit. Since the company has no risk fund or assets to mortgage, directors take an individual risk.

3.2 Meeting multiple demands of FPO members

As indicated earlier, the FPO members of Gujpro are from different locations, having different crops. In addition, some FPOs are established since several years and are supported by experienced NGOs or CSRs while others have been recently formed and are project-funded or self-initiated. There are several expectations on Gujpro from these diverse sets of FPOs. While the established FPOs expect Gujpro to help them explore national and international markets, the newly formed FPOs want capacity building and hand-holding support for developing a business plan and funding support for scaling up their operations. Meaningfully engaging all the FPO members and meeting their expectations with limited financial and human resources is one of the biggest challenges that Gujpro faces.

3.3 Tackling issues of regional representation and marketing

The board members, representing various FPOs, know their local markets and the prices of the commodities that they were dealing in than Gujpro. Thus, they expect that Gujpro help them with exploring state, national, and export markets for the commodities that they are dealing in. To illustrate the point, Kavitaben, the only woman member of the BoD, represented Kachchh and its member FPOs. She says that earlier, pastoral and farmer communities were well represented in Gujpro as collectives. In fact, milk has already been taken care of by National Dairy Development Board (NDDB) and Gujarat Cooperative Milk Marketing Federation (GCMMF) so Gujpro needed to promote farming collectives in Kachchh. In the current times Kachchh is an underrepresented region in Gujpro, and there is a huge potential for promoting commodities such as pomegranate and dates in the region. A feasibility analysis study for pomegranate and dates as well as an ecosystem mapping and infrastructure mapping was carried out by Gujpro.

Similarly, BoD members and representatives of Somnath Farmer Producer Company (a member FPO of Gujpro) share their expectations from the federation by stating that Gujpro should "help market the produce and provide linkages to other entities in the market and support ecosystem."

3.4 Challenges to leadership

During 2017–18, there was a brief change in leadership of Gujpro which caused an upheaval within the organisation. It left some scars which still seem to be hurting the organisation, its members, and its reputation. Kuldeep quit Gujpro to start his own agribusiness and was replaced by another CEO. The new CEO was business-savvy, coming from a corporate world, and believed in scaling up at all costs. He took Gujpro to new heights wherein it achieved a turnover of Rs. 1,680 million as compared Rs. 350 million in the previous year, an enormous jump of five times. However, this had its own cost – governance and financial systems and democratic processes were compromised upon. It became driven by the CEO, and the members started feeling alienated. The members soon realised the pitfalls of a short-term gain vis-à-vis long-term stability. The board members with support from the expert director decided to take control and not renew the CEOs contract. They requested Kuldeep to re-join and steady the ship to which he agreed.

3.5 Strengthening of existing systems

Mohan Sharma (executive director, DSC), who was earlier an expert director on the Gujpro, felt that Gujpro needs to evolve systems that will help arrive at sustainable business plans and value-chain interventions. He is of the view that there is a need for an expert director who could help in strengthening the governance and management systems of Gujpro.

The management systems also need to be streamlined: monthly checking of stocks, earnings, profits, costs, and so on. Project-based accounting should also be practised. There is also a need to reduce cash transactions, to cut on costs, and to reduce risks. While indirect expenses need to be reduced, it would be difficult to cut HR expenses as that would lead to sub-optimal business. Interaction with the BoD members and CEO of Somnath Farmer Producer Company revealed that Gujpro needed to focus on "good governance and financial checks and balances" as both are "essential for the functioning of the Gujpro."

3.6 Managing with limited human resource

The company has hired the services of a chartered accountant for external audit and also hired the services of a company secretary to adhere to the legal compliances as per the requirements of the Ministry of Corporate Affairs (MCA). Besides Kuldeep, the CEO, the Gujpro team has a procurement officer who acquires the produce from FPOs as well as other private entities. There is one staff member who looks after the administration, finance, and accounts. One person has been hired for the coconut business while a field officer does job work at the groundnut processing unit in Keshod and seed production.

4. Evolving the business model of Gujpro

Gujpro deals with a variety of products such as cereals, pulses, oilseeds, spices, fruits, and vegetables. Except for seeds, it does not deal with inputs such as fertilisers and pesticides as this is taken care of by the respective FPOs members. As seen from Table 16.4, Gujpro has tried out a variety of interventions including linkages with various government and private

Table 16.4 Revenue sources of Gujpro from 2014 to 2021

Break up of Revenue (Rs. in Million)	2016–17	2017–18	2018–19	2019–20	2020–21	Total Rev.
(A) Groundnut and Groundnut products						
Sale of groundnut	329.99	1,613.11				**1,943.10**
Sale of groundnut pods			117.46			**117.46**
Sale of groundnut seeds			3.13			**3.13**
Sale of groundnut oil			0.02	0.16	0.33	**0.51**
Groundnut – blanch peanut				24.67	0.00	**24.67**
Groundnut – peanut kernel and other by-products				17.39	7.84	**32.11**
Total A	**329.99**	**1,613.11**	**120.62**	**45.63**	**11.53**	**2,120.88**
(B) Trading in other commodities						
Sale of gram			194.71		16.88	211.58
Sale of wheat					10.84	10.84
Sale of *toor*			128.07			128.07
Sale of mustard			331.65			331.65
Total B			**459.72**			**682.14**
(C) Warehouse rent + gunny bag sales						
Godown/ warehouse income			39.51	10.01	2.22	51.74
Sale of gunny bags	15.70	69.33	23.70	1.34	0.33	110.41
Total C	**15.70**	**69.33**	**63.21**	**11.35**	**2.55**	**162.14**
(D) Fruits and vegetables						
Mango sales (export to UK)	0.71					0.71
Sale of Kesar mango (domestic)	0.05	0.01			2.31	2.37

Break up of Revenue (Rs. in Million)	2016–17	2017–18	2018–19	2019–20	2020–21	Total Rev.
Sale of coconut and other vegetables					1.85	1.85
Satvik Grahak Bazaar				0.03	0.31	0.34
Total D	0.76	0.01	0.00	0.03	4.47	5.27
Grand total (A + B + C + D)	346.45	1,682.45	838.26	57.02	46.28	2,970.60

entities to help the FPOs in scaling up and increase its own revenue. During the first two years, that is, 2014–15 and 2015–16, Gujpro did not carry out any business activities.

In the initial years, since Gujpro had little experience in marketing and trading, they hired marketing consultants. As price information was not readily available to the member FPOs at that time, Gujpro registered itself at trade portals such as India Mart and TradeIndia. In 2015, it tried out many initiatives such as "Mango without makeup" campaign wherein it procured mangoes from its member FPOs and sold them in Ahmedabad. In 2016, it exported mangoes worth Rs. 7,00,000 to the UK.

From 2016 to 2018–19 the main activity for earning revenue was organising sale of different commodities such as groundnut, gram, wheat, *toor*, and mustard under the price support scheme of the central government (procuring at minimum support price) facilitated by NAFED and Small Farmers Agribusiness Consortium (SFAC). The revenue from gram, wheat, *toor*, and mustard was Rs. 682.14 million which constitute ~23% of its total revenue till date (see Table 16.3).

Since 2019–20 MSP sale has been discontinued as the Government of Gujarat decided to work only with the Civil Supply Department. Thus, besides trading in groundnut, it started production and sale of high-value blanched peanut and opened a retail shop in Ahmedabad.

In 2020–21, Gujpro added some new products to its kitty. It revived the sale of Kesar mangoes and successfully sold mangoes worth Rs. 2.31 million to urban households from Ahmedabad and Anand. This story has been earlier published.[1] Similarly, coconuts worth Rs. 1.85 million were also sold in the urban market. In addition, it also procured wheat and gram from the FPOs and sold it in the open market. Revenue from these along with the rent of warehouses at Gandhidham block of Kachchh district and sale of gunny bags to NAFED and SFAC was close to Rs. 167.41 million till date, constituting ~5.6% of the revenue (see Table 16.3). However, as is clear from the table, groundnut has been the main commodity on which Gujpro has focused through several market channels such as MSP sales, private partnerships, and throughout levels of value addition such as whole pod, blanched, oil, by-products, and so on.

4.1 MSP procurement – a double-edged sword for Gujpro and its member FPOs

Gujpro was first invited to participate in the PSS of the central government during Kharif 2016 by the Department of Agriculture and Cooperation, Government of Gujarat. It was appointed as a state-level agency for NAFED for procurement of groundnut. From 2016–17 to 2018–19, besides groundnut, Gujpro also dealt with commodities such as *toor*, gram, and mustard. As seen from Table 16.5, Gujpro procured 5,95,491 quintals produce worth Rs. 2970 million through 16 FPOs which benefitted 33,670 farmers.

The MSP experience was both a boon and a bane for Gujpro and its partners. The FPOs gained first-hand exposure working on a huge scale on postharvest aggregation and sale of agriculture commodities. It helped Gujpro and the FPOs in building their capacities on quality control of produce, in managing logistics and human resources, and in managing procurement operations. The difference in MSP rate as compared to market rate was in the range of Rs. 300 to Rs. 500 per quintal which was a substantial amount. Since more farmers were inclined on selling the produce under MSP, it increased the visibility of Gujpro and FPOs in their respective areas. More farmers were interested in becoming members of FPOs, and the impact of MSP procurement on the farmers was much more than the other activities that the FPOs were involved in. Moreover, it enhanced the balance sheet, which helped Gujpro and FPOs to secure loan from mainstream financial institutions like NABKISAN, FWWB, Samunnati, and Ananya Finance.

However, on the downside, although Gujpro directly dealt with NAFED and the government, the FPOs were also impacted. The farmer payments

Table 16.5 Details of MSP procurement taken up by Gujpro on behalf of member FPOs

Commodities	Procurement (in MT)	Sales Value (in Rs. Million)	Number of Farmers Benefited
Groundnut (2016–17)	7,820.00	329.90	4,465
Toor (2016–17)	2,699.60	136.30	2,466
Groundnut (2017–18)	33,985.28	1,785.40	18,178
Toor (2018–19)	2,349.92	136.20	2,337
Gram (2018–19)	4,404.30	207.60	2,283
Mustard (2018–19)	8,290.05	377.10	3,943
Total	59,549.15	2,972.50	33,672

and incidental costs were not immediately released by NAFED. Hence, the state government gave a revolving fund to all state-level agencies to pay to farmers immediately. There were considerable delays in payments by NAFED which affected the operations of Gujpro and the FPOs. Also, unjustified deductions in incidental costs like transportation and labour created problems for the FPOs.

Since the operations were carried out on a large scale in every block with exposure to thousands of farmers, criticism of the work done by FPOs also followed. Slow pace of work, poor quality of produce purchased, and so on were the issues raised by media, politicians, and the farmers. Hence, from 2019 to 2020, the state government decided to work only with the Civil Supply Department.

4.2 Groundnut – the mainstay of Gujpro's business model

Groundnut trading and value addition has been one of the most successful ventures of Gujpro. From 2016–17 to 2020–21, Gujpro has had a turnover of Rs. 2,120.88 million from groundnut and its products which constitute about 71.40% of its total business till date. In 2016, Gujpro with its FPO members procured about 8,000 MT groundnut at MSP for NAFED which increased to about 34,000 MT in 2017–18 but fell to 4,400 MT in 2018–19 totalling 46,400 MTs. From 2016 to 2019, Gujpro also sold certified groundnut pods to a Fair-Trade buyer VNKC Agrocom Private Ltd. The sale of groundnut through MSP and Fair Trade was a major source of revenue for Gujpro and its FPO members. But even here, there is fluctuation in the prices each year. In 2019–20, it was a good business decision to export dehulled/blanched peanuts of about Rs. 24.7 million and earn profits. However, in 2020–21, the peanut prices went down, and the transaction was non-profitable. So Gujpro stored 100 MT groundnut in cold storage and leveraged it to get warehouse receipt loan of Rs. 10 million from NAB-KISAN. Also, 50 MT groundnut was processed at the processing unit near Keshod. It doubled its sale from groundnut oil from Rs. 1,63,000 to Rs. 3,27,000.

However, groundnut also proved to be a major problem for Gujpro and its members. The NAFED had made timely payments in the previous years; however, in 2019–20 these proved to be very costly for Gujpro and its members, and till date the pending recovery from NAFED is Rs. 12 million. Similarly, Gujpro had dealings with VNKC Agrocom Private Ltd. (largest exporter of peanuts) since 2016. In 2019, Gujpro did job work on a large scale with the VNKC, and initially timely payments were made by the company. However, in 2020 the company defaulted, and over Rs. 30 million is yet to be recovered from the company. Kuldeep and the board members of Gujpro have made several attempts to recover the money from the company. However, the company has declared itself bankrupt, and Gujpro has filed a case against them to recover the pending dues. Thus, the pending trade receivables as on 31 March 2021 is Rs. 45.6 million.

Thus, while Gujpro has made considerable strides in the groundnut value chain and it has also tried to diversify its product portfolio, it has yet to find a sustainable business model, i.e. interventions that are profitable to the organisation and also cater to the varied needs of its FPO members.

4.3 Satvik Grahak Bazaar

The retail shop "Satvik Grahak Bazaar" was started as a pilot in 2019 thinking that higher income to farmers will come by moving up the value chain and reaching the customer directly. Trade and primary processing have profit margins ranging from 0.5 to 2%. Even in secondary processing the margins have dropped from 8–10% to 3–5%, and farmers get only 1–1.5%. Tertiary processing and packaging of products for sale through retail outlets help in directly reaching to the consumer and better sustained earnings for the farmers. Satvik mainly stored non-pesticide management (NPM) products developed by FPOs such as spices, cookies, pickles, and so on. But then liabilities increased as the marketing efforts were costly, and Covid-19 further added to the problem. The retail shop demanded too much time, and given the paucity of funds and human resources, it was temporarily closed. However, there is a plan to restart the same if the situation improves.

4.4 Benefits of Gujpro to FPO members

Gujpro enjoys high trust among its FPO members, and they greatly value its efforts in scaling up and exploring new markets. Despite the difficulties faced by members in recovering their dues from NAFED and VNKC Agrotech Pvt Ltd, they have continued their relationship with Gujpro. FPO members, such as the Somnath FPC, Krishidhan FPC, and Avirat Agro FPC, have exhibited a sense of ownership and have supported the CEO and the staff as and when required, drawing from their own vast experiences with the various stakeholders in the ecosystem.

Member FPOs, apart from business, benefit through government liaising – when meetings happen with the secretary, Department of Agriculture (Government of Gujarat), NABARD, and so on. Also, hand-holding and risk sharing happens, especially in the case of weak FPO members. FPOs often need quick payments, and Gujpro tries to ensure the same. Gujpro helps the FPOs in developing business plans and also provides guidance and motivation to them. If a commodity produced by an FPO is not bought by Gujpro, it tries to contact and arrange another buyer. Gujpro also anchors a WhatsApp group for its FPO members wherein they share their problems, products, government schemes, virtual webinars, and the like on a regular basis.

However, not many FPOs are capable of deploying enough working capital and expertise into the trade. Kuldeep Solanki, the CEO opines,

> [O]ne decision that might help in involving more FPOs is that Gujpro pays the interest on Working Capital loans taken by FPO members, in return for a promise to trade through Gujpro. This will help Gujpro raise enough funds for the trade as Working capital is one of the biggest constraints for expanding its business to other regions.

4.5 Managing business risks

Gujpro takes unsecured loans that require guarantors as it does not have assets to take a loan of a few million rupees. Thus, unsecured loans need to be taken, even though these are risky. For NABKISAN loan, SFAC is a guarantor, but with other NBFCs such as Samunnati Finance, some other person or entity has to be the guarantor. Mostly, a director would act as one. This is a personal guarantee, and very few directors are willing to take such a risk. The risk is genuine, and if default happens, the director's own creditworthiness would suffer. Kuldeep himself has also provided a personal guarantee of Rs. 1.5 million.

The Chairman Sureshbhai feels that Gujpro could have mobilised funds from member FPOs, in theory, just as FPOs mobilise member equity from FIGs and SHGs. But for that to happen, all or most FPOs should be financially strong, which is not the case. Out of the 30 member FPOs, only 18–20 are active and have enough surplus to meet their operational costs.

Recovery of long-pending dues from NAFED and VNKC Ltd is a major challenge for Gujpro and its members. In spite of all their efforts, there is a substantive pending amount which is impacting their current operations. The current outstanding loans need to be paid, and the losses need to be recovered.

5. Financial performance of Gujpro

The key parameters based on audited financial statements for six years, plus unaudited statement for 2020–21, are presented in Table 16.6.

Gujpro's revenue has grown sharply till 2017–18 and then seen a sharp dip. This is because of the high revenue generated through MSP transactions. Gujpro's transactions with NAFED have led to this surge and dip of revenue; however, the actual income in such cases is the commission or fee that the procurement agency offers. In the case of Gujpro it was 0.5%. Since 2019–20, FPOs role in MSP sales have been discontinued by the Government of Gujarat, and this has compelled Gujpro to trade in various commodities on its own. As a result, in 2020–21, there was a loss of Rs. 2.57 million but to Gujpro's credit; they have been able to absorb this loss due to strong reserves and surplus (Rs. 20.93 million). Notably, despite significant challenges all

Table 16.6 Key financial parameters of Gujpro (Rs. in thousands)

Key Parameters/ Year	2014–15	2015–16	2016–17	2017–18	2018–19	2019–20	2020–21
Total revenue	2.97	10.05	3,552.16	16,864.77	8,487.71	577.51	490.35
Total expenses	2.97	10.02	3,545.23	16,806.53	8,325.64	573.25	516.01
Profit after tax	0	0	4.78	43.21	162.13	0.43	−25.7
Long-term borrowings	0	0	30.01	0.04	862.16	289.01	0

the long-term debts have been cleared by Gujpro, and the working capital has been managed well by the leadership including the CEO and the BoD members. This shows a profound understanding of the risks involved and a great rapport with the member FPOs (particularly among the BoD members and the management) – thus, displaying a great deal of member allegiance.

6. Plans for the future

Gujpro needs to work towards strategic partnerships. This will help in achieving Rs. 200–250 million turnover and also share the risk. As compared to private entities, FPOs have the challenge of finding partners. For this, Gujpro needs to develop its strengths *viz.* a strong backward linkage with member FPOs and try to find partners that are willing to cover the weaknesses in the market front. Such partnerships can be general partnerships with Gujpro or based on a project such as groundnut value chain, organic products or multiple trading centres, and export business through private support. Diversification of crops might help. Procurement from other regions, for example, coconut from Karnataka, will help in revenue generation. Gujpro also plans to work on seed production for commodities such as wheat, maize (Syngenta), groundnut, and so on with its member FPOs and find a market in other regions such as South India.

Till 1 March 2022 Gujpro had a turnover of Rs. 97.3 million from the sale of groundnut, wheat, soybean, coconut, and so on. It has added seeds – groundnut, wheat, and hybrid maize to its basket of activities. It has recently entered into a collaboration with Samunnati Finance Ltd and launched the FPO 360 project in March 2022.

The project aims to scale up the operations of FPOs and fill their resource and capacity gaps. The FPOs will procure the member produce such as wheat and cumin from the farmers, set up collection centres, ensure quality checks, and deliver the produce at the warehouses set up by Gujpro at a pre-agreed price including the commission of the FPO. Samunnati through Gujpro will share the financial cost of hiring and running the collection centre and the human resource cost, while Gujpro will provide the requisite training and support to the FPO members. When the market is favourable, Samunnati will sell the produce in consultation with Gujpro. The profit will be shared in pre-agreed proportions between Samunnati, Gujpro, and the FPO. Similarly, the losses if incurred will also be shared in pre-agreed proportion between the three parties. Thus, it seems that this is a win-win project for all the three partners especially for Gujpro as it will help it to pay off the pending loan of Rs. 35 million to Samunnati, earn profits, and provide capacity building services to its FPO members.

7. Conclusion and reflections

Gujpro is a very active state-level federation and constantly engages with its members, buyers, government, and financial institutions. Its potential for growth is quite high, and this is recognised by not only its members but also other stakeholders. It has also tried to create an enabling environment for the FPOs in the state. However, it is not formally recognised by the state government as the apex body of FPOs in the state.

Gujpro so far has been focusing on supporting member FPOs through capacity, compliance, market linkage, value addition, and so on. The business models taken up and value chains developed also seem to depend on what the member FPOs have to offer at a given point of time and also the capacity of the member FPOs. While such an approach is helpful to the FPO, a long-term business model and plan are essential for the success of Gujpro itself.

Governance at Gujpro is still based mostly on trust and good faith. An important lesson can be learnt from one of its own members, namely Somnath Farmer Producer Company, Kodinar, where there are strict checks and balances in place to streamline the management and operations of the FPO. The directors, promoters, and member farmers are on the same page regarding the importance of such checks and balances. Member FPOs have evolved, and thus, what may have started as a mentor-mentee relationship now becomes business partnership. There is no harm in learning a few 'tricks of trade' and trying to implement it within Gujpro.

There is very little capacity building on non-business aspects such as governance or financial systems of member FPOs. Hence, Gujpro needs to work on these aspects so that there is member allegiance between Gujpro and the new members. With new guidelines coming in and government support being increased to primary FPOs, what can federations expect? Gujpro is exploring with Deepak Foundation and AKRSPI on a pilot project wherein the grant received by them would be given to Gujpro, and in turn Gujpro would train the FPO staff for 3–4 years to stabilise the business of these FPOs. This would be a win-win situation for Gujpro as well as the FPOs as Gujpro would get working capital and the FPOs could benefit through capacity building and hand-holding support and also be involved in processing commodities such as groundnut on behalf of Gujpro. Many of the FPO members of Gujpro have entered value chain and commodity trade only through Gujpro.

As in the case of primary FPOs, the government also needs to provide grants for state-level federations such as Gujpro for the initial 3–4 years. It requires working capital support for Rs. 70–80 million and funds for hiring skilled staff for 3–4 years.

Gujpro has participated in policy dialogues along with IRMA and others for creating an enabling environment for FPOs at the state and national levels. It has also advocated with the State Agriculture Department to set up a Center for Support of FPOs. Such a centre would help in coordinating with FPOs and promoting a pro-FPO policy in the state. If such a centre is developed by the state government, Gujpro can play a larger role in capacity building of the FPOs. However, there has not been much success so far pertaining to some state-level policy for FPOs and federations of FPOs that would have promoted 'ease of doing' business and 'ease of seeking' resources (both monetary and non-monetary) for such enterprises.

With the 10,000 FPO central sector scheme being implemented and FPO federations of Maharashtra and Madhya Pradesh having being selected as cluster-based business organisations (CBBOs) for the promotion of new FPOs in their respective regions, one wonders if Gujpro deliberately kept away from expressing interest for CBBO role in Gujarat. Kuldeep did consider applying as a CBBO. However, Gujpro ultimately decided not to do so currently as the main role of the CBBO is to facilitate and build the capacities of new FPOs. This is quite demanding in terms of time and human resources. Thus, given the current financial and human resources situation, Gujpro decided to focus on business development and financial growth so as to service its pending loans.

A member FPOs of Gujpro based in Banaskantha is itself a CBBO and has been given the responsibility of forming five new FPOs in the region. Kuldeep feels that Gujpro can play a role of providing technical support to these new FPOs rather than trying to create new FPOs on its own. However, off late, the board of Gujpro is in favour of applying for CBBO and forming new FPOs as this will enable Gujpro to expand its business and also directly influence the production as per its requirements. Thus, Kuldeep is in favour of applying as CBBO whenever there is a call for a second round of applications.

Note

1 IRMA staff facilitated Gujpro to sell its mangoes at the institute campus during the 2020 lockdown during Covid-19 and wrote a reflective piece on the experience. https://www.smallfarmincomes.in/post/conscious-consumerism-institutions-of-india-s-milk-capital-enable-fpo-sell-mangoes-during-lockdown

Reference

Bikkina, N & Sarin, A (2013). *Sajjata Sangh: A network of NGOs*. Ahmedabad: IIMA/PSG0112

17

REIMAGINING PRODUCER ORGANISATIONS IN INDIA

C. Shambu Prasad, Ajit Kanitkar,
and Deborah Dutta

How effective have FPOs in India been in making markets work for small and marginal farmers? As new-generation institutions are they able to nurture hopes and ambitions of responsible businesses that could, in the long run, lead to reduced wealth inequality? Have they provided greater voice to farmers as active participants, not passive beneficiaries, in addressing agrarian distress and as vehicles for agricultural transformation? Has there been sufficient investment in capital and capacity by the government and others in translating these ambitious goals? The collection of 15 detailed case studies on the growth and management of FPOs provides evidence and insights that could help ground truth policy propositions on FPO design. In this chapter we collate data and synthesise lessons from the individual case studies to present practical insights and heuristics on FPO design and sustainability to policymakers, FPO promoters, and researchers on what it takes to run successful FPOs.

This chapter is organised around nine sections delving into interconnected aspects of incubation, inclusion, business models, governance, capacity building, performance assessment, and policy implications, as synthesised from an overall analysis of all the cases in the volume. Our analysis throws light on the importance of pre-incubation and social mobilisation in building strong FPOs. The analysis also helps us appreciate the serious governance and leadership challenges these enterprises face in balancing the social and enterprise aspects of the business as they strive to represent the voice of smallholder tribal and women farmers in the market. While the FPOs do face serious issues of access to capital, any assessment of the performance of FPOs needs to go beyond their balance sheets and understand these institutions as 'start-up collectives' in the making. The cases reaffirm the faith in these institutions as important, though not the only, vehicles for agrarian transformation that continue to face significant challenges of capital and capability. They also provide insights on reimagining producer organisations, for instance, as sustainable transition intermediaries in agriculture.

266

DOI: 10.4324/9781003308034-17

In bringing together diverse cases through a co-production process we hope our collective effort would inspire newer directions in producer organisation research.

1. Incubating farmer organisations

Farmer organisations are rarely '*swayambhu*', or self-created, and need careful catalysing (Shah, 1996) or in today's terminology, incubation. Many FPOs in the volume have a long history of incubation, often several years before the official date of registration of the company. Patient efforts by many Civil Society Organisations (CSOs) such as Samaj Pragati Sahyog (SPS), Professional Assistance for Development Action (PRADAN), Development Support Centre (DSC), and Grassroots were working with farmers in their respective regions since 2005 and were pioneers in taking up the enterprise model when the FPO ecosystem was underdeveloped. Communities were mobilised around watershed, forestry, sustainable agriculture, livestock, and women's thrift and credit groups – self-help groups (SHGs) as key livelihood mechanisms to enhance incomes. The institutional arrangement of an FPO is an extension and an organic continuation of this process of social capital formation. Support through grants from philanthropic foundations and government funds have provided the seed money for incubation. Livelihood programmes such as the World Bank–supported DPIP (District Poverty Initiative Program) in Madhya Pradesh or Jeevika in Bihar have created fertile grounds for mobilisation. Networks of producers such as the Sahaja Samruddha, a network of seed savers of farmers, constituted the social capital in Desi Seed. These significant 'hidden costs' of incubating producer companies are not reflected in balance sheets but critical for FPO growth. Even for FPOs registered in 2016 such as Pandhana and Kazhani, prior project and institution building by their promoting institutions has been key to their future growth.

In contrast to this organic mode a newer, and increasingly more dominant, pattern of FPO formation is that of the promoting institution forming an FPO *without* any prior experience of intervention in the geography or any prior development efforts with the community. Hasnabad in Telangana, Bhangar in West Bengal, Mahanadi in Chhattisgarh, and Navyug in Uttar Pradesh are examples of this newer incubation process. These resource institutions were selected, through competitive bids, for project implementation by an agency like the Small Farmers Agribusiness Company (SFAC) or as part of state schemes with a mandate to form a company. Absence of any social capital coupled with their own inexperience in that region posed multiple challenges. The time frame and exit strategy imposed by the project of the donor speed up forming, storming, and norming processes of organisation building. Mobilising equity from members takes time and requires trust building and sharing of a vision. If these processes are compromised for speedy registration, it could lead to members not owning up the producer organisation.

In challenging ecosystems like remote tribal areas like Bastar the Mahanadi FPO case shows that mobilising grants through multiple sources is important to build capacities and resilience in establishing a niche in the marketplace. Target-based approaches undervalue the importance of incubation processes and the need to build business acumen through constant experimentation and innovation. The cases reiterate insights from FPO reviews in India that have pointed to the need to shift focus from promotion to incubation and the danger of FPOs born weak and with little business acumen thus hampering their future growth prospects (Kanitkar, 2016; Neti and Govil, 2022).

2. Building inclusive and purposeful producer organisations

There is a predominance of FPO promotion by CSOs in the volume that have historically favoured building institutions with higher representation of women, marginalised communities such as tribals, and a greater voice of small and marginal farmers. The cases provide insights on mechanisms that can enable greater inclusion and a significant shift away from the 'elite capture' by large male farmers of older cooperatives in India. The 15 FPOs operate in India's largely rain-fed tracts beyond high irrigation crops of rice, wheat, and sugar and have consciously sought to include greater gender participation either by design or through periodic reviews. Krushidhan, for instance, increased women members from 16% to 27% after a gender specialist reviewed the FPO. While gender participation in the FPO federations has been low, of the 12 individual FPOs, six were completely women owned, three FPOs were led by woman chief executive officers (CEOs), two of which were not women-led boards (Kazhani and Mahanadi).

2.1 Engendering FPOs: envisioning futures beyond tokenism

Pre-existing SHG initiatives by state livelihood interventions such as the Bihar State Livelihoods Project Society (that incubated Jeevika) or CSOs provided the base for building women-led FPO. SHG members were motivated to become members of producer groups (PGs), and village-level skilled extension workers were leveraged by Jeevika FPC and Pandhana to build federated structures. These women-led institutions have shown significant resilience and are now able to negotiate better market access and reduce transaction costs and have established their identity as dignified producers. The increasing confidence of women in handling business takes time, but their participation helps significantly in transforming agrarian relations and discovering newer business models.

Rather than aiming for ambitious growth, FPOs like Mahila Umang have managed to manage steady revenue through cautious investments, thus enabling the members to develop business acumen without taking too many risks. Interestingly, gender inclusion has also gone hand in hand with other forms of inclusion and innovations. Three chapters in the book trace the journey of FPOs led by tribal women in rain-fed areas. The cases underscore the need to understand gender-specific constraints, leverage their expertise, and build on pre-existing networks to mobilise communities. The journey of Ram Rahim FPO promoted by SPS indicates that the larger goal of farmers transiting to sustainable agriculture found greater acceptance among women who learnt non-pesticidal management (NPM) cultivation practices and led other members towards lower dependence on agrochemical inputs. The all-woman board also oversaw a major shift away from commodity trading through NCDEX and introduced low-cost spiral graders that can be easily operated by women and children.

The lack of lucrative market linkages in remote hills and tribal areas of Uttarakhand and Jharkhand led the women to adapt the FPOs on creating a stable community of shareholders than high growth and often fluctuating revenues. Umang Mahila followed an explicit gender-inclusive strategy with 70% of staff and the managing director being women. Strengthening the participation of women members need not lead to exclusivity. PRADAN followed a strategy of co-opting men in the community to support women as equal members, acknowledging the fact that cultural shifts take time and both Ram Rahim and Jeevika have depended on male CEOs as open-market hires.

Promoting institutions might be better advised to undertake gender analysis even before forming the FPO as the case of Pandhana FPO demonstrates. The gender study on small livestock-holding study highlighted the contradiction of women's high contribution in small livestock care, but little involvement in decision-making, or in access to technical skills, new knowledge, or marketing. The findings led the promoting institution, Aga Khan Rural Support Programme (AKRSP), to change its strategy from mixed groups to formation of exclusive women's Pashupalak Samuhs (PPS). They leveraged the aptitude and knowledge of tribal women as small livestock farmers to create market linkages and input services. Marketing and selling of livestock in distant markets in the night proved to be a barrier for women, and women found local markets as more lucrative.

Hasnabad women's collective offers a sobering lesson on why good intentions are not enough to tide over capacity building issues, and it may be more pragmatic to build a basic support system before attempting ambitious social change initiatives. Thus, despite being committed to gender and inclusion goals, balancing expectations in a volatile external environment owing to dependence on MSP procurement turned out to be more difficult than anticipated. FPO federations continue to see low involvement of women at a decision-making level as gendered spaces compound with larger geographies and need for wider interaction. Acknowledging and supporting women's participation is a normative shift that needs sensitisation of men and empowerment of women.

The cases also highlight that inclusion of women, tribals, small and marginal farmers happens at several levels. Parameters for inclusion include class, caste, and gender representation across various levels of the organisation, ranging from basic membership to access to decision-making bodies. Explicit targeting helps in increasing their role and participation in internal decision-making of smaller groups and later at the board level too. However, inclusion is not to be seen as an end but an important vehicle or means for transformation of agrarian relations. Mature institutions are better able to balance trade-offs with other core aims, such as financial performance, strong leadership, and smooth governance. As a strategy, FPOs may also include a certain proportion of men, and even large farmers (as in Krushidhan where large farmers provided loans for the greater common good), as they seek a larger share of the market and have more agency in negotiating better market spaces even as small and marginal farmers though comprised 72% of overall membership.

The cases also suggest that inclusion as a practice needs to go beyond tokenism in terms of having the odd woman or tribal in the board and invest in FPO design processes and capacity building of members and BoDs. Women-led boards can provide spaces for reworking business models (Ram Rahim and Mahila Umang) and pursue and include sustainability as an important parameter for future growth.

2.2 FPOs as sustainable transition intermediaries

A less-discussed dimension in FPO debates involves balancing growth and financial sustainability with larger ecological concerns around food systems and environmental sustainability. FPOs usually try and reduce the production costs for the farmers through arranging for quality inputs (fertilisers, seeds, and so on) at a competitive price. With increasing evidence of the ecological costs of agriculture, are FPOs (and their ecosystem partners) working towards sustainable agriculture or are they becoming a mechanism for promoting an agricultural model based on the last-mile delivery of agrochemical inputs? Can FPOs act as 'transition intermediaries' (Groot-Kormelinck et al., 2022) for getting its members into sustainable agriculture or will their outreach mechanism be appropriated by 'business-as-usual' corporate interests? The cases in the volume indicate FPOs can play an active role in enabling sustainable transitions if factored early. Transition is not a binary between pure organic and chemical but a spectrum of possibilities. For some FPOs like Desi Seed, Ram Rahim, Mahila Umang, and Kazhani, sustainability is seen as a differentiator for their produce in markets with their products being branded as organic or pesticide-free or driven by fair trade considerations. Desi Seed has embedded sustainability in its design and grew out of the organic and seed saver movement in Karnataka with an emphasis on preserving agrobiodiversity and human well-being.

In many challenged geographies, hills, and remote rain-fed areas, the creation of natural capital is a pre-requisite for consolidating social capital and using the same for business sustainability. FPOs like Krushidhan, Mahanadi, and Ram Rahim have reported significant reduction in the use of chemical fertilisers and inputs by members. They also provide agricultural extension support to farmers for enabling the transition to sustainable agriculture. Among FPO federations Gujpro has had forays into both fair trade markets and even setting up a retail outlet in Ahmedabad for promoting sustainable agricultural products from farmers. However, sustaining them has been a challenge. Madhya Bharat, another federation, has links with the Responsible Soya initiative and promotes sustainable agriculture, but this is not a line of business.

Social enterprises like Safe Harvest and EarthynGreen pro-actively procure from FPOs and are building farmer brands. In the absence of differentiated markets for organic or pesticide produce at local levels FPOs find it difficult to promote sustainable agriculture as a core activity. Among barriers identified in embedding sustainability have been orientation of promoting institution towards sustainability; ability to access grants to enhance capacities to further farmer-led agro-ecological extension; financial investments for creating consistent value for 'organic' or 'natural' across the value chain including scale-appropriate technologies for processing; and investments in marketing and brand building to create and capture value for safer products among consumers.

Overall, while there is evidence of promotion of organic agriculture or natural farming by FPOs through agricultural extension during the production process, rooting sustainability in FPO operation and design is still at a very early stage. FPOs have competitive advantage in promoting sustainable agriculture given their farmer base and their linkages with stakeholders with the necessary technical knowhow. Embedding sustainability would need FPO boards and CEOs to rethink their business models and come up with innovations that might favour stability over scale. The decrease in input costs through sustainable agriculture, as experienced by many farmers, with costs of imported chemical fertilisers spiralling in recent years could be an important driver for this transition.[1] FPOs could indeed reposition themselves as new-generation 'transition intermediaries'.

3. In search of a business model

As member-owned and governed organisations, the choice of the business model is critical for both the member and the management-governing systems in an FPO (Shah, 1995). There are multiple trade-offs that need to be balanced while selecting a business model that includes profit margins generated (more profits for company or distribution of residuals among member farmers based on patronage); the number of farmers served (procure from all or only those that the FPO can work with profitably in the market); types of members served (small or large land owners); managerial capacities to undertake business activity (professionals from outside or from within the region), and so on.

Most FPOs in India have been providing quality inputs (seeds, chemical fertilisers, and pesticides) at lower costs as a key element of their business model. FPOs also assist farmers in sale of organic inputs or bio-fertilisers, provide drip irrigation equipment, operate custom hiring centres, and could potentially provide other services such as crop insurance, Kisan Credit Cards, earning some revenue through commissions or margins. Agricultural extension, a much-valued and under-stated service to members by FPOs, however rarely translates into revenue for FPOs. Services include both information and knowledge on good package of practices (PoPs), sustainable agriculture that are often extended to non-members as well. The number of farmers impacted through Krushidhan's extension services, for instance, was ten times more than their membership. With lower or no willingness to pay for extension services FPOs depend on grants received by promoting institutions to take up these activities. A good FPO business model requires leveraging both grants and debt.

Unlike input services and agricultural extension where all members benefit, there is significant trade-off in the procurement of outputs and processing and value addition. Some of the FPOs (Krushidhan and Hasnabad), and all federations, have undertaken procurement on behalf of the government's minimum support price (MSP) operations. Typically, such an activity has the potential to include most of the members (inclusive) and is comparatively risk-free (margins or service fee on transaction is assured by the government buyer), and farmers are assured of a better price. However, to undertake an MSP operation, the FPO needs certain managerial capacities to organise village-level procurement and working capital to pay to farmers till payments from the government are received. Government procurement agencies are not consistent in ensuring that MSP intervention happens every single year and often default on payments with no continuity across seasons. Krushidhan that procured groundnuts at MSP is now experimenting with contract farming in potato and MAHAFPC sees itself transiting from Business to Government (B2G) to Business to Company (B2C). Despite uncertainty MSP operations help FPOs as they provide an opportunity to expand business, reach a large number of members (and non-members too) and make them ready for largescale procurement that helps them negotiate better with big market players.

FPOs also venture into activities such as seed production that is seasonal, can include only a few crops and limited to a few members yet adding value to both farmers and the FPO through sale of quality seeds (Madhya Bharat and Desi Seed). Seed production requires good agricultural experience, connect with government and certifying agencies and attention to quality. A business model focused on production and sale of organic products requires more managerial capacity at both the production and marketing ends to communicate to producers and consumers the value that can command higher price (Ram Rahim, Mahila Umang, Kazhani and Desi Seed).

Output marketing presents significant challenges with members expecting the FPO to provide market linkages to all commodities they produce. For instance, the FPO in Bihar marketed maize produce of its members but had to take a call on providing the same for wheat and *mentha* that had different value chains. FPO business models are dynamic and co-evolve based on the diversity of the crops that members produce, complexities in the value chain of each crop, choice of market destination (local, regional and international) and decisions to select appropriate intervention in the value chain (store and sell or store, process and sell). They depend on situated decisions taken by FPO management and leadership based on management capacities present within the FPC and availability of capital for operations.

A few FPCs experimented and even pioneered selling on the NCDEX exchange but discontinued in subsequent years (Ram Rahim and Jeevika). The export of bananas for the Kazhani FPO was profitable for some of its members and while good for the profitability of the organisation, was less inclusive in terms of reaching out to more producer members. The FPO had to also rejig its business model after the pandemic due to disruptions in the supply chain. These challenges make the search for the ideal business model elusive for most of the FPOs in their journey even after about five to seven years. Table 17.1 summarises the business models of the 12 FPOs (federations are dealt with separately).

The first four FPOs are into multiple commodities and products constantly seeking newer opportunities and tie-ups. The next three are based on focused value chains on a single product type (seeds, vegetables and fruits and goatery). Jeevika and Mahanadi have reached a limit of single commodity and want to diversify and Navyug, KBS coop and Hasnabad are operating on low profits and looking for a breakthrough. A significant learning from the cases is that business models are worked out through constant iteration with other stakeholders over the years. Mere aggregation of produce and linking with existing market players, as is often advocated for FPOs, does not yield value unless there is a good and consistent buyer as in the case of Bhangar with Sufal Bangla (a government enterprise), or Ram Rahim with Safe Harvest (social enterprise). FPOs are becoming smarter with experience and diversification is a key risk mitigation strategy. Output markets involve significant market risks and returns too. Rather than search for ideal business plans FPOs are better advised to build and develop business acumen and design and build for resilience rather than seek the mirage

Table 17.1 Business models of FPOs studied

FPO	Business model summary
Krushidhan	Diversified multi-commodity chains; backward integration in wheat, groundnut and cattle feed; processing and marketing of spices and pulses locally (own brand); potato contract farming with ISCON Balaji
Ram Rahim	Value in production and sale of safe and pesticide free produce through local food park facilities to process and pack, marketing through social enterprise.
Kazhani	Exporting high-value bananas, value-addition for millets, inter FPC-trading in paddy; strong extension through KVK.
Mahila Umang	Diversified lines – HimKhadya brand for safe foods mainstay, value-added fruit preservatives, and honey (Kumaoni) and hand-knits as off farm.
Desi Seed	FPO buy back of organic seeds from member farmers sold leveraging Sahaja Samruddha's network to customers.
Bhangar	Vegetable business leveraging proximity to Kolkata, marketing tie-up with Sufal Bangla (government retail outlet) through own vehicles.
Pandhana	Extension and health care support to goats; goat sale in local markets to reduce risk; direct to consumer for processed goat and poultry
Jeevika	Transparent grading in maize value chain, forward linkages to commodity exchanges. Diversifying into seed production, mentha oil and banana.
Mahanadi	Custard apple focused value addition through pulping and sale to businesses and customers (Bastar Fresh brand)
Navyug	Mango sales with private traders, also direct with consumers through federation (UP-PRO); MSP centre for wheat and paddy, potato sale to ITC
KBSSSL	Consistent agri-input business (seeds & bio-inputs), sale to traders for output of tomatoes and later mangos and watermelon.
Hasnabad	Single commodity pulses with several models including MSP, direct to traders, processing and then to consumers, recovering from losses

of super-profits. How have FPOs management and leadership addressed the significant capability (management and governance competences) and capital constraints (Mahajan, 2015)?

4. Managing growth and FPO governance

Like any commercial organisation, FPOs need to plan and manage growth though with the additional challenge that complex business decisions are made by less literate and first-time Board members and CEOs. How are strategic decisions made in the FPO and by whom? How invested are the BoDs in taking decisions on raising capital, choice of business lines, output markets, timing of payments to farmer members and suppliers and so on. The Board is expected to play multiple roles that may be supervisory, compliance related, fiduciary or operational. FPO Boards are often constituted to enable inclusion and thus need to balance social and commercial goals; maintain interests of small farmers; balance the needs of different villages or clusters; balance the demands of the market with those of the members. How 'member central' have the FPOs been? We seek to understand managerial and leadership capability through their member systems (comprising the members and the BoDs) and their operating systems (comprising the Chief Executive Officer (CEO) and staff).

Our analysis of the 15 FPOs provides commonalities, and differences, on the structural aspects of governance and nature of decision-making. Most FPOs (7 of 12) have federated structures with members organised into informal, often unregistered, farmers interest groups (FIGs) and self-help groups, and then federated them further to form village-level structures (such as village organisation or producer organisations), or clusters of SHGs/FIGs, that are finally federated at the level of FPO.[2] In most FPOs, decision-making has been decentralised so as to identify and empower leaders at all levels. Table 17.2 summarises the two systems for governance – the member system and the operating systems.

Table 17.2 Member and operating systems of the FPOs

FPO Name	Member system	Operating System
Krushidhan	Nine BoDs – from active Kisan club members across clusters (2 women); one expert Director	CEO deputed from DSC in 2013; 11 employees; BoDs actively involved in operations
Jeevika	Women BoDs (10–15) from Producer Groups (PGs) of 30–40 SHG members	Professional CEO heads a PC Management Committee that meets monthly with state livelihood manager and executive committee members from blocks
Bhangar	Eight BoDs including a woman	CEO from community active in all operations
Ram Rahim	Six women BoD representing SHG federations	External CEO management professionals (serve for 2–3 years) supported by 9 employees
Mahanadi	11 BoDs and two nominated (CEO and Vrutti rep)	Woman CEO oversees operations; Sub-committees of BoD meet weekly
Mahila Umang	Seven women BoD, rotational leadership and shadow team	Woman MD, managers for each vertical, 13 full time professionals

(*Continued*)

Table 17.2 (Continued)

FPO Name	Member system	Operating System
KBSSSL	Cooperative with 9 women BoDs with a 3 tier federation of women SHGs	President as CEO, earlier professional from PRADAN, one supervisor per 100 farmers works with President and Board
Hasnabad	Nine all-women BoD, 10th pass or below	CEO and one staff
Pandhana	10 all-women BoDs *Pashusakhis*, GBMs 50–60% participation non-members invited	CEO (male, para veterinarian worked with AKRSP), two staff, BoDs active in operations
Kazhani	12 BoDs (progressive farmers) meet monthly; often visit daily	Woman CEO from KVK of Myrada; Directors involved in all operations (one husband of CEO)
Navyug	5 BoDs (one woman), meet every quarter	CEO trained by Basix with FPC since inception
Desi Seed	Six BoDs (one woman) meet every quarter	CEO senior management in manufacturing, one marketing professional; Board involved in production targets, organic certification
Maha	Seven BoDs (down from 11) representing three regions of Maharashtra, met seven times in 2020–21	Chairman and MD CEO since inception; 19 staff members; three sub-committees led by a separate BoD; Active engagement of consultants
Madhya Bharat	10 BoDs (one woman) representing 13 districts of MP; three expert directors (one active)	CEO with significant FPO experience and 16 staff, three verticals – seed, marketing and community mobilisation
Gujpro	Seven board members (one woman) representing all regions, quarterly meetings; No expert Director since 2018	CEO since inception, open-market hire for two years did not work; Four staff; Supportive Board involved in recovering dues and operations

The FPOs have a minimum of five and maximum of 12 BoDs selected based on inclusivity (regions or clusters) and enabling ease of business operation. Gender representation in the selected FPOs is higher than the universe of FPOs in India. Monthly BoD meetings are most common though one in a few cases every quarter. While Producer Companies have the provision of having expert directors, but for Krushidhan, Madhya Bharat and Mahanadi most FPOs have not chosen to use this provision effectively. In practice the promoting institution has been playing this role de facto and from a governance perspective it would be desirable that this role is formalised, and the advantage of the Company form taken more seriously.

Unlike milk and bigger cooperatives where the management is completely run by professionals and the Board often keeps away from most operational decisions, in the FPOs studied, the CEO is often from the community or region and the Board is often involved in day-to-day operations. The choice of local CEOs (MD in MAHAFPC and president in KBSS) from the region ensured that churn or attrition is relatively low and they are often agricultural graduates from the community. Promoting institution staff and member farmers also acquired expertise to manage the business (Mahanadi's CEO from Vrutti or Krushidhan from DSC). Some like Ram Rahim, Jeevika and Desi Seed have preferred professionals from outside. But for a brief period in Gujpro, all CEOs of the Federations and Krushidhan and Kazhani have had the same CEO since inception. CEO salaries have mostly been borne, or augmented significantly, by the promoting institutions and have not followed the institutional architecture of recent government schemes that significantly underpay CEOs.

Unlike traditional cooperatives BoDs of the FPOs have been significantly invested in the operations of the FPOs and need to be seen as good practices. In a few cases their roles have been formalised as being part of at least one additional committee. Kazhani even has BoD members coming to the office every day and taking part in operations during the post-harvest marketing season. Many FPOs work with a combination of fulltime staff for key activities for procurement, marketing and administration and bookkeeping and some other staff on part-time basis. Newer practices like having task-based consultants, like in MAHAFPC, are likely to percolate to other FPOs too. The emerging HR practices will need to be studied more closely to redesign suitable governance structures for FPOs.

Practice indicates that CEOs have operated more as stewards of the farmers and directors than as opportunistic 'agents' of the promoting institution (the principal). Despite the rhetoric of an 'exit strategy' for the promoting institution (PI), our study shows that except for Navyug (where BASIX exited in 2018, four years after the establishment of the FPC), in all the cases the role of PI has evolved with changing roles from being a 'parent' to a 'partner'. Association continues through physical proximity (Krushidhan shares the office premises of DSC), or through placing the CEO from its own personnel (Bhangar, Mahanadi, and Kazhani), or by compensating the CEO or the MD (Ram Rahim and Kazhani), or by having representatives as part of the BoD as expert directors (Krushidhan and Desi Seed).

In FPOs that are very new or are still not viable, the PI provides ecosystem support by helping FPOs link to funding agencies, market partners, and infrastructure services. The ability of the member and operating systems to engage and co-evolve with other stakeholders of the emerging FPO ecosystem seems key for managing FPO growth. For this the member system represented by the BoDs, the operating system of the

CEO and staff or employees, and other key stakeholders, including the PI, need to be aligned with the enterprise's mission and together have the skills and the foresight to enter right businesses. Building BoD and CEO capabilities continues to be a key challenge and continues to be underinvested.

5. Assessing financial performance of FPOs

How have the FPOs performed and how have they addressed capital constraints? In our assessment we first present a snapshot of their performance (equity, revenue, profit/loss, and reserves and surplus) in the financial year 2020–21 (Table 17.3). We then disaggregate the information of the 12 FPOs to look at the trends in equity, revenue, profit and loss, and reserves and surpluses over the years. Financial performance of FPO federations is dealt with separately. All data has been sourced through the annual filings and reports of the FPO to the Ministry of Corporate Affairs (MCA) by the individual FPCs. The KBS Cooperative in Jharkhand is the only cooperative among the 15 cases, and data has been obtained from the organisation directly.

The snapshot masks the diversity of the FPOs in age (older FPOs have not benefitted from new policy architecture since 2014), commodities working with, promoting institutions' ability to access capital, and so on. Some FPOs have had access to long-term grants, a few have used capital from their SHG federations, and some have had support for infrastructure from state government-level schemes. A few broad trends are worth noting.

Unlike earlier cooperatives membership size is modest with nine of the 12 having over 1,000 members and only two above 4,000 (Krushidhan operates in several districts of Gujarat, and Ram Rahim builds on existing SHG networks). Good market linkages, like in Bhangar and Ram Rahim, are critical for profitability. Hasnabad, as indicated in the case, went for a hasty expansion of membership in anticipation of the SFAC equity grant. The broader picture that emerges is that there is no direct correlation between the size of the FPO and profitability, and a lot depends on their business plans, business acumen, and the commodity.

Member equity in cooperatives is seen as critical for the growth and health of the producer collective. Of the 12 FPOs the equity ranged from a low of Rs. 0.1 million for the remotely located FPO Mahanadi in Bastar to a high of Rs. 7 million in Ram Rahim. Interestingly, while Ram Rahim also works with tribals and its members are women, its healthier equity is largely due to building, and tapping into, the social and financial capital of the SHGs in the region. Kazhani's higher equity per member is explained in part by the commodity, banana, and the opportunity to export their product. However, it is also clear that the FPOs do face a serious capital constraint for further growth.

278

Table 17.3 Performance summary of FPOs in financial year 2020–21

Name of FPO	Members	Equity/Share Capital in Rs.	Revenue in Rs.	Net Profit/ Loss in Rs.	Reserves and Surplus (R&S) in Rs.	Total Equity (Share Capital + R&S) in Rs.
Krushidhan	4,409	4,408,500	85,045,944	16,641	425,756	4,834,256
Jeevika	1,206	375,600	15,884,230	(1,448,248)	9,480,436	9,856,036
Bhangar	1,751	1,486,600	134,036,052	891,276	3,055,567	4,542,167
Ram Rahim	5,000	7,055,740	85,347,394	3,293,074	2,007,133	9,062,873
Mahanadi	613	110,000	6,839,649	12,196	150,264	260,264
Mahila Umang	1,000	215,880	14,030,936	82,310	3,951,025	4,166,905
KBS Coop	2,680	245,400	16,716,037	1,283,834	6,187,725	6,433,125
Hasnabad	1,004	1,457,000	34,612	(1,349,450)	(5,603,682)	(4,146,682)
Pandhana	552	300,950	2,995,488	787,335	356,705	657,655
Kazhani	1,000	1,987,000	13,494,000	34,000	6,817,000	8,804,000
Navyug	1,005	1,313,000	5,359,636	38,089	(104,145)	1,208,855
Desi Seed	500	346,850	5,595,000	652,194	1,091,617	1,438,467
Maha FPC	600	3,860,000	510,646,801	88,639,097	91,155,526	95,015,526
Madhya Bharat	137	4,997,380	299,966,471	544,585	2,003,815	7,001,195
Gujpro	29	840,000	49,031,651	(2,569,512)	18,359,705	19,199,705

From Table 17.3 it is evident that seven of the FPOs have revenues of over Rs. 10 million in 2020–21. The average revenue is Rs. 3 million with a low of Rs. 34,612 (Hasnabad) and a high of Rs. 134 million (Bhangar). While there could be ways to increase revenues of these business entities, the sobering message is that few FPCs in India can match the growth and revenues of milk producer companies or superstar FPOs like Sahyadri (Lalitha et al., 2022). The FPO credit-need market is large, largely untapped, and has been estimated at Rs. 6000 million with significant institutional credit access issues (GIZ, 2020; Murray, 2021; NAFPO, 2022). As business enterprises, the FPOs seem to be making very modest profits. Seven of the FPOs made profits that were less than Rs. 0.1 million, three (Bhangar, Pandhana, and Desi Seed) were in the range of Rs. 0.1 million to 1 million, and only two (Ram Rahim and surprisingly KBS Coop) were able to make profits more than Rs. 1 million. None of the FPOs studied paid dividends though Mahila Umang paid patronage bonus for five years and Jeevika in one profitable year.

Both Navyug and Hasnabad have eaten into their reserves and had negative reserves. Overall, the financial health of the FPO could be gauged by the total equity of the FPO, a combination of member equity and the reserves built over time. All FPOs had a positive total equity except for Hasnabad that seemed to be significantly in the red. The total equity for the other 11 FPOs were from a low of Rs. 0.2 million for Mahanadi to a maximum of Rs. 9.85 million for Jeevika. The net positive total equity of the FPOs (see Table 17.2 last column) indicates that overall the FPOs are 'bankable' and do have the capacity to borrow and repay (except for Hasnabad that has not recovered from the market shock in 2016–17 where it purchased from its members at high cost and the market fell subsequently).

5.1 FPO performance trends

The longer-term trends of FPOs for the period 2014–15 to 2020–21 for equity, revenue, profit and loss, and reserves and surpluses have been further analysed to compare the FPOs and explore the changes over time. Some FPOs having shareholder equity less than Rs. 0.5 million have not got back to members, or increased membership, to raise their equity. Both Mahila Umang and KBS Coop are FPOs in operation for over 10 years, but they seem to leverage resources through other means. Desi Seed in contrast has increased member equity at least three times since inception. Among the older FPOs, both Ram Rahim and Krushidhan have raised equity more than four times. The need to increase share capital has been recognised by some of the younger FPOs such as Kazhani and Navyug.

Figure 17.1 shows the revenue trends of five of the 12 FPOs with revenues more than Rs. 20 million. Bhangar is the only FPO where revenues

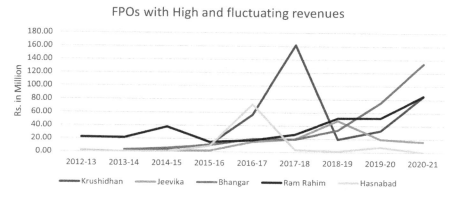

Figure 17.1 FPOs with high and fluctuating revenues

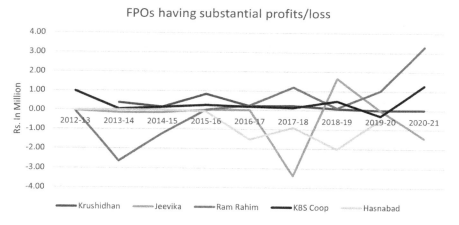

Figure 17.2 FPOs having substantial profits/loss

have consistently grown with no 'bad year'. Among those with revenues less than Rs. 20 million Mahila Umang is the only FPO where revenues have been relatively stable but for a fall during Covid. The dominant 'roller-coaster' trend of revenues in the journey of FPOs is one of the significant findings of the study. Some of the huge spikes, as seen in Krushidhan, are due to MSP procurement in a particular year. While MSP is usually good for farmers and their incomes, the inconsistency of procurement processes across years, unlike in rice and wheat, means that FPO business models can be significantly impacted in the long run if there is an over-dependence on MSP.

Figure 17.2 shows the trend of FPOs with significant profit or loss. Seven of the 12 FPOs had never seen profit (or loss) above Rs. 1 million. Only three

FPOs – Krushidhan, Bhangar, and Mahila Umang – have not had any loss year in over eight years of operation. However, except Hasnabad all the other FPOs have shown significant resilience in overcoming their losses and making profits in subsequent years. The important lesson for stakeholders in the eco-system, thus, is to appreciate the significant risks and challenges in FPO operations. The fluctuating maize and *toor dal* markets affected plans for Jeevika and Hasnabad FPCs that had planned for a windfall based on market trends. Initial years of experimentation for Ram Rahim came at a cost, and it was after a stable buyer and business model that the company has been able to grow.

Table 17.4 shows the reserves and surpluses of the FPOs collated over time. An analysis of the reserves and surpluses over the years shows that only three FPOs – Bhangar, Mahila Umang, and KBS Coop – have had positive reserves and surpluses in all years. Despite lower revenues and stable equity capital, a feature of Mahila Umang has been healthy reserves and surpluses at an average of Rs. 2.94 million. Jeevika, KBS Coop, Bhangar, and Kazhani have had average reserves of over Rs. 1 million. Krushidhan started with a negative for four years while Ram Rahim and Hasnabad had negative reserves in nine of the 10 years.

Grants often do not feature in the balance sheets of the FPOs as sometimes they are routed through the promoting institutions. Some government schemes, especially in horticulture, support creation of community assets such as a vehicle on subsidy or a processing plant that helps the FPO growth. The CEO salary in most cases continues to come from the promoting institution, and not all FPOs are able to generate enough surpluses to keep a CEO for a longer period from own finances. For FPOs to be successful business enterprises there is a need for significant investments in capacity building of both BoDs and CEO to manage the FPO and access to debt capital and grants to help them grow.

6. Assessing and sustaining FPO federations

Apex federations of cooperatives, referred to as the Amul model, with the primary cooperatives at the village level linked to district unions and then federated into apex cooperatives like the Gujarat Cooperative Milk Marketing Federation (GCMMF), have been in operation in India since 1970s and inspired several replications later in oilseeds and tree growers though with limited success. The logic of vertical integration across a particular value chain both provides economies of scale, especially in marketing of produce, and enables cooperatives to be domain central with a significant share and voice in the commodity. Replication of the Amul model in pulses, as we have seen in the Hasnabad case (Chapter 9), is challenging for individual FPOs. Twenty FPO federations were registered between 2014 and 2020, and only eight of them were reported active (Singh, 2021). This volume is the first of its kind that has looked at three

Table 17.4 Reserves and surpluses of FPOs 2012–21 (Rs. in million)

Year	2012–13	2013–14	2014–15	2015–16	2016–17	2017–18	2018–19	2019–20	2020–21
Krushidhan		-0.353	-0.186	-0.140	-0.013	0.318	0.390	0.399	0.426
Jeevika	1.010	0.870	0.740	2.250	2.260	-1.110	10.870	10.800	9.480
Bhangar			0.245	0.376	0.450	1.157	1.608	2.164	3.060
Ram Rahim		-2.886	-3.916	-3.891	-3.638	-2.436	-2.316	-1.286	2.007
Mahanadi				-0.106	-0.048	0.012	0.105	0.138	0.150
Mahila Umang		0.125	3.514	3.660	3.773	3.788	3.815	3.869	3.951
KBS Coop	-0.047	-2.886	2.322	2.580	2.752	2.891	3.362	3.362	6.188
Hasnabad	0.000	0.000	0.008	-0.165	-1.689	-2.596	-4.605	-4.266	-5.604
Pandhana					0.002	0.025	0.031	-0.431	0.357
Kazhani					-0.049	0.061	0.178	1.210	6.817
Navyug				-0.011	-0.040	0.032	0.170	0.142	-0.104

Source: Collated from case authors and audited reports of the FPOs

Table 17.5 FPO federations snapshot 2020–21

	MAHAFPC	Madhya Bharat	Gujpro
Authorised capital (AC) (Rs. in million)	10	10	2.5
Paid-up (PU) capital (Rs. in million)	2.3	5.0	0.86
PU capital as % of AC	23.2	50.02	34.4
Members	600	137	30

of them in detail. Table 17.5 presents a snapshot of the three FPO federations since 2014.

While all FPC federations started at the same time, MAHAFPC is on a fast growth trajectory adding over 100 FPCs every year in the last two years. On the other hand, Gujpro has faced challenges in dealing with output markets with only 30 members. Unlike individual FPOs where the average percentage of the paid up capital of the authorised capital is 65.4% (with some FPOs like Krushidhan and Hasnabad above 97%), the FPO federations, it appears, are yet to realise the full potential from members. Unlike individual FPOs that are eligible for state support, FPO federations have received none but for the initial grant from SFAC of Rs. 1 million. FPO federations are market facing, and the equity is insufficient to deal with significant volumes, and they also face working capital challenges. In an underinvested scenario, keeping members interested in the federations operations remains a challenge. Table 17.6 presents the snapshot of growth of FPO federations since 2014.

The FPO federations revenues were in the range of Rs. 49 million (Gujpro) to 510 million (MAHAFPC), and the profits were quite wide with Gujpro posting significant loss of Rs. 2.5 million and MAHAFPC a good profit of Rs. 88 million. While there are variations across the three federations based on their membership and business model, there are more commonalities in terms of consistent increase in equity and reserves and surpluses. The revenues though have had significant spikes in the case of Gujpro and Madhya Bharat. This is largely due to the MSP procurements in the years that were not followed in the subsequent years at the same vigour. While Madhya Bharat and MAHAFPC continue to take up MSP procurement with the state governments and NAFED, Gujpro has not been able to do so as the state government is also yet to make full payments to the FPC.

The overall picture is that many FPOs are caught in a vicious cycle of wanting to raise equity to improve performance, and members would like to be assured of returns before increasing equity. The reserves and surplus are moderate, and profits are not substantial. Conventional banks tend to be more conservative and do not lend based on their lower-equity base. FPOs, while asset light, have been able to build assets and have been able to leverage them for better market linkages. With better ecosystem services some FPOs, especially federations, have leveraged warehouse finance through

Table 17.6 Financial growth of FPO federations 2014–21 (Rs. in million)

Year		2014–15	2015–16	2016–17	2017–18	2018–19	2019–20	2020–21
Equity	MAHAFPC	0.10	0.10	0.10	1.53	2.00	2.32	3.86
	Madhya Bharat	0.57	1.60	4.73	4.88	4.96	4.98	5.00
	Guipro	0.10	0.16	0.17	0.24	0.24	0.82	0.84
Revenue	MAHAFPC	0.10	4.27	2.00	42.85	106.21	15.54	510.65
	Madhya Bharat	0.74	19.18	79.29	232.63	1545.46	62.88	299.97
	Guipro	0.30	1.01	355.22	1682.45	848.77	57.75	49.03
Profit and Loss	MAHAFPC	0.00	0.19	-0.71	1.94	0.35	0.74	88.64
	Madhya Bharat	0.02	0.10	0.73	0.14	0.19	0.88	0.54
	Guipro	0.00	0.00	0.69	1.79	16.21	0.43	-2.57
Reserves and Surpluses	MAHAFPC	0.00	0.19	0.52	1.42	1.78	12.52	91.16
	Madhya Bharat	1.47	0.97	0.62	0.69	0.81	1.46	2.00
	Guipro	0.00	0.16	0.48	4.80	20.98	20.93	18.36

agencies like Arya Collateral or Non-Bank Finance Company (NBFC) like Samunnati. FPO federations have played an important role in enabling greater market access to FPOs, especially in public procurement, leveraged government schemes for the benefit of individual FPOs, and continue to play an important advocacy role in state and national forums in favour of smallholders. Beyond financial performance a key element of understanding producer organisations is their ability to govern and manage for growth even as they face significant capability constraints.

7. Assessing impact: beyond finance and search for newer metrics

The impact of producer organisations is often beyond what is reported in the financial statements. The evaluation of impact of producer organisations would require more robust farmer-level information systems and independent assessments with stronger baseline data that has not been done for the FPOs studied. However, the 15 cases provide ample evidence of diverse tangible and intangible benefits that have been summarised under the following five heads.

7.1 Farmer-first institutions

FPOs in India have been able to provide an institutional form beyond the Primary Agricultural Credit Societies (PACS) that in many parts of India have bypassed small and marginal farmers and have rarely served as multiservice centres beyond credit. As farmer-first local institutions they are filling a key institutional void with declining public and private investments in agriculture, especially in rain-fed areas. FPOs helped lower or mitigate the risk for farmers by providing agricultural extension services, setting up custom hiring centres, and primary processing units. Over a period, FPOs have experimented with and developed diversified product lines. Krushidhan, for instance, took up contract farming for small farmers, ventured into seed business, provided MSP for farmers, and marked their presence as a serious market player by taking up a shop in the local market (*mandi*).

7.2 Empowered negotiators

A more visible impact that is across the cases is the new normal in member-local trader relations. By expanding the options for marketing by the FPOs members have been able to negotiate better, and fairer, price for their produce with local traders. As new institutions FPOs can play the role of 'market makers' but will be ill-advised to pursue ambitious ideological goals of 'eliminating the middlemen' given their limited resources and market share. FPOs, federations, are providing 'voice' to farmers in advocating policy shifts in favour of small farmers and by creating demand for markets and services. A few FPOs have their own brands – Bastar Fresh (Mahanadi FPO); Kumaoni, Himkhadaya, and Umang Handknits (Mahila Umang); Muskan (Pandhana); Kazhani (Kazhani); Umang (Navyug), and Sahaja Seeds (Desi Seed) – and retail outlets (Mahila Umang, Kazhani) that add value to members through differentiated products and markets.

7.3 Economic empowerment

Member farmers have realised better incomes by being part of the FPO. Members, and even non-members, benefit directly through reduced input costs and improved agricultural extension services. The KBSSSL in Jharkhand working through PRADAN assures Rs. 40,000–50,000 per year additional farm income for the members. Subsistence farmers in Mandla FPC, a part of the Madhya Bharat Federation, have been able to earn Rs. 8,000–16,000/season extra through the FPO operations. FPOs linked to markets that command better prices through newer value chains of fair trade, organic or export markets (Gujpro, Ram Rahim, Mahila Umang, Kazhani) though FPOs are often unable to do this for all members or on all crops. An estimate of benefits through collective aggregation and marketing through MSP in groundnut in the Krushidhan FPO indicates that for every rupee earned by the company farmers get Rs. 22.5.

7.4 Social empowerment

FPOs provide many intangible benefits that include risk mitigation of production and improved health of the farming community that is difficult to measure as they occur over a long time frame. The empowerment experienced by the members, especially women and tribals, is a positive fallout of FPO presence. Women used their agency to rework power relations and see the increased capability as empowerment with dignity (Mahila Umang). Collective action at the village, cluster, and FPO levels has provided an opportunity for tribal women to engage with formal male-dominated markets (Ram Rahim and Pandhana), the confidence to take up any task including those involving working with line departments and the banks (Jeevika, Hasnabad). This aspect was witnessed by many authors during field interactions and strengthens the case for FPOs as social enterprises.

7.5 Potential transition intermediaries

An emerging, though not extensive, theme of impact is the increasing benefit of FPOs on the planet. FPOs like Desi Seed, Ram Rahim, and Mahila Umang value this contribution and have sufficient experience and data to report this more proactively. If FPOs need to present themselves as business enterprises of the future they might want to reflect on their own triple bottom lines of people, profit, and planet and find proxies and suitable metrics that capture the social and environmental return on investments.

Producer organisations need to track and compute metrics that capture these tangible and intangible benefits to better communicate their overall impact that goes beyond balance sheets. Efficient operations in the value chain by the FPO lead to a virtuous cycle of greater trust of members and higher demand for services including value addition resulting in better farm incomes, sometimes to non-members too.

8. Policy and ecosystem

The discussions on business models, performance, innovations, inclusion, and impact from the cases point to important policy implications as producer organisations attract increasing interest from governments worldwide, and the Government of India plans an ambitious expansion of 10,000 FPOs by 2024. Recent landscape reports on the FPO ecosystem in India have highlighted how new FPO policies in India have favoured quantity and targets over quality, paying limited attention to ground realities and learnings from over 16 years of FPC promotion. The creation of FPCs has not been sufficiently producer driven or 'bottom-up', and the new scheme has been criticised for a lack of focus on women producers and not recognising CSOs to be well placed as promoting institutions (Neti and Govil, 2022; Govil and Neti, 2021; Singh, 2022). The FPOs in the volume, in operation for over five years, have been atypical in terms of inclusion and with greater investments in governance and management than many of the FPOs that have come up in the last few years in India. Some of the FPOs, especially the federations, can be considered as pioneers in this space and were set up when the FPO ecosystem was at a very early stage with many stakeholders insufficiently connected or involved. We summarise a few key policy implications from the detailed studies of 'older' FPOs to inform both research and policy on creating robust and resilient producer organisations.

8.1 FPOs as social enterprises and rural start-ups

Are FPOs the new collective institutions of the 21st century? With their origin or promotion outside the state and market, and civil society organisations playing an active role in incubation, the case studies highlight the tensions in transformation that these new producer organisations face in seeking an entrepreneurial route to farmer welfare. The case studies in the volume encourage us to go beyond the restrictive framework of conventional cooperative literature and seek to engage with newer frames of FPOs as social enterprises (Kaushik, 2022) within the social and solidarity economy (Utting, 2016). Recent entrepreneurship literature and insights on lean start-ups, effectuation, and the importance of experimentation and failing fast and forward (Ries, 2017; Read et al., 2016), the cases suggest, apply to FPOs as well. Future public policies need to recognise FPOs as start-ups, if only to be more open to failures, and acknowledge the significant social learning in building alternative business models.

8.2 FPOs not panacea for agricultural distress

Public policy in India has viewed FPOs as a single-stop solution and *the* institution that could resolve multiple issues plaguing the farm sector. As nascent institutions it would be a folly to overburden them with expectations and treat them as a panacea for all ills in the agricultural sector. FPOs cannot resolve structural challenges in the sector of decreased public investment (Ramakumar et al., 2022), the search for a frame of intervention beyond productivity and populism (Kumar et al., 2020) and declining state capacity (Prasad, 2021). The danger of policy pushing smallholder organisations to overextend themselves without fully recognising constraints was pointed out by Ton et al. (2007) and is playing out in the Indian context. It is important to recognise that many issues that FPOs face are beyond the ambit and capabilities of members, board of directors, or CEOs and relate to the larger ecosystem that determines their access to credit and addressing capability issues.

8.3 Building a supportive ecosystem

Public policy needs to shift from being prescriptive with quantitative targets to working with partners and stakeholders in creating a supportive and enabling ecosystem. Features of this ecosystem support should recognise and build on the following ideas that cover their design, finance, governance, and management:

1 Social capital is critical to resilient FPOs and business success. Investing and orienting in collective institutions, such as SHGs, farmer clubs, water user associations, to federate to formal FPOs is more likely to lead to yield results, and the transformation to jointly owned businesses can take time.
2 Market facing social enterprises can lead to exclusions of different kinds and designing institutions for inclusion is as important as seeking efficiency.
3 Diversification is a key part of mitigating risks, and FPOs have shown how engaging with multiple commodities, while complex, is a better route than aiming to capture value in a single commodity value chain. Newer prescriptive policies such as the 'One District One Product' run counter to the rationale of member-owned institutions and farmers being more actively involved in decision-making.

4   In managing post-incubation growth there is a need to explore blended finance (comprising grants, investments, debt at low costs, and commercial capital at a later stage) in a more proactive manner that is suited to the life cycle of the FPO. Given the continuous demands on capital of an FPO that cannot be met by low member equity, newer sources need to be explored, and targeted grants from government agencies and corporate social responsibility (CSR) foundations could help.

5   Capacity building support to nurture managerial and governance capacities within the organisation is currently low and is significantly under-invested in comparison to schemes like the National Rural Livelihoods Mission (NRLM). While there are many service providers in this space, the content and pedagogy of their capacity building efforts need a greater focus on skilling new entrepreneurs in rural areas.

6   Engaging with stakeholders early and often is critical for creating local ecosystems that enable growth of FPOs. These include the need to align bankers, financial institutions, agricultural markets (*mandis*) to meeting, and possibly servicing, the demands for compliance, capital, and capability that the FPOs face.

7   As the number of FPOs grows the demand for such apex federations that negotiate and lobby on behalf of member FPOs will increase. The evidence from the three federations indicate that they need significant support, and the current policy architecture provides none.

8   FPOs are to be seen as public goods, and state support is essential for their survival and growth. They are potentially better investments than individual farm loan waivers. Excessive compliance requirements that treat these fledgling institutions on par with bigger and well-resourced corporations in the producer company format do not create a level-playing field for FPOs. Public partnerships of the kind seen in the MAHAFPC case between NAFED and MAHAFPC to create infrastructure in rural areas might do more to create opportunities for collectives of farmers than populist policies that tend to favour individual loan waivers.

9   The onus of success is often too much on the BoDs or the promoting institution of the FPO. It is however important to recognise that FPOs are more complex than collective institutions of the past like the SHGs and their federations. The challenge for incubators, including academic institutions, is to create innovation spaces for knowledge dialogues that enable the education and reorientation of different national institutions such as NABARD, NCDC, SFAC, donors, and the officers in the departments in the state and central government entrusted with the task of promoting FPOs. This is critical to bridge the gap between FPOs and other institutions *viz.* academic institutions, agricultural colleges, Krishi Vigyan Kendra (KVKs), and so on.

9. Conclusions: reimagining producer organisations as social enterprises

The collection of 15 cases organised around the four themes of enabling market access through collectives, building inclusive institutions towards innovation and autonomy, and sustaining FPO federations provides seeds of hope for farming futures in India and elsewhere. Producer organisations can be seen as organisations of the future spearheading alternative economic systems that embed purpose, people, and planet in the search for appropriate business models and profit. The 15 cases in the volume provide hope that 'another world is possible' through such institutions. However, beyond reaffirming faith there is a need to look more closely at institutional changes in the ecosystem that can drive innovation for greater impact. These need to be backed by adequate investments that can bring about empowerment of rural producers while transforming our food systems. The grounded understanding of the growth and management challenges of producer organisations show that there is a need for thinking beyond conventional disciplines and silos that have shaped the farmers collectives' discourse and actively seek newer interdisciplinary perspectives such as those emerging from stakeholder theories of the firm and rarely extended in management research to collective enterprises. By situating the individual FPOs within their local and regional ecosystems and exploring how these FPOs have co-evolved with stakeholders the cases also encourage us to rethink producer organisations as responsible and inclusive businesses or as social enterprises that could benefit from ongoing discussions in critical management studies, political economy, and economic sociology.

The book presents a strong case to go beyond conventional economic assessments of producer organisations' performance and explore multiple metrics that might enable capturing the rounded impact as a social enterprise. With the Government of India notifying a framework for a social stock exchange[3] that unfortunately currently does not include FPOs the time is not far when FPOs would go beyond the confines of conventional cooperatives seeking government aid to positioning themselves, through a reimagined narrative, as responsible businesses or 'start-up collectives' that can access capital more widely. None of the cases are celebrated success stories; it is in their everyday negotiation with markets and states that these nascent institutions reveal the complex and interconnected contexts of newer agroecological, socio-economic, and political realities. Public policies chasing large quantitative targets for promotion seem to ignore the ground realities in the consistent and collective efforts required to establish FPOs as rural start-ups.

The ecosystem for supporting and enabling FPOs in India continues to grow with increased state and even private sector interest and support

(NAFPO, 2022) even as the search for 'ease of doing' business in rural India continues to be elusive, as these cases show. Realising greater farm incomes though is contingent to going back to the basics of creating strong and resilient member-owned organisations. Farmers in India, and elsewhere, continue to face uncertain futures due to increased impacts of climate change, high dependence on fossil fuel-based inputs that continue to spiral, and incomes that do not rise commensurately. The pandemic has affected many agricultural markets, and the FPOs in the volume have shown significant resilience in overcoming the disruption through innovation and growth. FPCs have the potential to be harbinger of change in the stressed real context where a large number of educated youths who otherwise have dropped out of agriculture can engage with 'new' agricultural initiatives that are based on technology and ecological practices and reorient agriculture as honourable profession that assures decent livelihood and income.

Notes

1 The Government of India is expected to spend $32 billion in fertilizer subsidy in 2022–23 up to 62% from 2021–22 in rupee terms. https://indianexpress.com/article/opinion/columns/what-india-needs-to-do-to-reduce-its-fertiliser-bill-7987006/. A significant thrust of the government's natural farming initiative is to save on fertilizer subsidy though FPOs currently are not seen as integral to it. https://natural-farming.niti.gov.in/.
2 Shareholding in most cases is with individual farmers, not with the groups, except in Ram Rahim and Umang Mahila where the SHGs are shareholders.
3 For the notification, see https://www.livemint.com/market/stock-market-news/sebi-notifies-framework-for-social-stock-exchange-11658861357504.html

References

GIZ (2020). *Guidebook on lending to farmer producer organisations*. New Delhi: Deutsche Gesellschaft für Internationale Zusammenarbeit (GIZ) GmbH.
Govil, R & Neti, A (2021). Farmer producer companies: From quantity to quality. In B Sen (Ed.), State of India's Livelihoods Report 2021 (p. 172). ACCESS Development Services.
Groot-Kormelinck, A, Bijman, J, Trienekens, J & Klerkx, L (2022). Producer organizations as transition intermediaries? Insights from organic and conventional vegetable systems in Uruguay. *Agriculture and Human Values*. https://doi.org/10.1007/s10460-022-10316-3
Kanitkar, A (2016). *The logic of farmer enterprises* (Occasional Publication 17). Anand: Institute of Rural Management Anand (IRMA).
Kaushik, R (2022). Understanding cooperatives as social enterprises. *Economic and Political Weekly*, 57(5), 24–30.
Kumar, R, Aggarwal, NK, Vijayshankar, P & Vasavi, AR (2020). State of rural and Agrarian India Report: Rethinking productivity and populism through alternative approaches. *Network of Rural and Agrarian Studies*. Retrieved from http://

www.ruralagrarianstudies.org/wp-content/uploads/2020/11/State-of-Rural-and-Agrarian-India-Report-2020.pdf

Lalitha, N, Viswanathan, PK & Vinayan, S (2022). Institutional strengthening of farmer producer organizations and empowerment of small farmers in India: Evidence from a case study in Maharashtra. *Millennial Asia.* https://doi.org/10.1177/09763996221098216

Mahajan, V (2015). Farmers' producer companies: Need for capital and capability to capture the value added. In S Datta, V Mahajan, S Ratha, et al. (Eds.), *State of India's livelihoods report 2014* (pp. 87–108). New Delhi: Oxford University Press.

Murray, E (2021). *FPOs as harbingers of agricultural transformation: The significance of credit.* Anand: Institute of Rural Management Anand.

NAFPO (2022). *State of sector report: Farmer producer organisations in India.* New Delhi: Authors UpFront.

Neti, A & Govil, R (2022). *Farmer producer companies. Report on inclusion, capitalisation and incubation* (No. 2; p. 48). Bengaluru: Azim Premji University.

Prasad, CS (2021). Consultation or consultants? *Seminar, 748,* 46–50.

Ramakumar, R, Surya, A & Das, R (2022). *Public spending on agriculture in India: 2010–11 to 2019–20: A project report* (p. 66). Bengaluru: The Foundation for Agrarian Studies.

Read, S, Sarasvathy, S, Dew, N & Wiltbank, R (2016). *Effectual entrepreneurship.* New York: Routledge. https://doi.org/10.4324/9781315684826

Ries, E (2017). *The startup way.* New York: Currency.

Shah, T (1995). Liberalisation and Indian agriculture: New relevance of farmer co-operatives. *Indian Journal of Agricultural Economics, 50*(3), 488–509.

Shah, T (1996). *Catalysing co-operation: Design of self-governing organisations.* New Delhi: Sage Publications.

Singh, S (2022). *How can India's farmer producer companies better serve small-scale farmers?* London: International Institute of Environment and Development. Retrieved from https://www.iied.org/20856iied

Singh, V (2021). *Understanding of Farmer Producer Company (FPC) Consortiums in the Indian context: Exploratory study on second level institutions in the FPC ecosystem.* New Delhi: Rajiv Gandhi Institute of Contemporary Studies.

Ton, G, Bijman, J & Oorthuizen, J (Eds.) (2007). *Producer organisations and market chains: Facilitating trajectories of change in developing countries.* Wageningen: Wageningen Academic Publishers.

Utting, P (2016). *Mainstreaming social and solidarity economy: Opportunities and risks for policy change.* Retrieved from https://base.socioeco.org/docs/paper-mainstreaming-sse-12-november-2016-edit-untfsse.pdf

INDEX

and procurement linkages 75–76; pandemic and beyond 79; risk of selling perishable produce 69–70; timeline of 73
Bharatiya Agro Industries Foundation (BAIF) 8
Bhartiya Samruddhi Investments and Consulting Ltd (BASIX) 187; business development services 189–190; institution development services 188–189
Bidhan Chandra Krishi Viswavidyalaya 77
Big Basket 58, 195
Bihar Agriculture Investment Promotion Policy (BAIPP) 63
Bihar Rural Livelihoods Project (BRLP) 51–52
Bihar Rural Livelihoods Promotion Society (BRLPS) 52
bio-inputs, adoption of 96
BISCOMAUN 67
board of directors (BoD) 60; Bhangar Vegetable Producer Company Limited 73; Desi Seed Producer Company Limited 202, 206; farmer producer organisations 7, 10, 12, 14, 18, 247, 274–276, 278, 282, 290; Hasnabad Farmer Service Producer Company Limited 147, 153, 156; Indira Kabadwal of village Kafra 121; input aggregation 147–148; Jeevika Women Agri Producer Company Limited 53–54, 57, 60–62, 66–67; Krishi Bagwani Swawlambi Sahakari Samiti Limited 130, 139, 142–143; Krushidhan Producer Company Ltd 31–32, 35, 42, 44, 46–48; Madhya Bharat Consortium of Farmer Producers Company Limited 239–240; MAHA Farmers Producer Company Ltd. 223–224; Mahanadi Farmer Producer Company Limited 99, 102–103, 108–109; Navyug Kisan Producer Company Ltd. 191–192, 200; Pandhana Pashu-Palak Producer Company Limited 168–170; Ram Rahim Pragati Producer Company 88–89, 91, 96; Somnath Farmer Producer Company 255
brainstorming workshops 35
Business Acceleration Unit (BAU) 100

business model: Gujpro Agri-business Consortium Producer Company Ltd. 255–261; Krishi Bagwani Swawlambi Sahakari Samiti Limited (KBSSSL) 134–138; Madhya Bharat Consortium of Farmer Producers Company Limited (MBCFPCL) 234–237; MAHA Farmers Producer Company Ltd. (MAHAFPC) 218–220; Mahanadi Farmer Producer Company Limited (MFPCL) 105–107; and member centrality in 218–220; reimagining producer organisations in India 271–274; salient feature of 220–221
Business-to-Business (B2B) marketing 39, 105, 121
Buy Fresh Buy Local 122

capacity building programmes 124, 175, 248, 266, 269–270, 282, 290; Bhangar Vegetable Producer Company Limited 82; Desi Seed Producer Company Limited 209, 215; farmer producer organisations 8, 14, 18; Gujpro Agri-business Consortium 247, 249, 254, 263–264; Hasnabad Farmer Service Producer Company Limited 146; Jeevika Women Agri Producer Company Limited 52, 61, 67; Kazhani Farmer Producer Company 183; Krishi Bagwani Swawlambi Sahakari Samiti Limited, 130, 143; Krushidhan Producer Company Ltd 44, 47–48; Madhya Bharat Consortium of Farmer Producers Company Limited 233; Mahanadi Farmer Producer Company Limited 101–103, 109; Mahila Umang Producer Company Limited 124; Navyug Kisan Producer Company Ltd 187; Ram Rahim Pragati Producer Company 92, 95–96
capacity building support 289
Capital Adequacy Ratio (CAR) 65
capsicum 75
Catalyst Management Services (CMS) 100
Centre for Digitisation of Financial Inclusion (CDFI) 199
chemical pesticides 35

13; longer-term trends of 280–282; on markets and member farmers 97; meeting multiple demands of 254; not panacea for agricultural distress 289; as social enterprises and rural start-ups 288–289; stage for state-level federation of 248–249; sustainable transition intermediaries 270–271

farmers: geographical regions/clusters, balancing of 43–44; intangible benefits 42; members *vs.* non-members 43; men and women, participation of 44; social and commercial goals, balancing of 42; socio-economic conditions of 244; tangible benefits 41–42

farmer suicides 3–4, 21, 24, 202

Farming Futures project 18

federation 96, 129, 154, 211, 217, 230; business model and member centrality in 218–220; cluster-level 52; emerging 230–231; FPCs 194; FPO 11–12, 16, 20, 233–234, 240, 245–246, 268, 271, 278, 282–291; marketing 221, 247–264; new initiative 225–227; paddy procurement for state 155; revenue model for 224; SHG 52, 85, 89, 91–92, 130, 140; SHG-VO-CLF 53; supportive ecosystem for FPO 233–234

feminisation 13, 114

field visits 16

Food Security Fund (FSF) programme 59

food sovereignty movements 2

forests, degradation of 114

fresh fruits and vegetables (F&V) 69

general body meeting (GBM): annual general body meeting (AGM) 133, 153, 170, 190, 239, 253, 276

General Power of Attorney (GPA) 153

goat marketing 165

goat rearing 159

Gobichettipalayam 174

gobindobhog rice 76

Godrej Agrovet 88

Goel, Sudhir Kumar 228

governance structure: Bhangar Vegetable Producer Company Ltd

(BVPCL) 73–75; Desi Seed Producer Company Limited 206–207; Gujpro Agri-business Consortium Producer Company Ltd. 252–255; Jeevika Women's Agri Produce Company Limited (JWAPCL) 59–61; Kazhani Farmer Producer Company Limited 182–184; Krishi Bagwani Swawlambi Sahakari Samiti Limited (KBSSSL) 132–134; Krushidhan Producer Company Ltd. (KPCL) 42–49; Madhya Bharat Consortium of Farmer Producers Company Limited (MBCFPCL) 237–240; Navyug Kisan Producer Company Ltd. (NYPCL) 190–192; non-timber forest produce (NTFP) 108–109; Pandhana Pashu Palak Producer Company Limited (PPPPCL) 169–170

government role 6

Grassroots 267; financial overview 123–126

Green Agro Products 179

GREEN (Genetic Resource, Ecology, Energy and Nutrition) Foundation 210

grocery items, sale of 176–177

grocery retail services 156

Gujarat Cooperative Milk Marketing Federation (GCMMF) 11, 254, 282

Gujarat Rajya Krushak Manch (GRKM) 249

Gujpro Agri-business Consortium Producer Company Ltd.: conclusion and reflections 263–264; evolving business model of 255–261; financial performance of 261–262; governance and leadership 252–255; journey of 250–252; plans for future 262–263; Sajjata Sangh and need for primary producer collectivisation 247–248; state-level federation of FPOs 248–249

Gumla 128

Gumla Gramin Poultry Co-operative Society Ltd. (GGPCS) 140

Hasnabad Farmer Service Producer Company Limited (HFSPC): challenges in running FPC 154–155; direct sales to consumers 150–152; efforts to turn around FPC 155–158; human resources for managing

156; input aggregation 147–148;
marketing of pulses 148–149;
members' ownership and patronage
for services 153; promotional grant
from SFAC to ALC India 145–146;
struggle in accessing working capital
152–153; three-year business
plan 147; unpredictability in MSP
operations 149–150; women-
owned FPC in rain-fed subsistence
agriculture region 146
HimKhadya 119
hub-and-spoke model 122
Human Development Index (HDI) 83
Human Development Report 99
Hytech 91

income tax 6
incubation 12, 18, 20, 28–33, 40,
46–47, 62, 100–101, 111, 129, 180,
266–268, 288, 290
Indian Council of Agriculture Research
(ICAR) 140
Indian Farmer Fertiliser Cooperative
(IFFCO) 11, 67
Indian Himalayan Region 114
Information and Communication
Technologies (ICTs) 185
Institute of Rural Management Anand
(IRMA) 5, 145
Integrated Nutrient Management
(INM) 247
Integrated Pest Management (IPM) 247
Inter-Departmental Working Group on
Organic Agriculture (IDWG/OA) 202
International Crops Research
Institute for the Semi-Arid Tropics
(ICRISAT) 146
intra-basin trade 115

Jai Kisan 180
Jain, L. C. 5
Jal-Jungle-Jameen 117
Jeevika Women's Agri Produce
Company Limited (JWAPCL):
accounting and auditing compliances
63; annual action plan of 59;
beginnings 53; books of accounts
maintenance 63; current status and
road ahead 66–67; diversification
and experimentation 57–59;
ecosystem support 62; financial

capabilities 62–65; financial linkages
63; financial performance 63–65;
governance structure 59–61; impacts
of 65–66; management 61–62;
pivoting to maize (2016–19) 54–57;
quiet early days (2009–15) 54; rural
livelihoods via farmer producer
companies in Bihar 51–53; share
capital mobilisation 62; social
impacts 66; tangible and intangible
assets 65
Jharkhand Opportunities for
Harnessing Rural Growth Project
(JOHAR) 143
Jharkhand Self-supporting Cooperative
Societies Act 130, 139
Jharkhand Women's Poultry Self-
Supporting Co-operative Federation
Ltd. 140
Jitban 67

Kabadwal, Indira 121
Kalesindh Farmer Producer
Company 242
Kambde, Meerabai 96–97
Kanker 99
Karnataka Organic Farming Policy
2017 211–212
Kazhani Farmer Producer Company
Limited: collective marketing of
rice 176; conclusion 185–186; crop
insurance 175–176; end-to-end
solution for farmers 184–185; forays
into bulk marketing of banana 177;
foundation of strong SHG network
174–175; key business strategies
177–182; leveraging support from
ecosystem 184; millet processing
177; overview of 177; sale of grocery
items 176–177; shareholder outreach
and governance 182–184
Khagaria district 51
Khan, Abdul Jabbar 70, 75
kharif crops 84
krishak mitras 102
Krishi Bagwani Swawlambi Sahakari
Samiti Limited (KBSSSL): adaptive
management and convergence
128–129; business model of
134–138; conclusion 142–143;
convergence of interventions
139–140; governance and

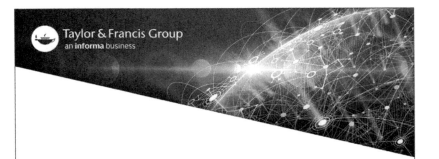

Printed in the United States
by Baker & Taylor Publisher Services